ETRUSCAN Life and Afterlife

ETRUSCAN

A Handbook of Etruscan Studies

Life and Afterlife

Edited by Larissa Bonfante

Wayne State University Press DETROIT

Published with the assistance of the J. Paul
Getty Trust and the Dr. M. Aylwin Cotton
Foundation.

98 97 96 95 94   9 8 7 6 5

Library of Congress Cataloging-in-Publication Data

Etruscan life and afterlife.

   Bibliography: p.
   Includes index.
   1. Etruscans. I. Bonfante, Larissa.
DG223.E75   1986   937'.5   86-5457
ISBN 0-8143-1772-3
ISBN 0-8143-1813-4 (pbk.)

Contents

Illustrations

Contributors

Larissa Bonfante, who commissioned the essays for this collection, translated Chs. 2, 4, and 5. She teaches classics and archaeology at New York University and is the author of *Etruscan Dress* (1975), *Out of Etruria* (1981), and, with her father, the linguist Giuliano Bonfante, *The Etruscan Language: An Introduction* (revised Italian translation, *Lingua e cultura degli Etruschi,* 1985). She is presently at work on a book on ancient Greek and Roman dress.

Marie-Françoise Briguet, of the Centre National de la Recherche Scientifique, is Chargé de Mission at the Musée du Louvre in Paris. She has worked especially with the Louvre collection of Etruscan sculpture.

Nancy Thomson de Grummond is associate professor of classics at Florida State University. Both art historian and archaeologist, she often bridges this gap with her publications on the influence of ancient art in the Renaissance. She has edited *A Guide to Etruscan Mirrors* (1982) and the *Dictionary of the History of Classical Archaeology;* she is the founder and publisher of *Archaeological News.*

Friedhelm Prayon teaches archaeology at the University of Tübingen in Germany. The author of *Frühetruskische Grab- und Hausarchitektur* (1975) and *Alt-Phrygische Plastik* (in press), he also specializes in Anatolian archaeology and in Roman architecture.

Emeline Richardson is professor emeritus of classical archaeology at the University of North Carolina at Chapel Hill and the dean of Etruscan studies in America. Her books include *The Etruscans* (1964) and *Archaic Etruscan Bronzes* (1983).

Mario Torelli is professor of archaeology at the University of Perugia, an editor of *Dialoghi di Archeologia,* and author of numerous books and articles, including *Elogia Tarquiniensia* (1975), *Typology and Structure of Roman Historical Reliefs* (1982), and *Lavinio e Roma* (1984). He has excavated the Greek sanctuary at Gravisca (the Etruscan port of Tarquinia) and, with John G. Pedley, the sanctuary of Santa Venera at Paestum.

David Enders Tripp studied Etruscan archaeology with Donald Strong at the Institute of Archaeology of the University of London. As a numismatic researcher and photographer, he has assisted The Johns Hopkins University and the Walters Art Gallery. He is currently preparing the British Museum's collection of Etruscan coins for publication.

Jean MacIntosh Turfa excavated at Murlo with Kyle M. Phillips. Her Bryn Mawr dissertation on Etruscan-Punic relations will soon be published. Her fascicle on the collections of the museums of Liverpool and Manchester has been prepared for the Corpus of Etruscan Mirrors.

Preface

Archaeological discoveries about the Etruscans in the last thirty years have so increased, and are adding to our knowledge of the Etruscans at such a rapid pace, that one stands more of a chance of learning of a new find from the newspaper than from a book. The discovery of a coin or the reading of an inscription can change our picture of their history overnight.

The wealth of recent finds and the lively state of the field could, we thought, be made accessible to a wider English-speaking public by a handbook whose text would help dispel some of the mystique of the Etruscans' enigma and isolation, still being propagated in much of the writing on this ever-popular subject, and whose notes and bibliography would allow further work in various areas. Several distinguished colleagues agreed to provide surveys of their particular fields, in simple language, following the French tradition of *haute vulgarisation,* thus minimizing the danger described by Christopher Hawkes in *Greeks, Celts and Romans* (p. XL): "Single-author and single-subject books, if they aim at an exhaustive treatment, are more prone today than ever before to erosion by newer work, and the wider their field and the more parts it covers, the more so."

Serviceable, up-to-date notes and bibliographies are designed to make all these chapters useful for a varied audience of scholars from other disciplines and graduate students, as well as a wider interested public.

The Etruscans provide an excellent opportunity of turning archaeology into history: this we tried to do, in our chapters, according to our individual directions. Nancy Thomson de Grummond traces the interest in and knowledge of the Etruscans from the earliest days. Mario Torelli provides an independent account of Etruscan history, based on

monuments and sources. Jean MacIntosh Turfa belies the cliché of the Etruscans' traditional "isolation" by surveying the material evidence for their trade with the Phoenicians, Greeks, and other neighbors in the Mediterranean. Marie-Françoise Briguet, Friedhelm Prayon, David Tripp, and I survey Etruscan art, architecture, coinage, and daily life, respectively. Emeline Richardson contributes what she calls a "primer" in the Etruscan language, a basic archaeological introduction to the Etruscan language, meant to help newcomers read the inscriptions on many of the monuments illustrated and to see these with the interdisciplinary approach so characteristic of, and necessary in, Etruscan studies.

The study of the Etruscans in England and America in these last few years has been made much easier by the availability of new books on the Etruscans in English. Two especially, both in paperback, have made an enormous difference. Pallottino's classic work *The Etruscans* (1978), edited for an English-speaking audience by David Ridgway, provides context and questions within which new finds and new publications can be understood and evaluated. Otto Brendel's *Etruscan Art* (1978), completed by Emeline Richardson, constitutes a highly original view of the style, artistic context, and continuity of their monuments. Two other books must also be mentioned, both beautifully illustrated: *Etruscan Cities* (1978), and most recently *The Etruscans* (1983), by Maja Sprenger, Gilda Bartoloni, and Max and Albert Hirmer, which makes available photographic and bibliographic documentation for all the chief Etruscan artistic monuments.

Our book, designed to complement more popular works, and to lead students back to the standard texts, as well as to more specialized literature in the field, illustrates two current tendencies in Etruscan studies responsible for recent progress: specialization and collaboration. The ideal of collaboration, both international and interdisciplinary, comes closest to being achieved in archaeology: we constantly depend on the work of others as we pursue our special goals. Neither the Etruscans nor we who study them are now so isolated. In fact, Italy's celebration of 1985 as the Year of the Etruscans shows that Etruscan past lives in the memory of the general public as well as scholars.

In Memoriam

It is with particular sadness that we record the death of members of an earlier, courageous generation to whom we owe much more than knowledge, and of younger ones, whom we had hoped to count on far into the future. In the last fifteen years these great scholars in the field of Etrusco-Italic studies have died: Axel Boethius (1969), Otto J. Brendel (1973), Ranuccio Bianchi Bandinelli (1975), Maja Sprenger (1976), Luisa Banti (1978), Andreas Alföldi, Michelangelo Cagiano de Azevedo, Martin Frederiksen, R.M. Ogilvie, John Ward-Perkins (1981), Edith M. Wightman (1983), M. Aylwin Cotton, Hans Jucker, Richard E. Linington, H.H. Scullard (1984), Aldo Neppi Modona (1985), George M.A. Haufmann, Dorothy Kent Hill (1986).

Acknowledgments

I am grateful to museums, institutions, and individuals, including the authors of this book, who graciously provided illustrations and permissions. Special thanks go to: Robert Bianchi, Giorgio Buchner, Mauro Cristofani, Adriana Emiliozzi Morandi, Nancy de Grummond, Richard DePuma, Johannes Felbermeyer, Ellen Macnamara, David Mitten, Cristiana Morigi Govi, Francesco Nicosia, Massimo Pallottino, Paola Pelagatti, Martin Price, David Ridgway, Francesca Serra Ridgway, Francesco Roncalli, Stephan Steingräber, Judith Swaddling, Mario Torelli, Silvana Tovoli, Bluma Trell, and Jo Goldberg, who prepared the maps. I am also grateful to the Trustees of the British Museum, the Soprintendenza alle Antichità dell'Etruria Meridionale, the Soprintendenza Archeologica della Toscana, the Museo Civico Archeologico, Bologna, the Deutsches Archaeologisches Institut (DAI) in Rome, the Musée du Louvre, and the Liverpool Museums. The encouragement and assistance provided the editor in the publication of the volume by The Dr. M. Aylwin Cotton Foundation are gratefully acknowledged. Finally, the illustrations would have been much fewer without the generous support of the Getty publication grant.

Abbreviations

Full bibliographical information is found either below or in the Selected Readings at the end of this volume.

AA: *Archäologischer Anzeiger*

ActaAntHung: *Acta Antiqua Academiae Scientiarum Hungaricae* (Budapest)

ActaArch: *Acta Archaeologica*

AGI: *Archivio Glottologico Italiano*

Aigner Foresti, Ostalpenraum und Italien: L. Aigner Foresti, *Der Ostalpenraum und Italien: Ihre kulturellen Beziehungen in Spiegel der anthropomorphen Kleinplastik aus Bronze des 7. Jhs. v. Chr.* (Florence 1980)

AJA: *American Journal of Archaeology*

AJAH: *American Journal of Ancient History*

AnnPisa: *Annali della R. Scuola Normale Superiore di Pisa, Sezione di Lettere*

ANRW: *Aufstieg und Niedergang der Römischen Welt* (Berlin, New York 1972–)

AntCl: *L'Antiquité classique*

ArchCl: *Archeologia Classica*

ArchEph: *Archaiologike Ephemeris*

ArchJ: *Archaeological Journal*

ArchNews: Archaeological News (Tallahassee Archaeological Society)

ArchReports: Archaeological Reports, in *Journal of Hellenic Studies*

ASAtene: *Annuario della R. Scuola Archeologica di Atene*

ASCS: American School of Classical Studies

ASMG: *Atti della Società della Magna Grecia*

Aspects of Italic Culture: Published as *Italian Iron Age Artefacts in the British Museum.* Sixth British Museum Classical Colloquium, December 1982, ed. J. Swaddling (London 1985)

AthMitt: *Mitteilungen des deutschen Archäologischen Instituts, Athenische Abteilung*

Aufnahme 1981: *Aufnahme fremder Kultureinflüsse in Etrurien und das Problem des Retardierens in der etruskischen Kunst.* Etrusker-Symposion Mannheim 1980 Schriften des Deutschen Archäologen-Verbandes 5 (Mannheim 1981)

Babelon-Blanchet, Catalogue des Bronzes Antiques: E. Babelon, J.-A. Blanchet, *Catalogue des Bronzes Antiques de la Bibliothèque Nationale* (Paris 1895)

BABesch: *Bulletin von de Vereeniging tot Bevordering der Kennis van de Antieke Beschaving*

BAC: *Bulletin archéologique du Comité des travaux historiques et archéologiques*

BAntFr: *Bulletin de la Société nationale des antiquaires de France*

Banti, Etruscan Cities: L. Banti. *The Etruscan Cities and Their Culture* (Berkeley and Los Angeles 1973)

BCH: *Bulletin de correspondance hellénique*

BdA: *Bollettino d'Arte*

Beazley, EVP: J.D. Beazley, *Etruscan Vase Painting* (Oxford 1947)

Becatti-Magi: G. Becatti, F. Magi, *Monumenti della pittura antica scoperti in Italia.* 1. *La pittura etrusca di Tarquinia* (Rome 1955)

Bianchi Bandinelli-Giuliano, Etruschi e Italici: R. Bianchi Bandinelli, A. Giuliano, *Etruschi e Italici prima del dominio di Roma* (Milan 1973)

BiblArch: *The Biblical Archaeologist*

Bibl.Nat.: Bibliothèque Nationale

BICS: *Bulletin of the Institute of Classical Studies*

Boardman, Greeks Overseas: J. Boardman, *The Greeks Overseas,* revised ed. (London 1980)

Boethius: A. Boethius, *Etruscan and Early Roman Architecture* (Harmondsworth 1978)

BollMonMusGallPont: *Bollettino dei Monumenti Musei e Gallerie Pontifici*

Bonfante, Etruscan Dress: L. Bonfante, *Etruscan Dress* (Baltimore and London 1975)

Bonfante, Etruscan Language: G. Bonfante and L. Bonfante, *The Etruscan Language: An Introduction* (Manchester and New York 1983)

Bonfante, Out of Etruria: L. Bonfante, *Out of Etruria: Etruscan Influence North and South.* BAR S103 (Oxford 1981)

Bordenache-Battaglia, Ciste prenestine I: G. Bordenache Battaglia, *Le Ciste prenestine I* (Rome 1979)

Brendel, Etruscan Art: O.J. Brendel, *Etruscan Art*

Brendel Essays: *In Memoriam Otto J. Brendel. Essays in Archaeology and the Humanities,* ed. L. Bonfante and H. von Heintze (Mainz 1976)

Brit.Mus.: British Museum

Brown, Etruscan Lion: W. Llewellyn Brown, *The Etruscan Lion* (Oxford 1960)

BSA: *British School at Athens, Annual*

BSL: Bulletin de la Société de Linguistique de Paris

Buonamici, *Epigrafia etrusca:* G. Buonamici, *Epigrafia etrusca* (Florence 1932)

Cahiers Bérard: *Cahiers du Centre Jean Bérard*

Camporeale, *Commerci di Vetulonia:* G. Camporeale, *I commerci di Vetulonia in età orientalizzante* (Florence 1969)

Camporeale, *Tomba del Duce:* G. Camporeale, *La Tomba del Duce di Vetulonia* (Florence 1967)

Canciani-von Hase, Tomba Bernardini: F. Canciani and F.-W. von Hase, *La tomba Bernardini di Palestrina. Latium Vetus II* (Rome 1979)

Caratteri dell'ellenismo: *Caratteri dell'ellenismo nelle urne etrusche. Prospettiva,* Suppl. I (Florence 1977)

CIE: Corpus Inscriptionum Etruscarum

Civiltà del Lazio Primitivo: *Civiltà del Lazio Primitivo* (Rome 1976)

Colloquii del Sodalizio: *Colloquii del Sodalizio* (Rome)

Contributi: *Contributi introduttivi allo studio della monetazione etrusca.* Atti del V Convegno del Centro Internazionale di Studi Numismatici 1975 (Naples 1976)

CP: Classical Philology

CR: Classical Review

CRAI: Comptes Rendus de l'Académie des Inscriptions et Belles Lettres

Cristofani, *L'arte degli Etruschi:* M. Cristofani, *L'arte degli Etruschi. Produzione e consumo* (Turin 1978)

Cristofani, *Etruscans:* M. Cristofani, *The Etruscans* (London 1979)

Crossroads: *Crossroads of the Mediterranean.* International conference held at Brown University, 1981, ed. T. Hackens, R. Holloway, N. Holloway (Louvain-la-Neuve and Providence, R.I. 1983)

CSE: Corpus Speculorum Etruscorum

CSEL: Corpus Scriptorum Ecclesiasticorum Latinorum

CUE: Corpus delle urne etrusche di età ellenistica (Florence 1975–)

DAI: Deutsches Archäologisches Institut

DialAr: Dialoghi di Archeologia

D.H.: Dionysius of Halicarnassus, *Antiquitates Romanae*

Dumézil, *Archaic Roman Religion:* G. Dumézil, *Archaic Roman Religion* (Chicago 1970)

EAA: Enciclopedia dell'arte antica, classica e orientale

ES: E. Gerhard, A. Klügman and C. Körte, *Etruskische Spiegel* (Berlin 1840–1897)

EtCl: Études classiques

Ficana: *Ficana. Una pietra miliare sulla strada di Roma.* Exhibition Catalogue (Rome 1981)

Gempeler, *Etruskischen Kanopen:* R.D. Gempeler, *Die etruskischen Kanopen* (Einsiedeln 1974)

Giglioli, *Arte etrusca:* G.Q. Giglioli, *Arte etrusca* (Milan 1935)

Die Göttin von Pyrgi: *Die Göttin von Pyrgi.* Akten des Kolloquiums zum Thema. Archäologische, linguistische und religionsgeschichtliche Aspekte, Tübingen, 1979 (Florence 1981)

Grant, *Etruscans:* M. Grant, *The Etruscans* (New York 1980)

Grazer Beiträge: *Grazer Beiträge. Zeitschrift für die klassische Altertumswissenschaft*

Greeks, Celts and Romans: *Greeks, Celts and Romans. Studies in Venture and Resistance. Archaeology into History* I. (London and Totowa, New Jersey 1973)

Guide to Etruscan Mirrors: N.T. de Grummond, ed., *A Guide To Etruscan Mirrors* (Tallahassee, Florida 1982)

Harden, *Phoenicians:* D.B. Harden, *The Phoenicians* (London and New York 1963)

von Hase, *Seminar Marburg 5* (1979): F.-W. von Hase, "Zur Interpretation villanovazeitlicher und frühetruskischer Funde in Griechenland und der Ägäis," *Kleine Schriften aus dem vorgeschichtlichen Seminar Marburg 5* (1979)

Helbig, *Führer*[4]: W. Helbig, *Führer durch die öffentlichen Sammlungen klassischer Altertümer in Rom,* vols. 1–4, ed. H. Speier (Tübingen 1963–72)

Hellenische Poleis: *Hellenische Poleis,* ed. E.C. Welskopf (Berlin 1973–74)

Herbig, *Götter und Dämonen:* R. Herbig, *Götter und Dämonen der Etrusker,* ed. Erika Simon (Mainz 1965)

Heurgon, *Daily Life:* J. Heurgon, *The Daily Life of the Etruscans* (New York 1964)

Higgins, *Jewellery:* R.A. Higgins, *Greek and Roman Jewellery*[2] (London 1980)

***Hommages Benoît* II (1972):** *Omaggio Fernand Benoît,* 4 vols. Istituto Internazionale di Studi Liguri (Bordighera 1972)

Hommages Grenier: *Hommages A. Grenier* (Paris 1962)

IBR: D. Ridgway, F.R.S. Ridgway, eds., *Italy Before the Romans* (London, New York and San Francisco 1979)

JAOS: Journal of the American Oriental Society

JdI: Jahrbuch des(k.)deutschen archäologischen Instituts

Jeffery, *LSAG:* L.H. Jeffery, *The Local Scripts of Archaic Greece* (Oxford 1961)

JHS: Journal of Hellenic Studies

Johnston, *Trademarks:* A. Johnston, *Trademarks on Greek Vases* (Warminster 1979)

JRS: Journal of Roman Studies

LCM: Liverpool Classical Monthly

LIMC: Lexicon Iconographicum Mythologiae Classicae

LSJ: H.G. Liddell, R. Scott, H. Stuart Jones, *Greek-English Lexicon.* 9th ed. (Oxford 1940)

MAAR: Memoirs of the American Academy in Rome

Macnamara, *Everyday Life:* E. Macnamara, *Everyday Life of the Etruscans* (London and New York 1973)

MadrMitt: Mitteilungen des Deutschen Archäologischen Instituts, Madrider Abteilung

MarbWPr: Marburger Winckelmann Programm

von Matt, Moretti, Maetzke: L. von Matt, M. Moretti, G. Maetzke, *The Art of the Etruscans,* foreword by D. Strong (London 1970)

Mayer-Prokop: I. Mayer-Prokop, *Die gravierten etruskischen Griffspiegel archaischen Stils* (Heidelberg 1967)

MEFRA: Mélanges d'Archéologie et d'Histoire de l'École Française de Rome. Antiquité

Mélanges Heurgon: L'Italie préromaine et la Rome républicaine. Mélanges offerts à J. Heurgon (Rome 1976)

MemLinc: Memorie della R. Accademia Nazionale dei Lincei

Milani, *Mus.Arch.*: L.A. Milani, *Il R. Museo Archeologico di Firenze* (Florence 1912)

MonAnt: Monumenti Antichi

MonPiot: Monuments et mémoires publiés par l'Académie des Inscriptions et Belles-Lettres, Fondation Piot.

Mostra dell'Etruria Padana: Mostra dell'Etruria Padana e della città di Spina I (Bologna 1961)

Mueller-Deecke: K.O. Mueller and W. Deecke, *Die Etrusker* (Stuttgart 1877; rev. A.J. Pfiffig, 1963)

MusHelv: Museum Helveticum

NSc: Notizie degli Scavi di Antichità

Ogilvie, *Commentary*: R.M. Ogilvie, *A Commentary on Livy, Books 1–5* (Oxford 1965)

ÖJh: Jahreshefte des österreichischen archäologischen Instituts

Out of Etruria: L. Bonfante, *Out of Etruria. Etruscan Influence North and South.* BAR International Series 103 (Oxford 1981). With two chapters on language by G. Bonfante. (See also Bonfante, *Out of Etruria*)

Pairault, *Recherches*: F.-H. Pairault, *Recherches sur quelques séries d'urnes de Volterra à représentations mythologiques* (Rome 1972)

Pallottino, *Etruscans*: M. Pallottino, *The Etruscans* (Harmondsworth 1978).

Pallottino, *Saggi di Antichità*: M. Pallottino, *Saggi di Antichità* (Rome 1979)

ParPass: La Parola del Passato

PBSR: Papers of the British School of Archaeology at Rome

Pfiffig, *Etruskische Sprache*: A.J. Pfiffig, *Die etruskische Sprache* (Graz 1969)

Pfiffig, *Religio Etrusca*: A.J. Pfiffig, *Religio Etrusca* (Graz 1975)

Pfister-Roesgen: G. Pfister-Roesgen, *Die etruskischen Spiegel des 5. Jhs. v. Chr.* (Frankfurt am Main 1975)

Pliny, *NH*: C. Plinius Secundus, *Naturalis Historia*

Popoli e Civiltà (Pop. e Civ.): Popoli e civiltà dell'Italia antica 1–7 (Rome 1974–78)

Prayon: F. Prayon, *Frühetruskische Grab- und Hausarchitektur* (Heidelberg 1975)

Prima Italia (1981): Prima Italia. Arts italiques du premier millénaire av. J.C. (Brussels 1980–81)

ProcPhilSoc: Proceedings of the American Philosophical Society

ProcPS: Proceedings of the Prehistoric Society. Cambridge

Pyrgi: Scavi nel santuario etrusco di Pyrgi (Rome 1964)

RA: Revue archéologique

Rallo, *Lasa*: A. Rallo, *Lasa. Iconografia e esegesi* (Florence 1974)

Rasmussen, *Bucchero*: T. Rasmussen, *Bucchero Pottery from Southern Etruria* (Cambridge 1979)

Rathje, "Banquet Service": A. Rathje, "A Banquet Service from the Latin City of Ficana," *Analecta Romana*

Istituti Danici 12 (1983) 7–29

Rebuffat-Emmanuel, *Le miroir étrusque*: D. Rebuffat-Emmanuel, *Le miroir étrusque d'après la collection du Cabinet des Médailles* (Rome 1973)

REA: Revue des études anciennes

REE: Rivista di Epigrafia Etrusca, continuing survey of inscriptions, published in *Studi Etruschi*

REL: Revue des études latines

RendPontAcc: Atti della Pontificia Accademia Romana di Archeologia, Rendiconti

Richardson, *Etruscans*: E.H. Richardson, *The Etruscans* (Chicago 1964)

RivFC: Rivista di Filologia e d'Istruzione Classica

RivIstArch: Rivista del R. Istituto d'Archeologia e Storia dell'Arte

RivScPr: Rivista di Scienze Preistoriche (Florence)

RivStorAnt: Rivista Storica dell'Antichità

RömMitt: Mitteilungen des deutschen archäologischen Instituts. Römische Abteilung

RSF: Rivista di Studi Fenici

RSL: Rivista di Studi Liguri

RStO: Rivista degli Studi Orientali

Seminar Marburg: Kleine Schriften aus dem vorgeschichtlichen Seminar Marburg

de Simone, *Griechische Entlehnungen*: C. de Simone, *Griehische Entlehnungen im Etruskischen* vols. I–II (Wiesbaden 1968–70)

Snodgrass, *Archaic Greece*: A. Snodgrass, *Archaic Greece. The Age of Experiment* (London, Melbourne and Toronto 1980)

Sprenger-Bartoloni: M. Sprenger, G. Bartoloni, M. Hirmer, A. Hirmer, *The Etruscans: Their History, Art and Architecture* (New York 1983)

StDocHistIur: Studia et Documenta Historiae et Iuris

Steingräber, *Etruskische Möbel*: S. Steingräber, *Etruskische Möbel* (Rome 1979)

StEtr: Studi Etruschi

Strøm, *Etruscan Orientalizing*: I. Strøm, *Problems Concerning the Origin and Early Development of the Etruscan Orientalizing Style* (Odense 1971)

StRom: Studi Romani

Studi Banti (Rome 1965): *Studi in onore di Luisa Banti,* ed. G. Camporeale (Rome 1965)

Studies Robinson, I: *Studies Presented to David M. Robinson* I (St. Louis, Missouri 1951)

Thesaurus: Thesaurus Linguae Etruscae I (Rome 1978).

TLE: M. Pallottino, *Testimonia Linguae Etruscae*[2] (Florence 1968)

Torelli, *Elogia Tarquiniensia*: M. Torelli, *Elogia Tarquiniensia* (Florence 1975)

Warmington, *Carthage*: P.H. Warmington, *Carthage* (Harmondsworth 1964)

Webster, *Potter and Patron*: T.B.L. Webster, *Potter and Patron in Classical Athens* (London 1972)

Maps

Sources for the maps: for Map 1, L. Banti, *The Etruscan Cities and Their Culture* (Berkeley and Los Angeles 1973), p. 3; for Map 2, K.W. Weeber, *Geschichte der Etrusker* (Stuttgart 1979), p. 38; for Maps 3, 4, 6, and 7, M. Pallottino, *Genti e culture dell' Italia preromana* (Rome 1981), figs. 1, 3, 19, and 2; for Map 5, G. Bonfante and P. Ferrero, *Grammatica Latina* (Milan 1976), map 2; for Map 8, A.J. Pfiffig, *Die etruskische Sprache* (Graz 1969), map 2; for Map 9, W. Culican, *The First Merchant Venturers* (New York 1966), fig. 1.

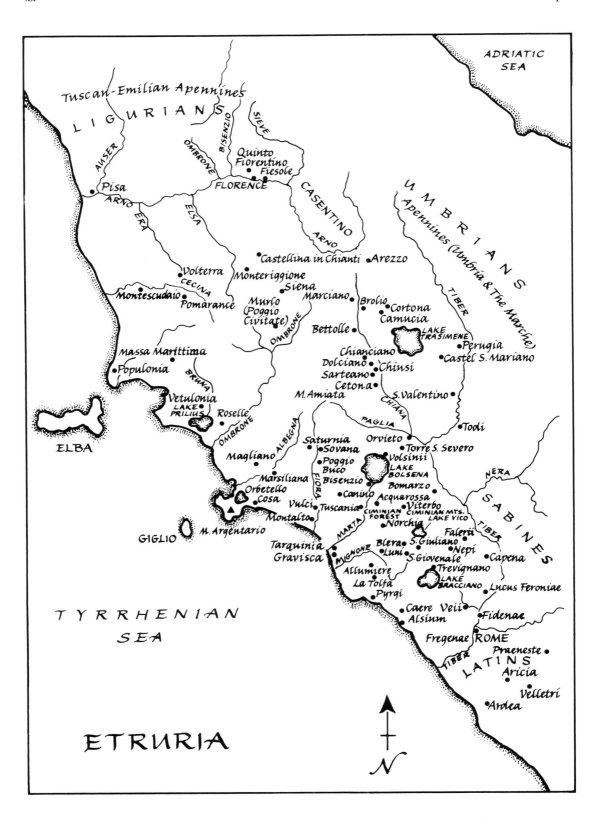

Map 2 xxi

ETRUSCAN CITIES
and
THEIR BOUNDARIES

Map 4   xxiii

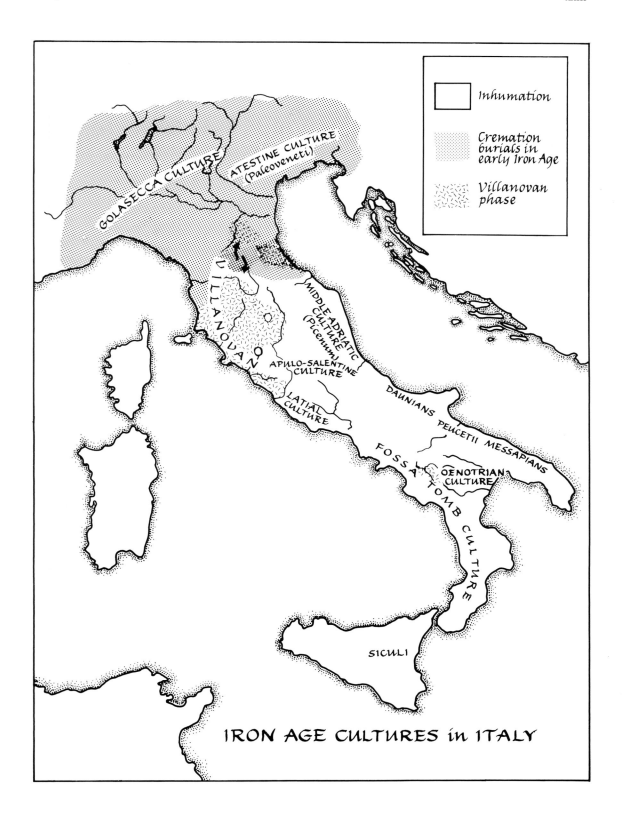

Inhumation

Cremation
burials in
early Iron Age

Villanovan
phase

GOLASECCA CULTURE

ATESTINE CULTURE
(Paleoveneti)

VILLANOVAN

MIDDLE ADRIATIC
CULTURE
(Picenum)

APULO-SALENTINE
CULTURE

LATIAL
CULTURE

DAUNIANS PEUCETII MESSAPIANS

FOSSA TOMB CULTURE

OENOTRIAN
CULTURE

SICULI

IRON AGE CULTURES in ITALY

Map 5

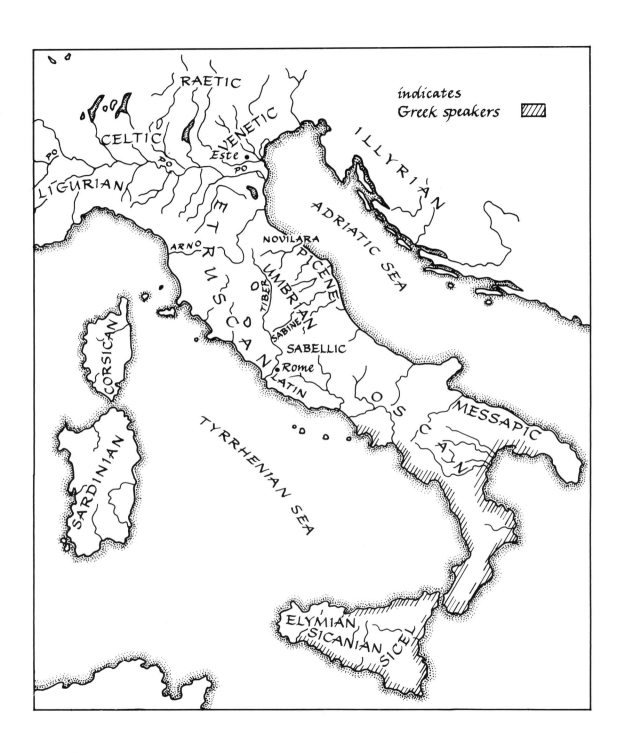

indicates
Greek speakers

RAETIC

CELTIC

VENETIC

LIGURIAN

PO

PO

PO

Este

ILLYRIAN

ADRIATIC SEA

ARNO

NOVILARA

ETRUSCAN

TIBER

UMBRIAN

SABINE

PICENE

SABELLIC

Rome

LATIN

O

S

C

A

N

MESSAPIC

TYRRHENIAN SEA

CORSICAN

SARDINIAN

ELYMIAN
SICANIAN

SICEL

Map 6

XXV

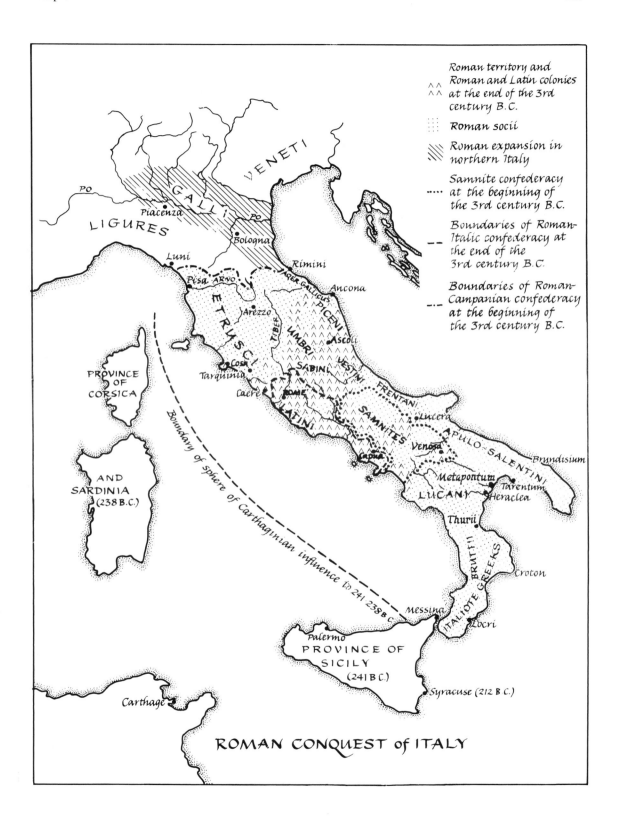

ROMAN CONQUEST of ITALY

RAETIA

XI
TRANSPADANA

X
VENETIA ET HISTRIA

DALMATIA

PO

IX
LIGURIA

AEMILIA

VIII

PO

ARNO

ADRIATIC SEA

ETRURIA

VII

UMBRIA

VI
PICENUM

TIBER

SABINI ET IV
SAMNIUM

V

CORSICA

II
APULIA
ET
HIRPINI

CALABRIA SALLENTINI

LATIUM
ET CAMPANIA

TYRRHENIAN
SEA

III
LUCANIA
ET BRUTTII

SARDINIA

N

SICILIA

REGIONS of ITALY
ORGANIZED UNDER AUGUSTUS

Map 8

xxvii

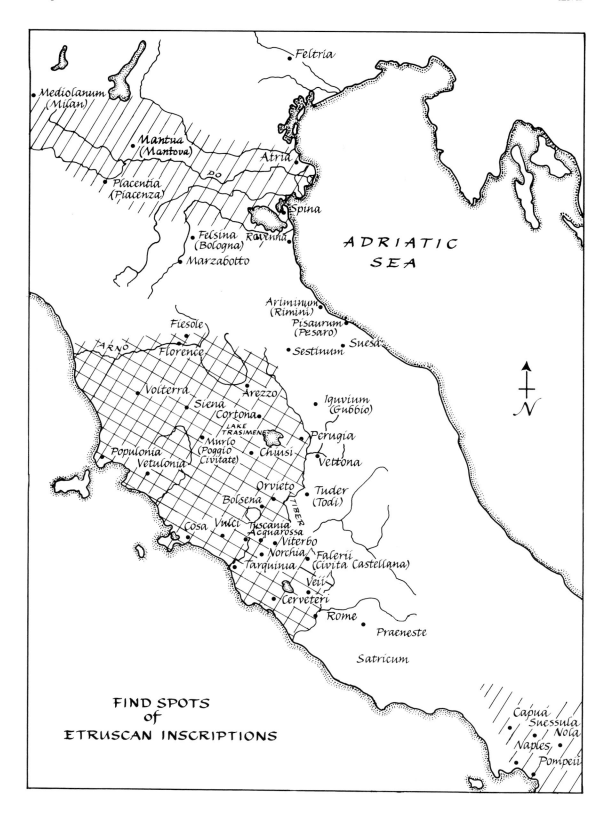

FIND SPOTS
of
ETRUSCAN INSCRIPTIONS

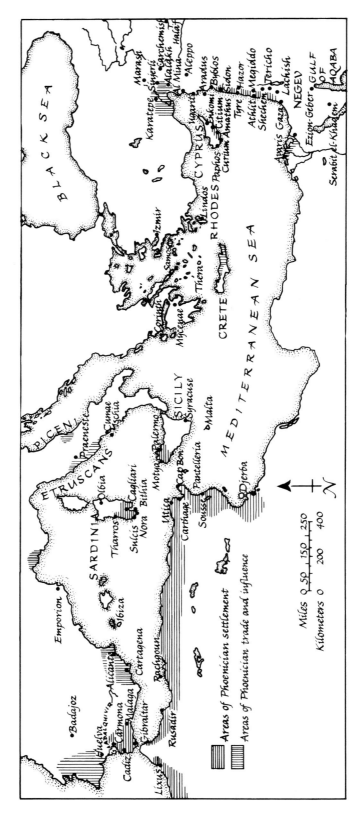

ETRUSCAN Life and Afterlife

Introduction / Etruscan Studies Today

LARISSA BONFANTE

The eight essays in this volume attempt to cover the history, customs, art, and architecture of the Etruscans, standard headings under which we are accustomed to study a civilization. This coverage, however, is incomplete. We face a peculiar situation with regard to the Etruscans: there is no literature. What we know most about, their monuments, has to be "read" in order to gain information about their history, their religion, and their daily life. The unevenness of the coverage therefore reflects, in part, the state of our knowledge.

There is much we do not know. But a great deal can be revealed by a new way of seeing, thanks to the work of individual scholars, past and present, as Nancy de Grummond makes clear in the first chapter on the history of Etruscan studies. For too long, even in the present century, such ultimately sterile problems as the "origin" of the Etruscans and the "mystery" of their language occupied the energies of scholars as well as the fantasies of laymen. In recent years several scholars have, by their individual efforts, redirected the focus of the study. Luisa Banti, for example, insisted on the individual character of the various Etruscan city-states; a proud Florentine herself, she understood what it meant to be a citizen of a community whose culture radiated well beyond its physical boundaries. Jacques Heurgon, in his classic work on the daily life of the Etruscans, an original survey and outstanding example of *haute vulgarisation,* made this subject respectable and visible. Massimo Pallottino also changed our way of looking at the problem of Etruscan origins. In the various editions of his fundamental book *The Etruscans,* he has identified many problems and set new directions. He is responsible for many of these advances, directly through his own scholarship and indirectly by his leadership, most recently as president of the Istituto di Studi Etruschi.[1]

The efforts of these and other scholars seem finally to have set the Etruscans firmly into a historical setting, out of the isolation to which their "mystery" condemned them, and to have made a wider public conscious of their reality. Anyone who has traveled to the Etruscan sites and has seen the rocky hills where their cities stood and the mounds which mark their cemeteries, so well described by George Dennis, has no doubt of their existence and begins to imagine, as D.H. Lawrence did, something about the world they lived in and their relation to their neighbors in Italy and beyond.[2]

We are entering a new phase of Etruscan studies. This book, focusing directly on the Etruscans, may be one of the last to treat the Etruscans as a separate culture rather than as one of the many groups inhabiting pre-Roman Italy (Map 3). There is now much more interest in their foreign relations, described in Jean MacIntosh Turfa's survey (Ch. III) of the Etruscans' international contacts. In fact, this awareness of the Etruscans' identity as one of many peoples living in a complex world has made it possible to understand the evidence in a wider context and, for the first time, to write the history of the Etruscans, as may be seen in Chapter II, by Mario Torelli.[3]

Though there is still controversy about the chronology and composition of the Etruscan people, recent discoveries confirm the theory that the history of the Etruscan people extends at least from the Iron Age in Italy to the end of the Roman Republic—in chronological terms, from about 1000 B.C. to the first century B.C.. The sites of the chief Etruscan cities of historical time were continuously occupied from the Iron Age (Villanovan period) on (Maps 1–2). Much confusion would have been avoided if archaeologists had used the name "proto-Etruscan" (meaning "early Etruscan"), instead of Villanovan, to refer to this Iron Age material, excavated first at Villanova, near Bologna, in the mid-nineteenth century and later at all the major Etruscan sites (Map 4).⁴ The people who lived in central Italy between the Arno and Tiber rivers spoke a language first known to us from a thousand or so inscriptions of the seventh century B.C., and so this is the date when we begin to refer to them as the historical Etruscans. They surely did not suddenly start to speak Etruscan: what happened was that they learned to write from their Greek neighbors at Pithekoussai (Ischia) and Cumae and thus recorded their peculiar language (Maps 5, 8).⁵ The use of writing, borrowed from the Greeks, officially marks the beginning of the historical period in Italy. A chapter in this book, by Emeline Richardson, introduces us to their writing and language.

The complexity of our picture of the Etruscans also reflects the historical reality of their great variety: like the contemporary Greek polis, or a Tuscan city of the Renaissance, each Etruscan city was characterized by its individualism and independence. One of the results was disunity. There never was an Etruscan empire; there was an Etruscan people, who shared a language, a religion, a geographical location, and certain customs and costumes that made them recognizably different from other people in Italy and in the Mediterranean. They also shared a name. The Etruscans knew themselves as Rasenna or Rasna. The Greeks knew them as Tyrrhenians and gave this name to the sea the Etruscans controlled to the west of the Italian peninsula (the Adriatic derived its name from Adria, or Atria, a settlement of Etruscans and Greeks on the eastern coast). The Romans called them Tursi, Tusci, or Etrusci. The name of one of the streets of Rome, the Vicus Tuscus near the Capitoline Hill, long preserved the memory of their residence in the city.⁶

One of the most fascinating aspects of Etruscan studies is the way in which progress has depended on the accidents of archaeological discoveries and on the point of view from which the material is considered. There has been much recent activity in both discovery and discussion, and there will continue to be for some time. Change has been rapid. It is no coincidence that in the last twenty years excavation has brought to light evidence that has

transformed our view of the Etruscans and illuminated previously unknown aspects of their civilization. It is hoped that this book will prepare the reader to participate in the ongoing recovery of this important area of ancient history and to want to find out more about this ancient people so important to our past.

For the sake of convenience ten new trends in Etruscan studies are surveyed in this Introduction. The first six relate to new methodology that is proving fruitful; the next four sections pertain to particular periods and subjects that have received new emphasis. Within each area, the acrimony of the controversy often is a measure of the intensity of the interest aroused.

Restoration, Conservation, and Exhibition

The disastrous flood of 1966 in Florence marks the beginning of an aggressive campaign of restoration and conservation of objects in museums. This concern for the restoration of ancient monuments is paralleled by the concern of archaeologists with careful excavation techniques and the application of scientific methods.⁷ When the disaster of the flood struck in Florence, the Soprintendenza reacted promptly and heroically. There were many losses, but important gains were made when objects were cleaned and revealed surprises. In 1967, Soprintendente Guglielmo Maetzke officially announced the establishment of the Centro del Restauro in Florence. Now this world-famous laboratory has almost completed the cleaning and restoration of the material in the topographical section of the Museo Archeologico in Florence (on the ground floor of the building, this material was the worst hit by the flood).⁸ The laboratory has been responsible for such striking achievements as the cleaning of the terracotta sarcophagus of the Bride and Groom in the Louvre.⁹

Museums are now trying to clean and restore, as far as their budgets will allow, their older collections. Such cleaning often involves the removal of nineteenth-century "restorations" which concealed the true nature of the object. The year 1971 saw the publication of one of the most remarkable monuments of situla art and a document of the life of women in Italy in the seventh century B.C., long preserved in Bologna in the Museo Civico Archeologico. Recent cleaning of this bronze "tintinnabulum," or pendant, part of a woman's tomb furnishings, uncovered for the first time its incised decoration, which illustrated, appropriately enough, scenes of women busy at their woolwork and included a picture of the most ambitious loom known from antiquity, a two-storied affair, with a nobly dressed lady in the top story seated on a high-backed chair.[10] The cleaning of two seventh-century Etruscan terracotta statuettes in the British Museum revealed that the heads on the ladies did not belong. Female heads had been attached to male bodies in order to achieve the "complete" work nineteenth-century buyers (including museums) demanded. Together with a third statuette in Rome, the statuettes break down into two female heads, one male head, and three male bodies. We can therefore reconstitute one complete male statuette (fig. IV–39); but we shall never know what the female bodies looked like, for the missing fragments were discarded.[11]

These newly cleaned pieces are presently exhibited in new settings in several major museums. After World War II, the museum of Villa Giulia in Rome was the first to design a new exhibit space, and it is still a model. The architects' brilliant solution, carried out within the spaces of the Renaissance villa of Pope Julius III, was shocking and controversial. In fact, much of the public bitterly denounced the solution. The use of transparent plastic rather than conventional plaster to complete the limbs of such statues as the Apollo of Veii is an example: the outcry was so great that the transparent material was removed and never tried again. Other museums have followed suit in creating new settings for their Etruscan collections: the Louvre, the Museo Etrusco Gregoriano in the Vatican, and the British Museum.[12]

Corpora and Other Publications

Not since the nineteenth century have there been so many corpora in the course of publication. The pursuit of order in scholarship leads once more to the compilation of collections of scattered materials, like the nineteenth-century compendia. The new works emphasize objectivity, tending to replace drawings with photographs and organization by subject matter with a topographical and chronological context. We still depend on the earlier publications, however, for the newer contributions complement rather than replace these, produced as they are, for the most part, by committees rather than by individuals.

An ambitious international project, the *Lexicon Iconographicum Mythologiae Classicae* (*LIMC*), deals with the classical subject matter so popular in Etruscan art and is already immensely useful.[13] Under the aegis of the Istituto di Studi Etruschi, the publication of the *Corpus Inscriptionum Etruscarum* (*CIE*) has resumed;[14] new corpora—of Etruscan mirrors (*CSE*),[15] Hellenistic cinerary urns (*CUE*),[16] and painting[17]—are under way, as is the *Thesaurus Linguae Etruscae*.[18] The corpus of Praenestine cistae collects and catalogs these objects so closely related to Etruscan art.[19]

Many new series—too numerous to list—have been established for the publication of material in older collections, in museums as well as in private hands.[20] For museums and collections in Rome, the new fourth edition of Helbig's guide is an invaluable aid. The publication of existing collections not only provides us with important "new" monuments, but also with tomb groups and contexts that give a history for many of the monuments previously known only in isolation. Prayon's archival research, for example, has led to the identification of the Tomb of the Five Chairs in Cerveteri, where five terracotta statuettes originally were represented seated on high chairs, attending a funerary banquet (fig. VIII–1).[21] The accessibility of all this material—older as well as newly excavated—is making it much easier to carry out new studies using reliable data and statistics in a variety of areas.

History of Archaeology

A study of the history of the discipline of archaeology (its techniques, ideas, fashions, and personalities) is a necessary part of archaeological research.

This kind of study involves digging in archives for the identification of collections and tomb groups, and searching out the pedigree and provenance of single monuments in order to uncover the forgeries and reveal the true discoveries of the past. Art historians have long been interested in the survival and revival of antiquity and its influence on the art of later periods and have often explored the history of archaeology. Now archaeologists are having to make judgments on the work of their predecessors as they are excavating in the field and in archives.[22]

Ultimately "man himself is at the center of archaeological studies and interpretation, both affected by and affecting the discoveries that are made."[23] Recent interest has focused on the historical context in which a number of eighteenth- and nineteenth-century forgeries were carried out and on the personalities involved. The famous Praenestine fibula, which has for a century been honored as bearing the earliest Latin inscription and the best example of archaic Latin, "Manios med vhevhaked" ("Manius made me"), is now supposed by many to have been forged in collusion with learned scholars who conspired to pass it off as genuine.[24] The history of museum collections and private collections, which makes fascinating reading, is providing the background for exhibits such as that of the Vatican collections shown in New York and elsewhere in the United States.[25]

Exhibits, Catalogues, and Colloquia

In 1955, an important exhibit of Etruscan art in Zurich renewed interest in Etruscan studies on the international level.[26] In Italy, those were euphoric postwar years. While the arts and literature blossomed, ancient historians and archaeologists turned away from the country's imperial past, encouraged throughout the thirties and early forties by Mussolini,[27] and concentrated once more on early Rome and the Etruscans.

Marxist scholars have claimed credit for the current interest in "material culture" that informs archaeological work in Italy today. But this approach is not new; the Germans in the last century were already studying what they called *Realien*—the actual physical objects and what they can tell us about the daily life of the people who used them (a practical approach especially suited for the study of Etruscan remains). This trend preceded the theoretical, philosophical approach of the period between the two world wars.[28]

Giacomo Boni's careful excavation of the prehistoric Roman huts on the Palatine at the turn of the century was paralleled by the work of Etruscan scholars. Public enthusiasm went hand in hand with scholarly accuracy, for example, in the foundation of the museum of Etruscan topography in the Museo Archeologico in Florence. L.A. Milani, who organized it in 1897, described this collection as unique in its grouping of objects by provenance and tomb groups and found its success to lie in the fact that "people are beginning to be more interested in simple things than in great ones, and to prefer grave furnishings to the monuments of great art."[29] At the same time, the discovery of the magnificent work known as the Apollo of Veii in 1916 also publicized and encouraged scholarly as well as amateur interest in the Etruscans.

Much of the groundwork for our present interdisciplinary, concerted work on Etruscan art and culture was laid during the twenties. The Istituto di Studi Etruschi was founded in 1932, but its journal, *Studi Etruschi,* had started to appear regularly in 1927.[30] Since the Etruscan exhibit of 1955 many others have taken place, each marking a new turn on the road, summing up past knowledge, making it available in catalogue form, and spurring research in new directions.[31] In the United States, several important exhibits have included Etruscan material: one held in Worcester, Massachusetts, in 1967, focused on monuments of Etruscan art in America.[32] These exhibits, often accompanied by colloquia or symposia, brought together, either physically or in print, the chief scholars in the field.

Italian exhibitions and catalogues have also been devoted to other peoples of ancient Italy, such as the Sabines (a most important inscription was discovered to be in the Boston Museum of Fine Arts), or to areas such as that of situla art (appropriately carried out as an international project). One of the most influential exhibitions recreated a chronological period: "Roma Medio Repubblicana" (1973) brought together material from Rome and the neighboring area illustrating the culture of the fourth through second centuries B.C., thereby at last ordering a vast number of monuments either vaguely classified as Hellenistic or oscillating in time and space between the fourth and first centuries B.C. or even later.[33] Exhibits displaying the finds from early Latium have been of great importance. Designed to represent Italy at the "Europalia" in Brussels in 1980, "Prima Italia" exhibited a group of monuments from Italy of the first millennium B.C. The exhibit and accompanying catalogue (1981) are particularly useful for their reflection of the peoples and the levels of civilization in ancient Italy, in sharp contrast to the contemporary situation in Greece. They also illustrate the modern tendency to look for interconnections among these various peoples and for some historical and geographical unity underlying and formed by the ever-changing, often chaotic variety in each of its phases. Typical, as we have seen, is the attempt to see the world of the Oscans, Sabines, Etruscans, Latins, Gauls, etc., in a wider context. This same concern was also expressed by the colloquium held at the British Museum in December, 1982, in preparation for the installation of the permanent exhibition galleries of Italic art, designed to parallel those of Minoan, Mycenaean, and Greek art. The topic was neither, as it might once have been, Etruscan art, nor Roman, but "Aspects of Italic Culture."[34]

Interdisciplinary Collaboration

The study of the Etruscans in a wider context is, in part, made possible by the cooperative nature of Etruscan studies. More than any other field, "Etruscology," as the Italians call it, has cut across disciplinary barriers. This is so by necessity. Historical evidence is practically nonexistent and hard to interpret. Linguistic and archaeological evidence often does not agree. But the danger of not crossing boundaries is illustrated by the contrast so often wrongly assumed to exist between "Villanovan," an archaeological term, and "Etruscan," a linguistic definition. The resulting inconsistency could have been avoided by an integrated approach. Now anyone who studies the Etruscans has to make use of a variety of evidence, from an inscription to the shape of a tomb to a fashion represented in a tomb painting. Massimo Pallottino's famous *Etruscologia*

showed how all this evidence could be woven together to form a picture. Recently a historian of early Italy, E.T. Salmon, has broken new ground by writing a book on the Romanization of Italy using the considerable linguistic evidence at hand to build up a historical picture of Italy's changing culture from the fourth to the first century B.C.[35] The meetings of the Istituto di Studi Etruschi typically include linguists, art historians, archaeologists, and epigraphists. One area in which the interdisciplinary approach has been increasingly fruitful is the study of the sculptured funerary urns of the Hellenistic period, which were made in the north Etruscan cities of Volterra, Chiusi, and Perugia. The realistic "portraits" of the deceased on the lids of these terracotta or stone urns, the inscriptions recording their names, and the mythological relief representations on the front of the caskets have to be studied together to give a consistent picture, though the particular study of their language and their art is the business of specialists.

Interdisciplinary studies are particularly necessary for the understanding of Etruscan religion, social structure, legal systems, economics, and political organization; of the place of women and the identification of slaves; of aristocrats and craftsmen; of members of the middle class, freedmen, clients and refugees, priests, magistrates, traders, peasants, warriors; of clans and families; and of villages, towns, and cities in the various periods of Etruscan history. A social history of Etruria has yet to be written, but we are beginning to piece together such a narrative.[36]

Nonfunerary Archaeology

Revolutionary for our understanding of the Etruscan cities has been the discovery of early habitation sites: houses at Acquarossa, where stone and tile-covered roofs existed side by side with the thatched-roof huts, an isolated architectural complex at Poggio Civitate (Murlo) near Siena, whose interpretation is controversial (palace or sanctuary?), and buildings at Castelnuovo Berardenga in the north. (Both Acquarossa and Murlo were destroyed around 500 B.C., probably in connection with the growth of Chiusi.) The study of the roads and landscape of Etruria, in great measure the province of British archaeologists, is closely related to this interest.[37]

The great sanctuary at Graviscae has changed our view of Etruscan-Greek relations, as have excavations of sanctuaries in Latium and central Italy in general. The publication of numerous collections of terracotta votive gifts from sanctuaries of this area, drawing upon objects found in both new excavations and existing museum collections, is further contributing to the serious study of ex-votos dating from the fourth to the first century B.C. A Hellenistic settlement at Cetamura del Chianti, presently under excavation, is providing new information about Etruscan town planning, including hydraulics, fortification, and street patterning. Systematic excavation and publication of other later habitation sites is needed to tell us more of developments from the fourth century B.C. on.[38]

Early Italy, Bronze and Iron Ages

Within Italy, extremely successful excavations and studies are expanding the prehistoric and protohistoric picture in their various areas. The results have recently been made accessible to English-speaking readers, primarily through David and Francesca Ridgway's collection of papers by some of the most involved scholars, both Italian and non-Italian (*Italy before the Romans*). As certain chronological periods receive special attention, the history of ancient Italy is extended farther and farther back in time. Within this framework, the Mycenaean presence becomes ever more substantial. The history of early metallurgy, too, has shown this technique to have been extraordinarily advanced in the second millennium B.C.[39]

International Relations

Important finds and publications have transformed our knowledge of pre-Roman Italy and of the history of the people who spoke and wrote Etruscan, whose well-harbored, mineral-rich, fertile land attracted the Greeks westward to settle near its borders at Pithekoussai, and whose cities developed

the culture that almost united Italy long before the Roman conquest. The historical relations of the Etruscans with their neighbors in Italy, the Mediterranean, and Europe can now be seen much more clearly, and scholarly syntheses are bringing the results of this revolution in thinking about Etruscan history before the public. The seven-volume *Popoli e civiltà dell'Italia antica* (1974–78) presents the syntheses in detail, and a number of exhibits and catalogues have furnished important information.[40]

PHOENICIAN AND PUNIC

In 1964 the discovery of three inscribed gold tablets from about 500 B.C., found between two temples at Pyrgi, the harbor of Cerveteri (two in Etruscan, one in Phoenician [or Punic?]), gave us a glimpse of events which could be fitted into the Greek and Roman historical record: Aristotle's remark on close ties between Etruscans and Carthaginians and Polybius's record of a Carthaginian treaty with Rome in 509 B.C.[41] Much remains to be done in this area; we shall certainly be learning more about relations between Etruscans and Phoenicians and Etruscans and Carthaginians—barbarians, that is, non-Greeks, in contact with a world known to us through Greek eyes (Map 9).

GREEK

The first western Greeks settled at the island of Pithekoussai, an emporium for trade rather than a colony proper, around 775 B.C. (Map 3). Hundreds of eighth-century graves and their contents are revealing details of lively trade and contact between Greeks and Etruscans, as well as between Greeks and peoples from the eastern Mediterranean in this period. Here and elsewhere, the attraction of Etruscan metal—a trade which probably existed before the arrival of the Greeks—is evident. Greek civilization and urbanization were developing in this very period, and the formation of the Greek polis may well have been encouraged by this kind of trade and contact.[42]

A study of the language illustrates the kind of

contact that took place between Etruscans and Greeks. Greeks brought to Etruria the alphabet, civilized customs such as drinking wine at symposia, the equipment for it, many words for vases, and technical terms.[43] Etruscans apparently learned to grow olives from the Greek colonies of southern Italy: an early vase is inscribed *aska eleivana* ("olive-oil bottle"), and the Greek word for the olive residue, *amurca,* came into Latin via Etruscan. Other Latin words which came from Greek by way of Etruscan in the early period include *groma,* a surveyor's instrument, and *triumphus,* a victory rite and parade. Such evidence shows that when the Greeks brought civilization to Italy, it was readily adopted by the Etruscans, who were well on their way to urbanization and therefore ready to take on the outward signs of this culture of cities. They handed it over in turn to their neighbors, the Latins.

The question of the formation of the city at this point in history is currently being discussed.[44] Of concern to both historians and archaeologists are the origin and growth of the cities of Italy, in particular, the native origin of the Etruscan cities and their relationships with the civilization of Greece in the Iron Age and Orientalizing periods, and in later times, down to the fourth-century *koine* (cultural unity) and the Hellenistic culture of the late Roman Republic.

The presence of immigrant Greeks in the sixth century B.C. is attested to by inscriptions and especially by Mario Torelli's excavation of a Greek sanctuary on Etruscan soil at Graviscae, the port of Tarquinia. The study of other kinds of archaeological evidence, for example, trade in Greek vases, is also forming a much clearer picture of Greek-Etruscan relations in all periods.[45]

LATIUM

Most recent, and most sensational of all, have been the finds made in ancient Latium. Publications dealing with these reflect the current realization that it is as impossible to separate history and archaeology as it is to view Rome's civilization as separate from that of her neighbors: the study of

the protohistoric and Archaic period in Rome and Latium has been completely transformed by these startling discoveries. Archaeological activity has gone hand in hand with a general revival of interest in the remote past of Rome and Latium, involving historians and philologists as well as archaeologists and resulting in a lively debate on the historical implications of these discoveries.[46]

The focus shifted from early Rome to other sites in Latium when a series of salvage excavations started to bring to light remains of the necropolis of Castel di Decima (from 1971 on), Osteria dell'Osa (from 1971 on), and one on the Via Laurentia (from 1976 on). Excavations of the settlements, the necropolis, and the sanctuary were carried out at Pratica di Mare from 1955 on, at the cities of Gabii and Ficana from 1976 on, and at Satricum since 1977.[47] Out of these emerges a picture of Latium made up of a group of independent settlements on the way to achieving urbanization. Among these, but not ahead of them, is Rome.[48] Spectacular exhibits have brought the material from these sites before a wide public.[49] Discovered at various sites of ancient Latium, these finds have revealed tombs as wealthy in the seventh century B.C. as contemporary ones in Etruria: the silver and amber dress of a lady in a tomb from Decima is as magnificent as anything found in any Etruscan tomb.[50] No longer must the rich seventh-century Bernardini and Barberini tombs of Praeneste be attributed to Etruscan lords, though scholars are still divided as to whether the name Vetusia, inscribed on a silver bowl from the seventh-century Bernardini Tomb, is Latin or Etruscan.[51]

We can see more clearly the differences between Latium and Etruscan cities. We can also confirm the Etruscans' reputation for luxurious living, as recent excavations and study are identifying the contrast between Etruscan and Latial ideology through the furnishing of the tombs.[52] For instance, the wealthy Latial tombs of the seventh century B.C. give way, at the end of the century, to poorer burials. After the seventh century, even the former custom of burying rich furnishings with the deceased in aristocratic tombs disappears. What accounts for this drastic change? Since there do not seem to be economic reasons, it has been plausibly suggested that it results from the enactment of sumptuary laws like those of the XII Tables forbidding extravagant funerals. The XII Tables may thus reflect much earlier laws. Rather than dating from the mid-fifth century B.C., they seem to belong, as far as the archaeological record is concerned, to the time of Tarquinius Priscus, over one hundred years earlier, and thus seem to be contemporary with the laws of Solon in Athens.[53]

Rome, of course, remains the center in Latium best known to us, for we have literary sources which relate events from Rome's past, while Rome's neighbors become visible largely through the material culture which new excavations are making available. From early times, Rome, facing the Etruscans directly across the Tiber, was the Latin city most exposed to the influence of the wealthy, sophisticated culture of the Etruscans. This influence has in recent years been shown to be highly visible, reflected as much in the archaeological record as in the accounts of such historians as Livy and Dionysius of Halicarnassus. This influence affected the outward forms of culture: the alphabet and writing; the insignia of honor of Roman kings and magistrates, including the triumphal procession with its music, costume, royal connotations, and its goal, the Temple of Jupiter on the Capitoline Hill; anthropomorphic images of the divinity; and the words for luxury objects and for technical knowledge (kylix, *groma*, etc.).[54]

A new view of the series of the kings of Rome has resulted from all this. In the post-World War II period, scholars expressed a more or less qualified belief in the historicity of the last three Etruscan kings of Rome, while the earlier four were considered mythical. The Sabine element in the tradition in particular was vigorously denied by Poucet, who considered anachronistic the traditional stories of the early kings—the dual kingship of the Sabine king, Titus Tatius, who ruled together with Romulus, and the "Sabine dynasty" of Numa Pompilius and Ancus Marcius. Reluctantly, it was conceded that the tales of the kings embodied historical elements and that one must avoid the extreme position of Ettore Pais, who dismissed the whole tradition of the monarchy as pure fiction.[55] The kings' names, for example, are as one would expect in that period:

Romulus had only one; his successor, Numa Pompilius, had two, reflecting a more developed social order. Numa's second name was, furthermore, clearly Sabine in form: in Latin it would have been Quintilius.

Giacomo Boni's excavations of the early hut foundations on the Palatine at the beginning of the century[56] set a physical stage for the history of early Rome which had long been considered fictional. Today the pendulum has swung away from the earlier skepticism, and scholars regularly use the names of all the kings, including Romulus, in reconstructing the stages of Rome's growth and the history of her neighbors.[57] The rich site of the necropolis of Decima has been tentatively identified with the city of Politorium mentioned by Livy, and the names of other cities of the *prisci Latini,* the "early Latins," have been connected with recently excavated sites. The traditional accounts of Livy and Dionysius of Halicarnassus seem to have been confirmed by, and have in turn given meaning and structure to, the archaeological discoveries. Scholars today take the written sources seriously, including the chronological framework.

This is not to say that historians and archaeologists are in agreement. In fact there is much healthy, and some acrimonious, controversy about the interpretation and reconciliation of literary and archaeological evidence. An example of disagreement, within the covers of this volume, is the question of the beginning of coinage in Italy. Mario Torelli, in his chapter on history, accepts the recent attribution of the introduction of a form of coinage to King Servius Tullius, on the basis of Pliny's statement, "*Servius rex primus signavit aes*"; a type of cast bronze bar has been identified with such *aes signatum*. Both identification and attribution have recently been disputed, as we learn in David Tripp's chapter on coinage. Not all these disagreements can be resolved by new discoveries, and scholars must be satisfied with a relative certainty.[58]

An account can be given of the formation of early Rome that unites both archaeological knowledge and the tradition. Under Romulus, the early settlements of the Forum and the Palatine coalesce in the eighth century B.C.: this would be Romulus's "foundation." In a second phase, Rome absorbs most of the settlements north of the Alban Hills; she comes to take the lead among the cities of Latium, eventually destroying Alba Longa in the time of Tullus Hostilius. The dual kingship of Romulus with Titus Tatius, the Sabine king, and the Sabine "dynasty" of Numa Pompilius and Ancus Marcius, which reflect Rome's relations with the neighboring Sabines to the north, are supported by linguistic and archaeological indices in spite of Poucet's skepticism. Along with the remarkable development of the centers of power at Satricum, Ardea, Lanuvium, Politorium (Decima), Tivoli, and Praeneste comes the growing influence of Etruscan culture and power, the growth of Rome and urbanization. This story is told in the histories of Livy and Dionysius of Halicarnassus and need not be repeated here. Even the story of Aeneas has been given more credit since the discovery of the so-called Tomb of Aeneas at Lavinium and the growing evidence of a Mycenaean presence in Italy.[59]

THE NORTH

A study of the influence of Etruria in the north has been made possible, as well as desirable, by the extraordinary rate at which excavation and publication have been carried out in both Italy and central Europe since 1970. Relations between Italy and central Europe were studied in the last century by scholars both in Italy and the "Vienna School." At issue, then and in more recent times, has been the question of chronology: which was earlier, the southern or the northern culture?[60] Now that careful study has resolved this chronological question,[61] scholars can try to understand the reciprocal influence and the character of the various cultures which were in contact with the historical Etruscans and their ancestors, the prehistoric Iron Age Villanovans. Otto-Hermann Frey, with his publications on situla art (in particular *Entstehung der Situlenkunst,* Berlin 1969), settled once and for all the early date of situla art and showed how Etruscan influence of the seventh-century Orientalizing period affected the distinctive bronzes of a region that includes northeast Italy (the Veneto and the Po Valley), the Alps, and the territory beyond, in modern Austria, Switzerland, and Yugoslavia (Maps 3–6).[62] The

people who lived in this area developed a common culture during the course of the seventh century B.C. or earlier. At the center of lively exchange between north and south, the situla people flourished: they grew rich from their trade in amber, clustered around their princes in townlike settlements, and began to adopt the external features of city life or "civilization" from their neighbors, the Etruscans. Yet they remained independent, speaking their various Indo-European languages and celebrating their own way of life on the bronze buckets they decorated with scenes of the aristocratic life of their princes, used for wine at heroic banquets, and buried with valiant lords in their graves. They borrowed from the Etruscans, as the Romans did, many of the signs of honor and culture: aristocratic symbols such as the helmet, the custom of drinking wine at symposia, dress and honorary costumes, the use of the human figure in art, and, later, the use of writing. It is from their inscriptions, written in an Etruscan alphabet, that we have come to know their languages, though the scarcity of these inscriptions, compared to the enormous quantity of Etruscan inscriptions (some thirteen thousand), reflects the relatively minor importance of writing among these people and their failure to develop city life, or a full-fledged civilization. In this region, as in central Europe, the local Iron Age cultures persisted—here they reached a state on the way to urbanization—and real cities did not develop until the time of Roman conquest.

The relationship of the Etruscans to the Celts, their longtime northern neighbors (Maps 3, 6) and (from the fourth century on) their enemies, has in recent years been closely studied from the archaeological as well as the historical and linguistic point of view. An important exhibition held in Rome in 1978, "I Galli e l'Italia," collected material and interpretations on the Gauls in Italy. The language of the Gauls, spoken in areas of Italy near Etruria, also sheds light on their life and historical relations. The influence of Italy on the Celtic art of the Continent was masterfully placed in proper perspective by Paul Jacobsthal's *Early Celtic Art* (1944) and other, more recent studies.[63] The interest in the situation in Italy in the fourth century B.C. and the early republic will focus more attention on these

Gallic inhabitants of Italy and their relations to their neighbors in their new homeland as well as their linguistic and cultural identity with the Celts of Europe. At the same time, increasing scholarly attention is being paid to the Celts as one of the nonclassical peoples of antiquity. It is worth asking what, if anything, these "barbarians" had in common with each other in various periods of their history, and what their relations with the Greeks, the Romans, and each other were.[64]

The Fourth-Century *Koine*

For Greece, a clearer picture of the poorly documented and obscure fourth century B.C. is emerging with the sensational finds from Vergina and the controversy over the tomb identified by some as that of Philip II.[65] The exhibit and catalogue of *Roma Medio Repubblicana* (1973) crystallized interest in contemporary events in Italy. The existence of a fourth-century *koine,* within which framework close relations existed between Etruria and Campania, as well as other regions (their relationship still has to be determined more precisely), is one of the most interesting questions facing archaeologists of Italy today. More than anyone else, the late British historian Martin Frederiksen devoted his career to its study.[66]

Scholars have noted the changes that took place during the period in Etruscan religion, art, society, and dress; specific instances will be found in various chapters of this book. In this period "ethnic" differences were emphasized, and local "history" was codified. The local heroes from Vulci depicted in the fourth-century François Tomb from Vulci and other representations of Etruscan "historical" art illustrate this moment in Etruscan and Roman history.[67] In Latium, at Lavinium, we seem to see "history" being made: a seventh-century grave, the so-called Tomb of Aeneas, was opened in the fourth century, and an offering was made. The tomb was then closed again, and a little "chapel," or *heroon,* was built over it to mark it as special.[68]

Iconographical studies have yielded valuable information and insights about this complex picture. As always, what we know best about the Etruscans,

their art, presents a difficult challenge. It has to be faced directly, without the benefit of contemporary explanations. Lately, Greek myths and Etruscan divinities, and figures decorating engraved mirrors and relief urns have attracted attention.[69] In particular, the restoration and identification of terracotta pediments have made monumental public art available to us. We learn that a favorite theme, the siege of the city gates by the Seven Against Thebes, with the two sons of Oedipus fighting on opposite sides, occurs as early as the mid-fifth century B.C. on one of the temples at Pyrgi. Represented is an unusually gruesome scene, unknown in Greek art: Tydeus gnaws at the head of his enemy Melanippus, as Athena shrinks back in horror and Zeus prepares to strike him down with a thunderbolt.[70] Another pedimental decoration, from a temple at Telamon dated about 150 B.C., has recently been carefully studied and restored. The results are exhibited in Florence.[71] Its subject, again the battle of the Seven Against Thebes, is also a favorite on Hellenistic urns. The Etruscan Fury Vanth is present as the fratricide of Eteocles and Polyneices is played out before their father, Oedipus. Severed heads are shown, either fastened onto gates or being thrown by the enemy against the city walls. Notable throughout is the recurring Etruscan preoccupation with scenes of blood, dismemberment, and sacrifice. In the fourth century B.C. there appear in the art of the Etruscan cities, Campania, and farther south a number of other motifs, rare in Greek art, which take their place in a specifically Italic *koine:* the *kourotrophos,* or mother with child; the representation of the soul as someone swathed in bandages; the sacrifice of the Trojan prisoners; Herakles by a spring or fountain; and Marsyas tied to a tree; evidently the last image shows the Roman sterile tree, or *arbor infelix,* of Indo-European tradition. Another distinctly Italian motif occurs in representations of severed heads, as we have seen.[72]

The End of the Etruscans

The late republican period and the Romanization of Italy have been examined in numerous recent studies. At the other end of the chronological scale from Etruscan origins, they constitute a controversial topic related to the question of Roman imperialism, emphasized by both Marxist and non-Marxist historians.[73] Complex cultural, social, and political changes took place from about 200 B.C. to the time of Augustus in all the regions of Italy. There is still much we do not know. In the case of the Etruscans, the evidence available (archaeological, artistic, epigraphical, and linguistic) can be supplemented with a few passages in the Roman historical record.[74] When and how did Romanization take place? The major Etruscan cities, Perugia, Cortona, and Arezzo (Livy 3.37.12), along with other northern centers, continued to be important in this later period after the southern cities had faded. Why? Attempts to answer these and other questions form the core of a number of studies, from William Harris's history *Rome in Etruria and Umbria* (1971) to *Studies in the Romanization of Etruria* (1975), a collective volume by the Finnish Institute in Rome. A colloquium in Göttingen, "Hellenismus in Mittelitalien" (1977), examined various aspects of the interaction between Hellenistic and local elements in the face of the Roman presence.[75]

As Torelli points out in his historical survey (Ch. II), more work needs to be done on the architecture of this period. Progress is being made, meanwhile, in the study of certain late monuments, largely due to the fruitful collaboration between archaeologists and linguists. In some northern cities these last years of Etruscan culture were a time of great activity in specialized craftsmanship, especially in the manufacture of cinerary urns. The urns of Perugia, Chiusi, and Volterra were long scorned by archaeologists as mass-produced objects of little artistic value. Now the tide has turned. The hundreds of cinerary urns, miniature sarcophagi for cremation burials, are today much studied from a variety of aspects: the typology of the portrait figures reclining on the lids, the iconography of the mythological relief scenes carved on the front of the urn, and the organization of the workshops which produced them. Volterra has yielded over six hundred of these burial urns (cremation persisted in the northern cities) and some one thousand lids. Many of these have inscriptions, which constitute the single most important source for a study of the Ro-

manization of the city. The end of their production includes Latin inscriptions alongside Etruscan and coincides with the Romanization of Etruscan culture. Elsewhere, too, on grave markers (cippi) and other monuments from Cerveteri, the presence of contemporary Latin and Etruscan inscriptions on the same kind of monument—Latin inscriptions appearing on monuments of clearly Etruscan type, or containing Etruscan names—shows the close linguistic connection and cultural interpenetration between these peoples in the later period.[76]

The importance of language in the process of Romanization is aptly stressed by E.T. Salmon:

Paradoxical though it may seem, the very multiplicity of languages in pre-Roman Italy may have helped to promote its unification. Its Alpine rampart and the surrounding seas make the country a natural and largely self-contained geographical unit. But, at the dawn of its history, some forty languages and dialects were spoken within its comparatively narrow confines. As its many tribes gradually became less simple and primitive and their mutual intercourse more constant and complex, the need for a *lingua franca* amid the babel of tongues became increasingly urgent.[77]

Recent archaeological discoveries and the evidence of the languages—Umbrian, Faliscan, Venetic, Oscan, and others written in the Latin and Etruscan alphabets learned from their neighbors[78] (Map 5)—allowed Salmon to study the relationship between language and citizenship through the four hundred years (350 B.C.–A.D. 2) which culminated in Rome's unification of Italy, when Latin was used as the common language. The author shows that Rome's prestige, rather than force, was the decisive factor in this Romanization and in the adoption of Latin. It was a complex, gradual, and uneven changeover. Salmon's consideration of its various phases brings up questions of ethnic identity, bilingualism, double citizenship, political connotations of language, revival of native vernaculars, local speech, and national outlook—all aspects of Romanization relevant to the end of the Etruscan language and culture in the Etruscan cities.

In this area the question of interpretation of Rome's politics and policies is again, as might be expected, controversial. Against the charge of aggressive imperialism often brought against Rome, Michael Crawford has recently cited, as the crucial factor among the manifold reasons for Rome's success, "the generosity and flexibility of the ways in which she gradually bound the rest of Italy to herself and the manpower upon which she could call as a result."[79]

Etruscans thus gave up their language and their customs and became Romanized. Their ideas and influence did not wholly disappear, however. Marta Sordi notes the religious fear of the imminent destruction of their city that gripped the Romans several times during periods of crisis—they feared that the capital would be moved to Veii in the fourth century, after the Gallic disaster, or later, with Antony and Cleopatra, to Alexandria. Sordi attributes this fear, along with the accompanying sense of guilt, to the influence of Etruscan beliefs in a limited series of eras, or "generations," which had been allotted to each people.[80]

The crisis of the civil wars in Rome in the first century B.C. coincided with Etruscan beliefs about the end of one of the last of these cycles and their own imminent end. To each of these eras the gods had allotted a certain number of years. "When such a period comes to an end and another begins an amazing sign is sent from earth or heaven."[81] A prophecy by the nymph Vegoia, which seems to date from 91 B.C., warned that the eighth saeculum had ended. It announced a series of coming disasters if boundary stones were moved and if their greed and avarice drove men to try to take land which was not theirs.[82] Foretelling the evils of the civil war in 88 B.C., the nymph evidently expressed a religious view of history and insisted on the Etruscan, and Roman, ideas that punishment was visited on a people because of a *scelus,* or crime. A similar idea is found in the poetry of the Augustan period, for example, Vergil's mysteriously apocalyptic Fourth Eclogue. In the Christian period, it was elaborated by Saint Augustine and others. The Romans had evidently adopted certain Etruscan religious ideas which fitted in with their own deeply moral world view.[83]

In 44 B.C., an Etruscan haruspex proclaimed the end of a saeculum. The comet that appeared after Caesar's death, he said, had signaled the end of the ninth saeculum. The Etruscans, and their haruspices, were aware that their end as a people was at hand. Then in A.D. 19, according to the historian Dio Cassius, a trumpet blast sounded, and a prophecy announced that a nine-hundred-year period was ending.[84] The Etruscan world disappeared, leaving only the names of cities and lands; echoes in Roman religion and art; and the noble traditions of ancient Etruscan families.[85]

Notes

Full bibliographical information on references listed in the Abbreviations list or in the Selected Readings is found in those places.

1. Banti, *Etruscan Cities;* Heurgon, *Daily Life;* Pallottino, *Etruscans.*

2. G. Dennis, *The Cities and Cemeteries of Etruria*³; D.H. Lawrence, *Etruscan Places* (London 1929).

3. H.H. Scullard's history (1967), still basic, was entitled *The Etruscan Cities and Rome.* Now K.-W. Weeber, A. Hus, M. Torelli, and M. Grant have written independent histories of the Etruscans. (For bibliography, see Selected Readings at the end of this volume.)

4. D. Ridgway, "The Etruscans" (Edinburgh 1981; forthcoming in the new edition of *CAH*) 4.

5. Pallottino, *Etruscans,* Part 3, "The Etruscan Language"; Bonfante, *The Etruscan Language.*

6. On the name of the Etruscans, see G. Devoto, *StEtr* 28 (1960) 276; J. Heurgon, *MEFRA* 83 (1971) 9–28; C. de Simone, *StEtr* 40 (1970) 153–81; L. Aigner Foresti, "*Tyrrhenoi* und *Etrusci,*" *Grazer Beiträge* 6 (1977) 1–25. On the Vicus Tuscus, see Ogilvie, *Commentary;* Pallottino, *Etruscans* 109; M. Cristofani, "Il ruolo degli Etruschi nel Lazio antico," in *Greci e Latini nel Lazio antico* (Rome 1982) 39.

7. Such journals as *Journal of Field Archaeology* and *Archaeometry* reflect this recent interest. Since World War II, when the application of scientific methods to Etruscan archaeology gained momentum, the Fondazione Lerici Prospezioni Archeologiche has brought to light thousands of tombs in Tarquinia and Cerveteri by the development of geophysical techniques of prospecting. The resulting material is being published and exhibited: e.g., *Gli Etruschi e Cerveteri* (Milan 1980), with full discussion and bibliography. See Pallottino, *Etruscans* 279–80, and *passim.*

8. *Restauri Archeologici. Mostra dei restauri sulle opere d'arte del Museo Archeologico di Firenze* (Florence 1969), with introduction by G. Maetzke; *Nuove letture di monumenti etruschi dopo il restauro* (Florence 1971), with contributions by L. Vlad Borelli, M. Cristofani, and others. The systematic restoration and study of objects in the Museo Archeologico proceeds apace: one of the latest monuments to be restored, exhibited, and published is the famous

François Vase from Chiusi: see M. Cristofani, *Il vaso François* (Florence 1981). See also the ongoing surveys in *StEtr* and *Prospettiva*.

9. See M. Briguet's account (infra Ch. IV).

10. C. Morigi Govi, *ArchCl* 23 (1971) 211–35; *Prima Italia* (1981) 97–99, no. 59, with bibliography.

11. Bonfante, *Etruscan Dress* 95–97, 150, figs. 14–16; F. Prayon, *RömMitt* 82 (1975) 165ff.; *Prima Italia* (1981) 94–96, no. 56.

12. For the Vatican collection, see F. Roncalli, "Il reparto di antichità etrusco-italiche," in *BollMonMusGallPont* 1 (1959–74) 53–114 (offprint). The Boston Museum of Fine Arts and the Walters Art Gallery in Baltimore have new Etruscan rooms, and the Toledo Museum has added some impressive Etruscan pieces to its collection.

13. For an account of the *LIMC* project and a review of the first volume, *Aara–Aphlad* (Zurich and Munich 1981), see the review by B.S. Ridgway, *AJA* 86 (1982) 599–600.

14. M. Cristofani, *CIE* II¹, fasc. 4 (Florence 1970) 5607–6324: for the history of the *CIE*, see review by L. Bonfante, *JRS* 66 (1976) 243–44.

15. Four fascicles of the *Corpus Speculorum Etruscorum* have already appeared: see G. Sassatelli, *CSE* Italia 1, 1–2, Bologna, Museo Civico (Rome 1981); H. Roberts, *CSE* Denmark 1 (Odense 1981); L.B. van der Meer, *CSE* Netherlands (Leiden 1983). A full account of matters pertaining to Etruscan mirrors is found in *Guide to Etruscan Mirrors*.

16. M. Cristofani, M. Cristofani Martelli, E. Fiumi, A. Maggiani, and A. Talocchini, *CUE I: Urne volterrane, 1: I complessi tombali* (Florence 1975). See review by L. Bonfante, *ArchNews* 6 (1977) 125–27.

17. This project is under the direction of Francesco Roncalli and Richard Bronson.

18. *Thesaurus Linguae Etruscae I: Indice Lessicale*, ed., M. Pallottino, M.P. Angeletti, C. de Simone, M. Cristofani, and A. Morandi (Rome 1978). For recent bibliography on the Etruscan language see Bonfante, *Etruscan Language* 157–65.

19. *Le ciste prenestine I. Corpus*, ed., G. Bordenache Battaglia, with the assistance of A. Emiliozzi (Rome 1979).

20. *Musei e Collezioni d'Etruria* 1: A. Emiliozzi, *La Collezione Rossi Danielli nel Museo Civico di Viterbo* (1974); *Monumenti Etruschi, Istituto di Studi Etruschi ed Italici* 2, *Veio* 1; *Museo Topografico dell'Etruria* I; M. Cristofani, *Le Tombe da Monte Michele nel Mus. Arch. di Firenze* (Florence 1969). For material in Bologna see C. Morigi Govi, "La collezione etrusca," in *Pelagio Palagi artista e collezionista* (Bologna 1976) 291–311; *Cataloghi del Museo Civico di Bologna* I, R. Pincelli and C. Morigi Govi, *La necropoli villanoviana di San Vitale* (Bologna 1975); *Ancient Italy Before the Romans* (Ashmolean Museum, Oxford 1980), by A.C. Brown, with bibliography by D. Ridgway.

21. For the study of older museum collections see M. Cristofani, M. Martelli, and M. Collarata, *Palazzo Vecchio: Committenza e collezionismo medicei* (Florence 1980) 27–42 (catalogue of the Etruscan collection of the Medici). See also *La Città degli Uffizi* (Florence 1982) 33–41. For Prayon, see supra n. 11.

22. N.T. de Grummond, "Towards a History of Archaeology: New Books," *ArchNews* 11 (1982) 11–14. For art-historical focus, see N. Dacos, "Sopravvivenza dell'antico," in *EAA* Suppl. (1970) 741–46. For the history of Etruscan archaeology, see M. Martelli, "Il Revival etrusco," in *Palazzo Vecchio* (Florence 1980) 19–26; M. Cristofani, "Storia di un problema," in *L'arte degli Etruschi*, 3–28; D. Ridgway, "Archaeology in Sardinia and Etruria," in *ArchReports 1979–80*, 63.

23. N.T. de Grummond, *ArchNews* 11 (1982) 12.

24. For inscription, see A.E. Gordon, *The Inscribed Fibula Praenestina: Problems of Authenticity* (Berkeley and Los Angeles 1975); D. Ridgway, "Manios Faked?" *BICS* 24 (1977) 17–30; M. Guarducci, *MemLinc* 24 (1980) 415–574. On nineteenth-century forgers of Praenestine cistae, Marinetti and Pasinati, see G. Bordenache Battaglia, *Le ciste prenestine* I (Rome 1979), xviii, 120–22, 126, 129.

25. *The Vatican Collections. The Papacy and Art* (New York 1982).

26. *Mostra dell'arte e della civiltà etrusca* (Milan 1955), with introduction by M. Pallottino. The exhibit, which opened in Zurich, traveled to Milan, Paris, The Hague, Oslo, and Cologne during 1955–56.

27. A focus which resulted in the restoration of the Ara Pacis and the splendid museum of casts which made up the *Mostra della civiltà romana*.

28. On the study of *Realien*, see L. Bonfante, "Margarete Bieber, 1879–1978: An Archaeologist in Two Worlds," in *Women as Interpreters of the Arts* (Westport, Connecticut, and London 1981) 256. For theoretical discussion of the character of native, "Italic" art as opposed to Greek art during the Fascist period, see Cristofani, *L'arte degli Etruschi* 19; and for the danger of concentrating on "material culture" to the exclusion of art, see p. 23.

29. Milani, *Mus.Arch.* 31–32.

30. M. Pallottino, *Etruscans* 30; *Civiltà artistica etrusco-italica* (Florence 1971) 49–51.

31. E.g., *Arte e civiltà degli Etruschi* (Turin 1967), with introduction by M. Pallottino. Ten years after the first exhibition, this one opened in Vienna, Stockholm, and Turin (1966–67).

32. R.S. Teitz, *Masterpieces of Etruscan Art* (Worcester, Massachusetts, 1967); see also D.G. Mitten and S.F. Doeringer, *Master Bronzes from the Classical World* (Cambridge, Mass., St. Louis and Los Angeles, 1967–68); D. von Bothmer, *Ancient Art from New York Private Collections* (New York 1961); M.A. De Chiaro, *Etruscan Art from West Coast Collections* (Santa Barbara, California, 1967) and *Re-Exhumed Etruscan Bronzes* (Santa Barbara, California,

1981); N.T. de Grummond, "Reflections on the Etruscan Mirror," *Archaeology* 34 (1981) 54–58 (Tallahassee, Florida, exhibition).

33. On the Sabines, see *Civiltà arcaica dei Sabini nella valle del Tevere I–III* (1973–77), Vol. I (1973). For the inscription from Poggio Sommavilla in Boston, see Vol. III, 97. On situla art, see *L'Etruria Padana e la città di Spina* (Bologna 1960); *Arte delle situle dal Po al Danubio* (Florence 1961); *Situlenkunst* (Vienna 1962). On culture in Rome, see *Roma Medio Repubblicana*, F. Coarelli, ed. (Rome 1973).

34. *Aspects of Italic Culture*. Another colloquium was held at Mannheim in 1980: *Aufnahme* (1981). See also *Crossroads* (1983). For international collaboration and the study of the variety of cultures and reciprocal influences in Italy, see also *Un trentennio di collaborazione italo-francese nel campo dell'archeologia italiana. Atti dei Convegni Lincei 54* (Rome 1983).

35. For the use of archaeological evidence by historians see Scullard, *The Etruscan Cities and Rome*, with review by L. Bonfante, *AJA* 73 (1969) 252–53. See also Harris, *Rome in Etruria and Umbria;* the review of Harris's book by H.S. Versnel, *Bibliotheca Orientalis* 33 (1976) 106–108 can be read in connection with Mario Torelli's chapter on Etruscan history in this book, since it focuses on points of controversy and interpretation; E.T. Salmon, *The Making of Roman Italy* (London and Ithaca, New York, 1982).

36. On social history in general, see Grant, *Etruscans* 117; Pallottino, *Etruscans* 124–37; Torelli, *Elogia Tarquiniensia*, with reviews by T.J. Cornell, *JRS* 68 (1978) 167–73; J. Heurgon, *StEtr* 46 (1978) 617–23. On the anthropology of early trade, M. Cristofani, "Il 'dono' nell' Etruria arcaica." The study of tomb groups has been particularly enlightening, but these must be interpreted with care: see Colonna, "L'ideologia funeraria" (infra n. 52). See also G. Buchner, *IBR* 129: "None of the tombs so far excavated at Pithekoussai can be assigned to the highest social class, that of the warrior aristocracy: indeed, not a single weapon has been found. It would, however, be wrong to deduce from this that Pithekoussai was inhabited exclusively by traders and artisans. . . . The lack of warrior tombs merely means that we have not yet happened to find a family plot of the noble class."

37. See Ch. V, Architecture, for Acquarossa and Murlo; see also Rathje, "A Banquet Service"; T.W. Potter, *A Faliscan Town in South Etruria. Excavations at Narce 1966–71* (London 1976), with foreword by John Ward-Perkins, and bibliography; T.W. Potter, *The Changing Landscape of South Etruria* (London 1979), on a survey instigated by John Ward-Perkins, and review by B. Jones, *Antiquity* (1981) 143–44. For bibliography on topographical studies and field surveys, see T.J. Cornell, "Rome and Latium Vetus," *ArchReports 1974–79*, 72–73; R.V.D. Magoffin, *A Study of the Topography and Municipal History of Praeneste*

(originally published Baltimore 1908), reprinted in *Studi su Praeneste. Reprints di Archeologia e di Storia Antica* (Perugia 1978) 47–143.

38. See bibliography on votive offerings, Ch. VIII. On Cetamura, see N.T. de Grummond, "Etruscan Waterworks at Cetamura del Chianti," *AJA* 88 (1984) 246; C. Sowder, "Utilitarian Pottery from Cetamura del Chianti," *ArchNews* 13 (1984) 13, 17, n. 3.

39. *IBR,* with contributions by R. Peroni, "From Bronze Age to Iron Age"; M.A. Fugazzola Delpino, "The Proto-Villanovan: A Survey"; J. Close-Brooks, "Veii in the Iron Age," with D. Ridgway; and G. Buchner, "Early Orientalizing: Aspects of the Euboean Connection." For early metallurgy, see D. Ridgway, F. Serra Ridgway, and E. Macnamara, "The Bronze Hoard from S. Maria in Paulis, Sardinia," in *Aspects of Italic Culture,* and E. Macnamara, D. Ridgway, and F.R. Ridgway, *British Museum Occasional Paper* No. 45 (1984). For the Mycenaean presence in Italy, see L. Vagnetti, ed., *Magna Grecia e mondo miceneo. Nuovi documenti. XXII Convegno di Studi sulla Magna Grecia, Taranto 1982* (Tarentum 1982).

40. *Popoli e civiltà,* 6, *Lingue e dialetti* (1978); see also *Prima Italia* (Rome 1981), with introduction by M. Pallottino; the maps are taken from M. Pallottino, *Genti e culture dell'Italia preromana* (Rome 1981), reviewed by L. Bonfante, *AJA* 86 (1982) 593. For the art, see Bianchi Bandinelli-Giuliano, *Etruschi e Italici.*

41. See Chs. II–III.

42. See Ch. III and A. Rathje, "Oriental Imports in Etruria in the Eighth and Seventh Century B.C.: Their Origins and Implications," *IBR* 145–83 with bibliography. On the Phoenicians and Carthaginians in the West, see the account and bibliography in J.M. Blázquez, F. Presado et al., *Historia de España Antigua I. Protostoria* (Madrid 1980) 277–520, 587–97; and F. Jordá and J.M. Blázquez, *Historia del Arte Hispanico* I¹. *La Antigüedad* (Madrid 1978). On the Greeks in the West see D. Ridgway, *L'alba della Magna Grecia* (Rome 1984); G. Buchner, "Early Orientalizing: Aspects of the Euboean Connection," in *IBR,* 129–44; and G. Buchner and D. Ridgway, *Pithekoussai* I–II (forthcoming). For the origin of the *polis,* see A. Snodgrass, *Archaic Greece* (Berkeley 1980) 32; O. Murray, *Early Greece* (Glasgow 1980) 74–75; and R. Hägg, ed., *The Greek Renaissance of the Eighth Century B.C.: Tradition and Innovation.* Proceedings of the II International Symposium at the Swedish Institute in Athens, June 1981. *Acta Inst. Ath.* 30 (Stockholm 1983).

43. Here and in what follows, I have relied on Martin Frederiksen's summary, "The Etruscans in Campania," in *IBR,* 284–90. For alphabet and language, see M. Cristofani, "Recent Advances in Etruscan Epigraphy and Language," in *IBR,* 373–412; C. de Simone, *ANRW* I² (1972) 514.

44. For example, a seminar organized by *DialAr* in

Rome in 1977; cf. *DialAr* 7 (1973) 122ff.; *DialAr* 8 (1974–75) 162–64; G. Colonna, in *Civiltà del Lazio primitivo* (Rome 1976) 25–36; see also various contributions in "Lazio arcaico e mondo greco," *ParPass* 32 (1977) 172–77; C. Ampolo, *La città antica* (Rome, Bari 1980). Still basic is Numa Denis Fustel de Coulanges, *The Ancient City* (Baltimore and London 1980 [originally published in Paris in 1864], with introduction by A. Momigliano and S.C. Humphreys). Further bibliography in L. Bonfante, *Out of Etruria,* esp. 49, and *passim.* See supra n. 42.

45. Cristofani, *L'arte degli Etruschi,* on Greek and Etruscan craftsmen and workshops; see also Chs. II–III. For a Greek inscription in Delphi mentioning the Etruscans, see M. Cristofani, *Xenia* 8 (1984) 13.

46. T.J. Cornell, "Rome and Latium Vetus," *ArchReports 1979–80,* 71–89, with preceding bibliography.

47. *Civiltà del Lazio primitivo* (Rome 1978); *Naissance de Rome* (Paris 1977). This exhibit was held in Bucharest and Budapest in 1980.

48. Archaeological discoveries have in large measure confirmed Andreas Alföldi's views on the position of Rome in the Latin League, cited with approval in A. Momigliano's review, *JRS* 57 (1967) 211–16: see A. Alföldi, *Early Rome and the Latins* (Ann Arbor 1965). See also his *Die Struktur des voretruskischen Römerstaates* (Heidelberg 1974); and *Römische Frühgeschichte. Kritik und Forschung seit 1964* (Heidelberg 1976).

49. *Ricerca su una comunità del Lazio protostorico. Il sepolcreto dell'Osteria dell'Osa sulla via Prenestina* (Rome 1979); *Ficana. Una pietra miliare sulla strada per Roma. Mostra itinerante, 1975–80; Enea nel Lazio* (Rome 1981). Supra n. 47.

50. *Civiltà del Lazio primitivo* (Rome 1976) 287, cat. no. 91.

51. G. Colonna, in *Civiltà del Lazio primitivo* 33, assigns them to local princes. The discussion concerning Vetusia and bibliography are to be found in F. Canciani and F.-W. von Hase, *La tomba Bernardini di Preneste. Latium Vetus* II (Rome 1979) 39–40, no. 23.

52. G. Colonna, "L'ideologia funeraria e il conflitto delle culture," *Archeologia Laziale IV. Quarto incontro di studio del comitato per l'archeologia laziale. Quaderni del centro di studio per l'archeologia etrusco-italica* 5 (1981) 229–32; see also L. Quilici, *Roma primitiva e le origini della civiltà laziale* (Rome 1979) 286.

53. M. Cristofani, "Il ruolo degli Etruschi nel Lazio antico," in *Greci e Latini nel Lazio antico* (Rome 1982) 27–48; Colonna, "L'ideologia funeraria," 229. On the XII Tables and Greek influence in the sixth century B.C., see also D. van Berchem, "Rome et le monde grec au VIᵉ siècle avant notre ère," in *Mélanges d'archéologie et d'histoire offerts à A. Piganiol* (Paris 1966) 739–40. For comparisons between Rome and Athens around 500 B.C., see C. Ampolo, "Analogie e rapporti fra Atene e Roma arcaica. Os-

servazioni sulla Regia, sul Rex sacrorum e sul culto di Vesta," *ParPass* 141 (1971) 443–60.

54. M. Cristofani, "Artisti etruschi a Roma nell'ultimo trentennio del VI secolo a.C.," *Prospettiva* 9 (1977) 2–7; L. Bonfante, *JRS* 60 (1970) 49–66; *Out of Etruria* (1981) 93–110 (orig. publ. 1970), and bibliography: 154–56. For Etruscan religion, see Dumézil, *Archaic Roman Religion,* Appendix; and Pfiffig, *Religio Etrusca.*

55. Still basic for the whole discussion are A. Momigliano, *JRS* 53 (1963) 96ff. (see now *Settimo Contributo,* [Rome 1984]), and G. Dumézil, *Mythe et Epopée* I (Paris 1968) 269–70. E. Peruzzi and his book *Le origini di Roma* I–II (Vol. I, Florence 1970; Vol. II, Bologna 1973) were criticized for ideas which seemed idiosyncratic, such as considering Romulus and Titus Tatius as real people, exaggerating Sabine influence in early Rome; many of his ideas are now seriously discussed. See also E. Peruzzi, "La lingua greca nel Lazio preromano," in *Greci e Latini nel Lazio antico* (Rome 1982) 9–26; J. Poucet, *Recherches sur la légende sabine des origines de Rome* (Louvain 1967); E. Pais, *Ancient Italy* (London 1908).

56. See G. Boni, *NSc* 1907. E. Gjerstad's *Early Rome* I–VI (Lund 1953–73) was based on some of Boni's notes, as well as re-examination of the remains. But his radical lowering of the regal chronology has not been accepted: for criticism, see infra n. 58. See also the review by Inez Scott Ryberg, *AJA* 66 (1962) 427–30.

57. See M. Pallottino's lucid account, in *Naissance de Rome* (Paris 1977) and "The Origins of Rome: a Survey of Recent Discoveries and Discussions," *IBR* 197–222 (originally published in *ANRW* I¹ [1972] 22–47). The traditional account of each king's reign is now being re-evaluated in the light of this new tendency. For Aeneas and Romulus, see T.J. Cornell, *Proceedings of the Cambridge Philological Society* 21 (1975) 1–32; "The Foundation of Rome in the Ancient Literary Tradition," in *Papers in Italian Archaeology* I. *BAR* S 41 (Oxford 1978) 131–40; E. Tiffou, "Notes sur le personnage de Romulus," in *Mélanges Heurgon* (Rome 1976) 991–93. On the Tarquins and Servius Tullius, see M. Pallottino, "Servius Tullius à la lumière des nouvelles découvertes archéologiques et épigraphiques," *CRAI* (1977) 216–35; T.N. Gantz, "The Tarquin Dynasty," *Historia* 24 (1975) 539–54; R. Ridley, "The Enigma of Servius Tullius," *Klio* 57 (1975) 147–77; R. Thomsen, *King Servius Tullius,* Humanitas 5 (Gyldendal 1980); J. Gagé, *Enquêtes sur les structures sociales et religieuses de la Rome primitive* (Brussels 1977); L.-R. Ménager, *MEFR* 88 (1976) 455–543; J. Poucet, "Le Latium protohistorique et archaïque," *AntCl* 47 (1978) 177–220; 566–601; "Archéologie, tradition et histoire: les origines et les premiers siècles de Rome," *EtCl* 47 (1979) 201–14, 347–63.

58. E. Gjerstad, *Early Rome* I–VI (Lund 1953–73), provides the most complete archaeological survey of early Rome (Vol. III discusses the Temple of Jupiter on the

Capitoline Hill). For criticism see T.J. Cornell, *CR* 29 (1979) 106–9; G. Colonna, *IBR* 223–35; D. Ridgway, *IBR* 187–93; further bibliography, *IBR* 187–235 *passim.* See bibliographical note to Ch. VI for the controversy on Servius Tullius and coinage. For the beginning of Greek coinage, see D. Kagan, "The Dates of the Earliest Coins," *AJA* 86 (1982) 343–60.

59. R. Bloch, in *ANRW* I[1] (1972) 19; G. Pugliese-Carratelli, *I Micenei in Italia* (Taranto 1967) 7–12; L. Vagnetti, in E. Peruzzi, *Mycenaeans in Early Latium* (Rome 1980) Appendix II, 151–66 (the author advises that this is already out of date); see now D. Ridgway, "Archaeology in South Italy, 1977–81," in *Archaeological Reports 1981–82* 82–83. For the "Tomb of Aeneas," see P. Sommella, *RendPontAcc* 44 (1971–72) 47–74; *Gymnasium* 81 (1974) 273–97. An archaic tomb of the seventh century B.C. was surmounted by a tumulus; sometime during the fourth century B.C. a square chamber with a monumental stone door was inserted into the mound, turning it into a *heroon.* T.J. Cornell in "Aeneas' Arrival in Italy," *LCM* 2 (1977) 77–83, believes that the Aeneas story was a later, learned reconstruction.

60. For the bibliography, see L. Aigner Foresti, "Forschungsübersicht," in *Der Ostalpenraum und Italien: Ihre kulturellen Beziehungen im Spiegel der anthropomorphen Kleinplastik aus Bronze des 7. Jhs. v.Chr.* (Florence 1980) 1–5.

61. F. Serra Ridgway, "The Este and Golasecca Cultures: A Chronological Guide," in *IBR* 419–87 (abstract of R. Peroni et al., *Studi sulla cronologia delle civiltà di Este e Golasecca,* 1975); W. Dehn and O.-H. Frey, "Southern Imports and the Chronology of Central Europe," in *IBR* 489–511.

62. L. Bonfante, *Out of Etruria,* with bibliography.

63. See *I Galli e l'Italia,* exhibition catalogue, ed. P. Santoro (Rome 1978); see esp. M. Michelucci, F.-H. Pairault-Massa, "I Galli e l'Etruria," 206–20. For battle scenes between Etruscans(?) and Gauls on funerary stelae from Bologna, see J. Stary-Rimpau, "Fremdeinflüsse in Bologneser Stelen," *Aufnahme* (1981) 86–87. For the language, see *I Celti d'Italia,* ed., E. Campanile (Pisa 1981), esp. A. Bernardi, "I Celti in Italia," 11–30; M.L. Porzio Gernia, "Gli elementi celtici del latino," 97–122. In addition to P. Jacobsthal, *Early Celtic Art* (Oxford 1944), see also T.G.E. Powell, *The Celts* (1958; new edition, with preface by S. Piggott, London and New York 1980); J.V.S. Megaw, *Art of European Iron Age. A Study of the Elusive Image* (Bath 1970); *Die Kelten in Mitteleuropa* (Hallein, Austria 1980), with contributions by O.-H. Frey, J.J. Mott, L. Pauli, and others.

64. A. Momigliano, *Alien Wisdom* (Cambridge 1975), on Greeks and Romans and their relations to Celts, Jews, and Iranians.

65. See *The Search for Alexander. An Exhibition* (Washington, D.C., 1980). The discussion to date is summarized by E. Borza, "Those Vergina Tombs Again," *ArchNews* 11 (1982) 8–10.

66. See B.M. Felletti Maj, *La tradizione italica nell'arte romana* (Rome 1977) Ch. 1; Bianchi Bandinelli-Giuliano, *Etruschi e Italici* part 4 (see esp. 223–24 for the parallel and separate development of a "cultural" Greek art and the surfacing of local, "native" elements); M. Frederiksen, "Campanian Cavalry: A Question of Origins," *DialAr* 2 (1968) 3–31; "The Etruscans in Campania," in *IBR* (1979) 277–311; *Campania,* N. Purcell, ed., British School at Rome (London 1984).

67. L. Bonfante, "Historical Art: Etruscan and Early Roman," *AJAH* 3 (1978) 136–62, with previous bibliography.

68. See supra n. 59. A protogeometric building or *heroon* recently discovered in Greece, at the Euboean site of Lefkandi, was built over the shaft grave of a "hero": see M. Popham, E. Touloupa, and L.H. Sackett, "The Hero of Lefkandi," *Antiquity* 56 (1982) 169–74; *Lefkandi* I. *BSA* Suppl. 2 (1980); D. Ridgway, *L'alba della Magna Grecia* (Rome 1984) 28–31, 177.

69. For Etruscan divinities, see Pfiffig, *Religio Etrusca.* Several have been the subjects of special studies: E.H. Richardson, "Moonèd Ashteroth?" *Brendel Essays,* 21–24; "Ariadne in Italy," *Studies in Classical Art and Archaeology* (Locust Valley, New York, 1982); "The Lady at the Fountain," *Miscellanea Maetzke* (Rome 1984) 447–54; A. Rallo, *Lasa. Iconografia e Esegesi* (Florence 1974). For bibliography on the mirrors, see *Guide to Etruscan Mirrors,* esp. R. De Puma, "Greek Gods and Heroes," and C. Sowder, "Etruscan Mythological Figures." For the urns, see F.-H. Pairault Massa, *Recherches* (Rome 1972); Cristofani, *L'arte degli Etruschi,* 206–12.

70. I. Krauskopf, *Der thebanische Sagenkreis und andere griechische Sagen in der etruskischen Kunst* (Mainz 1974) pl. 17; cf. J.P. Small, *Studies Related to the Theban Cycle on Late Etruscan Urns* (Rome 1981). Small's interpretations are controversial: see remarks by B. von Freytag Löringhoff, in *Talamone. Il Mito dei Sette a Tebe* (Florence 1982) 45.

71. *Talamone. Il Mito dei Sette a Tebe,* Catalogo della Mostra (Florence 1982), ed., F. Nicosia.

72. For Herakles nursed by Juno, and the importance of the *kourotrophos,* see Ch. VIII. For the sacrifice of the Trojan prisoners, see L. Bonfante, *AJAH* 3 (1978) 136–62, with references. For the *adligatus* and the *arbor infelix,* see A. Weis, *AJA* 86 (1982) 21–38. To these we can add the motif of the hero at the well, as on the Ficoroni cista (Anne Weis, private communication). For the log-built pyre, "an original Italiote motif," see M. Gualtieri, *AJA* 86 (1982) 478.

73. W.V. Harris, *War and Imperialism in Republican Rome, 327–70 B.C.* (Oxford 1979).

74. See T.J. Cornell, "Etruscan Historiography," *Ann-*

Pisa (1976) 411; see also Ogilvie, *Commentary; Early Rome and the Etruscans;* and J. Heurgon, *The Rise of Rome to 264 B.C.* (London 1973).

75. *Studies in the Romanization of Etruria.* Acta Instituti Romani Finlandiae V (Rome 1975); *Hellenismus in Mittelitalien. Kolloquium in Göttingen Juni 1974,* ed., P. Zanker (Göttingen 1976). See, e.g., J.-P. Morel, 471–501; "La céramique arétine ressortit en fait à une tradition étrusque."

76. See *CUE* (supra n. 16). For the considerable bibliography on these urns, see *Caratteri dell'ellenismo* (1977). For the cippi, see supra n. 14.

77. Salmon, *The Making of Roman Italy* (supra n. 35) 154. For the history of this type of study, see G. Devoto, "Storia politica e storia linguistica," *ANRW* I² (1972) 457–65. On the ancient historical "linguistic league" in Italy, see V. Pisani, in *Popoli e civiltà* 6 (1978), *Lingue e dialetti,* 17–127, esp. 21, 39; M. Bartoli, *Introduzione alla neolinguistica* (Geneva 1925) 41ff.; R. Jakobson, "Über die phonologischen Sprachbünde," in *Selected Writings.* I. *Phonological Studies* (The Hague 1962; orig. publ. 1931) 137–43; cf. 144–201.

78. G. Bonfante, "The Spread of the Alphabet in Europe," in *Out of Etruria,* 125; M. Cristofani, "Sull' origine e la diffusione dell'alfabeto etrusco," *ANRW* I² (1972) 466–89.

79. M. Crawford, *The Roman Republic* (orig. publ. 1978; Cambridge, Massachusetts, 1982) 42; cf. A. Hus, *Les Étrusques et leur destin* 289. For the Romanization of Italy see also P.A. Brunt, *Italian Manpower 225 B.C.–A.D. 14* (Oxford 1971).

80. M. Sordi, "L'idea di crisi e di rinnovamento nella concezione romano-etrusca della storia," *ANRW* I² (1972) 781–93.

81. Plutarch, *Sulla* 7; Harris, *Rome in Etruria and Umbria* 31–40.

82. Harris, *Rome in Etruria and Umbria* 36; J. Heurgon, *JRS* 49 (1959) 41–45. Pfiffig, *Religio Etrusca* 157–59; A. Rallo, *Lasa, Iconografia e esegesi* (Florence 1974) 64–65, identifies the Nymph Begoe mentioned by Servius (*ad Aen.* 6.72) with the Lasa Vecu shown and labeled on an Etruscan mirror.

83. Sordi, *ANRW* I² (1972) 786.

84. Dio Cassius 57.18.3–5; Harris, *Rome in Etruria and Umbria* 36.

85. Some examples of linguistic continuity in place names are remarkable, for example, the modern name Rasina, related to Etruscan Rasna; see S. Pieri, *Toponomastica della Toscana meridionale* (Siena 1969) 33–34; Ch. 1, "Nomi locali derivanti da nomi personali etruschi," 3–142. See also G. Devoto, "Divinità etrusche," in *Scritti minori* (Florence 1967) 164–71, on Fufluns, Pupluna (Populonia), *populus,* etc.; and G.B. Pellegrini, "Toponimi ed etnici nelle lingue dell'Italia antica," in *Popoli e Civiltà* 6 86–87, on names of Etruscan origin. On the *obesus Etruscus* of Catullus 39, see J.P. Small, "Verism and the Vernacular: Late Roman Republican Portraiture and Catullus," *ParPass* 202 (1982) 47–71. On the spirit of antiquarianism and religious revival of the early imperial age, statues, and epitaphs, see Torelli, *Elogia Tarquiniensia,* and review by T.J. Cornell, *JRS* 68 (1978) 167. On the importance of "linen books" with the pedigree and titles of the deceased beginning with the fourth century B.C. and their relationship to other documents preserved in aristocratic family archives and temples, see F. Roncalli, "Osservazioni sui *libri lintei* etruschi," *RendPontAcc* 51–52 (1978–79, 1979–80) 3–21.

I / Rediscovery

NANCY THOMSON DE GRUMMOND

At the last blow of the pickaxe, the stone which sealed the entrance of the crypt gave way, and the light of our torches lit those hollow rooms whose silence and darkness had not been troubled for more than twenty centuries. Everything was still the way it had been on the day the entrance had been closed, and ancient Etruria appeared to us just as when it was in its glory. On their funeral couches warriors, covered by their armor, seemed to be resting from the battles they had been waging against the Romans and our ancestors, the Gauls. Shapes, garments, cloth, and color, all were clearly distinguished for some minutes; then everything disappeared as the outside air came into the underground chamber, where our flickering torches were almost being blown out. The past which had been conjured up lasted no longer than a dream, and disappeared, as though to punish us for our foolhardy curiosity.

While these frail remnants turned to dust upon contact with the air, the atmosphere around us was becoming more transparent. We then saw that we were surrounded by another group of warriors, created by the artists of Etruria. Paintings decorated all the walls of the tomb and seemed to come to life in the trembling light of our torches. . . . On one side, the paintings recalled Greek myths, and the Greek names written in Etruscan letters left no doubt as to their subject. They had been inspired by the poems of Homer. Before my eyes, one of the bloodiest events of the *Iliad* was taking place, the sacrifice, by Achilles, of the Trojan prisoners over the tomb of Patroclus. In contrast, the fresco which formed a pendant with it no longer had anything Greek about it, except for the sophistication of the art, the modeling of the naked bodies, the bulging muscles, the expressiveness of the faces, animated by violent passions, and the skill with which the lights, the shadows and the halftones were rendered. As for the subject, it was obviously a local theme, as shown by the names, completely Etruscan in character, inscribed above each figure.[1]

I wish to thank the following persons for their kind assistance with my topic: Larissa Bonfante, David Butler, Charles Davis, W. de Grummond, John Elliott, Emeline Hill Richardson, Cheryl Sowder, Sandra Tison.

Such were the vivid impressions of the French excavator A. Noël des Vergers, when he and the archaeologist-artist Alessandro François first entered the now-famous François Tomb at Vulci in 1857 (figs. IV-96—97). His emotional response was typical of the heroic pioneers of Etruscan studies of the nineteenth century, who have left us abundant evidence in literature and art of the excitement of discovering the Etruscans in their underground tombs, of seeing paintings and statues come to life again after so long a sleep. Their particular brand of archaeology, combining artistic sensibility with scholarly acumen, has now disappeared with the advent of modern, more "objective" archaeology. But while the results of the latter type of scholarship will furnish the principal material of this book, it may be useful at the start to review the attitudes of past scholars, writers, and artists who have encountered the Etruscans. The study of their perspectives and methods, often so different from our own, can lead to greater flexibility in our modern approach, or at least to a proper sense of humility as we regard the many, many centuries of trial and error in Etruscan studies that have led to our present state of comprehension.

The history of Etruscan studies actually begins more than two thousand years before Noël des Vergers and François. The topic is thus very large and in fact has never been treated comprehensively; without doubt an entire volume would be required to deal with it in a truly complete way.[2] I shall only attempt to give an outline of the principal developments, beginning in antiquity and going through the Middle Ages and the Renaissance to modern times.

Naturally Greek and Roman scholars and writers

recorded a wealth of information about Etruscan culture. Historical material was gathered by a number of writers; perhaps the most notable of these were Dionysius of Halicarnassus, the Greek rhetorician and historian, who came to Rome to live in the first century B.C. and studied the earliest civilizations of Italy;[3] the Roman Livy (d. A.D. 17),[4] whose history of Rome from its founding necessarily dealt with the Etruscan rulers and cities closely involved with the city in its early centuries; and the emperor Claudius (ruled A.D. 41–54), who devoted an entire work of twenty books to Etruscan history, called *Tyrrheniká,* now lost.[5] This vast undertaking was written in Greek and was evidently intended for wide circulation in the Roman Empire; regularly scheduled readings of it took place at the famous library at Alexandria.

Curiosity about the Etruscans even took on a patriotic cast during the late republic and early empire, as many Romans looked back to an Etruscan ancestry and proudly sought to emphasize it. The prime example of this attitude is provided by Maecenas,[6] the generous patron of the poets of the court of the emperor Augustus, whose influence no doubt accounts, in part, for elements of a revival of the Etruscans in Augustan literature and art. Vergil's *Aeneid,* especially, is filled with references to the Etruscans, and it includes a historical reconstruction of their culture that verges on being archaeological.[7] In depicting the Etruscan leaders who allied themselves with Aeneas and the other founders of the Roman race (such as Tarchon, the founder of Tarquinia, according to tradition[8]) as well as those who opposed them (such as Mezentius, the cruel and tyrannical ruler of Caere[9]), Vergil conveys a vivid impression of their splendid equipment, their chariots, and their powerful navy; he also portrays convincingly the topography of the once heavily forested countryside of Etruria. That he was intimate with Etruscan religious practices is evident from his description of the warrior-priest Asilas from Tuscan Pisa, who was skilled in interpreting the messages of the gods through lightning, the flight of birds, the stars, and the entrails of animals.[10]

Of course, the Etruscan art of soothsaying had long been a prominent element in Roman religious practice. There must also have been a great deal of the material culture of Etruria still surviving in imperial times. The Augustan architect Vitruvius surely had the opportunity to observe actual proportions and details of construction of Etruscan temples still standing, when he prepared his description of the proper way to build a temple in the Tuscan style.[11] Pliny the Elder (d. A.D. 79) records his admiration of ancient Etruscan terracotta statues of the gods that were still visible in his day. He finds these noteworthy for their fine modeling and their durability; in a burst of nostalgia for the good old days in Italy, he characterizes them as "more deserving of respect than gold, certainly more innocent."[12] Elsewhere he indicates that bronze statuettes from Etruria were all the rage among collectors.[13] Horace provides evidence that the passion for collecting these had already begun in the first century B.C.[14] In addition to their appreciation of the major arts of sculpture and architecture, the Romans were aware, though perhaps dimly, of a very old tradition of wall painting in Etruria.[15] From remarks in Strabo[16] and Quintilian,[17] we can see that they had a fairly specific attitude about style in Etruscan representational art, which they likened to that of Egypt and early Greece for its "hardness" and rigidity.

The Etruscan language seems to have survived longer than other elements of the culture of Etruria,[18] not so much because it attracted the attention of philologists (Varro and a number of other scholars have left us information about Etruscan vocabulary and a few notes on pronunciation and grammar), but because of its connection with religion.[19] Long after it ceased being a living language, it was studied and spoken by priests in the Roman college of haruspices or soothsayers, much as Latin continued to be used into the twentieth century by priests of the Catholic church. As late as the reign of Julian the Apostate (A.D. 360–63), there were still haruspices at court,[20] and the last recorded instance of the use of the Etruscan language was in 408, when an Etruscan soothsayer emerged to conjure lightning, as the Visigoth king Alaric prepared to sack Rome.[21]

It is not surprising that many of the references to the Etruscans found in the Middle Ages relate in one way or another to religion or to magic. It is true that there are scattered references to their artistic achievements—for example, Isidore, bishop of Seville (d. 636), has brief remarks on the nature of Arretine ware,[22] the characteristic red-glaze pottery made during the early Roman Empire in the old Etruscan town of Arezzo. But Isidore devotes more space and enthusiasm to the Etruscan prophet Tages, reviewing the remarkable tale of how Tages sprang up from a ploughed furrow to reveal the truths of Etruscan religion, then fell back and was seen no more.[23] There are other cases in which the interest in Etruscan culture occurs within a religious context, for example, a whole series of Benedictine churches in the old south Etruscan territory which have a tripartite arrangement of the choir area. Modern art historians have traced this arrangement to the tripartite cella of ancient Etruscan temples in the region.[24] Others have remarked on the similarities in stylization and in decorative motifs found in Archaic Etruscan relief sculpture and in certain Romanesque ecclesiastical sculpture, but these similarities may be purely coincidental.[25]

By far the most remarkable descriptions of Etruscan remains in the Middle Ages occur in the *Chronicle of the Kings of England* by William of Malmesbury (d. about 1148). The author relates a story told to him in his boyhood by a Spanish monk who had visited Italy; the tale evidently pertains to a visit to an Etruscan tomb, but in its transmission from Italy to England and from one generation to another, it became filled with fantasy and magic. The monk reported:

I eagerly viewed many of the wonders of that country and impressed them on my memory. Among others I saw a perforated mountain, beyond which the inhabitants supposed the treasures of Octavian were hidden. Many persons were reported to have entered into these caverns for the purpose of exploring them, and to have there perished. . . . I, with my companions, about twelve in number, mediated an expedition of this nature. . . . We proceeded on our journey along the caverns in the mountain, in the best manner we were able. Everything was dark, and full of horrors; the bats, flitting from holes, assailed our eyes and faces: the path was narrow, and made dreadful on the left-hand by a precipice, with a river flowing beneath it. We saw the way strewed with bare bones. . . . Arriving at the farther outlet, we beheld a lake. . . . A bridge of brass united the opposite banks. Beyond the bridge were seen golden horses of great size, mounted by golden riders.[26]

The company desired to cross the lake, in order to seize some of the precious metal, but each time they made the attempt, a rustic figure made of brass would strike the water with a bronze club and cause clouds to fill the air. Disappointed, they returned through the caves, and found only a silver dish which they somehow divided among themselves. The story ends with a visit to a "Jew-necromancer," who uses his magic powers to bring back precious treasures from across the lake.

Amid the fantasy, we may discern various elements of real Etruscan remains. The description of the "perforated mountain," with its path running along a precipice and a river, calls to mind the rock tombs in the tufa region of southern Etruria, where the façades and openings to the tombs were cut into the cliffs (figs. I-17, V-18, V-22–23), high above ravines and streams. The descriptions of the precious metals and the bones seem like exaggerated accounts of the contents of Etruscan tombs, while the characterization of the places as "full of horrors" reminds one of the dreadful demons commonly found in Etruscan funerary art. The remarkable rustic with a club resembles no one so much as Herakles (in Etruscan, Hercle), who was a very popular figure in Etruscan bronze statuary (fig. I-1).[27]

The visit of William's monk presumably took place in the twelfth century, but there is also evidence in the *Chronicles* that Etruscan tombs were opened at an earlier date. The mathematician Gerbert, who became Pope Sylvester II (999–1003), took a great interest in the remains of classical antiquity—to such an extent that he kept near himself the head of an old statue which he consulted for advice about his future. ("For instance, when Gerbert would say 'Shall I be pope?' the statue would reply, 'Yes.' "[28]) William of Malmesbury relates another incredible tale, which must have its basis in a real experience in an Etruscan tomb, of how Gerbert used magic arts to enter into a subterranean palace. The setting of the tale is given as Rome, but the context has been regarded as Etruscan by modern scholars. So, too, in the case of the "perforated mountain" beyond which lay the "treasures of Octavian," one presumes that the Etruscans were unknown to William and his sources.[29] As William tells us:

The story culminates in the attempt of Gerbert and his assistant to secure some of the treasures, when, alas, all of the statues come to life and try to seize the intruders! The details of this bizarre "excavation" and the listing of the contents of the "palace" may, after all, be derived from the unearthing of some Roman imperial structure during the Middle Ages in the city of Rome. Yet the most illuminating comparisons for the various items in the underground chambers seem to be found among well-known Etruscan antiquities, such as the many sets of dice found in Etruscan tombs (fig. I-2)[31] or the huge wine crater (surely a "vessel of great weight and value"), chest-high, represented in the Tomb of the Lionesses (fig. I-3).[32] The description of the "king" and "queen" banqueting, with slaves in attendance, calls to mind the many banqueting scenes painted on the walls of the tombs of Tarquinia (cf. fig. IV-91),[33] and the emphasis on precious metals recalls once again the opulent contents of Etruscan tombs. The much-molested statue with the right hand extended may have had a gesture something like that of the famous bronze Orator (Arringatore) in Florence (fig. IV-65; the right arm is a restoration, but fully convincing),[34] or of numerous Roman statues of orators and generals of imperial times.

Through the centuries from the time of Gerbert onward there occur bits of evidence, visual and literary, to indicate that Etruscan tombs were investigated periodically. At the end of the medieval period and the beginning of the Renaissance, the artist Giotto seems to have seen Etruscan tomb painting, judging from the evidence of the frescoes

I-1. Statuette of Herakles. Bronze. Ht. 24.2 cm. Late fourth to early third century B.C. Toledo Museum of Art, Acc. 78.22, gift of Edward Drummond Libbey. (Toledo Museum of Art.)

There was a statue in the Campus Martius near Rome, I know not whether of brass or iron, having the forefinger of the right hand extended, and on the head was written, "Strike here." The men of former times supposing this should be understood as if they might find a treasure there, had battered the harmless statue by repeated strokes of a hatchet. But Gerbert convicted them of error by solving the problem in a very different manner. Marking where the shadow of the finger fell at noon-day, when the sun was on the meridian, he there placed a post; and at night proceeded thither, attended only by a servant carrying a lanthorn. The earth opening by means of his accustomed arts, displayed to them a spacious entrance. They see before them a vast palace with golden walls, golden roofs, everything of gold; golden soldiers amusing themselves, as it were, with golden dice; a king of the same metal, at table with his queen; delicacies set before them, and servants waiting; vessels of great weight and value, where the sculpture surpassed nature itself.[30]

I-2. Ivory dice. Etruscan, Hellenistic period. Rome, Villa Giulia. (Soprintendenza alle Antichità dell'Etruria Meridionale.)

I-3. Tomb of the Lionesses, Tarquinia, painted frieze on back wall showing dancers with crater.
520–510 B.C. (DAI.)

I-4. Giotto, fresco of *Justice,* detail of lower section with dancers and landscape. 1304. Padua, Arena
Chapel. (Alinari.)

I-5. Giotto, *The Hiring of Judas*. Padua, Arena Chapel. (Alinari.)

I-6. Late medieval devil with hammer, from a fresco at Stratford-upon-Avon. (From "A Dissertation on the Pageants or Dramatic Mysteries Anciently Performed at Coventry.")

I-7. Etruscan painting, detail, head of Charun. Tarquinia, Tomba dell' Orco.

which he executed in the Arena Chapel in Padua (first decade of the fourteenth century). In a fresco of Justice enthroned, a vignette at the bottom shows the good effects of Justice, as riders go by on horseback and dancers and musicians cavort among the trees (fig. I-4). The latter figures are dancing in an Etruscan style (cf. fig. IV-92), and the bits of landscape included are similar to the settings for dancers and musicians found in Etruscan tombs.[35]

Giotto also must have seen representations of the Etruscan demon Charun, who evidently served as model for the profile of Satan and also for that of Judas in the scene of the hiring of Judas to betray Christ. (figs. I-5, I-7).[36] Another late medieval specimen of an Etruscan-style demon comes from a fresco at Stratford-upon-Avon (fig. I-6), where a hideous devil brandishes a hammer, the characteristic weapon and attribute of Charun (cf. figs. IV-96, VIII-50).[37] Doubtless many similar examples could be cited from other countries and centuries, but there is not enough space here to make the full investigation, as yet lacking, of the extent of the influence of Etruscan demonology in the Christian world.

I-8. Nicola Pisano, relief panel of Nativity from pulpit. Marble. 33.5 × 44.5 in. 1260. Pisa, Baptistry. (Alinari.)

Giotto was not the first artist in Tuscany to look back to the ancient inhabitants of his region for inspiration. Nicola Pisano had quoted from Etruscan art when creating images of the reclining Virgin in the Baptistery at Pisa (fig. I-8).[38] The Virgin thus resembles the ladies reclining on innumerable ash urns and sarcophagi from antiquity, Etruscan and Roman alike (cf. figs. IV-43–44).[39] Similarly, Arnolfo di Cambio had imitated the Hellenistic dress and jewelry of Etruscan ladies in his enthroned Madonna and Child in the church of San Domenico at Orvieto (dated 1282).[40]

Nor were these artists by any means the last to study or be influenced by the ancient Etruscans; the roster of later artists of Tuscany who have been mentioned in this connection reads like a roll call of the most famous artists of the Renaissance—Brunelleschi, Ghiberti, Masaccio, Donatello, Alberti, Antonio Pollaiuolo, Leonardo, Michelangelo, Benvenuto Cellini, Giorgio Vasari, and Andrea Sansovino—and there were many other lesser figures as well.[41] All in all, there is an extensive body of material to support the proposal by the French scholar André Chastel that an "Etruscan Revival" took place in Renaissance Tuscany.[42]

These artists represent the wing of Renaissance studies in which antiquity was approached from the aesthetic point of view. The ancient Etruscan objects (along with Greek and Roman ones, of course) were to be studied and imitated because of their interesting and expressive motifs, because of their high quality, because of their truth to nature. This aesthetic attitude is unlike any approach encountered previously. Certainly it differs radically from the medieval point of view, which was centered around the religious and magical. In comparison with the attitude of the classical Greeks and Romans, the Renaissance added a new dimension, since so much emphasis was now placed on the objects as works of art. Essentially the Romans were interested in the Etruscans because the earlier culture was so inextricably tied to their own traditions and past history;[43] their concern for aesthetic questions was limited.

Nevertheless, in their feelings about the Etruscans, the Renaissance scholars and artists had much in common with the ancients. Their pride and curiosity about their ancestors was much the same as that observed in the Romans of the first century B.C., and we can identify a trend of historical research in the Renaissance that parallels the work of Livy, Claudius, and others in antiquity. This trend had a starting point rather similar to that of the ancients: the Renaissance scholars got involved in Etruscan history because they wished to describe the origin and development of their cities[44] and could scarcely neglect the Etruscan chapters of the story. Thus the medieval and Renaissance city of Corneto was identified as early as the time of Boccaccio[45] with the ancient city called Corythus, mentioned more than once in Vergil's *Aeneid* as a specifically Etruscan city and a cradle of Trojan and Italian civilization. This historical view of Corneto as Corythus was warmly praised by L. Vitelleschi, a member of a prominent Cornetan family, in a poem which he dedicated to the Florentine humanist Francesco Filelfo (d. 1481).[46] Vitelleschi believed that he had seen the ruins of ancient Corythus in modern Corneto and had even visited the palace of King Corythus, believed by some to be the founder of the city:

This mount is Corythus, the place of the first origins of ancient Troy, where now sits the wealthy city of Corneto. . . . The greatest monuments still exist, and they have been found in large numbers over extensive territory. There is a huge palace which was carved out of the white rocks. It was the great abode of a very great people. . . .

Carved benches are round about, openings allow daylight to penetrate the rooms. In a certain place is wrought a paneled ceiling beautiful to behold. It was, I believe, the court of the king Corythus. My eyes surveyed these carvings; they were memorable, but the long passage of time has diminished that ancient work. In addition, there are also effigies and sepulchres of ancient men; there are images of demigods and gods.[47]

An alternate tradition that Corneto contained the ruins of the Etruscan city of Tarquinii may be found as early as the fourteenth century in Petrarch[48] and eventually came to prevail in modern times, so that the medieval name of Corneto was abandoned and the city was renamed Tarquinia.

There is an air of romance in Vitelleschi's identification of the subterranean area (evidently an Etruscan tomb complex) as a palace and in his dating of the works to the time of the mythical king Corythus (which would actually be six or seven hundred years too early). An even more romantic spirit is evident in Ariosto's *Orlando Furioso* (first published in 1516), where the atmosphere of an Etruscan tomb is evoked when Orlando visits a rock-cut grotto, the abode of the fair virgin Isabel, or when Bradamante enters the secret cave and sepulcher of the wizard Merlin.[49] But compared with the fantasy-loving William of Malmesbury, Vitelleschi reveals a far more sober orientation in regard to Etruscan antiquities. Ariosto, after all, did not pretend to be writing history.

A much more analytical and truly archaeological vein of Etruscan studies occurs along with the aesthetic, historical, and romantic approaches already noted. It is evident at the surprisingly early date of 1282 within the pages of the work *Della composizione del mondo,* by Ristoro of Arezzo, who describes in great detail ancient vases which were then being unearthed in his own town.[50] Another example is a fifteenth-century description of the contents of an Etruscan tomb at Volterra by the humanist Antonio Ivano from Sarzana. In a letter of 1466 to a friend in Florence, he reports on the tomb, which had been opened outside the walls of Volterra on the road to Pisa:

Not far from the same hill some sepulchres have been discovered in a certain grotto; out of these there is left one made of marble; and their lids are carved to represent various likenesses of reclining figures and the ancient clothing of the bodies. But the sepulchres are very short and narrow, from which we [can] easily judge that these, like urns, preserved ashes, not bodies. There were also extant in the same grotto a number of vases shaped from clay, but they were partly broken. Indeed the various types of these pleased me very much. On the cover of the marble sepulchre was carved the figure of a venerable matron wearing a necklace and bracelets painted in light gold. On the front of another sepulchre a horseman was painted in a red color in the ancient manner. Two foot soldiers seem to accompany him. One goes ahead, carrying a sling on his shoulders. The other follows, carrying a shield. I believe that these sepulchres, which are now preserved by the diligence of the abbot of San Giusto, belonged to a single family only.[51]

This is an excellent report on the finds of the tomb, with its array of sculptured and painted urns and pottery, and allows us to suppose that Ivano was looking at the contents of a typical Volterran tomb of the Hellenistic period (cf. fig. IV-32). To be sure, he does not seem to have identified the material as Etruscan and in general has included only a very modest amount of inference in his careful inventory. He was evidently correct in assuming that the sepulchres were ash urns (to date, only two Etruscan sarcophagi have been found at Volterra) and was sensible to conclude that the tomb belonged to a single family.

There certainly were scholars in the fifteenth century who could identify Etruscan objects and inscriptions as such. Among these was the versatile genius Leone Battista Alberti (d. 1472). He reports on visiting the sites of ancient towns and tombs where he saw ancient grave stelae "dug up with Inscriptions on them, as is generally believed, in *Etrurian* characters, which are like both those of the *Greeks* and *Latins;* but no body can understand them."[52] Not surprisingly, in his *Ten Books on Architecture* Alberti also includes numerous observations on Etruscan architectural style. These comments are based on his reading of ancient sources and his study of the actual visual remains and are generally perspicacious. He observed that the Etruscans built their walls of squared stones, the largest that could be obtained; that they used the Doric order at a very early date; that they were said to have used a round plinth rather than a square one under their columns ("but I never met with such a Base among the Works of the Ancients"[53]). He discusses at some

length the proportions used by the Etruscans in their temples (the discussion is based on Vitruvius) and describes in some detail the Tomb of Lars Porsenna at Clusium, evidently following the report on this huge and bizarre structure given by Pliny the Elder[54] (Alberti had the good taste to criticize it as being overdone).

The influence of Etruscan architecture on Renaissance buildings has been noted by a number of writers, with perhaps the most interesting example falling within the oeuvre of Alberti himself. It has been argued that elements of his famous design for the façade of the Palazzo Rucellai in Florence (fig. I-9) were suggested by Etruscan urns in the shape of a building, such as the well-known one in the Museo Archeologico in Florence (fig. V-36).[55] The two structures illustrated have in common the usage of the arch with voussoir blocks flanked by pilasters and a wall articulated by horizontal courses of squared masonry, as well as the heavily projecting cornice contrasting with a flattish wall surface.

Another example of Etruscan influence occurs in the villa built for Lorenzo de' Medici at Poggio a Caiano, just outside Florence (1480s, fig. I-10), where the architect, Giuliano da Sangallo, appears to have imitated elements of an Etruscan temple (cf. fig. V-38).[56] The broad, low pediment and the widely spaced columns call to mind the porch of an Etruscan temple, and the ribbon motif in the pediment also has parallels in Etruscan art. In addition, on the terracotta frieze above the colonnade there is a serpent-bearing bearded figure, who has been compared with Charun and Tuchulcha.[57] The Medici interest in Etruscanizing motifs continued into the sixteenth century, when Pontormo painted a fresco in the great hall of the villa featuring the Etruscan deity Vertumnus (1520–21) and evidently experimented with motifs from Etruscan sculpture as he prepared the design for the fresco.[58]

The most famous of all Etruscan scholars of the Renaissance was the Dominican friar Giovanni Nanni, better known as Annio da Viterbo (1432–1502).[59] He was apparently the first to study the Etruscan language intensively and to profess to have translated the Etruscan inscriptions that he came across in his native Viterbo and elsewhere. He believed that Etruscan was derived from Hebrew,

I-9. Leone Battista Alberti, façade, Palazzo Rucellai, Florence. 1446–51. (Brogi.)

I-10. Giuliano da Sangallo, façade of first-floor loggia, Medici villa, Poggio a Caiano. 1480s. (Alinari.)

which was an honest enough error in a period when many scholars believed that all languages derived from Hebrew. But he also made a good many dishonest claims, and, as a result, his name is rarely mentioned with unqualified enthusiasm. It is certain that he is the creator of some literary forgeries—the most famous of these a Latin book on the history of Rome allegedly written in antiquity by Fabius Pictor; it included a map of the ancient city of Rome, the first such created in the Renaissance, which was as fanciful as Fabius's text.[60] The Etruscan inscriptions which he published have also come under suspicion, and there can be no doubt that his confident translations of them were absolutely wrong. His writings and lectures on ancient history were intensely patriotic and pro-Etruscan, and ap-

parently one of his main goals was to demonstrate that Viterbo was an early cradle of civilization. He summoned up a remarkable array of ancestors for the modern Viterbans; Hercules was not so surprising, but even the highly credulous must have gasped to learn that the foundation and development of Viterbo involved such personages as Isis and Osiris, Atlas, Electra, and Tyrrhenus;[61] the last supposedly brought the Farnese family to Tuscany.

Annio was the perpetrator of one of the first deliberate excavations of Etruscan material. His excavation was exceptional in that it was not just a hunt for buried treasure, nor was it accidentally or casually undertaken in connection with ploughing a field or digging foundations, like so many Renaissance digs. It was undertaken in a spirit of research, in an attempt to find out more about the inhabitants of ancient Italy. But unfortunately it seems to have been something of a hoax: the finds were planted in advance. When a tomb outside of Viterbo was opened in the presence of Pope Alexander VI, Annio was able to begin discoursing immediately on the sculptures found there and their connections with the earliest kings in Italy.[62]

Annio has been damned and scorned as a contemptible forger by scholars of the nineteenth and twentieth centuries, who perhaps have judged him a little too harshly. It is worth noting, nonetheless, that even in the sixteenth century many scholars were highly skeptical about his publications and ideas, and that his brand of scholarship does not seem to have been at all typical of Renaissance Etruscan studies.[63]

For a thoroughly responsible and perceptive treatment of newly excavated Etruscan material, we may turn to Giorgio Vasari, the Renaissance artist famous above all for his *Lives of the Artists*. Vasari, like Annio, was a native of an old Etruscan town (Arezzo), but he did not allow patriotism to conquer good sense. In the preface to the *Lives,* he reports on what must have been one of the most sensational discoveries of an antiquity in the Renaissance, when the Chimaera from his native Arezzo was brought to light (fig. IV-62):

In our time, that is in 1554, when trenches, fortifications, and ramparts were being made at Arezzo, there was found a bronze sculpture made as the Chimaera of Bellerophon. In this sculpture one can recognize the perfecting of that art which took place in antiquity among the Tuscans. [That it belongs to this culture] can be seen in its Etruscan style, but even more so in the letters engraved on one leg. Because there are but a few, it is conjectured—for no one understands the Etruscan language today—that they could thus signify the name of the artist, or of this sculpture, and perhaps also the date, according to the usage of those times. And this sculpture, because of its beauty and antiquity, has been placed by Duke Cosimo [de' Medici] in the hall of the new rooms of his palace.[64]

In this excavation report, Vasari tells us the time and place of the find, the material and subject of the piece, and the present location.[65] He identifies the cultural context in an impressive way, and in making conjectures, he is modest and does not make excessive claims. His honest appraisal of the

inscription (which, *pace* Friar Annio, belonged to an undeciphered language) allowed him to be sure that the piece was Etruscan, but he also supported his conclusion by analyzing style, a technique which he had learned well from his extensive study of the style of Renaissance artists. He discussed this matter in greater detail elsewhere (in his *Ragionamenti,* or *Discourses*), pointing out that the immature and archaic treatment of the hair of the Chimaera was a sign of an early date, and that the piece was therefore neither Greek nor Roman. (Vasari evidently was not acquainted with Greek art of the Archaic period or earlier.) Also in the *Ragionamenti* he discusses the subject matter in greater detail (the identification of the Chimaera was based on comparisons with ancient coins and examination of the creature's wounds and indications of suffering) and reveals more about the condition of the piece when found. All in all, he has handed down to us a great deal of information and a sensitive analysis of the find.

The Chimaera attracted much attention after its discovery, not only in the art world in Tuscany, but also beyond. Titian's impressions of the piece were recorded by Pietro Aretino, and Montaigne noted in his diary (1580) that he had seen the bronze sculpture placed on a column in the Palazzo Vecchio when he visited Florence.[66] Most famous of all is the mention of the Chimaera in the *Autobiography* of Benvenuto Cellini (probably completed in 1562).[67] The context has sometimes been thought to suggest that Cellini was involved in restoring the piece, but the passage must be read with caution. He refers to the discovery of the Chimaera and of a number of bronze statuettes, evidently Etruscan, along with it. He then describes how he and Duke Cosimo took tiny hammers and goldsmith's chisels and carefully cleaned the corrosion and dirt off of the small bronze figures; afterwards, the Duke asked Benvenuto to restore the missing parts of the statuettes. But it should be noted that Cellini does not state that he worked on the Chimaera itself, and since he never missed an opportunity to report on the commissions or deeds that brought him glory, it is probable that he had nothing at all to do with the restoration of the famous piece.

Besides the bronze Chimaera and the statuettes

from Arezzo, certain other important Etruscan bronzes first came to light in the sixteenth century. These include the large bronze Minerva now in the Museo Archeologico in Florence,[68] discovered at Arezzo some years before the Chimaera, and the Orator, also in the Florence museum, discovered at Sanguineta near Lake Trasimene in the territory of Perugia, in 1573.[69]

The earliest evidence for the study of bronze Etruscan mirrors dates to the beginning of the sixteenth century, and again the context is Florentine.[70] An anonymous drawing from the Codex Pighianus (Fig. I-11) shows a design from a mirror thought to have been discovered at Castellina in Chianti in 1507, with a representation of Odysseus (Uthste) threatening to decapitate Circe (Cerca). The composition bears a remarkable resemblance to Cellini's sculpture group of Perseus with the decapitated Medusa (fig. I-12).[71] Perhaps here Cellini was inspired by Etruscan mirrors just as later, in the seventeenth century, the French painter Poussin was to be influenced by adornment scenes from them; his painting of *Mars and Venus* in Toledo (fig. I-13) shares many motifs with the numerous ancient mirrors that show the toilette of Venus (fig. I-14).[72]

There is much other evidence of study of the Etruscans among the artists, humanists, and princes of the sixteenth century. Michelangelo made a famous drawing of the Etruscan god of the underworld, Hades (in Etruscan, Aita),[73] possibly upon the occasion of visiting an Etruscan tomb and examining its paintings, and in his creation of the tombs for the Medici family in their chapel in San Lorenzo, he seems to have been influenced by Etruscan sculptural and iconographic motifs.[74] Andrea Sansovino, like Michelangelo, was apparently acquainted with Etruscan urns and sarcophagi. In his Tomb of Cardinal Girolamo Basso della Rovere (fig. I-15; Santa Maria del Popolo, Rome),[75] he used a motif for the dead person which was unusual in Italian Renaissance tomb sculpture, but which is understandable if viewed within the context of imitation of antiquity. The deceased is not shown stretched out flat on his back with eyes closed and arms folded over the body in eternal repose, as is typical of reclining tomb figures of the Italian Renaissance. Instead, the upper portion of the body is

I-11. Drawing after an engraved Etruscan mirror discovered in a tomb near Castellina in Chianti in 1507, showing (*left to right*) Uthste (Odysseus), Cerca (Circe), and Velparun (Elpenor). Sixteenth century. Codex Pighianus, Tübingen University Library.

somewhat raised, and the knees are pulled up, as in Etruscan sculpture (cf. fig. I-23). But while the deceased in Etruscan art enjoys the afterlife fully alert and awake, Sansovino attempted to retain a note of repose in the Renaissance work by using the closed eyes and drooping head, and the result has been criticized as awkward: "If Girolamo . . . sleeps, it is the painful sleep of a headache—all sense of taking rest is gone."[76]

We may examine one final example of Etruscan influence in the sixteenth century. At Bomarzo, in the bizarre pleasure garden laid out for the eccentric Renaissance humanist and prince Vicino Orsini (created mostly in the third quarter of the century), we find Etruscan art, architecture, and even landscape quoted and imitated in a very unusual way.[77] The garden was intended to astonish and delight the visitor and is filled with remarkable pieces of sculpture and architecture which Orsini likened to the seven wonders of the world. The sources of his inspiration were diverse, even exotic, since he took an interest in the culture of faraway times and

I-12. Benvenuto Cellini, Perseus with the head of Medusa. 1545–54. Loggia dei Lanzi, Florence. (Alinari.)

I-13. Nicholas Poussin (attributed), *Mars and Venus*. 1630–40. Toledo Museum of Art, Acc. 54.87, Gift of Edward Drummond Libbey. (Museum photo.)

I-14. *The Toilette of Malavisch*. Engraved Etruscan mirror. 350–325 B.C. British Museum. (*ES* 213.)

I-15. Andrea Sansovino, tomb of Cardinal Girolamo Basso della Rovere. Sixteenth century. Rome, Santa Maria del Popolo. (Anderson.)

I-16. Mask of ogre, entrance to a building in the Parco dei Mostri, Bomarzo. 1550–75. (G. Bonfante.)

places. The Etruscan sources, while somewhat exotic and unusual within the total context of the
study of antiquity in the Renaissance, were certainly
also intimately familiar to Orsini himself. It has
been plausibly suggested that he had visited Etruscan cemeteries north of Bomarzo; from these he
could have derived the generally "Etruscan" atmosphere of his park, displaying massive stone features
within a picturesque and often uncultivated landscape. In imitating the Etruscan countryside and its
remains, he also had his workmen create a rock-
carved tomb façade in Etruscan style, intentionally
broken and overturned to look like a ruin in the
landscape. Etruscan precedents have also been identified for decorative motifs in the pedimental sculptures of the tomb façade and for other monuments
of the park. Especially notable is the huge head of
an ogre (fig. I-16), one of twelve colossal sculptures
placed about the garden (among the others are an
elephant with a tower on its back, a dragon, a huge
tortoise, two giants wrestling, and a sphinx). The
weird head rises up out of the ground with its
mouth wide open; one may enter the "door" of the
mouth and sit on one of the benches running

I-17. Entrance to the Tomb of the Statues, Ceri. Seventh
century B.C. (Prayon.)

I-18. Tomb of the Shields and Chairs, Cerveteri, with furniture carved out of the rock. First half of sixth century B.C. (DAI.)

around the chamber; in the center is the dining table. The horror of the ogre's head recalls once again Etruscan demonology, and the interior of the head has been thought of as an Etruscan tomb jokingly transformed into a dining room.[78]

Almost a century later, the mood of grotesquerie and enchantment in the landscape around Bomarzo seized the German archaeologist-antiquarian Athanasius Kircher, as he visited various sites gathering material for a projected work, *Itinerarium Etruscum,* which was unfortunately never realized.[79] Referring to his explorations around "Polimartium" (i.e., Bomarzo) and the "Ager Viterbensis" (the territory around Viterbo), he reports a visit to an Etruscan tomb (cf. fig. I-17). There he viewed the chambers and the pieces of funerary furniture hewn

out of the rock (cf. fig. I-18) and recorded the local tradition that the place was actually constructed for habitation. The Etruscans did indeed attempt in many cases to make the eternal abodes of the deceased resemble their actual dwellings. But Kircher's penchant for speculation goes too far when he compares these "habitations" to the grottoes of the fabled troglodytes, weird cave-dwelling creatures whose customs and manner of speech were barbarous and sinister.[80] The following passage describes the phenomena which Kircher encountered and his anthropological interpretations:

In the year 1659, when I was exploring Etruria, it happened . . . as I was on my way to survey the Ager Viterbensis that I crossed a certain field in which smoke fumes came forth, all the way from one side to the other. As one aston-

I-19. Etruscan mirror. Third or fourth century B.C. Paris, Cabinet des Médailles, Bibliothèque Nationale. A drawing of the front of the mirror, now at Windsor Castle, made in the seventeenth
century and included in Cassiano dal Pozzo's "Paper Museum," or Museum Chartaceum, is shown
at the left. The mirror has been dedicated to the dead by scratching *suthina*, "for the grave," across
the reflecting surface. The subject engraved on the back, shown at the right, is an Etruscan version
of the building of the Trojan horse (here called *Pecse*, Pegasus) by Sethlans (Hephaestus) and his
assistant, Etule. (Bibl. Nat.)

ished at such a sight, I supposed that there were trenches
of sulphur in that place. And so I asked my companion to
reveal what fumes of that type might betoken. He smiled
and said, "These fumes which you see are not exhalations
of the earth, but they are fumes which obtain release in
these fields through the chimneys of subterranean habitations." And immediately after a brief space he showed
me an opening, through which lay an entrance into the
aforesaid grottoes. And so we entered and found all things
disposed in a manner not different from that of the Troglodytes of Melita; [there were] bedchambers, benches, and
compartments cut out of the living rock, much more spacious than those of Melita.[81]

Another ambitious project in Etruscan studies
that failed in the seventeenth century turned out
ultimately to be far more successful than Kircher's
"Etruscan Itinerary." Early in the century the Scotsman Thomas Dempster had come to Italy, after a

tempestuous career in England and France, where
he had become famous not only as a scholar and
a poet, but also as a swordsman. In between his
numerous quarrels and duels, he somehow found
time to serve as professor of civil law at the University of Pisa and to prepare a major study, the first
since antiquity, on the Etruscans. The commission
to do the book came from Cosimo II de' Medici,
Grand Duke of Tuscany (d. 1620), who was interested in the ancient Etruscan civilization that had
once flourished in his domain. The result was a
manuscript, *De Etruria regali libri septem* ("Seven
Books on Etruria of the Kings"), which was presented to the Grand Duke, but did not command
sufficient attention to be published. The manuscript
lay ignored for almost a century, until it was discovered in Florence by an Englishman, Thomas Coke.

Coke sponsored the publication of the manuscript, with copious notes and corrections by the Italian scholar Filippo Buonarroti and with handsome copperplate illustrations never envisioned by Dempster.[82]

Much of Dempster's text is based on literary rather than archaeological evidence, and it focuses especially on the written classical sources of information about the origin, customs, history, cities, and language of the Etruscans. Evidently he had never visited many of the cities which he mentions, but his treatment of the language does take into account both inscriptional evidence from Etruscan artifacts and the glosses found in classical sources. From these Dempster was able to compile a small Etruscan vocabulary, one of the earliest attempted.[83]

As noted previously, Etruscan mirrors attracted attention from an early date.[84] In the seventeenth century a number of individuals—scholars, artists, collectors—studied them. Poussin must have learned about them from his friend and advisor Cassiano dal Pozzo, secretary to the Cardinal Barberini, who, in turn, may have first become interested in the ancient mirrors found at Palestrina (Praeneste), which was acquired by the Barberini family in 1623.[85] Cassiano included a drawing of an Etruscan mirror (fig. I-19) in his ambitious "Paper Museum" ("Museum Chartaceum"), a gathering of illustrations of all the notable antiquities to be seen in his day. The piece, showing an Etruscan version of the building of the Trojan horse, evidently belonged at the time to the great French polymath N.C.F. de Peiresc; it is today in the Bibliothèque Nationale, Paris.[86] Another well-known Etruscan mirror, the "Patera Cospiana," today in the Museo Civico Archeologico, Bologna (fig. I-20), first came to light in the seventeenth century at Arezzo.[87]

In general, however, interest in the Etruscans waned in the seventeenth century. The lack of excitement over Dempster's *De Etruria regali* seems to be a good indicator of the scholarly climate. Probably the main reason for a decline in Etruscan studies in this period is that Florence, previously a focal point for such interests, had yielded to Rome in artistic leadership. The scholars and artists who flocked into Rome in the seventeenth century were fascinated above all with *Roman* antiquity, as is evident from the history paintings they commis-

I-20. Etruscan mirror, the so-called Patera Cospiana, with the birth of Minerva from the head of Tinia (Zeus), discovered at Arezzo in the seventeenth century. Bologna, Museo Civico Archeologico.

sioned or created. Aeneas, Constantine, Germanicus, Romulus—these and other Romans were the heroes of the great historical sequences and individual works created by Rubens, Poussin, and Pietro da Cortona, and only occasionally did an Etruscan figure find a place. Rubens, for example, depicted the Roman Mucius Scaevola casting his right hand into fire in the presence of the Etruscan king of Clusium, Lars Porsenna, in order to show his contempt for physical torture,[88] and Rembrandt created a design for a scene showing the decapitation of the sons of Brutus and the other conspirators who tried to restore the Etruscan king Tarquinius Superbus to power in Rome.[89] But in such works as these, the interest was clearly centered in the Roman figures and on Roman history.

The eighteenth century presents a dramatic contrast. During this period a veritable mania for the Etruscans developed. The term *Etruscheria* is often

I-21. G.-B Piranesi, frontispiece to *Osservazioni sopra la lettre de M. Mariette* (1765).

applied to this phenomenon, which actually materialized as a result of Dempster's *De Etruria regali* finally being published.[90] The work was an instant and spectacular success, particularly in the region of Tuscany, as was natural. In the old Etruscan town of Cortona, a recently founded academy, the Accademia degli Occulti, reacted to the book by changing its name to the Accademia Etrusca (1726) and by deciding to call its president *lucumone,* after the Etruscan word for king (preserved in Latin as *lucumo*). This academy was to play a major role in eighteenth-century study of the Etruscans, with its regular meetings and scholarly discussions and its *Dissertazioni,* published on various subjects over a period of more than fifty years.[91]

These eighteenth-century academicians lead the way to modern scholarship. Admittedly they often do not measure up to the rigorous scholarly standards prevailing today and have sometimes been scorned as pseudo-scientific. Some of their theories, which they paraded as scholarship, were indeed preposterous. For example, Greek vases found in Etruscan tombs and the Greek temples of southern Italy were thought by many to have been created by Etruscans and therefore to constitute evidence of the ultimate Etruscan origin of similar temples and vases found around the Mediterranean and, in fact, of all Greek civilization.[92] Once again a patri-

otic fervor for this Italian civilization poured forth, with the result that the Etruscans were credited with the invention of everything from architecture to law, literature, navigation, philosophy, and science.[93] One ardent supporter of native Etruscan art was the artist-archaeologist G.-B. Piranesi, who repeatedly asserted the superiority of the art of ancient Italy over that of Greece. One of his treatises on the subject, directed at the French critic Mariette, had for its frontispiece a design featuring the ruggedly simple Tuscan Doric order (fig. I–21). Elsewhere he included Etruscan motifs in his book of recommended designs for chimneypieces; his chimney designs later influenced Robert Adam in creating designs for a series of "Etruscan Rooms."[94]

In general Etruscan scholars of today have admiration and respect for the eighteenth-century archaeologists, who did not themselves have, after all, the great backlog of sifted theories and data that we have now to serve as a basis for new departures. Above all, respect for them is based on their tendency to inject purpose, method, and system into their approach to the Etruscans. Extensive excavations were undertaken—around Volterra, Siena, Cortona, and Arezzo—as part of the realization that more information was needed to support theories. Etruscan collections were formed and museums were founded, such as the Museo Guar-

I-22. Antonio Francesco Gori, illustration of cinerary urn from Chiusi, second century B.C., with relief representation of a man fighting with a plow. (*Museum Etruscum* [1737–43], pl. CLVII, I.)

I-23. Antonio Niccolino D'Abbati, illustration of cinerary urn with relief representation of the combat of the Greeks with the Trojans. (Gori, *Museum Etruscum*, pl. CXXXII.)

nacci[95] at Volterra and the Museo dell'Accademia Etrusca at Cortona, and material was grouped for study in a way that went considerably beyond the "Paper Museum" of Cassiano dal Pozzo, for example. There was also a keen awareness that all of this material had to be published in a systematic way and made available to other scholars. The plates which Buonarroti added to Dempster's treatise were part of this trend, but probably the most notable effort was the series of publications of the Florentine Antonio Francesco Gori, with his richly illustrated *Museum Etruscum* in three volumes (Florence 1737–43; fig. I–22; cf. fig. I–23), and his works on the Museo Guarnacci at Volterra (1744) and on the museums at Florence and Cortona (1750).[96] In addition, monographs were written on individual aspects of Etruscan customs (e.g., the dissertation on Etruscan clothing by Lorenzo Guazzesi of Arezzo, one of the *lucumoni* of the Accademia Etrusca).[97] Treatises dealing with pre-Roman Italy in general also appeared. Perhaps the most admired of these eighteenth-century scholars today is the philologist and historian Luigi Lanzi, who finally laid to rest the misconception that the Greek vases found in Etruscan tombs were themselves Etruscan, in a study on "ancient painted vases popularly called Etruscan" (published in Italian, 1806).[98] An even more important contribution was his *Saggio di lingua etrusca e di altre antiche lingue d'Italia* (1789), in which the author provided a summation of the knowledge of the Etruscans at that time as part of his treatise on the Etruscan language and other languages of Italy.

The *Etruscheria* of the eighteenth century was an especially Italian phenomenon, although it is true that since the seventeenth century other Europeans (e.g., Dempster, Kircher) had begun to take an interest in the Etruscans. Succeeding these were such figures of the eighteenth century as the German J.J. Winckelmann, who was known above all for his work with the history of Greek art, but whose encounter with the Etruscans is witnessed by his membership in the Accademia Etrusca;[99] the famous French antiquarian the Comte de Caylus, who published Etruscan antiquities along with Egyptian, Roman, and Gallic material;[100] and Josiah Wedgwood, who called his neoclassical ceramic factory in Staffordshire "Etruria." It was founded in

1769, and the first vases issued by the factory have the legend *Artes Etruriae Renascuntur:* "The Arts of Etruria Are Reborn."[101]

It was in the nineteenth century that Etruscan studies became truly international. The French, the British, and the Germans now came in throngs to Italy and joined forces with the Italians to initiate a heroic age in Etruscan studies, characterized by fervent activity in travel, discovery, and publication. For the first time, too, the general public began to take an interest in this ancient civilization. Unfortunately, along with all of this interest came a wave of opportunism in regard to Etruscan antiquities. Treasure hunters, dilettantes, and hucksters flocked through Etruria, and their rape of Etruscan sites provides a gloomy backdrop for the brilliant progress made in scholarship and the many responsible excavations that did take place in the nineteenth century.

The importance of the French school in Etruria during this period has already been brought out in connection with the spectacular discovery of the François Tomb. The British contribution mainly took the form of a series of travel books that served to make the general public aware of the achievement and significance of the Etruscans. Most important among these popularizers were a Scotsman, James Byres; an English clergyman's wife, Mrs. Hamilton Gray; and the traveler and explorer George Dennis.

Byres, a worthy successor to his compatriot Thomas Dempster, had come to Rome as a very young man in 1756 and spent most of his life there.[102] Trained as an artist and then as an architect, he earned his reputation as well as his living as an antiquarian and dealer, guiding generations of English lords on the Grand Tour through the ruins of ancient Rome—Edward Gibbon was one of his customers—and giving advice on the purchase of antiquities. It was he who bought the Portland Vase from the Barberini family and then sold it to William Hamilton, thus starting it on its journey to the British Museum. His interest in Roman antiquities led Byres to an appreciation of Etruscan art, especially following discoveries of painted tombs in Tarquinia in 1763. He began work on a book on Etruscan tombs and started on the etchings that were to illustrate it, but was unable to convince publishers back in London that there was a real demand for such a volume. Like Dempster, he failed to see his work published in his own lifetime; it was finally issued in London in 1842, as *Hypogaei or Sepulchral Caverns of Tarquinia the Capital of Antient Etruria.*

A market was created for Byres's material, however, after the splash made by Mrs. Hamilton Gray's book, *Tour to the Sepulchres of Etruria in 1839.* This lady had had the good fortune to be guided through the cemeteries of Veii, Cerveteri, and Tarquinia in a tour through Etruria and was able to describe for the English public these newly discovered paintings and art objects. Her interest in seeing and telling about (and, if possible, acquiring) the showier material being recovered is reflected, for example, in her report of the discourse of a learned bishop, who compared the Etruscans favorably to the Egyptians: "He spoke of funeral feasts and games, which were painted in the sepulchres—statues which were carved upon the coffinlids—crowns of gold that had been buried with the dead, and vases, and ornaments, of which he had been a purchaser to a very large amount, particularly of a pair of earrings belonging to a priestess, of large pendant carbuncles set in the purest and most delicately wrought gold."[103] Her book also provided useful, if somewhat superficial information for the prospective tourist, and her occasionally giddy and gushing prose was enormously successful.

After the books of Mrs. Hamilton Gray and Byres came the beautifully written classic, George Dennis's *Cities and Cemeteries of Etruria* (London 1848).[104] His work, like that of Mrs. Hamilton Gray, provides a vivid account of the writer's own personal experience, but as a piece of scholarship it is a far more enduring work. Still the best single guide to Etruscan cities and tombs, it is also important today because it gives reliable, precious information about monuments which have since been lost. The successive editions of his work incorporated descriptions of the latest sensational finds being made, conveying the excitement, without losing any of the precision, as tomb after surprising tomb was opened.

The German school of professional and scientific archaeologists working in Italy in the nineteenth century was especially important. The central figure was Eduard Gerhard, whose genius for organizing culminated in his foundation of the international Istituto di Corrispondenza Archeologica (1829), an organization which was joined by the ablest scholars and archaeologists of all countries. The regular meetings and publications of the Institute—*Bollettino, Annali,* and *Monumenti Inediti*—created a climate highly favorable for the dissemination of information about new finds and the presentation of new studies of existing material, as well as suggesting new projects.[105] Gerhard's personal influence may be felt behind many of these projects, especially those which involved codification, or initial publication of known materials. A good example is his own corpus of Etruscan mirrors, *Etruskische Spiegel,* issued between 1840 and 1897.[106]

He formed a large personal collection of Etruscan mirrors (many of which were published in *Etruskische Spiegel*) and freely gave advice to others interested in acquiring mirrors as well as other Etruscan antiquities.[107] The versatile artist-collector Pelagio Palagi, from Bologna, profited from Gerhard's advice in adding Etruscan material to his collection, and probably also obtained from Gerhard the illustrations of paintings from the Tomb of the Baron at Tarquinia (fig. IV–94), which served as inspiration for Palagi's Gabinetto Etrusco at Castello di Racconigi (fig. I–24).[108]

We have noted the reactions of various writers, travelers, and scholars to the opening or entering of Etruscan tombs. As a final example, we may add to these descriptions one by Gerhard himself, made in May of 1829. We are once more at Vulci, upon the exciting occasion of the first excavations taking place on the property of the prince of Canino, Lucien Bonaparte (brother of Napoleon). These excavations were the result of a peasant's chance find and were important above all for the vast quantity of pottery which they yielded:

There was revealed on a desolate stretch of land six miles long between the small towns of Canino and Montalto an extensive Etruscan burial place, perhaps that of ancient Vulci. Insignificant-looking grottoes lying more or less near the surface were filled with the most beautiful Greek vases, many of them painted. At many different points of this extensive site excavations have been carried on constantly and successfully. Two other owners besides the Prince de Canino share in the interest, Sig. Candellor and Sig. Feoli, but the prince being the largest landowner has the greatest share. Besides the shepherds in this neighborhood one hundred workmen have been employed

I-24. Pelagio Pelagi, detail of wall decoration, Gabinetto Etrusco, Castello di Racconigi. (Museo Civico Archeologico, Bologna.)

daily in excavating under his personal supervision since last November. . . . Your correspondent, who speaks as an eye-witness, can never forget the wonderful spectacle when he first beheld from the hill of Campomorto (the site belonging to Sig. Feoli) the numerous excavations scattered over the neighboring plain on all sides, with the huge tumulus (*La Cucumella*) in the centre. On closer examination his astonishment only increased. The various bands of laborers, who had come from distant parts, chiefly from the Abruzzi and Romagna, were distributed under foremen from their own provinces; and three tents formed the central point, into which poured the incessant stream of newly found vases or vase fragments still covered with damp soil.

Attempts were made at once to put the fragments together, in the tent occupied daily by the prince and his family; these were then sent to Musignano, the prince's country house, and handed over to experienced restorers. Their work continued day and night.[109]

Gerhard's description, written in a preliminary form for the Prussian Official Gazette, is interesting for its emphasis on details about the circumstances and methods of conducting these excavations and on the artifacts recovered (as opposed to the tombs themselves). His ardent enthusiasm about the handling of the site was premature, for we know from descriptions of later work at Vulci, notably by Dennis, that the finds were sometimes treated in a very brutal way. Etruscan bucchero pottery, for example, which had little or no artistic appeal at the time (and therefore no market value), was deliberately smashed by the diggers, on orders from their overseer.[110]

The Italian scholars of the nineteenth century, who developed the tradition in publishing that had begun with Gori and Buonarroti in the previous century, continued to bring out magnificent publications displaying Etruscan artifacts, tombs, and inscriptions, such as the six volumes of the *Monumenti Etruschi* of Francesco Inghirami (1821–26).[111]

Followers of Luigi Lanzi contributed to the study of the language by publishing the monumental *Corpus Inscriptionum Italicarum,*[112] while Luigi Canina created valuable records for posterity as he wandered up and down the Etruscan countryside making drawings of tombs and other remains. His *Antica Etruria marittima* appeared between 1846 and 1851. The work of these men, along with that of Dennis and Gerhard, of Noël des Vergers and François, places us at the threshold of modern scholarship.

The progress of Etruscan studies in modern times—during the last hundred years or so—is not, properly speaking, part of this essay. Instead the results of the previous century's work are incorporated in the other chapters of this book where it has a bearing on the topics. An excellent survey of modern scholarship on the Etruscans has been made by Massimo Pallottino in his basic handbook *The Etruscans,* and a guide to the latest developments is provided in the pages of *Studi Etruschi,* the annual journal published by the Istituto di Studi Etruschi in Florence. It is already clear that the current pace of new excavations and publications is furious, making it difficult for specialists and the general public alike to keep up to date. Possibly when the history of this period is finally written, it will be seen as yet another period of "Etruscan Revival," comparable to the Augustan Age in Rome, the Renaissance in Medicean Florence, and the eighteenth century with its *Etruscheria.*

Notes

1. A. Noël des Vergers, *L'Etrurie et les Etrusques* (Paris 1862–64) II 47–48, trans., L. Bonfante. Noël des Vergers took the romanticized detail of the disappearance of the bodies in contact with the air from C. Avvolta, *AnnInst* 1 (1829) 96. For these and further references see L. Bonfante, "Historical Art: Etruscan and Early Roman," *AJAH* 3 (1978) 136–37, 153, n. 4.

2. The longest study is that of A. Hus, "Les Étrusques vus par les autres ou le mythe étrusque," in *Les Étrusques et leur destin* (Paris 1980) 297–349. There are many useful references in R. Weiss, *The Renaissance Discovery of Classical Antiquity* (Oxford 1969), *passim,* and F. Weege, *Etruskische Malerei* (Halle 1921). James B. Wellard, *The Search for the Etruscans* (New York 1973) must be used with caution.

The study of the Etruscan language is discussed by B. Nogara, "Gli studi etruscologici dal Rinascimento fino ai nostri giorni," in *Gli etruschi e la loro civiltà* (Milan 1933). A series of studies deals with the Medici and Renaissance Florence: A. Chastel, "L' 'Etruscan Revival' du XVᵉ siècle," *RA* (1959) 165–80; *idem,* "Le Musée Etrusque et l' 'Etruscan Revival'," in *Art et humanisme à Florence* (Paris 1959) 63–71; G. Cipriani, *Il mito etrusco nel rinascimento fiorentino* (Florence 1980); *Palazzo Vecchio: committenza e collezionismo medicei* (Florence 1980) 19–42 (catalogue of the exhibition with entries on Etruscan antiquities by M. Cristofani and M. Martelli). See also M. Cristofani, *La scoperta degli Etruschi. Archeologia e antiquaria nel Settecento* (Rome 1983). Many of the individual artists and scholars who studied the Etruscans through the centuries are treated in *Dictionary of the History of Classical Archaeology,* ed. N. de Grummond (forthcoming, Greenwood Press). See the entries on Annio da Viterbo, Thomas Dempster, A.F. Gori, F. Inghirami, George Dennis, James Byres, Eduard Gerhard, and others.

3. *Roman Antiquities,* Chs. 1–6, deal with the Etruscans. A. Andrén, "Dionysius of Halicarnassus on Roman Monuments," *Hommages à Léon Herrmann,* Coll. Latomus 44 (1960) 98.

4. Livy, *The Early History of Rome, 1–5,* trans., A. de Sélincourt (Harmondsworth 1960). For commentary, see J. Heurgon, ed., *Tite-Live, Ab Urbe Condita, Liber Primus* (Paris 1963); Ogilvie, *Commentary.*

5. Suetonius, *Claudius* 42: "Denique et Claudius scripsit historias, Tyrrhenicon viginti, Carchedoniacon octo." Cf. A. Momigliano, *Claudius. The Emperor and his Achievements* (Oxford 1934; Italian originally published 1932) 11–16.

6. Heurgon, *Daily Life,* 318–28.

7. See R. Enking, "P. Vergilius Maro vates etruscus," *RömMitt* 66 (1959) 71–72; J. Gagé, "Les Étrusques dans l'Enéide," *Mélanges d'archéologie et d'histoire* 46 (1929) 115–44.

8. *Aen.* 8.506, etc.

9. *Aen.* 7.648, etc.

10. *Aen.* 10.175.

11. Vitruvius, *De architectura* 4.7.

12. Pliny, *NH* 35.158.

13. Pliny, *NH* 34.34.

14. Horace, *Epistula* 2.2.180.

15. Cf. Pliny, *NH* 35.18.

16. *Geographica* 17.1.28.

17. *De institutione oratoria* 12.10.1.

18. Pfiffig, *Etruskische Sprache,* 7–9.

19. Pfiffig, *Religio etrusca,* 380–82.

20. Pfiffig (supra n. 19) 381.

21. Zosimus 5.41.

22. Isidore of Seville, *Etymologiae* 20.3.5.

23. Isidore of Seville (supra n. 22) 8.9.34–35.

24. Weege, *Etruskische Malerei* 17.

25. Weege (supra. n. 24) 17.

26. *William of Malmesbury's Chronicle of the Kings of England* (London 1847), trans., J.A. Giles, 178.

27. Bronze statuette of Herakles in the Toledo Museum of Art. Cf. statuette in the collection of the W.R. Nelson Gallery of Art, Atkins Museum of Fine Arts, Kansas City, Missouri; see also D.G. Mitten and S.F. Doeringer, *Master Bronzes from the Classical World* (Greenwich 1967) 179.

28. *William of Malmesbury's Chronicle* 181.

29. Thomas Wright, "On Antiquarian Excavations and Researches in the Middle Ages," *Archeologia* 30 (1844) 440.

30. *William of Malmesbury's Chronicle* 176.

31. See Pallottino, *Etruscans,* 292, pl. 95 for inscribed dice from Tuscania, in the Vatican, Museo Etrusco Gregoriano; E. Brizio, "Il sepolcreto gallico di Montefortino," *MonAnt* 9 (1899) 682; and D.J. Hamblin, *The Etruscans* (Time-Life Books, New York 1975) 18 for dice in the Regolini-Galassi Tomb, Cerveteri; Helbig, *Führer*⁴ 2956 for dice from Praeneste, Barberini Collection.

32. Brendel, *Etruscan Art* 184, fig. 120.

33. Brendel, *Etruscan Art* 185–93, figs. 120–22, 178–79, 185–86.

34. See T. Dohrn, *Der Arringatore* (Berlin 1968).

35. P. Colacicchi, *All the Paintings of Giotto,* II (New York 1963) pl. 167; Brendel, *Etruscan Art* 192–93, figs. 127–28.

36. F. de Ruyt, *Charun: Démon étrusque de la mort* (Brussels 1934); Colacicchi, *All the Paintings of Giotto,* II, pl. 129.

37. C.M. Gayley, *Plays of our Forefathers* (New York 1908) 130.

38. F. Hartt, *History of Italian Renaissance Art* (New York 1979) 37, fig. 31; L. Becherucci-G. Brunetti, *Il Museo dell' Opera del Duomo* I (Florence [1971?]) 219–220, pls. 16–17.

39. C. Gambetti, *I coperchi di urne con figurazioni femminili nel Museo Archeologico di Volterra* (Milan 1974).

40. Weiss, *Renaissance Discovery* 14; A. Lazzarini, "Coscienza etrusca in Orvieto medievale," in *Sopravvivenze e memorie etrusche nella Tuscia medievale* (Orvieto 1964) 59.

41. See esp. the articles cited by Chastel, supra n. 2, and also infra nn. 55, 58, 65, 66, 73, 75. See also M. Martelli, *Prospettiva* 10 (1977) 58–61.

42. Supra n. 2.

43. D. Musti, *Tendenze nella storiografia romana e greca su Roma arcaica,* Quaderni Urbinati 10 (Rome 1970).

44. E.g., Leandro Alberti, *Descrittione di tutta Italia* (1561).

45. Boccaccio, *Genealogia deorum* 6.1 (written 1351–60).

46. M. Pallottino, "Tarquinia," *MonAnt* 36 (1937) cols. 19–20.

47. Trans. N.T. de Grummond from the Latin text cited by Pallottino (supra n. 46).

48. Weiss, *Renaissance Discovery* 119.

49. Ariosto, *Orlando Furioso* 13.89–90 (Isabel); 3.6 ff. (Merlin).

50. *Della composizione del mondo* (edition of Milan 1864) 255.

51. Trans. N.T. de Grummond from the MS in the Biblioteca Riccardiana, Florence, MS 834, folia 212ʳ and 212ᵛ.

Cetera haud procul ab eodem colle reperta sunt in quodam antro aliquot sepulcra ex quibus unum marmoream extat, quorum sculpta tegmina iacentum varias effigies et vetustos corporum habitus representant. At brevia sunt admodum, et angusta, ex quo facile iudicamus ea tamquam urnas cineres preservasse: non corpora. plura etiam vasa fictilia, sed semifracta in eodem antro extabant, quorum quidam varie species me satis oblectarunt. In sepulcri autem marmorei tegmine sculpta est imago venerabilis matrone torquem, et armillas auro levi pictas habens. In facie uno alii sepulcri rubro colore pictus est eques more prisco quem pedites duo comitare videntur, unus procedit balistam humeris, alter sequitur scutum ferens. Hec ego sepulcra unius tantum familie fuisse arbitror, que nunc Abbatis sancti Iusti diligentia preservat.

J.R. Spencer, "Volterra, 1466," *ArtBull* 48 (1966) gives an untrustworthy transcription and translation of the MS.

52. Leone Battista Alberti, *Ten Books on Architecture,* trans., James Leoni (1755), reprint, Alec Tiranti Ltd. (London 1955) 169.

53. Alberti, *Ten Books* 7.2; 6.6; 7.7; p. 143.

54. Alberti, *Ten Books* 7.4; Pliny *NH* 26.91.

55. C.C. Van Essen, "Elementi etruschi nel Rinascimento toscano," *StEtr* 13 (1939) 498–99; L. Heydenreich and W. Lotz, *Architecture in Italy 1400 to 1600* (Harmondsworth 1974) 33–34, pl. 22.

56. Heydenreich and Lotz (supra n. 55) 133–35, pl. 138; A. Boethius, *Etruscan Architecture,* esp. 37, fig. 22.

57. Chastel, *Art et Humanisme à Florence* 224.

58. K. Weil-Garris Posner [Brandt], "Comments on the Medici Chapel and Pontormo's Lunette at Poggio a Caiano," *Burlington Magazine* 115 (1973) 641–49.

59. See esp. Weiss, *Renaissance Discovery* 94 and the bibliography there cited. Annio's magnum opus was issued at Rome, 1498, as *Commentaria supra opera diversorum auctorum de antiquitatibus confecta.*

60. Weiss, *Renaissance Discovery* 94.

61. Weiss (supra n. 60) 126.

62. Weiss (supra n. 60) 114.

63. Weiss (supra n. 60) 120.

64. Trans. N.T. de Grummond, from *Le vite de' più*

eccellenti pittori, scultori e architetti, ed., Milanesi (Florence 1878) vol. 1, 221–22.

65. M. Pallottino, "Vasari e la Chimera," *Prospettiva* 8 (1976) 4–6.

66. See Pallottino (supra n. 65) 4 on Titian; Montaigne, *Journal de Voyage en Italie . . . 1580 et 1581* (Paris 1955), ed., M. Rat, 88–89.

67. See Benvenuto Cellini, *Autobiography,* Ch. 43. See also M. Cristofani, "Per una storia del collezionismo archeologico nella toscana granducale. 1.I grandi bronzi," *Prospettiva* 17 (1979) 6, 10. Evidently only the tail was missing at the time of discovery (and none of the paws, contrary to what is often stated), and this was restored by Carradori in the eighteenth century.

68. Cristofani (supra n. 67) 4–15, *passim.*

69. Supra n. 34.

70. N.T. de Grummond in *Guide to Etruscan Mirrors,* Ch. 1, "The History of the Study of Etruscan Mirrors."

71. See Hartt, *Italian Renaissance Art* 588, fig. 719. I wish to thank Ruth Rubenstein and Elizabeth McGrath of the Warburg Institute, who discovered this similarity and pointed it out to me.

72. L. Bonfante and N.T. de Grummond, "Poussin e gli specchi etruschi," *Prospettiva* 20 (1980) 72–80.

73. See E. Panofsky, "The Mouse That Michelangelo Failed to Carve," in *Essays in Memory of Karl Lehmann* (Locust Valley, New York 1964) 249–50.

74. Supra n. 58.

75. J. Pope-Hennessy, *Italian High Renaissance and Baroque Sculpture* (London 1970) 55, fig. 58.

76. G. Davies, *Renascence, The Sculptured Tombs of the Fifteenth Century in Rome* (London 1910) 176. Cf. J.C. Carter, "The Tomb of the Siren," *AJA* 78 (1974) 138.

77. See J. Oleson, "A Reproduction of an Etruscan Tomb in the Parco dei Mostri at Bomarzo," *ArtBull* 57 (1975) 410–17. and the bibliography there cited.

78. E. Battisti, *L'Antirinascimento* (Milan 1962) 129.

79. Battisti, (supra n. 78) 411.

80. Cf. Herodotus 4.183.

81. Trans. N.T. de Grummond from A. Kircher, *Mundi Subterranei* (Amsterdam 1678) II, 128.

82. See M. Cristofani, "Sugli inizi dell' 'Etruscheria': La pubblicazione del *De Etruria Regali* di Thomas Dempster," *MEFRA* 90 (1978) 577–616; A. Momigliano, "Ancient History and the Antiquarian," in *Studies in Historiography* (New York 1966) 18–19.

83. *De Etruria Regali* I (Florence 1723) 88–91. Cf. Nogara, supra n. 2, 4–5, and Weiss, *Renaissance Discovery* 120, on Sigismondo Tizio, who compiled a short vocabulary in the late fifteenth century.

84. Supra nn. 70, 72. [See also, on Etruscan mirrors used for magic purposes in the thirteenth and fourteenth centuries, F. Orioli, "D'un uso non conosciuto degli specchi mistici d'Etruria nei secoli XIII e XIV," *Giornale del R. Istituto Lombardo di Scienze Lettere ed Arti,* I (1841) 1–18;

reprinted in *Spighe e Paglie. Opera periodica pel Prof. Francesco Orioli* (Corfu 1845) 244ff. We owe this important reference to the kindness of Adriana Emiliozzi Morandi.— *Ed.*]

85. Bonfante and de Grummond, "Poussin e gli specchi etruschi," 76.

86. D. Rebuffat-Emmanuel, *Le miroir étrusque d'après la collection du Cabinet des Médailles* (Rome 1973) 8–9. Bonfante and de Grummond, "Poussin e gli specchi etruschi," n. 22.

87. G. Conti, "La 'Patera Cospiana,'" *ArchCl* 28 (1976) 49–68.

88. R. Oldenbourg, *P. P. Rubens,* Klassiker der Kunst (Stuttgart, n.d.) pl. 151.

89. O. Benesch, *The Drawings of Rembrandt,* III (London 1955) 139, no. 479, fig. 600.

90. See S. Ferri in *EAA,* s.v. "Etruscheria." The printed date of publication is 1723, but the two volumes, including the plates, were not actually released to the public until three years later. For the major scholars working on the Etruscans in the eighteenth century (and also the nineteenth), see the useful summary of J. von Vacano, "Die Wiederentdeckung der Etrusker im 18. und 19. Jahrhundert," in *Kunst und Leben der Etrusker* (Cologne 1956) 39–45.

91. *Accademia Etrusca di Cortona, Mostra Documentaria 1727–1976* (Cortona 1977); E.W. Cochrane, *Tradition and Enlightenment in the Tuscan Academies, 1690–1800* (Chicago 1961) esp. 166–72, 197–98.

92. Cochrane, *Tuscan Academies* 193–94.

93. Supra n. 92.

94. J. Wilton-Ely, *The Mind and Art of Giovanni Battista Piranesi* (London 1978) 77, fig. 128, frontispiece for the *Osservazioni sopra la lettre de M. Mariette* (1765) 116, fig. 136, Etruscan motifs from *Diverse maniere d'adornare i Cammini* (1769) fig. 213, Robert Adam, Etruscan Room at Osterley Park.

95. See E. Fiumi, *Storia e sviluppo del Museo Guarnacci di Volterra: La collezione di urne del Museo Guarnacci nel XVIII e XIX secolo* (Florence 1977), with introduction by G. Maetzke. This essay was also published in *CUE.* 2.*Urne volterrane, 2.Museo Guarnacci:* parte prima, ed., M. Cristofani (Florence 1977) 11–22.

96. A.E. Gori, *Musei Guarnacci antiqua monumenta etrusca* (Florence 1744); *Museum Florentinum,* 12 vols. (Florence 1731–62); *Museum Cortonense* (Rome 1750).

97. Cochrane, *Tuscan Academies* 182.

98. M. Cristofani, "Winckelmann, Heyne, Lanzi e l'arte etrusca," *Prospettiva* 4 (1976) 16–21, and the bibliography there cited.

99. W. Leppmann, *Winckelmann* (New York 1970) 196. See further M. Cristofani, "Winckelmann a Firenze," *Prospettiva* 25 (1981) 24–30.

100. *Recueil d'antiquités égyptiennes, étrusques, grecques, romaines et gauloises* (Paris 1752–67).

101. *Wedgwood by Rathbone. A Reprint in Its Entirety with added Index of Old Wedgwood by F. Rathbone* (Merion, Pennsylvania 1968) 41.

102. See B. Ford, "James Byres—Principal Antiquarian for the English Visitors to Rome," *Apollo* (1974) 446–61; Elaine P. Loeffler, "A Lost Etruscan Painted Tomb," in *Essays in Memory of Karl Lehmann* (Locust Valley, New York 1964) 198–203; J. Wellard, *The Search for the Etruscans* (New York 1972) 47–52.

103. Mrs. Hamilton Gray, *Tour Through the Sepulchres of Etruria*² (London 1843) 3–4.

104. The best edition is the third (1883). In general on Dennis, see D.E. Rhodes, *Dennis of Etruria* (London 1973).

105. A. Michaelis, *A Century of Archaeological Discoveries* (London 1908), trans., B. Kahnweiler, 57–62.

106. The publication continues to be essential though the new corpus is in publication, sponsored by the Istituto di Studi Etruschi (see supra, Introduction, n. 15).

107. N.T. de Grummond, in *Guide to Etruscan Mirrors* Ch. I.

108. See the catalogue *Pelagio Palagi, artista e collezionista* (Bologna 1976) with the section by C. Morigi Govi, "La collezione etrusco-italica," 291–95 for an excellent survey of the intellectual climate at the time of Gerhard and Palagi, and the catalogue of the Etruscan objects, 296–311 (entries by C. Morigi Govi and Silvana Tovoli).

109. Quoted in Michaelis, *A Century of Archaeological Discoveries* 63–64.

110. G. Dennis, *The Cities and Cemeteries of Etruria* I, 431–33.

111. See G. Cressedi, in *EAA,* s.v. "Inghirami, Francesco."

112. A. Fabretti, *Corpus Inscriptionum Italicarum* (Turin 1867); *Supplemento* 1–3 (Turin 1872–78). See further *CIE* (Leipzig, Florence 1893–1980), and *Thesaurus Linguae Etruscae* I. *Indice Lessicale* (Rome 1978). For recent work, see Pallottino, *Etruscans* 189–234; Cristofani, in *IBR* 373–412, with full bibliography; Pfiffig, *Etruskische Sprache;* Bonfante, *Etruscan Language.*

II / History: Land and People

MARIO TORELLI

The Land

The geography of Etruria is closely connected to the history of the Etruscan people. The two main rivers in Italy, the Tiber and the Arno, along with the Apennines and the sea, form Etruria's boundaries (Maps 1–2). They enclose a large area, favored by the mild Mediterranean climate, with a wide variety of land formations. Both the plains and the gentle rolling hills are well watered and good for growing the crops which were most important in antiquity: grain, vines, olives, and flax. There are also lush valleys with rivers, ideal for raising livestock. Other important natural resources are the mountain forests, once rich in wood which could be used to build houses and ships, and stone, which could be quarried and cut into square blocks. Most valuable of all in early times were the mineral deposits in various areas of Etruria: in the hills of La Tolfa, in the Colline Metallifere (the metal-bearing hills), and especially on the island of Elba, where iron was mined in very large quantities up to Roman times.

This environment was extremely favorable for Etruria's economic development once the primitive agriculture of the prehistoric period had given way to a more profitable use of the soil and the mining of iron and silver had created improved economic conditions. At first, the location of the leading Etruscan cities seems to contradict this rosy economic picture since they are not directly by the sea. Instead, all the great coastal cities except Populonia are situated on low-lying hills some five to ten miles away from the shore. Only smaller harbor towns such as Alsium and Pyrgi are on the coast, as well as Punicum serving Caere (Cerveteri), Graviscae serv-

ing Tarquinia, Regisvilla serving Vulci, and so on. All ancient sources and legends (such as the one told in the Homeric Hymn to Dionysus) describe the Etruscans' famed seamanship—as pirates. Piracy was by no means an Etruscan monopoly, however, so the cities were sited inland where they could prosper without the threat of a sea-borne attack.

Agriculture, mineral resources, and a very active trade (for this is what piracy actually meant in antiquity) were the economic bases of Etruscan civilization and of Etruscan history. They account for the remarkable development of a culture which, along with that of the Greek colonies of southern Italy and Sicily, was the most influential in bringing civilization to Italy. Modern historians have alternately emphasized agriculture or commerce as the main economic base. Actually, there is no real contrast between the two. The most strikingly luxurious objects archaeologists have found in Etruria, such as the gold and ivory objects discovered in tombs of the Orientalizing period of the seventh century B.C., and the enormous quantity of Greek vases, mostly Corinthian and Attic, from the cities and necropoleis of Etruria, were all products of direct or indirect trade with the world outside. Etruria's great wealth was always the fertility of its fields, as the historian Livy points out in his account of the expedition undertaken by the Roman general Fabius Rullianus beyond the dense Ciminian Forest toward Chiusi (9.35). Agriculture and commerce developed about the same time. Only if we consider them together can we understand repeated ancient references to Etruscan piracy and to the wealth of their mineral resources, as well as to the development of the prosperous inland cities in the fifth century B.C. and the colonization of the fertile fields of Campania to the south and the Po Valley to the north—all inland areas which were precious for Etruscan agriculture.

Origins of the People

Ancient authors were arguing about the origin of the Etruscans long before modern historians confronted this issue. The level of civilization which the Etruscans reached very early on, unrivaled by the other inhabitants of the Italian peninsula, evidently aroused the curiosity and interest of the first Greek writers. The Etruscans seemed different from the other peoples of Italy. To the Greek way of thinking about history, just as the origin of a polis or city-state was to be explained by a mythical hero as founder, so the origin of a people had to be explained as the result of a migration, under the leadership of a mythical founding hero, a chief who had originally led them to their lands. Herodotus tells the story of the origins of the Etruscan people as a migration of part of the people of Lydia (1.94)—in saying this he quotes the Lydians—led by King Tyrsenos, from whom they took their name. The migration was due to a famine which took place shortly before the Trojan War (about 1200 B.C.). In contrast, the Greek historian Hellanicus, quoted by Dionysius of Halicarnassus (1.28), stated that the Tyrrhenians of Etruria were, in fact, the Pelasgians, a mysterious, wandering, ancient people who, after roaming about the Aegean, finally landed on the coasts of Italy. For Anticleides, too—quoted by the geographer Strabo (5.2.4)—the people who had come to Italy led by Tyrrhenus were Pelasgian, of the same stock which had settled the Aegean islands of Lemnos and Imbros. The earliest authors are therefore unanimous in stating that the Etruscans came from the east (although they are much less certain whether to connect them with the Lydians or the Pelasgians), and they place their arrival in mythological, heroic times, before the beginning of written history. The only exception is Dionysius of Halicarnassus, a Greek author of the time of Augustus. After carefully reviewing the theories of the historians who preceded him, he expresses a new one of his own (1.25–30). The Etruscans, he states,

were autochthonous, that is, they did not come from anywhere else—they had always been settled in Etruria. This was the view of the Etruscans themselves, whom he had consulted. And, in fact, the Etruscans did not call themselves Tyrrhenians at all—they referred to themselves as Rasenna.

Modern controversy over the origin of the Etruscan people is based on these ancient ideas, as well as on some hundred and fifty years of excavations in Etruria. Contemporary historians, starting from theoretical premises similar to those of the ancient authors, have also stated their conclusions in terms of either migration or autochthony. Those who support the theory of an Oriental origin, claiming that the Etruscans came from Asia Minor, have based their argument mainly on the authority of the ancient sources. Some have attempted to find confirmation in archaeology, considering the possibility that the Etruscans' arrival in Italy coincided with the so-called Orientalizing phase of Etruscan art. This idea is, however, contradicted by the study of the monuments unearthed by archaeology, for these reflect a gradual development from the art of the Iron Age to that of the Orientalizing period. Furthermore, according to the ancient tradition, handed down in all the written sources, the Etruscans were already in Italy before the Orientalizing period.

Earlier in this century, archaeological evidence led scholars to consider that the Etruscans might have emigrated from the north. There are undoubtedly similarities between the Iron Age cultures of central Europe and those of Etruria. Those who put forward this theory also drew attention to a statement by Livy (5.33.11) that the Raetians, a people of the Alpine regions of northern Italy, represented a fossilized surviving remnant of an originally Etruscan people. Yet the northern theory does not hold up under scrutiny. In the first place, not only Etruscan culture but the culture of other peoples in Italy and in Europe bears a close resemblance to the culture of central Europe. Furthermore, Livy's reference to the Raetians connected them not with an alleged Etruscan northern migration but rather with the well-attested Etruscan colonization of the Po Valley, an expansion which was swept away by the later Gallic invasions of the fifth and fourth centuries B.C. A variation of the autochthonous theory of Dionysius of Halicarnassus has recently been revived in a different form. According to it, the so-called Villanovan culture of the Iron Age belonged to Italic peoples, while those of the late Neolithic and Bronze Ages belonged to an Etruscan people, a Mediterranean race who spoke a pre-Indo-European language. Yet this theory too is implausible since the Villanovans did not live in the area later occupied by the Italic peoples. Instead, Villanovan settlements everywhere precede the Etruscan cities of the historical period.

Despite the conflicting theories, we do know that the sequence of the prehistoric and protohistoric cultures of Italy appears to be continuous from the Bronze Age throughout the early part of the Iron Age, without any interruptions which might have been caused by invasions or the arrival of a new people. On the other hand, all the earliest Greek sources, those least likely to have been influenced by political or ideological considerations (unlike Dionysius of Halicarnassus, writing about the Romans who were sensitive about their own origins and relationship to the Greeks) refer to the close relationship between the Etruscans and Aegean peoples such as the Pelasgians and Anatolian people such as the Lydians, and, in particular, between the Etruscans and the pre-Greek inhabitants of the islands of Lemnos and Imbros. The inscription on a stele from Lemnos (fig. VII-5) shows that the language in which it was written—and which was apparently spoken on that island—was closely related to the Etruscan language. Yet both the language of the stele and the Etruscan language were as isolated and distinct from the other languages of the Aegean area as Etruscan was from any other language spoken in the Mediterranean.

There is one other historical event tied to the origin of the Etruscans. Records of the Pharaohs Amenhotep and Ramses III, whose reigns spanned the years 1230–1170 B.C., mention a failed attempt to invade Egypt by sea and by land, an attempt by a group of people which the Egyptians called the "Sea Peoples." Identification of this motley group of barbarian tribes is difficult. Several of them can be identified with some assurance: the Achaeans (Jqjwšw), the Philistines (Prst.w), and the Lycians

(Rk.w). Others are less certain: are the Sqrš.w the Siculi of Sicily? And are the Šrdn.w the people of Sardinia? Or of Sardis, in Asia Minor? Among these names there appears that of the Trš.w, according to some scholars "Tyrsenoi" or "Tyrrhenians"—that is, the Etruscans. Though the identification is controversial, the date of the attempted invasion would seem to coincide with the date implied by Herodotus for the arrival of the Lydians in Italy. The Trš.w of the Egyptian sources may or may not be the ancestors of the Etruscans of Italy. In any case the arrival of any people in Italy in the prehistoric period (including the hypothetical arrival of the Etruscans) can only be imagined as an arrival of small groups of people. Even if they brought with them a different culture and a superior technological and military knowledge, their numbers were small, and they brought no radical or noticeable change to the gradual development of culture in Italy, to which they apparently soon adapted without leaving a trace, save perhaps their non-Indo-European language. A migration or invasion such as that envisaged by ancient authors and modern scholars would also fail to explain the history of early Etruscan culture as we know it. We must rather think in terms of their gradual transformation into a people with their own special culture, economy, and social structure. This transformation seems to have taken place in Italy, from the end of the Bronze Age throughout the Iron Age.

The Earliest Settlements

The cultural pattern in Italy during the Bronze Age was much the same throughout the peninsula, though the so-called Apenninic culture differed from that of the north or that of the Po Valley or Sicily. It is characterized by moderate-sized settlements, most without fortifications but all situated near a small or medium-sized source of running water. Their economy seems to have been based on an agriculture which supplied its own needs and on the breeding of livestock. Contacts with the outside world were mostly with the Mycenaeans (especially in the region of the Puglia, but also on the Tyrrhenian coast, in Campania and Etruria). A widening of cultural relations with the north occurred in the late Bronze Age (the so-called sub-Apenninic period) in the twelfth and eleventh centuries B.C. Larger and more stable settlements now tended to be located on hilltops for ease of defense. This transformation quickened in the late Bronze Age, in the eleventh and tenth centuries B.C., when a new culture, that of the so-called proto-Villanovan period, made its appearance. While aspects of its material culture and, to a lesser degree, its settlement were still related to the culture of the preceding, sub-Apenninic phase, the proto-Villanovan exhibited new features. There were strongly fortified habitats and cremation burials in urn fields like those of central Europe, sometimes under mounds, in ossuary urns of rough impasto ware of a more or less biconical shape. The type of fibulae found in these burials is shaped like a so-called violin bow or a simple bow.

Scholars have for some time recognized, as the name itself implies, that there was a close relationship between this proto-Villanovan culture and the subsequent Iron Age culture called Villanovan. The two have a number of features in common: the type of burial and the rites connected with it; the craft of bronzeworking; the pottery, decorated with geometric motifs made up of broken lines and right angles—quite different from the meander decorations of the pottery of the Apenninic people—and the preference shown by the people of the sub-Apenninic period for undecorated surfaces. Yet up to now archaeologists have not been able to prove real continuity, either in the form of continuous settlements or of continuous territory. The culture of the proto-Villanovan period seems to have been scattered over the whole peninsula, from Lucania in the south to the Veneto region in the north, from the Marche on the Adriatic coast to Campania in the west. In some areas, evidence for the late Bronze Age is missing; others, such as Latium, in this same period show evidence of a different culture. In contrast, the culture of the Villanovan period has a clearly defined area: not only Etruria proper, but also, in the north, a part of the Po Valley around Bologna and Rimini and to the south a region in Campania around Capua and Salerno (Maps 3–4). With the coming of the Villanovan phase, the cul-

tural picture of the territory occupied by the historical Etruscans acquires stability and continuity: nearly every Etruscan city shows evidence of having been inhabited in the Villanovan period. Villanovan culture thus provides the link between the protohistorical period and the historical period in Etruria.

In its earliest phase, roughly the ninth century B.C., this culture was relatively uniformly distributed over the whole area. Recent study, however, has revealed certain regional differences, such as particular types of fibulae, or safety pins, found in tombs, which allow us to trace several interesting interrelations between various regions. For instance, cremation urns in the shape of huts, found within an area of Latium and Etruria in the proto-Villanovan and the proto-Latial periods, are found in a larger area in the Villanovan period. The area, which ranged from the original territory around Vulci and Tarquinia to that around Lake Bolsena and, in a later period, to the coast, reached as far north as Vetulonia and as far south as Pontecagnano. These local differences resulted from the influence of the local traditions, as well as from a wide variety of contacts which united different areas, even some which were quite distant from each other. In spite of these variations, this early period of Villanovan culture was remarkably homogenous, allowing us to assume that its economic and social structures were also quite uniform.

The area was evidently occupied by a closely knit network of hut villages. Unfortunately, few are well known, as excavation has been nearly impossible, since most Villanovan settlements have been buried by the successive building phases of classical and medieval towns and cities. Our knowledge of them comes mainly from a study of their cemeteries. Most villages were on hills, though some were in valleys or near the coast. Their inhabitants worked the soil or took advantage of other natural resources, such as fishing. Because many of these villages tended to be close together and were often concentrated along a single large plateau, it is clear that their social structure had gone beyond that of the tribe, and that they shared a mutual interest. Such a bond foreshadows the birth of the Etruscan poleis, or city-states. This development can be traced in the principal cities of Etruria, such as Vulci, Tarquinia, Veii—all of their origins were firmly based on this earlier Villanovan phase.

Eighth Century B.C.

The first phase of the Villanovan period revealed by the cemeteries is characterized by a fairly egalitarian social structure, in which the division of labor takes place mostly, if not wholly, according to sex. The grave gifts deposited alongside cremation urns are quite poor, and reflect social distribution: men were warriors, and women were the custodians of the house and spinners. Soon, however, this relative financial equality between individuals disappeared. In the second phase of the Villanovan period, during the eighth century B.C., certain groups begin to exhibit greater wealth. The tombs now contain many metal objects, arms, armor, and objects of daily use. After an interruption of many centuries, vases were once again imported from Greece, especially from the area of Euboea and the Cyclades; these vases are dated earlier than those of the earliest Greek colonies in the West. Archaeological evidence also shows exchange with the East and with Sardinia, both of actual objects and of decorative styles and motifs. The increased wealth of individuals and groups shows the beginning of the social stratification from which the powerful and splendid aristocracy of the following century would emerge.

This division of Etruscan society into different groups or classes also brought with it a new division of labor, beginning with agriculture, but gradually extending to the crafts. The potter's craft, for example, had been until this time one of many activities carried on within the individual households. Now pottery-making became an independent industry, like metalworking. This independence led to the diffusion and adoption of important technical advances, such as the potter's wheel. It is likely that similar advances, such as the extraction of metals or carpentry, were made in other fields too, though the lack of archaeological evidence does not allow us to trace such developments. It is clear that a more specialized division of labor and formation of groups of craftsmen continued to increase throughout the Archaic period, at least up to the end of the sixth century B.C.

Increased wealth, divisions into groups or classes, and division of labor did not, however, occur at the same time throughout the entire Villanovan-Etruscan area. From the beginning of the eighth century B.C. the different regions developed at different rates. Southern Etruria, having as its center Tarquinia, Veii, and Vulci, seems to have taken on a leading role. Following these were the principal centers of Etruscanized Campania, Capua, and Pontecagnano. The area around Bologna was slowest to develop; the central and northern Etruscan region also lagged behind. This difference resulted from the progressive superiority of certain centers within the more advanced regions. Many of the smaller settlements around the larger centers disappeared, or at least they decreased in wealth and population. In this proto-urban stage the population tended to be concentrated in centers which would eventually become cities.

The social and economic picture of this period becomes clearer in the light of historical developments in the Italian peninsula at the time. The most important event was the beginning of Greek colonization in the west. Starting in about 775 B.C. with the colony of Pithekoussai, Greek colonies gradually filled the coastline of southern Italy. It is no coincidence that the earliest colony, Pithekoussai, was nearest to Etruria. Greek and Oriental imports, which certainly came by way of Pithekoussai, as well as pottery made or inspired by Euboean and Cycladic craftsmen, are proof that Pithekoussai served as a trading center for the peoples of the peninsula, particularly for Campania and the southern Etruscan area. The lively interest in trade displayed by the people of southern Etruria closely coincided with their progressive differentiation into social groups or classes. Certainly some of the luxurious objects placed in the tombs of individuals belonging to higher classes are the result of a trading activity based on Etruscan mineral wealth. This state of affairs confirms what ancient sources tell us about the "piracy" of the Etruscans; in antiquity, piracy and trade were not always clearly differentiated. Many texts, in fact, speak of Etruscans as synonymous with pirates. Such Etruscan "piracy" goes back to the eighth century B.C. The historian Ephorus tells us that the seas were infested by Tyrrhenian pirates at the time of the foundation of the Chalcidian colony of Naxos in Sicily in 736 B.C.

The Orientalizing Period

We can see the great wealth accumulated in the major centers of southern Etruria during the eighth century B.C. in its most splendid form in the gold, silver, and bronze objects and in all the complex, exuberant, and varied decoration of the art of the Orientalizing period in the seventh century B.C. The Orientalizing style of art had its beginnings in Greece, stimulated by frequent contact with the cultures of the East: Lydia, Urartu, Syria, Palestine, Assyria, and Egypt (Map 9). In Etruria this composite, eclectic style acquired an even more luxuriant character, in accord with the provincial, marginal character of the area, but this style also expressed the love of luxury, the boldness, and the enterprising spirit of the Etruscan aristocracy. Burial practice, which had already shifted from cremation to inhumation in the eighth century B.C., no longer included individual graves; instead, a number of chamber tombs were hollowed out within large funerary mounds or tumuli (see Ch. V), reflecting the change from tribal to aristocratic family groups. These truly princely tombs contained huge treasures, the status symbols of this newly developed aristocracy. Often situated beneath enormous mounds or in high places, these tombs reproduce the interiors of Etruscan houses. Originally a series of rooms was laid out along a single straight line. Later, near the end of the century, they were laid out according to elaborate plans borrowed from the East. The celebration of a funeral banquet according to the Greek custom was gradually introduced, with all its complex symbols and its cultural context. Hunting, an aristocratic sport, became, from the beginning of the Orientalizing period, a mark of nobility. Early in this period, within the first decades of the seventh century, the use of writing was adopted. It was derived either directly from the Chalcidian Greek alphabet of Cumae, or inde-

pendently, like the Chalcidian alphabet, from other model alphabets of this period.

These aristocrats were proud of their conquests and of their economic, social, and cultural progress. Even though their power still derived from agriculture, they now lived not in the country but in the larger centers (Maps 1–2). These urban centers began to look more and more like cities, though it was only at the beginning of the sixth century that they would actually have strong fortified walls, impressive temples and public buildings, and a complex road system. The cities of southern Etruria were in the forefront of this development. Caere was first, followed by the other great metropolises of the south (though there were variations): Veii, Tarquinia, and Vulci. Certain northern cities, Rusellae, Vetulonia, and Populonia, became more prominent because of their choice locations near the mineral deposits, but they remained culturally dependent on the cities of the south. The cities of Etruscanized Campania, especially Pontecagnano, also grew in importance during this period. On the other hand, inland cities from Orvieto to Chiusi and from Volterra to Perugia developed more slowly and were still tied to Villanovan traditions, only incidentally touched by Orientalizing influences. The Po Valley in this period was even slower to develop.

In the past Etruscan culture had greatly influenced the peripheral, non-Etruscan regions; now it drew these even closer into its orbit. Falerii, the capital of the Faliscan-speaking region on the right-hand shore of the Tiber, whose language was closely related to Latin, became Etruscanized. Praeneste, the principal inland center of communications between Etruria and Campania, was in the hands of Etruscan families in the first half of the seventh century B.C. Later, in the second half of the seventh century, Rome was ruled by the Etruscan dynasty of the Tarquins.

In the meantime, economic and social transformations continued. In southern Etruria at the end of the seventh century a more complex social system evolved. The clear-cut rule of a few groups over the mass of the population had become more accentuated with, among other things, the introduction of the cultivation of olive trees. This practice apparently led to those forms of organization and legal systems which, in Rome at least, implied the existence of a kind of serfdom and a personal relationship between the aristocrats and the rural population. *Fides,* "trust" or "loyalty," and a religious sanction of the oath guaranteed to the aristocrats the complete loyalty of those subservient to them and a percentage of the profits from their lands; to the rural people, it guaranteed ownership of their land and the protection of the prince. (Literary sources often mention this *servitus,* even as late as the Hellenistic period.) In the seventh century B.C. *servitus* seems to have been firmly established, though its origins are to be found even earlier, in the social differentiation so clearly evident in the eighth century. This relationship can be compared to the forms of dependence in the Greek world— the helots of Messene, the *klarotai* of Crete, the Thessalian slaves, the *mariandynoi* of Heraclea Pontica—as well as to the system of *clientela,* or serf-class, of Rome. The legal forms involved must have been military in origin. The Roman "family" of the Fabii with their dependents (*clientes*) waged a personal war against Veii in 477 B.C.; this was apparently the latest example of a custom which was normal two hundred years earlier. Such changes in the society were then hastened by the move to the hoplite tactics, which, judging from artistic representations and archaeological evidence, came to Etruria around the middle of the seventh century B.C. This type of warfare called for large, heavily armed groups of soldiers to be drawn up in close-set ranks, in the form of a phalanx. It brought with it important changes in the social and economic system, for it opened the way for the richer aristocrats, eliciting fierce competition among the various groups or clans. This rivalry was only partly modified by dynastic-type alliances carried out by way of marriages and exchange of gifts. On the other hand a new tyrannical style of kingship and the increasing importance of defense encouraged ever-growing concentrations of populations in more defensible positions, especially in the new cities (and in those *oppida,* or towns, which had grown during urbanization).

Other economic, social, and cultural changes set the stage for further transformations in the sixth century. During the last decades of the seventh century the Etruscans accepted Greek culture in all its forms. The ground plans of houses followed Eastern patterns, and aristocratic residences, opening out on large inner courtyards, were adorned with architectural decorations which imitated Greek models. Etruscan cities, which had been protected by simple wooden embankments or earthworks, were now surrounded by fortified walls in cut stone, sometimes topped by sections of sun-baked bricks. The earliest sanctuaries were probably organized around open-air altars; later they included temples built like simple dwelling units. Greek myths inspired by Greek tradition were also represented in Etruscan art, and the style of life imitated that of the Greeks, with its ritual emphasis on banquets and ceremonial games. Due to the unquestioned power of the aristocracy in Etruria all these new customs were included within the aristocratic way of life. Only a few elements, such as the "state" religion, were not entirely absorbed by the aristocratic world. In southern Etruria, then, between the end of the seventh and the beginning of the sixth century B.C., city life seems to have been firmly established, though under the strict economic and social control of the aristocracy.

Sixth Century B.C.

During the sixth century B.C. a special political and social pattern developed in Etruria which was to determine its history. Veii, Caere, Tarquinia, Vulci, and Orvieto in the south were city-states of the first rank, rivaling the wealthiest of the Mediterranean in their extent. In northern Etruria, Vetulonia's decline encouraged the further growth of another coastal city, Populonia. Chiusi was on its way to becoming a major center, and other inland cities were steadily growing in importance. The Etruscans controlled the Po Valley and Campania, as shown by the epigraphical and archaeological evidence (Maps 3, 8). In this period they seem to have settled many colonies, especially in the Po Valley. For example, the city excavated near modern Marzabotto, with its regular orthogonal plan—we do not know its name—was founded in the sixth century and developed considerably in the fifth century B.C.

Unfortunately we do not know much about political developments in Etruscan history of the Archaic period; archaeology allows us to trace only long-range developments. Yet we can make certain assumptions. We can compare the events which took place in early Roman history. By the end of the seventh century Rome was already ruled by Etruscan kings, said to have come from the city of Tarquinia. They may have been individual generals, condottieri, rather than real Etruscan kings. Even so, the dynasty of the Tarquins at Rome reflects the great interest the southern Etruscan cities had in controlling the plains of Latium, not only because of the economic importance of the Latin cities but also because of the need to guard the route to Campanian territory under Etruscan control.

Coalitions and alliances among Etruscan cities and the predominance of particular city-states can now be reconstructed from archaeological evidence (similarities in the manufacture of certain products, for example, or specialized imports). In the seventh century B.C. such archaeological finds document a rivalry between Caere and Tarquinia for the hills of Caere; the territorial expansion of Vulci can be reconstructed from its growing wealth and from the parallel decline of the city of Marsiliana. Archaeological exploration of smaller settlements shows that the boundaries of most larger city-states known to us from historical sources were fixed in the sixth century B.C. (Map 2). Unfortunately, the day-to-day political struggles, the battles, and the wars between various city-states are almost completely unknown to us. Only rarely do hints in the literary sources or inscriptions allow us to catch glimpses of these complex political and social events. For instance, Macstrna, a figure represented on the wall paintings of the François Tomb at Vulci, is mentioned in Roman times by the emperor Claudius in a speech preserved both in a passage of Tacitus's *Annals* (11.23–24) and in an inscription found at Lyons in 1528—the *Tabulae Lugdunenses*. He is equated with the king of Rome known in the Roman tradition as Servius Tullius. A contemporary sixth century B.C. inscription from Veii also seems to refer to characters of this legend, the Vibenna brothers. The Lyons wall paintings from Vulci depict Macstrna and the brothers Avle and Caile Vipinas, along with other heroes, presumably from Vulci. They are fighting with other men identified by inscriptions which give not only their names but also the names of the cities they come from: Volsinii, Sovana, Falerii, and Rome. The man from Rome bears the interesting name Cneve Tarchunies Rumach (Cnaeus Tarquinius of Rome). According to tradition, the legendary Roman figure of Servius Tullius, born of either divine or slave parents, interrupted the dynasty of the Tarquins. The Etruscan version adds a historical context, not mentioned in the Roman sources: the existence of a coalition of most of the cities along the Tiber against Vulci. Further evidence is a votive gift found in the sanctuary of Apollo at Veii. According to the inscription, this was offered by Avle Vipinas. Slightly earlier in date is an inscription identifying an Avile Acvilnas, who offered votive gifts in this sanctuary of Apollo, as well as in another sanctuary (at Ischia di Castro) in the territory of Vulci. We therefore have evidence of Vulci's interest in the valley of the Tiber River, and perhaps in Veii.

The international picture of foreign enmities and alliances was wider in scope. Etruscans from Caere joined in an alliance with the Carthaginians in a sea battle against Greek refugees from Phocaea settled in the city of Aleria in Corsica at the time of the so-called Cadmean victory in the sea around Sardinia, in 540 B.C. During the beginning of the crisis in the following century, central Italy was torn apart by a series of political and military blows: the fall of the Tarquins at Rome, the attack on Rome by Porsenna, king of Chiusi, and the great battle of Ariccia, fought by the men of Cumae and Latium against the Etruscans.

Meanwhile, complex social changes were taking place within the aristocratic family system, which up to now had been relatively flexible. The myth of Demaratus, a Greek exiled from Corinth, who came to the Etruscan city of Tarquinia where he received asylum and married a noble Etruscan wife, Tanaquil, illustrates the acceptance of foreigners into Etruscan society. This is confirmed by inscriptions of the late seventh century. From Tarquinia comes an inscription with the name of Rutile Hipucrates, a Greek by the name of Hippocrates, who kept his old name as a family name, adding as a praenomen Rutile (in Latin, Rutilus). Another inscription from Caere bears the name of Kalatur(us) Phapenas. This man was of Latin origin, originally named Fabius, with the common Latin first name Calator, but he gave his name an Etruscan form. Also from Caere is an inscription with the name of Ramutha Vestiricina. The form of her family name, Vestiricina, which was typical of the Osco-Sabellian language, indicates that this was a lady of Italic, non-Etruscan origin who had taken an Etruscan name, Ramutha. During the sixth century, this readiness to admit strangers decreased, and restrictions were put on the granting of citizenship. Excavations of the port city and trade center of Graviscae have shown that foreigners were kept outside the large cities. As crafts and trade became more important, there were more people who did not fit into the client relationship on which the economic and social power of the aristocracy was based. Thus a kind of urban demos, something like the Roman plebs, arose and was soon in conflict with the rule of the aristocracy. There is evidence of such a demos in Caere and in Orvieto, in the huge cemeteries, or necropoleis, cities of the dead, whose urban plans were made up of individual lots, now obviously cheaper and more modest in size and furnishings. At Orvieto, the names of the deceased show that many of the owners of these "middle-class" tombs were of foreign origin, Italic or Latin.

These social transformations, similar to those which gave rise, in Rome, to the political, demographic, and military reforms attributed to the tyrannical rule of king Servius Tullius, were accompanied by the first attempts to introduce a form of coinage. The so-called *aes signatum,* or cast bronze bars (not yet circular in shape), bore type which showed a dry branch (see coins, Ch. VI). In the political sphere, there is evidence of a conflict between social groups and internal struggle among the aristocracy which on the one hand shook up the ancient monarchic organization and on the other encouraged the rise of tyrants. These conflicts affected both the internal development of the individual city-states and the international political situation (as shown in the legend of Macstrna). Yet there is no reason to think that changes in the type of government coincided in the various city-states. In the sixth century, monarchy seems to have prevailed almost everywhere. It is to this period that the insignia and institutions of kingship, which Roman tradition attributed to the Etruscans, can be traced. It is also probable that the Etruscan cities, like those of Latium, shared a religious rather than a political bond in the league or federation which they joined. This federation met at the Fanum Voltumnae (sanctuary of Voltumna), near Volsinii, at least as early as the fifth century B.C. By analogy with the Latin League, which was a federation of various cities of Latium, we can imagine that the Etruscan League stemmed from ancient tribal institutions. Though written sources often mention a league of twelve cities, this number is probably a conventional one. In fact twelve cities, or any other number, could scarcely have formed the basis of the organization before the urbanization of the sixth century B.C. had been completed.

The Crisis of the Fifth Century

This complex process of internal and external transformation in the Etruscan world came to a head during the first half of the fifth century B.C. Several serious crises had already weakened the Etruscan hegemony. The loss of control of Rome and Latium deprived the cities of Etruria of stable, permanent contacts with the Etruscanized Campanian area. Central Italy was troubled by the movements of Umbro-Sabellian tribes heading for the plains of the Tyrrhenian coast. After invading southern Latium at the end of the sixth century B.C., they would destroy Etruscan rule in Campania by 424 B.C. and conquer Cumae by 420 B.C. The ancient Etruscan dominion over the sea, already weakened by Greek raids in the sixth century B.C., was finally destroyed by the fleet of Syracuse in a sea battle waged in front of Cumae in 474 B.C. Greek trade, which had flowed into the harbors of southern Etruria without interruption throughout the sixth century, bringing a huge quantity of products, especially vases, lapsed between 475 and 450 B.C. and was mostly redirected toward Spina, the trading center of the Po Valley.

The economic hardship which resulted from these military disasters must have had reverberations throughout the southern Etruscan cities. As at Rome, the oligarchic republican governments which had developed from the excessive power of the aristocracy were probably challenged by the reaction of tyrants (such as Thefarie Velianas named on the gold tablet from Pyrgi, figs. III-3, VII-10).

There was, then, a period of crisis brought about by international instability and by internal tensions. The archaeological evidence shows the consequences of these disturbances. Tombs shrank in number and decorative quality. Shortly before 450 B.C. at Caere, at Tarquinia, and at Orvieto the great cemeteries became poorer, and the offerings and furnishings of the tombs fewer and cheaper. Tomb paintings now consisted of tired reproductions of the models of the first quarter of the century. Craftsmanship suffered as well. There was a growing standardization, an impoverishment of the types and decoration of both bronzes and ceramics (particularly evident is the gradual but steady decline in the quality of bucchero, that peculiarly Etruscan fabric). The quality of the few monuments of large-scale sculpture declined, as did that of the even fewer examples of small sculpture. Some of this impoverishment may have been due to sumptuary laws limiting conspicuous consumption, as in the Twelve Tables of Roman Law, about 450 B.C. These laws are an unmistakable sign that the political struggle and the social conflicts have become harsher, bringing about a lowered production on the part of craftsmen and merchants and reducing their income. The growth of the economic and political power of the demos, or common people, stopped; at the port of Graviscae, archaeological evidence shows that commercial exchange came to a standstill in this period. At the same time, the foundation upon which the aristocratic rule of the city-states was based, already weakened by long, exhausting wars, was further endangered. The southern Etruscan cities especially suffered. Those of central and northern Etruria, which remained almost untouched by the expansion of Greek sea trade and were perhaps less torn apart by internal social pressures, seem to have been less vulnerable to economic distress.

The information from ancient sources deals almost exclusively with the wars against Rome waged by Veii and her allies from Capena, Fidenae, and Falerii during the periods between 485 and 475 B.C. and 438 and 425 B.C. After a ten-year siege, modeled, according to tradition, after the Trojan War, Veii finally succumbed to Rome in the early fourth century. During this war, Veii was ruled by a king. (There is no real reason to doubt this, despite the skepticism expressed by some scholars.) The new evidence of gold tablets from Pyrgi (figs. III-3, VII-10) and of so-called *elogia,* or epitaphs, of the members of the Spurinna family seems to indicate that oligarchic government at Caere and at Veii—if it ever existed—was indeed quite unstable and was substituted by the rule of kings or tyrants of the Greek type, based on "democratic" consensus. In Rome in the fifth and fourth centuries B.C., history tells of unsuccessful attempts at such a takeover on the part of two men, Spurius Cassius and Manlius Capitolinus. These tyrannical attempts are, for the most part, to be considered demagogic reactions to the difficulties encountered by subordinate urban groups and to that crisis of the serf classes of southern Etruria which would alter the economic and social situation in the following century. Even during this crisis faint traces of specific relationships between individual city-states of southern Etruria are revealed—relationships beyond those dictated by their form of government or political or social alliances.

Etruscan and Etruscanized cities near the Tiber formed a tightly knit unit, as shown by the sturdy alliance of Veii, Capena, and Falerii and the help given to Veii by Tarquinia (in 397 B.C.) and Volsinii (in 392 B.C.) immediately before and after the fall of the city in 396 B.C. Caere maintained a position of benign neutrality during the wars between Rome and Veii and became a close ally of Rome after the Gallic invasion of Rome in 387 B.C. There seems to have been a strong feeling of solidarity joining Volsinii and Veii, as on an axis. Tarquinia formed the coastal extension of this axis, which was set against another bloc of cities with Caere at its apex, strongly tied to the neighboring Latin cities. This political pattern not only continued after Veii was taken over by Rome but also determined the political history of the area during the entire first half of the following century.

The Recovery of the Fourth Century

In the last years of the fifth century B.C. distinct signs of recovery appeared throughout Etruria. Once more, Greek pottery was imported (though in far smaller quantities than in the sixth century B.C.), especially black-glaze pottery and the decorated fabrics then being manufactured in Attic workshops. Everywhere there was a new fervor of construction of grandiose public or religious buildings such as temples, city walls, and sanctuaries, as well as private houses and tombs, buildings of a new type, richly decorated. Crafts flourished once again. Figured vases imitated Attic and south Italian pottery of the late fifth century B.C.; bronze statues and statuettes followed in the great tradition of Etruscan bronze work; furnishings and decorations of public and private buildings attained a high artistic level. This recovery, which came in on a new wave of Greek culture, was slow but sure. It is most apparent in central Italy, from Chiusi to Volsinii and Falerii, but it is also evident throughout all the Etruscan cities. The significance and the origins of this fourth-century "Renaissance" are still not fully understood. The Etruscan cities were clearly benefiting from a recovery which was going on throughout the Mediterranean and, at the same time, were resolving some of the social and economic difficulties with which they had been struggling during the previous century. The transformation of the basic forms of society is especially marked in southern Etruria, where family tombs, for example, were now prepared for several generations. The adoption of coinage and the development of an economy based on money was a feature of civilization; until this moment it had been practically unknown, or known only in its embryonic stages, in this part of the ancient world. (Ch. VI). The ideals of the aristocracy were no longer expressed in the form of private ceremonies and activities, such as the symposium or funerary banquet, funeral games, and hunting, but rather in the public arena, for now the symbols of status were acquired by holding public office in one's city. Each of these public offices or magistracies was quite different in its function and level of honor, especially in the southern Etruscan cities, such as Tarquinia, Vulci, or Volsinii. A *zilath eterau*, that is, a "magistrate" (*zilath*) especially concerned with the "*etera*," (serf) classes, can perhaps be compared with the equivalent Roman "judge," or praetor, in charge of cases concerning *etera* or *servi*. This political organization and the appearance of new names, along with those of the aristocratic families, lead us to believe that at least in southern Etruria a new aristocracy had arisen, similar to the new nobility which in Rome was the result of the Licinian laws. This nobility included the remnants of the older aristocracy as well as the most financially successful members of the groups which had formerly opposed them.

Before such a social and economic change could have taken place, there must have been a reorganization of the landholding system. This would explain the situation in the cities of southern Etruria which arose at the end of the Archaic period and ended in the fifth century B.C. (It had no doubt been slowly developing in the northern cities as well during the fifth century B.C., in a way that is still not clearly understood or shown by the archaeological evidence.) The social struggle of the preceding historical periods, which was apparently the result of the hunger for land, eventually led to an expansion of the land controlled by the city-states, who took over that of smaller neighboring satellite towns (the *castella*, or fortified towns, often mentioned by ancient sources relating the wars between Rome and the Etruscan cities). Eventually this movement also led to the diminishing importance of the countryside in favor of the city. Both developments characterize the crisis of the fifth century B.C. and help to explain the struggle, within the Etruscan League, for the control of the whole group by one of them alone. Honorary inscriptions of Tarquinia of this period, recently studied, clearly illustrate this struggle in their insistence on military triumphs and honors.

While this partial and timid recovery of the late fifth century B.C. was going on, the Etruscans once again became active in the international world. In 413 B.C. they helped the Athenians with their ill-conceived and finally disastrous expedition against Syracuse, the Etruscans' eternal enemy. The fact that the expedition was commanded by the Tarquinian leader, Velthur Spurinna, shows that Tarquinia was the most important city of the Etruscan League at this time. It was also foremost in the mid-fourth century B.C., when the son or grandson of Velthur Spurinna, Aulus Spurinna, led an army of the twelve cities of Etruria against Rome. Provoked by Roman rule in the territory of Veii and the repressive actions taken against a king of Caere, this war led to the end of that alliance between Caere and Rome so well documented by the events following the invasion and the burning of Rome by the Gauls. Measures were also taken against the slave revolts at Arezzo. Such wars reveal the aristocratic character of the League's political actions. This aristocratic character also marks the Etruscan wars against Rome, which took place in a period (358–351 B.C.) when Rome was working out the alliance between patricians and plebeians made possible by the laws of 366 B.C.

The end of the war between Rome and Tarquinia perhaps signals the decline of Tarquinia's supremacy and Volsinii's rise. Such a changeover may be deduced from the presence in these two cities—and nowhere else—of the post of *zilath mechl rasnal,* an important magistrate known in Latin as the *praetor Etruriae*. At Tarquinia, this title appears around the middle of the fourth century B.C., in the epitaph of the Spurinna family in the Tomb of Orcus I and in another inscription of this date. At Volsinii, we find it at the end of the century (in the tomb of the Leinie family, Golini Tomb I). Later events, up to the time of the Roman destruction of Volsinii in 265 B.C., when the League seems to have been dissolved, show that the preponderance of power was held by the cities of central Etruria.

The Gallic invasions of the end of the fifth century B.C. and their later raids of the fourth century B.C., the fall of Veii into Rome's power in 396 B.C., and Tarquinia's military campaign against Rome in 358–351 B.C. constitute the significant events of the century before the series of attacks against Rome (Map 6). These began in 311 B.C. and ended in the third century B.C. with the defeat and submission of Etruria. In this period, which coincided with the most flourishing moment of the Etruscan cities after the greatness of the Archaic period, Etruscan society underwent a significant transformation, partly as a result of the influence of Greek culture, especially that of the Greek cities of southern Italy, but also as a result of the obvious conflicts

within the Etruscans' own economic and social structure. All this would eventually make Etruria an easy prey to Roman imperialism and expansionism. The results would soon be evident in the availability of Etruscan mercenary troops, soldiers no longer fighting for their own cities, but out for hire, such as those which were used at the end of the fourth and the early third century B.C. in the wars between Syracuse and Carthage.

Roman Conquest

Rome's campaign of expansionism first turned against Etruria. The victory over Veii in 396 B.C. was the first instance of Rome's annexation of a great city. It also made it possible for her to solve her internal social problems and to establish a solid base from which to set forth on her irreversible march across the peninsula. Rome was, for the rest of the century, almost wholly occupied with her wars against the south: Latium, Samnium, and Campania. The war against Tarquinia in the middle of the century almost resembles a war among Etruscan states, with Rome taking the place of Veii and the Etruscan cities (perhaps) testing the "revolutionary" intentions of their new neighbor along the right-hand shore of the Tiber, now that the internal conflict between patricians and plebeians was nearing resolution. Except for this brief interval of war, there was peace between Rome and Etruria until 311 B.C. Then, according to Livy (9.32.1), the Etruscan cities, that is, the Etruscan League, with the exception of Arezzo, besieged Sutri, the advance outpost of Rome. Scholars have wondered about these sudden hostilities. The concurrent end of Rome's military engagement in the south and the outbreak of the new Etruscan war (311–308 B.C.) would seem to suggest Rome's responsibility. Yet, the Etruscans appear to have taken the initiative in attacking Sutri. Perhaps the Etruscan League desired revenge, which had been Tarquinia's motive forty years earlier.

Despite the confused and uncertain events of the war, several facts can be ascertained: the siege of Sutri was lifted; one or two battles took place near Perugia; and, after these battles, there was a temporary truce with Perugia, Cortona, and Arezzo, as well as a separate forty-year truce with Tarquinia. Exactly forty years had passed since Tarquinia's last war against Rome in 351 B.C.

This separate truce with Tarquinia, along with the aid Etruscan ships gave to Agathocles against Carthage's blockade of Syracuse in 310 B.C., seems to support the conjecture that the Etruscan coastal cities stayed more or less out of the wars. The third treaty between Rome and Carthage (306 B.C.) barely balanced this situation, although the treaty considered Corsica a neutral zone between Carthage and Rome—and this at a time when archaeological evidence shows that Corsica was very much in Etruria's grip.

Rome's initial serious conflict with the city-states of central Etruria was followed by a series of events (which are not quite clear to us) in the ten years between the end of the war and the recurrence of hostilities which culminated in the terrible Etruscan defeat at Sentinum in 295 B.C. According to the historical sources for this period (hopelessly contradictory and often not to be trusted), the front widened, approaching Arezzo in 302 B.C. There the Romans intervened to settle a conflict between the aristocratic family of the Cilnii (Cilnium gens) and the plebeians (just as Aulus Spurinna, the judge, or *praetor Etruriae,* had done fifty years before). At Rusellae, too, raids took place. In 298 B.C. there was a brief conflict with Volterra and the people of Falerii. Finally, from 295 B.C. on, a whole series of battles were waged along the northern front between Etruria and Umbria. By now, the Roman armies moved freely over all of Etruria. The only hope for the Etruscans was to ally themselves with the other peoples still stubbornly resisting Rome, such as the Umbrians, Samnites, and Gauls.

The battle of Sentinum in 295 B.C.—leaving aside the dramatization of the story by our sources, and the uncertainty and confusion of the various versions—signaled the beginning of the end for the Etruscans. The battle ended in a crushing defeat; according to the Greek historian Douris, one hundred thousand men lost their lives. Even though Etruscan involvement may have been limited, from 294 B.C. on, after truces which were dearly bought by Volsinii, Perugia, and Arezzo, Rome's

onslaughts on individual Etruscan cities finally brought the remainder of Etruria to its knees. In 293 B.C., after a treaty which had been long respected, the people of Falerii rebelled, only to be subdued. Around 285 B.C. Volsinii revolted, once more to no avail. In 283 B.C. the Etruscans, allied with a local group of Gauls, the Boii, confronted the Romans in a desperate and decisive battle in the open field, near Lake Vadimo, and were defeated. In 281 B.C. Volsinii and Vulci were overcome, in 280 B.C. (perhaps) Tarquinia, and in 273 Caere. The Etruscans' defeat at Sentinum probably hopelessly divided them. The Romans took advantage of the acquiescence of the southern bloc of cities, Caere, Tarquinia, Volsinii, and Vulci, to defeat the northern cities.

The southern cities, or most of them, were then made to pay tribute and, in the case of Caere, Tarquinia, and Vulci, to give up some of their territory. During the third century B.C. the Romans took over land from Caere and settled the fortified garrisons or colonies of Fregenae (245 B.C.), Alsium (247 B.C.), Pyrgi (264 B.C.?), and Castrum Novum (264 B.C.?). In 181 B.C. they settled, in the area of Tarquinia, the colony of Graviscae; in the territory of Vulci they settled the Latin colony of Cosa (273 B.C.); later, in the second century B.C., the settlements of Saturnia and Statonia and the colony of Heba were established. Meanwhile a number of townships, Forum Clodii, Forum Cassii, and Forum Aurelii, were organized to serve Roman colonists isolated in the countryside on land which had been confiscated from these three Etruscan cities. Three roads, the Via Clodia, Via Cassia, and Via Aurelia, were built in the third and second century B.C. to facilitate communications in this southern Etruscan region.

Prelude to the Social War

The two centuries between Rome's conquest of Caere (273 B.C.) and the Social War (80 B.C.) are among the most obscure periods of Etruscan history. Historical sources are even scarcer than usual, and little of the archaeological record of this period has yet been properly worked on. The changes which occurred in Etruscan society, insofar as we can catch a glimpse of them when they are mentioned in Roman literature or revealed by archaeological discoveries, were very different in the south from those in the central and northern area. In the boundary zone between the Etruscan cities of the far south and those of the central region, the effects of the harsh terms imposed on Caere, Tarquinia, and Vulci were deeply felt during the next thirty years. By 265 B.C. Volsinii's social structure had completely collapsed. The *servi,* or serfs, took over, and the *principes,* or first families of the city, asked for Rome's intervention. After a brief siege Rome put down the rebellion. She destroyed the city of Volsinii and built a new one on the shores of Lake Bolsena, having first sacked the city and the sanctuary of Voltumna, which had been the seat of the Etruscan League. From the plunder of Volsinii the Romans brought home two thousand bronze statues. A remarkable document, dedicated by M. Fulvius Flaccus, the consul who celebrated the triumph over Volsinii, records the pillage. The monument, which was set up in the Temple of Fortuna and Mater Matuta in Rome, still bears the imprints of the feet and other traces of the many bronze statues which once adorned it. In 214 B.C. there was another revolt; this time the people of Falerii had set themselves up against Rome. The capital city of the Faliscan people suffered the same tragic fate as Volsinii.

These revolts show that the wars against Rome had created a new situation on the fringes of the area controlled by Rome. Along with the economic hardships caused by the harsh conditions of the peace treaty, there was a severe strain on the cities, especially where, as at Volsinii, the old class of the *servitus* had remained practically unchanged. Rome's confiscation of land from the Etruscan cities of the southern coast undoubtedly changed their economic and social organization radically. In all likelihood, however, the process of decay of the old social structure had already set in well before this time. The loss of so much land and the gradual breakdown of the control of the city-states over their original territory—new towns such as Tuscania, Axia, Blera, and others developed during the late Roman Republic—may well have been com-

pensated for by a different economy, based on slavery.

The kind of diplomatic ties Rome chose to have with the Etruscan cities in the third century B.C. were treaties of alliance which spelled out the specific obligations of the parties concerned. The Etruscan cities turned out to be remarkably loyal to Rome during the difficult period of the Roman wars with Carthage. During the final phases of the Second Punic War, between 212 and 201 B.C., when Rome was fighting Hannibal, Roman troops were stationed permanently in Etruria, usually two legions at a time. Though on several occasions there was talk of attempted defection on the part of one or more Etruscan cities, the rumored plots of the Etruscan aristocracy never did, in fact, take place. On the contrary, Etruscan troops fought as auxiliaries with the Romans (the *cohors Perusina* from Perugia in 216 B.C., for example, and the cavalry troops who fought in Apulia in 208 B.C.). Furthermore, in 205 B.C., all the more important Etruscan cities sent contributions to help prepare Scipio's expedition against Carthage. The list of the materials they sent, recorded in Livy's history (28.45), reflects the economies of the third-century city-states. Caere furnished grain and all kinds of food supplies; Tarquinia, linen for the ships' sails; Volterra, pitch and grain; Arezzo, famed for its bronze work, sent three thousand bronze shields and three thousand helmets, as well as fifty thousand throwing weapons, tools for forty long ships, and one hundred twenty thousand bushels of grain. Perugia, Chiusi, and Roselle contributed wood from their fir trees for building ships and grain.

From the Roman point of view, the treaties implied her support for, and political alliance with, the local ruling classes of the Etruscan cities; in turn, these ruling classes protected Roman interests against external and, above all, internal attacks. (The events at Volsinii in 265 B.C. seem to reflect such a situation.) When the war with Hannibal ended, leaving a wake of tragic destruction and economic upheaval throughout Italy, Rome's support was indispensable for the Etruscan cities. In 196 B.C. the praetor or general, Acilius Glabrio, put down a slave revolt which had seriously threatened Etruria, and returned the slaves to their masters. The military and political help of Rome were by now vital for the preservation of the privileges enjoyed by the oligarchic governments of Italy and of Etruria in particular. A good example is Rome's repression of the Bacchanalian conspiracy, a revolt which started in Etruria and spread throughout Italy from 186 B.C. on.

Such social restlessness reflects the severe crisis of the Etruscan institution of serfdom in the cities of central and northern Etruria in the first half of the second century B.C. Yet the archaeological record of this period shows that, from the middle of the century, Etruria benefited, though at a lower level, from the economic growth of Italy, especially Latium and Campania. This temporary prosperity also brought advantages to the lower classes, the small landowners who worked the land around Perugia, Chiusi, Volterra, and Arezzo. Among these men were a number of serfs or former serfs—inscriptions show that they bore family names derived from an original serf name. The first families of the northern Etruscan cities probably learned their lesson from the earlier revolts and compromised, allowing a partial integration of the lower classes into the political system. This was done, no doubt, in order to minimize the conflict and to satisfy, at least in part, the political and economic demands of the serf class. We do know that the system of serfdom did not disappear (though chattel-slavery had developed much less in the north than in the south) by a reference to serfs who had extensive property rights in a passage derived from the Greek writer Posidonius (quoted by Diodorus Siculus, 5.40) and also in a passage concerning the nymph Vegoia, one of the very few writings on Etruscan politics to have come down to us. The fact that these archaic economic and social institutions were essentially unchanged in the beginning of the first century B.C. helps to explain Etruria's actions during the Social War and the civil wars of Rome.

The Social War and Complete Romanization

The unification of Italy by Rome was preceded by the revolutionary attempt at land reform of the Gracchi (133–123 B.C.). As Plutarch tells us (quoting the younger brother, Caius Gracchus), Tiberius Gracchus was inspired to develop such a plan when he saw the desolation of the Etruscan fields as he traveled north from Rome on his way to Numantia to take part in the war in Spain. Given his itinerary, these fields must have been those of the coastal cities of southern Etruria. Here slavery and large estates (latifundia) run as businesses with cheap slave labor, using slaves of barbarian origin, had developed rapidly in the second century B.C. In fact, the list of colonies settled according to the provisions of the land reform law passed under Tiberius Gracchus includes several in Etruria, in the territory of Arezzo, Ferentum, and Tarquinia. The place names, which changed frequently in this period, imply that the Gracchi were active in land reform in Etruria, at least in the southern Etruscan area (even though not one of the boundary markers found at colonies settled under the Gracchan laws has as yet been found in Etruria).

The relationship of the Etruscan cities with Rome in the crucial years 90 and 91 B.C. has been the subject of controversy among scholars. In 91 B.C. the Etruscans, along with the Umbrians, protested the agrarian law of the tribune Livius Drusus, who set up land reform laws rivaling those of the Gracchi. They were evidently afraid of the revolution the law would bring to their economic system. The following year the Etruscans, who had not, until that moment, taken part in the Italic revolt raging around Rome, for the first time threatened to join the rebels. Soon, however, they accepted Roman citizenship. The new citizens were registered in wards, or rustic tribes, in a way that modern historians feel conferred a favorable political status upon them.

The worst moment for the Etruscans is certainly that of the civil wars, starting from 83 B.C., when they almost unanimously joined the faction of Marius, whether because of Etruscan client-patron ties with some of the leaders of the faction which declared against Marius's opponent, Sulla, or because of the dislike the local Etruscan aristocracy had for the centralized policy Sulla was advocating; or, perhaps, because of the social disturbances the Etruscan city-states suffered as a result of their newly granted Roman citizenship. The centers of resistance to Sulla were Chiusi, Arezzo, Populonia, and Volterra. At Chiusi, two battles were fought between the Roman generals Sulla and Papirius Carbo; at Arezzo, Carbo suffered his third terrible defeat. Populonia was subjected to a rigorous siege, as was Volterra, defeated by Sulla after a long siege between 80 and 79 B.C. Sulla's vengeance was fierce. Besides imposing a number of limitations on the privileges of citizenship, the dictator confiscated and distributed among his own veterans huge areas of the territory of the Etruscan cities, especially at Fiesole, Arezzo, Volterra, and Chiusi. He was thus satisfying the hunger of the soldiers of his twenty-three victorious legions for land. At the same time he was condemning a great number of dispossessed Etruscans to starvation. (Many of them joined the troops of the last rebels still holding out under the command of Sertorius in Spain or else emigrated to distant places such as Africa, where boundary stones of this period have been found inscribed in the Etruscan language.)

This time of terror and general social and ethnic upheaval, marked by a serious breakdown of morale and psychological disorientation (as shown by the frenzied pace at which prodigies are reported to have taken place in Etruria), left deep wounds in Etruscan society. The cities of southern Etruria seem to have settled down among the economic and political comforts which accompanied integration into Roman life. The northern cities, on the other hand, devastated by war and pillage at the hands of Sulla's men, never found peace. The cities were divided among the old and the new inhabitants. Their aristocracy, deprived of its ancient rights, did not marry into Roman society and was unable or unwilling to become integrated into it. Even Sulla's colonists, after having abused their position and repeatedly killed, raped, and looted the native population, soon squandered their money and sank deeply into debt. Many became bandits. At Fiesole, in 78–77 B.C., evicted landowners and local farmers revolted against them. Ironically, a follower of Sulla, M. Aemilius Lepidus, sent out as general by Rome to quell the uprising at Fiesole, instead found common cause with the rebels and incited another revolt. All these uprisings failed. Again in 63 B.C. Catiline's conspiracy, so

stubbornly fought by Cicero, found its adherents principally in Etruria, both among the hopelessly indebted colonists settled by Sulla and the members of the Etruscan communities who had suffered most from the dispossession of their lands. Twenty years later, the situation still remained turbulent. Even though the battle of Perugia between Octavian's troops (under the command of Agrippa) and the brother of Mark Anthony was a part of the conflict between the factions contending for supremacy at Rome, it was not by coincidence that it occurred in the heart of Etruria, with the participation of much of the local population. These Etruscan participants were subsequently severely punished by Octavian.

In spite of these troubles, during the period between the rule of Caesar and that of Augustus, a settlement was finally reached in Etruria (Map 7). The remnants of the local ruling classes were rapidly integrated into Rome's new political picture. Numerous colonies were settled by the triumvirate, and later by Augustus, throughout the whole of the Etruscan territory, from Arezzo to Lucus Feroniae, from Luni (near Carrara) to Castrum Novum, from Luca to Perusia (Perugia), from Rusellae to Siena, to mention only the major and best-known cities. Far from recreating the havoc wreaked by Sulla's colonies, these new colonies took part in the economic and social stabilization and reconciliation which now occurred throughout Italy. An ambitious urban building program transformed the appearance of every city in Etruria. City life was enriched by theaters, amphitheaters, basilicas, forums, and aqueducts. Almost universally, the economy is based on slave (?) *ergastula,* or workhouses, like that of the family of Volusius Saturnius discovered near Lucus Feroniae.

With Romanization complete, the atmosphere of restoration in the capital set the example for the reappearance of ancient local traditions. Nostalgia ruled: there was a thirst to rediscover the institutions and symbols of a past glory. The League of the Twelve Peoples reappeared (with fifteen members). In the piazze and forums of the cities memorials were dedicated to their bygone grandeur and fame; Tarquinia erected statues of the hero Tarchon, who was thought to have given his name to the city, as well as statues of the great *principes,* or leaders, the Spurinnae. The custom of rendering homage to the emperor's family was combined with the urge to glorify and preserve one's family's own legendary past, and so between the time of Caesar and that of Claudius scholars collected documents of Etruscan history, compiling and composing myths and genealogies, checking aristocratic family archives and ancient religious texts. This antiquarian historiography of the Augustan and Julio-Claudian period marks the end of the history of Etruria.

Bibliography

Ancient sources are cited in full in the author's book-length treatment of this subject: M. Torelli, *Storia degli Etruschi* (Rome and Bari 1981). Full publication information for books cited in short form here is found in the Abbreviations or in the Selected Readings to this volume.

GENERAL PUBLICATIONS

A. Alföldi, *Early Rome and the Latins* (Ann Arbor 1965).
M. Grant, *The Etruscans*.
W.V. Harris, *Rome in Etruria and Umbria*.
J. Heurgon, *The Rise of Rome to 264 B.C.* (London 1973).
———, *Daily Life*.
A. Hus, *Les Étrusques et leur destin*.
R.M. Ogilvie, *Commentary*.
———, *Early Rome and the Etruscans*.
H.H. Scullard, *The Etruscan Cities and Rome*.
K.-W. Weeber, *Geschichte der Etrusker*.

SPECIALIZED PUBLICATIONS

The Land

For the metal industry, see F.-W. von Hase, *RömMitt* 70 (1972) 155ff., and *L'Etruria mineraria. Atti XII Convegno Nazionale di Studi Etruschi, 1979* (Florence 1981).

The People

For general sources, see M. Pallottino, *L'origine degli Etruschi* (Rome 1946); F. Altheim, *Der Ursprung der Etrusker* (Baden-Baden 1950); H. Hencken, *Tarquinia, Villanovans and Early Etruscans* (Cambridge, Massachusetts,

1968); D. Musti, *Tendenze nella storiografia romana e greca su Roma arcaica. Quaderni Urbinati di Cultura Classica* 10 (Rome 1970); L. Aigner Foresti, *Tesi, ipotesi e considerazioni sull'origine degli Etruschi* (Diss. Graz 1972; Vienna 1974); and N.K. Sandars, *The Sea Peoples* (London 1978).

Earliest Settlements

For Bronze Age settlements, see S. Puglisi, *La civiltà appenninica* (Florence 1959); C.E. Oestenberg, *Luni sul Mignone e problemi della protostoria d'Italia* (Stockholm 1967); R. Peroni, *ParPass* (1969) 134ff.; T.W. Potter, *The Changing Landscape of South Etruria* (London 1979). For Mycenaean settlements in Italy, see W. Taylour, *Mycenaean Pottery in Italy* (Cambridge 1958); M.L. Ferrarese Ceruti, *RivScPr* 34 (1979) 243ff.; L. Vagnetti, in *Atti Convegno su Temesa* (Perugia 1981).

On the later Bronze Age, see H. Müller-Karpe, *Beiträge zur Chronologie der Urnefelderzeit nördlich und südlich der Alpen* (Berlin 1959); A.M. Bietti Sestieri, *ProcPS* 39 (1973) 383ff.; various authors, in *Atti XXI Riunione dell'Istituto di Preistoria e Protostoria, 1977* (Florence 1979); R. Peroni, ed., *Il Bronzo Finale in Italia. AMP* 1 (Bari 1980).

On the beginning of the Iron Age, see B. d'Agostino, in *EAA* VII (1966) 1173ff., and *EAA Suppl. 1970* (1973) 922ff., s.v. *Villanova, civiltà;* and M. Pallottino, *Genti e culture dell'Italia preromana* (Rome 1981). On Osteria dell'Osa, see A.M. Bietti Sestieri, *Ricerca su una comunità del Lazio protostorico* (Rome 1979). On the Villanovan at Pontecagnano, see B. d'Agostino, in *Seconda Mostra della Preistoria e della Protostoria nel Salernitano* (Salerno 1974) 87ff.; and, at Capua, W. Johannowski, *DialAr* 1 (1967) 159ff.

EIGHTH CENTURY B.C.

For general sources, see M. Torelli, in *DialAr* 8 (1974–75) 3ff.; G. Colonna, in *Contributi*, 3ff. On the necropolis of Quattro Fontanili, Veii, see J. Close-Brooks, *NSc* (1965) 53ff., and *StEtr* 35 (1968) 323ff. For trade, see D. Ridgway, *StEtr* 35 (1968) 311ff., and F.-W. von Hase, *Aufnahme* 9ff. On Sardinian bronzes from Vulci, see M.T. Falconi Amorelli, *ArchCl* 18 (1966) 1ff. On Populonia, see A. Minto, *NSc* (1926) 372ff. On Sardinia, see F. Lo Schiavo, *StEtr* 46 (1978) 25ff.; Camporeale, *Commerci di Vetulonia* 94ff.; *Kunst Sardiniens* (Karlsruhe 1980). On Phoenicians in Italy, see G. Garbini, *StEtr* 34 (1966) 111ff.; B. D'Agostino, *MonAntLinc*, ser. misc. 2 (1977) 44ff.; G. Buchner, in *Contributions à l'étude de la société et de la colonisation eubéennes*, Cahiers Bérard 2 (Naples 1975) 59ff.

On Greek colonization, see *DialAr* 3 (1969) 3ff.; D. Ridgway, *Greeks, Celts and Romans* (London 1973) 5ff.; N. Coldstream, *Geometric Greece* (London 1977) 92ff., 223ff.;

A. Mele, *Il commercio greco arcaico*, Cahiers Bérard 4 (Naples 1979); M. Torelli, *Studi M. Napoli* (1977); D. Ridgway, *L'alba della Magna Grecia* (Milan 1984).

THE ORIENTALIZING PERIOD

For general sources, see M. Cristofani, *ParPass* (1975) 132ff.; B. d'Agostino, *MonAntLinc* 2 (1977) 44ff. For the social system, see H. Rix, *ANRW* I² (1972) 700ff.; G. Colonna, *MEFRA* 77 (1970) 637ff., and *StEtr* 45 (1977) 175ff.; M. Cristofani, *Aspetti e problemi dell'Etruria interna. Atti VIII Convegno Nazionale di StEtr* (Florence 1974) 308ff.; C. de Simone, *Ann.Fond.Mus. C. Faina* 1 (1980) 26ff. (Orvieto); L.R. Ménanger, *StDocHistIur.* 46 (1980) 14ff.; T. Frankfort, *Latomus* 18 (1959) 3ff.; J. Heurgon, *Latomus* 18 (1959) 713ff.; D. Lotze, *Metaxù Eleuthéron kaì doùlon* (Berlin 1959); D. Musti, *Atti XVI Convegno Storia della Magna Grecia* (*HC,t^R,BA'(t)*Naples 1977) 23ff. (Locri). On "Palaces," see M. Torelli, in *Architecture et societé. Atti Convegno Int.* (Rome 1980).

SIXTH CENTURY B.C.

On urbanization, see C. Ampolo, *La città antica* (Rome, Bari 1980); Torelli, *DialAr* 8 (1974–75) 3ff. On Latium, see Torelli, *DialAr* n.s. 2 (1980) 3ff; Torelli, in *Miscellanea Dohrn* (Rome 1981). For craftsmanship and trade, see C. de Simone, *Die griechischen Entlehnungen im Etruskischen* (Wiesbaden 1968–70); G. Colonna, *ArchCl* 25 (1973–74) 132ff., *Scritti Neppi Modona* (Florence 1975) 165ff., *RömMitt* 82 (1975) 181ff., and *StEtr* 47 (1979) 163ff.; M. Torelli, *Studi Magi* (Perugia 1979) 305ff. On writing, see M. Cristofani, *Popoli e civiltà* 6 (1978) 403ff.

On hoplite reform, see A. Snodgrass, *Early Greek Armour* (Edinburgh 1964); P.F. Stary, *Aufnahme* 25ff. For thalassocracy and early trade, see J.G. Szilágyi, *ActaAntHung* 1 (1953) 419ff.; S. Paglieri, *StEtr* 28 (1960) 209ff.; M. Gras, in *Mélanges Heurgon* (Rome 1976) 341ff.; and *Le "bucchero nero" étrusque et sa diffusion en Gaule Méridionale* (Brussels 1979); F.-W. von Hase, in *Seminar Marburg* 5 (1979) 62ff. On social mobility, see C. Ampolo, *DialAr* 9–10 (1976–77) 333ff.

On Rome and Latium, see various authors, *ParPass* (1977). On Veii, see J.B. Ward Perkins, *PBSR* 16 (1961) 1ff.; L. Vagnetti, *Il deposito votivo di Campetti a Veio* (Florence 1971). On Orvieto, see M. Bizzarri, *StEtr* 30 (1962) 1ff. For Tarquinia see M. Pallottino, *MonAntLinc* 36 (1937) coll. 1ff. For Vulci, F. Messerschmidt, *Die Nekropole von Vulci* (Berlin 1930); *La civiltà arcaica di Vulci e la sua espansione. Atti del X Convegno Nazionale di Studi Etruschi* (Florence 1977). On Vetulonia, see D. Levi, *StEtr* 5 (1931) 13ff. *Roselle — Gli scavi e la mostra* (Pisa 1975). A. de Agostino, *NSc*

(1961) 63ff. On Volterra, see M. Cristofani, *NScSuppl* (1973). For Chiusi, see R. Bianchi Bandinelli, *MonAntLinc* 30 (1925) 210ff.

For Perugia, see C. Shaw, *Etruscan Perugia* (Baltimore 1939). On Cortona, see A. Neppi Modona, *Cortona etrusca e romana* (Florence 1977). On Arezzo, see P. Bocci, *StEtr* 43 (1975) 47ff. On Falerii, see A. Cozza and A. Pasqui, *Forma Italiae* II, 2 (Florence 1981). For Campania, see J. Heurgon, *Capoue préromaine* (Paris 1946). On Emilia, see G.A. Mansuelli, *StEtr* 25 (1957) 31ff.; Mansuelli, *Guida alla città etrusca e al museo di Marzabotto* (Bologna 1979); N. Alfieri, *Spina. Museo archeologico di Ferrara* (Bologna 1979). On Graviscae, see M. Torelli, *ParPass* (1977) 398ff. For Adria, see G. Colonna, *RivStAnt* 5 (1974) 1ff. On Archaic asylum, see D. van Berchem, *MusHelv* 17 (1960) 21ff.

For Ionian artists in Etruria, see M. Cristofani, *Prospettiva* 7 (1976) 2ff. On Servius Tullius, see A. Momigliano, *JRS* 53 (1963) 95ff.; M. Pallottino, *CRAI* (1977) 216ff.; J.C. Richard, *Les origines de la plèbe romaine* (Rome 1978). On Laris Velchainas, see M. Cristofani Martelli, *Scritti Neppi Modona* (Florence 1975) 205ff. On Avile Acvilnas, see C. Ampolo, *ParPass* (1975) 410ff. On Arath Spuriana, see M. Pallottino, *StRom* 27 (1979) 1ff. On Lavinium, see F. Castagnoli, *ParPass* (1977) 340ff. For the Comitium, see F. Coarelli, *ParPass* (1977) 166ff. For the Fanum Voltumnae, see G. Camporeale, *ParPass* (1958) 5ff. On Veii, see M. Santangelo, *BdA* 37 (1952) 147ff. On Lucus Feroniae, see M. Torelli, *Studi Pallottino* (Rome 1981). For the François Tomb, see R.T. Ridley, *Klio* 57 (1975) 147ff. On S. Omobono, see F. Coarelli, *DialAr* 2 (1968) 55ff. On Pyrgi, see M. Verzar, *MEFRA* 92 (1980) 35ff.; various authors, *Die Göttin von Pyrgi* (Florence 1981). On Montetosto, see M. Torelli, *Le délit religieux* (Rome 1981) 1ff. On Regia, see F. Brown, in *RendPontAcc* 47 (1974–75) 15ff.

THE CRISIS OF THE FIFTH CENTURY

For general sources, see D. Musti, *Economia greca* (Rome, Bari 1981) 47ff. See also bibliography for sixth century B.C. above. On Veii, see J.B. Ward Perkins, in *PBSR* 23 (1955) 44ff; *PBSR* 36 (1968) 1ff; L. Murray-Threipland and M. Torelli, *PBSR* 38 (1970) 62ff. On Falerii, see M.W. Frederiksen and J.B. Ward Perkins, *PBSR* 25 (1957) 67ff. For Cerveteri and Tarquinia, see G. Colonna, *StEtr* 35 (1967) 3ff. For Volsinii, see R. Bloch, *Recherches archéologiques en territoire volsinien* (Paris 1972). On Vetulonia and Roselle, see C. Curri, in *Forma Italiae* VII 4. *Vetulonia I* (Florence 1978).

On Bologna, see J. Stary-Rimpau, *Aufnahme* 75ff. On Marzabotto, see G.A. Mansuelli, *MEFRA* 84 (1972) 145ff. For Casalecchio, see B. Bouloumié, *MEFRA* 87 (1975) 7ff. On Spina, see S. Aurigemma, *La necropoli di Spina* (Rome 1960–65). For Adria, see G. Colonna, *StEtr* 42 (1974) 3ff.

On Campania, see M.W. Frederiksen, in *IBR* 277ff. See also *Lapis Satricanus* (Rome 1980); *I Galli e l'Italia* (Rome 1978); J. Heurgon, *Trois études sur le ver sacrum* (Brussels 1957); *Todi. Verso il museo della città* (Todi 1981); T. Salmon, *Samnium and the Samnites* (Cambridge 1967); *Sannio–Pentri e Frentani dal VI al I sec. a.C.* (Rome 1980). See also bibliography for Ch. V for individual cities.

THE RECOVERY OF THE FOURTH CENTURY

For general sources, see M. Humbert, *Municipium et civitas sine suffragio* (Rome 1978); Torelli, *Elogia Tarquiniensia;* M. Cristofani, *Popoli e civiltà* 7 (1978) 53ff.; *Roma Medio Repubblicana* (Rome 1973); J.P. Morel, "Atelier des petites estampilles," *MEFRA* 81 (1969) 59ff. On Gallic helmets, see F. Coarelli, *Mélanges Heurgon* I, 157ff.; M. Cristofani, *MemLinc* s. VIII, XIV 4 (1969) 213ff.; M. Torelli, *DialAr* 4–5 (1970–71) 431ff. See also M. Torelli, *The Typology and Structure of Roman Historical Reliefs* (Ann Arbor 1983). On votive terracottas, see A.M. Comella, *MEFRA* 93 (1981). See also bibliographies to Chs. IV and VI below.

ROMAN CONQUEST

For general sources, see W.V. Harris, *Rome in Etruria and Umbria* (Oxford 1971). For the Donario di Fulvio Flacco, see M. Torelli, in *Quaderni Ist.Top.Ant.Univ.Roma* 5 (1968) 71ff. On Populonia, see M. Cristofani Martelli, in *L'Etruria mineraria* (Florence 1981). On social changes, see H. Rix, *Das etruskische Cognomen* (Wiesbaden 1963); M. Torelli, *DialAr* 8 (1974–75) 3ff.; H. Rix, in *Caratteri dell'ellenismo,* 64ff.; M. Cristofani, *Caratteri dell'ellenismo,* 74f.

THE SOCIAL WAR AND ROMANIZATION

For general sources, see M. Torelli, *DialAr* 3 (1969) 285ff.; *RivFC* (1971) 489ff.; "Glosse etrusche: qualche problema di trasmissione," *Mélanges Heurgon* II, 1001–8; *Elogia Tarquiniensia;* and *Hellenismus in Mittelitalien* (Göttingen 1976) 87ff.; A. Carandini and S. Settis, *Schiavi e padroni nell'Etruria romana* (Bari 1979); J. Heurgon, *CRAI* (1969) 526ff.

III / International Contacts: Commerce, Trade, and Foreign Affairs

JEAN MACINTOSH TURFA

A succession of foreign contacts left their mark on the development of Etruscan culture. Commerce, in the form of exchange of technology and goods, had already occurred between the metal-rich Etruscans and the related Hallstatt cultures to the north in the Villanovan period (Map 4). The search for metals was common in the Mediterranean, since few regions had the necessary ores for the production of bronze, iron, silver, and gold.[1] Current research on Etruscan and Punic amphorae, on ancient shipping, and on metallurgy is filling in and, in some cases, changing radically our knowledge of Etruscan commerce. Thus a picture emerges for Etruscan relations with different peoples in the course of the various phases of their history.

I. Eighth Through Fifth Centuries B.C.

PHOENICIAN TRADE

The earliest in the quest for resources were the Phoenicians, whose ancestors may have scouted the Tyrrhenian Sea and Sicily even before the end of the second millennium B.C.[2] The Phoenicians were established in Sardinia by the date of the stone inscription found at Nora, the tenth or ninth century B.C.,[3] and by the eighth century B.C., they were prospecting from colonies scattered over the western Mediterranean and establishing trade relations with the metal producers and suppliers of Etruria and Latium (Map 9).[4] Phoenician merchants may have transported the Oriental curiosities found in the tombs of the *principes* of Tarquinia, Veii, and Vetulonia.[5] In the seventh century, the aristocrats of Praeneste, Vulci, and Caere, as well as of some of the Italic towns, Pontecagnano, Francavilla Marittima, were the proud recipients of flashy bronze and silver vases and bowls, faience or shell trinkets, decorated ostrich eggs, and ivories and glass. The best known of these are the bronze and silver bowls and plates of Phoenician manufacture from the Barberini and Bernardini tombs at Praeneste and the Regolini-Galassi Tomb at Caere. This metalwork was decorated with friezes showing characteristic Phoenician scenes: hybridized Assyrian/Egyptian motifs of royal hunts and warfare, exotic landscapes, and an occasional decorative hieroglyph.[6]

The Egyptian origin of certain goods also points to trade with Phoenician merchants. Ostrich eggs, raw ivory, and faience items, such as the Bocchoris Vase from the tomb of the same name at Tarquinia, are examples.[7] The polychrome reliefs on the vase show scenes and names that link it to souvenirs of hybrid Phoenician manufacture issued during the brief reign of Pharaoh Bokenranf (about 720–715 B.C.). It is interesting to note that the workshop had some commercial success—faience scarabs and vases naming Bokenranf (the Greeks called him

The author gratefully acknowledges helpful discussions and valuable information received during seminars at the University of Manchester, the University of Pennsylvania, and elsewhere. Special thanks go to A.J.N.W. Prag, T.B. Rasmussen, E. French, B.B. Shefton, A.W. Johnston, G. Warden, G. Buchner, D. Ridgway, B. Bouloumié, E. Macnamara, R. Stieglitz, S. Wolff, and L. Bonfante.

Bocchoris) reached the Phoenician colony of Motya in Sicily and the Greek emporium of Pithekoussai.[8] The Etruscan lady buried with the vase also had jewelry of Egyptian faience, as well as a complete set of Etruscan grave goods.

The presence of ostrich eggs in tombs of the early seventh to the early sixth century B.C. at sites such as Populonia, Vetulonia, Quinto Fiorentino, Vulci, Tarquinia, Caere, Rome, and in the region of the Marche shows that Phoenician purveyors of curiosities were quick to channel some of their customary trade goods into a new market.[9] Incense was another commodity supplied from the Red Sea area and shipped as far as Populonia, where some myrrh has been found in a seventh-century tomb.[10]

The supply of ivory objects and raw ivory[11] suggests a more complex involvement with the Levant. A few very fine pieces, such as reliefs and inlays for boxes or furniture found in two princely Praenestine tombs,[12] were imported from the same workshops that made some of the Nimrud ivories in the possession of the Assyrian kings. Some early Etruscan furniture, for example, heavy funeral couches at Populonia, seems to have been inspired by Near Eastern prototypes.[13] Itinerant craftsmen, natives of north Syria or their apprentices, may have been responsible for some of the carved ivories found in Etruria and for setting up Etruscan schools of ivories.[14]

One item of seventh-century Phoenician manufacture, a dark blue glass bowl found in the Bernardini Tomb at Praeneste, is similar to bowls made at Nimrud.[15] Beginning in the seventh century a native workshop for the production of glass beads (used to decorate fibulae) and unusual "porcupine vases," tiny colored glass jugs with spiny bodies, flourished. All these have been found in tombs of the wealthy.[16]

The Orientalizing style of Etruscan art generally was inspired and dominated by the influx of Phoenician goods and the hybrid Egyptian or Assyrian motifs in their decoration.[17] (Greek intermediaries may also have been involved.) Etruscan artisans added Oriental ornament to native objects in metal and pottery, such as the early bucchero or painted vases, and also imitated Oriental goods in their original media.[18] The costume and style of some early sculptures at Caere, Vulci, Tarquinia, and Chiusi suggest the Levantine influence on the

Etruscan elite: one of the earliest examples, a relief in the Tomb of the Statues at Ceri, is convincing evidence of such an origin for monumental sculpture in Etruria and other parts of Italy.[19] The elaborate gold jewelry found in the great tombs of this period is also distinctively Orientalizing.[20]

The earliest Phoenician imports were small trinkets, *athyrmata,* faience amulets, and the like, much in the manner of the trade beads used in more recent colonial enterprises.[21] Phoenician imports soon changed in character, however. Costly display pieces of bronze and gilded silver, toilet articles, perfume, and Oriental cosmetics, which seem to have been packaged in their ornamental flasks and carved shells, indicate the prestige of the Etruscans to whom they were sent.[22] The aristocratic classes of Latium, Caere, Tarquinia, Vulci, and other cities evidently obtained Oriental luxuries in order to show off their wealth and status, like the heroic gift giving of the Bronze Age.

A utilitarian lamp set in an Etruscan tomb at Populonia, the only ceramic object therein, may hint at a closer personal involvement with Phoenician or Punic travelers, for coarse Phoenician ware was apparently seldom exported; it has been found principally at settlement and colony sites.[23]

The Phoenicians evidently also dealt in perishable luxuries such as wine, precious woods (one thinks of the cedars of Lebanon), animals, like monkeys, agricultural products, perfumes, dyed or embroidered textiles, and slaves.[24] At the beginning of the sixth century B.C. they were supplying a wide range of manufactured goods to Etruscan and Italic cities, including blue and yellow glass beads, some shaped like the faces of bearded Semitic men (fig. III-1),[25] and faience amulets.[26]

The introduction of wine-making may also indicate the powerful influence of Phoenician contacts on Etruscan culture.[27] Some local amphorae and related coarse ware in seventh-century Italian fabrics seem to derive from Levantine shapes (the so-called Canaanite jar),[28] rather than from characteristically Greek transport amphorae. Etruscans apparently preferred other containers (perhaps wineskins) for domestic consumption. The Etruscan type of micaceous amphora does, however, appear in very great quantities in sixth-century ships wrecked off the coast of southern France. In one instance, dozens

III-1. Punic glass head bead or pendant, a type found in
Phoenicia, Carthage, Etruria, and the West. Seventh or
sixth century B.C. L. 2.5 cm. Corning Museum of Glass,
Corning, N.Y., Acc. 54.1.14. (Museum photo.)

kings.[29] The use of the chariot in war may also be
linked to the East, where that old-fashioned system
was retained by the Phoenicians even after it had
been superseded elsewhere.[30] The Etruscans' use of
chariots like those found in princely seventh-
century tombs points to a greater social influence
from the Near East than is suggested by the mere
purchase of contemporary trinkets. Other military
innovations were also adopted from the Near East,
and were then introduced by the Etruscans to Umbria, Latium, and Campania. Even prototypes for
the Etruscan warship may be traced to the eastern
Mediterranean.[31] Particularly intriguing is the
theory that the concept of a city-state, or polis, was
disseminated by the Phoenicians.[32]

What did the Phoenicians get in exchange for
their manufactured luxury goods and rare substances? The archaeological record here is very
scanty. Though few, if any, Etruscan products have
been found in the Levant, commodities like grain,
wood, leather, or unworked metal may well have
been exported from Etruria. Metals especially came
from the Colline Metallifere, Tolfa, or later, Elba.
New archaeometric techniques such as neutron
activation analysis of trace elements in manufactured metal goods may eventually tell us more.[33]
Another reason for our ignorance is that the extent
of excavation of Phoenician sites in the Levant is
not nearly so extensive as that of the Etruscan necropoleis. Nebuchadnezzar's destruction of Tyre in
573 B.C. may have put an end to Phoenician autonomy and resulted in Carthage's taking the lead in
the old mercantile empire. The influx of Oriental
trade goods into Etruria stopped rather abruptly at
the end of the first quarter of the sixth century, the
date when Etruscan bucchero appeared in quantity
at Punic, Cypriot, and Greek sites. The only de-
monstrably Phoenician product to reach Etruria
thereafter was a fine pale green glass amphora found
in the fifth-century Tomb of the Stool, Bologna.[34]
But since the Phoenician commercial system was
geared to exchanging manufactured goods or rare
substances for bulk raw materials, using Phoenician
ships rather than middlemen, it is not surprising
that relatively few Etruscan objects have been identified in Syria or Palestine. An Orientalizing belt
clasp in the British Museum is said to have come

of these amphorae were stacked in the hold of a
ship that sank off Cap d'Antibes (discussed later in
this chapter).

Yet Oriental influence on Etruria is perhaps best
demonstrated not by the introduction of exotic
trade goods and artistic motives but by the incor-
poration of Eastern customs into local society. Luxuries like parasols and fans in the representations
of important personages, such as the processions
and audiences of gods or magistrates that adorned
Etruscan buildings, separated the elite or persons of
status from the rest of society, as shown in the reliefs of the Assyrian and Persian (as well as earlier)

from Syria.[35] A small amount of *bucchero sottile* has been found at settlement sites at Monte Sirai, a Phoenician colony in Sardinia, and Ras el Bassit, a seventh- or sixth-century Greek emporium site in Syria.[36] Bucchero drinking vessels, especially the distinctive kantharoi, occur in early sixth-century contexts in the Phoenician colonies in Spain, Cyprus, Sicily, Sardinia, Carthage, and Utica.[37] None has as yet been recognized in Phoenicia proper. Such bucchero vases or sets of tableware were likely to have been adjuncts to the trade in prime commodities of raw materials.

GREEK CONTACTS: THE EUBOEANS OF PITHEKOUSSAI

From the Bronze Age on, the Greeks had been aware of the Phoenician commercial empire and traveled the Mediterranean to acquire the materials they needed.[38] In the eighth century B.C., difficulties on the island of Euboea (including perhaps the Lelantine War, whose date is uncertain) prompted Chalkidians and Eretrians (Euboeans) to establish trading posts, or emporia, on the coast of north Syria in order to participate in the Near East trade at its source. Two such sites have been excavated: Al Mina in Phoenician territory and Ras el Bassit in north Syria.[39] (Naukratis in Egypt and Emporion on Chios also served as trading posts.[40]) It may have been at a site like Al Mina that the north Semitic alphabet was adapted for use with the Greek language.[41] The emporia managed their own cottage industries as well as foreign commerce, and they were visited or inhabited by natives and other foreign traders. That the Euboeans seem to have had contact with a different set of Oriental merchants from those known to the Etruscans is suggested by the fact that north Syrian and even Cilician workshops are better represented on the eighth- and seventh-century Greek trade routes than are the crafts of the Phoenicians.[42] The Euboeans (and other Greeks) apparently followed Phoenician trade routes west to Italy, Sicily, and even Spain (Map 9),[43] but in establishing new emporia, they had to consider the spheres of influence already established by Punic colonies and natives.

Their first western site was the island of Pithekoussai in the Bay of Naples[44] (Map 3), chosen for its proximity to Etruria and the river valley system of Latium and Campania—probably the nearest site to the metal and agricultural regions not already controlled by hostile natives. Within a generation, Corinth had sent a colony to the next most advantageous location: Syracuse, in Sicily. It seems obvious, in the light of the discoveries at Pithekoussai, that the first Greek colonies in the west were also emporia, chosen for their strategic locations. Only afterward, in a second wave of emigration, did the canonical Greek colonies with *oikistai* (founders) and settler-families appear.[45]

Just before the foundation of Pithekoussai, Greeks (probably Euboeans) were apparently prospecting in the Tyrrhenian Sea; souvenirs of these trips appear in the votive deposits of the famous international sanctuaries at Delphi, Olympia, Dodona, and Samos, centers which thrived on commerce and international patronage in the Archaic period. The objects are mainly ornaments, arms, and armor; the latter were probably casual souvenirs rather than formal trophies of war, certainly not trade goods. There are helmets, round shields, horse-bits, and similar trappings of Villanovan design probably made in Tarquinia, Veii, Bisenzio, and Vetulonia.[46] Some of the weapons, like the miniature axes, are typical Italian votive offerings. (Interestingly enough, it was an Etruscan, King Arimnestos, who is remembered as the first foreigner to make a dedication [a throne] in the sanctuary of Zeus at Olympia [Pausanias V.12.5].[47])

From about 760 B.C., Euboean and Pithekoussan painted skyphoi began to appear in Italy, following the trade routes that linked Campania with the Tiber Valley. The cups were made in relatively large numbers during Phase IIA of the town of Veii.[48] From the last quarter of the eighth century, bronze fibulae of Etruscan or Italic manufacture were placed as donations in Greek sanctuaries: Olympia, Samos, Lindos, Perachora, Aegina, Pherai, and Exochi. It has been suggested that the production of specialized types of ornaments (*fibule con arco rivestito,* gold fibulae with elongated foot, and infants' gold funerary headbands) took place locally in response to the demands of native Italians for

III-2. Seal of the lyre-player group from Cilicia, found in Pithekoussai. Eighth century B.C. (*Greeks, Celts and Romans* 15, fig. 3.)

jewelry combining Orientalizing styles with Italic traditions.[49]

North Syrian (as opposed to Phoenician) relations with the Euboeans may be traced through Orientalizing metal ornaments of Etruria and central Italy, especially feline- and human-headed belt clasps.[50] The Euboeans apparently maintained their Near Eastern contacts, even at Pithekoussai, as shown by finds of north Syrian, Cilician, and even Phrygian goods, such as lyre-player seals[51] (fig. III-2). What is more, the presence of Orientals at the site is implied by infant burials in Near Eastern amphorae; some amphorae even bear Semitic inscriptions designating them for funerals.[52] The Euboeans adapted the north Semitic alphabet for their own use; the Etruscans no doubt acquired the western Greek alphabet through trade relations with the Euboeans, perhaps those of Pithekoussai.[53]

The trade routes originally followed the river valleys from Campania into Latium and up the Tiber Valley. The Etruscan demand for Greek goods was soon met with exports to Vulci, Tarquinia, and Bisenzio, including fine banquet vessels and large quantities of Corinthian miniature perfume vases.[54]

GREEK CONTACTS: IONIANS AND CORINTHIANS

Both Ionian and Corinthian vases were exported to Etruria and Latium throughout the seventh century, with quantities peaking about 625 B.C. From about 600–550 B.C. there was substantial trade in Laconian painted wares. The presence of contemporary Etruscan goods in Spartan territory[55] is interesting for the study of Laconian commerce: commodities exchanged by the Etruscans may have been raw materials. At first, only a small amount of Etruscan *bucchero sottile* reached Greece, notably at the seamen's shrine of Hera at Perachora, patronized by Corinthian travelers.[56] (A few pieces of bucchero made before 600 B.C. also occur at the Heraion on Samos and perhaps at Chios.[57])

Even after the use of coinage reached Etruria from Greece, early trade still functioned on a system of barter. The earliest coins in Etruria are Phocaean types of the late sixth century. The subsequent distinctive Etruscan minting of the early fifth century was clearly influenced by Greek prototypes, and the fact that the standard weight reflects the Attic-Euboeic unit is a strong indication of the economic influences on Etruria by the early fifth century.[58]

GRAVISCAE

In the seventh century, permanent Greek trading posts were established as the bases, or suburbs, of small towns along the Tyrrhenian coast in proximity to the major centers of Caere, Tarquinia, and Vulci. Etruscan cities of early metallurgical importance (Vetulonia and Populonia) show fewer Greek imports than might have been expected—perhaps it was the Phoenician trade at Vetulonia and Populonia which excluded the Greek latecomers. In the south, port towns whose names are known to us from literary sources have recently been excavated. Pyrgi (Santa Severa) was one of the ports of Caere. Graviscae, a Tarquinian port, was inhabited by Greeks from 600 to about 480 B.C. Cults to the Olympian gods—who would soon have a profound influence on Etruscan practices—were established in the sanctuaries connected with these harbor towns.[59] Inscribed dedications point to the worship of Aphrodite/Turan, Hera/Uni, and Demeter/Vei, as well as Apollo. Simple structures were at first grouped around a crude *naiskos,* or shrine; later, larger, more permanent buildings were arranged around an open square. Among the early votive offerings are some erotica as well as exotica, for instance, figurines and representations of a nude goddess. The cults of Turan at Graviscae and Uni/ Astarte at Pyrgi no doubt owe their inspiration to long-standing Levantine traditions of Astarte worship, which included the institution of sacred prostitution.[60] The worship of Hera and Demeter as goddesses concerned with women and the family seems to suggest a more permanent family character to the settlement and perhaps intermarriage of the Greek travelers with the Etruscan population.[61]

The majority of early Greek pottery imports (625–550 B.C.) at Graviscae are Ionian, but the site was quite cosmopolitan, judging from the names of those who inscribed dedications to the gods. Most graffiti, in the Ionic alphabet and dialect, are inscribed on Attic cups. These were made in large numbers from about 550 B.C. on, in both black- and red-figure styles. Etruscan dedications identify the goddesses involved. Some of the Greeks who offered gifts were Alexandros, Themistagoras, Eudemos (Attic?), Deliades, Lethaos, and Ublesios. Other worshippers were Paktyes, probably a Lydian, and Ombrikos (a Hellenized Umbrian?). The most famous Greek votary at Graviscae so far identified is Sostratos of Aegina, who dedicated a stone anchor to Apollo. This Sostratos is probably the same merchant mentioned by Herodotus (IV.152) as having traded with Tartessos in Spain.[62]

Graviscae's activities and imports correspond to developments in Tarquinia.[63] As a response to the influx of Greek goods, Tarquinia underwent a rapid Hellenization during the first quarter of the sixth century B.C. This process included production of Etrusco-Corinthian pottery and stone sculpture. Shortly thereafter the series of wall paintings in Tarquinian tombs began; these steadily increased in quantity and quality during the last decades of the sixth century. The presence of workshops established by Greek artisans, which was long assumed from a stylistic analysis of the paintings, was recently confirmed by the discovery of pigments among the offerings at Graviscae.[64] Upheavals in Persian-controlled Ionia apparently caused many professional artisans to flee to territories with Greek populations already catering to rich patrons.

The development of architectural terracottas has been attributed to growing relations between Etru-ria and the Peloponnese.[65] A significant school of Etrusco-Corinthian vase-painting at Tarquinia is also linked to Corinthian immigration.[66] At Caere, the itinerant Greek Aristonothos produced an interesting hybrid vase which depicts a naval battle (fig. III-3), now in the Louvre.[67] Ionian artists have been credited with the establishment of the later "Pontic" ceramic workshop at Vulci (figs. VIII-16, VIII-32) as well as with the production of the "Caeretan" hydriae (figs. IV-86–87). Etrusco-Corinthian, Pontic, and Caeretan fabrics have been found outside Etruria.[68] The largest numbers of Corinthian vases occur at Caere and Vulci, but many other cities, especially Tarquinia, made or received even larger amounts of local imitations of Corinthian wares. The available statistical evidence may show that emigrant Corinthian artists deliberately settled in cities which had little direct contact with Corinth, perhaps as political exiles seeking to hide their connection with the old regime.

The profound influence of foreign immigrants into Etruria as well as of Etruscan emigration is illustrated by the career of Lucumo, son of the Corinthian Demaratus, who, goaded by his Etruscan wife, moved to the more open society of Rome,

III-3. Naval battle on a vase signed by the Greek Aristonothos, Cerveteri. Ca. 670 B.C. Paris, Louvre. (Macnamara, *Everyday Life* fig. 86.)

where he became its king (Livy 1.34). Etruscan emigration is further implied by epigraphic evidence from Selinus in Sicily, such as a curse tablet of 500–475 B.C., which mentions a certain Turana. The name suggests she was an Etruscan woman who settled there.[69] In such places as the emporium quarter of Graviscae, foreign residents could mingle with Etruscans. Syncretism of Greek and Etruscan cults took place in sanctuaries established by immigrants, for example, at an extramural shrine built in the sixth century B.C. near Caere, which in the third century received Greek dedications to Hera.[70] Ionian influence seems clear in the choice of cults and myths designed to appeal to a heterogeneous population.[71]

The Etruscan aristocracy living in cities quickly assimilated many Greek customs. The Greek-style athletics depicted in the Tarquinian tombs and even earlier representations reflected real occasions. The Tomb of the Augurs, Tomb of the Olympic Games, and Tomb of the Chariots at Tarquinia, and the Tomb of the Monkey at Chiusi (in which was painted a monkey, no doubt imported) illustrate the stock program of Greek competition: boxing, wrestling, jumping, discus, javelin, and racing (cf. figs. IV-16, IV-30, VIII-23). Although technically related to Greek practice, these sports do not necessarily imply Etruscan acceptance of the spiritual and social ideal of the Greek athlete. In most cases, they were funeral games played by slaves or professional athletes as spectator sports before stands filled with noble men and women. Mixed in with these games were the darker activities of Phersu (fig. IV-48) connected with human sacrifice and with the Roman gladiatorial combats of a later period.

All these borrowings from Greek culture, sports, the hunt, and fine clothes, were aristocratic. The Greek legacy also had an impact on Etruscan weapons and warfare from about 650 B.C. until 400 B.C., as shown by Corinthian helmets, Argive shields, greaves, and the whole Greek panoply, Chalkidian and Ionian helmets. The tactics of warfare were adopted by Etruscan cities: the use of warships, cavalry organization, and the famous phalanx, a form of infantry formation. In many cases these tactics were passed on to their Italic neighbors.[72]

One of the principal Greek customs adopted by the Etruscan elite was that of banqueting on couches, with equipment of the type used at Greek symposia. During these parties the Etruscans used Greek vases for mixing and drinking wine and water in the Greek style. Etruscan copies of wine services, such as mixing bowls, table amphorae, water jars, and drinking cups, were made in large quantities in metal as well as pottery to meet a growing demand. Almost from the first contact with Ionian and Corinthian imports, the native Etruscan bucchero and impasto fabrics took on Greek shapes (see Ch. VIII).

In the sixth and early fifth centuries B.C., the tombs of Tarquinia, Caere, Vulci, and the other major cities were filled with great quantities of Rhodian, Corinthian, Ionian, Laconian, and (from about 500 B.C.) Attic vases. East Greek and Corinthian vases often must have served as containers for salves, perfumes, cosmetics, and condiments; others were intended for display or for use at table. The famous Chigi Vase found at Formello, a Corinthian olpe of about 650–625 B.C., is a masterpiece of early narrative painted in miniature style, which was surely purchased for its artistic value. The François Vase, a huge Attic crater from about 570–560 B.C., found near Chiusi, must have been sold as a conversation piece.[73] Panathenaic amphorae may have been heirlooms bought from the impoverished families of Greek athletes;[74] while Etruscans probably did travel to Athens, they were non-Greeks and would not have been allowed to compete in the games themselves. That traveling Etruscans did leave monuments in Greece, in the treasuries of Caere and Spina at Delphi, is attested by literary evidence.[75]

Special shapes, like the amphorae by the Athenian potter Nikosthenes, were produced especially for export to Etruria (fig. IV-80D). Their shapes imitated Italic or Etruscan ceramics; Etruscan kyathoi and kantharoi were also used as models by Greek potters.[76] Vases from the Perizoma Group produced from 530 B.C. onward portrayed athletes covered with white loincloths to satisfy the prudish Italian buyer.[77] The so-called Tyrrhenian and Pontic amphorae, made in Athens and Etruria, respectively,[78] are also indicative of the importance of foreign influence in the import and production of vases.

ETRUSCAN BUCCHERO EXPORTS: GREEK EXCHANGE OR ETRUSCAN PIRACY?

The Etruscan goods distributed throughout the sanctuaries and settlements of the major Greek cities are evidence of widespread trade. The finds, dating from the sixth century, differ from the eighth- and early seventh-century bronzes placed in the international sanctuaries in that they are mainly vases of bucchero, the majority of them those tall, two-handled cups which inspired the kantharoi of Athenian and Boeotian manufacture. Fragments of Etruscan bucchero have been found at nearly every major site except the international sanctuaries at Olympia, Delphi, Isthmia, and Nemea. The western colonies in Sicily yielded hundreds of examples; bucchero was also found in the cities of Magna Graecia and in the east.[79]

Even Athens imported Etruscan objects. The Athenian Acropolis produced part of a decorated bronze tripod from Vulci.[80] The Agora, however, has few examples of bucchero (what remains are mostly kantharoi),[81] for the bulk of Attic trade with Etruria seems to have occurred later than the production of bucchero. Attic vases of the later sixth and fifth centuries B.C. were therefore probably traded with other goods, like the Etruscan bronze utensils and candelabra admired by the Greeks.[82] The city of Vulci exported, within Italy and abroad, great numbers of tripods, spouted pitchers or Schnabelkannen (fig. III-4), and other high-quality utensils. Such exports were surely an economic advance over the export of partially smelted metal ores. The appliqué decoration in cast bronze on these utensils may have been derived from a Peloponnesian tradition, which would help to explain their popularity in Greece.[83]

The Laconian sanctuary at Amyklai and even the site of Vis in Dalmatia have fragments of Etruscan bucchero, as do Ithaca and Corfu.[84] The other Corinth-oriented site, Perachora, received kantharoi as part of its donations. Corinth has evidence of bucchero, almost exclusively kantharoi, in sanctuaries in the Forum and on Acrocorinth (sanctuary of Demeter and Kore), the Potters' Quarter, and on the site of what must have been an importer's shop on the Lechaion Road.[85] Two kantharoi, once vo-

tive offerings in a shrine in the Forum area, are incised with an Etruscan "A," as are many vases in Etruscan sanctuaries. It is tempting to interpret this mark as a dedication to the gods (Aiser), though others read it as a merchant's mark.[86]

The presence of bucchero in so many trading cities and its absence in the Panhellenic sanctuaries suggests the circulation of Etruscan merchants in ports from which their wares could be distributed commercially. We have noted that bucchero is missing from Olympia, Delphi, Isthmia, and Nemea. These sanctuaries were generally only visited for

III-4. Bronze "Schnabelkanne" from a tomb at Eygenbilsen. Sixth century B.C. Brussels, Musées Royaux d'Art et d'Histoire. (A.C.L.)

III-5. Bronze boat model from Sardinia, a type exported to Etruscan and Greek Italy. Seventh century B.C. 14.6 × 25.7 × 10.7 cm. Hirshhorn Museum and Sculpture Garden, Smithsonian Institution, Acc. HMSG 1966, 5348. (Museum photo.)

cult and athletic purposes, and while they did receive important foreign goods and donations, they did not attract bucchero tableware. Other types of Etruscan goods, such as fine bronzes, art objects, and the trophies of war—perhaps the donations of Italian travelers—do appear in these sanctuaries.

The phenomenal distribution of bucchero occurred during a brief but distinctive phase of Etruscan commerce and seems to lend credence to the Greek view of Etruscans as very active, and unwelcome, seafarers. The Greek competition called them pirates; this definition seems to have denoted any power able to compete for the markets of the Mediterranean.[87] Apparently any seafarer could be a pirate if the opportunity presented itself. The Etruscan merchantman, according to representations on seventh- and sixth-century vases, had a fighting deck and crew of marines to protect its cargo (fig. III-3). The Etruscans even had a specially designed merchantman with a massive spur set above its round, galley-like bow to prevent warships from coming close enough to ram.[88]

Greek jealousy would also have been fueled by military and naval incidents such as the battle over the Corsican site of Alalia in 535 B.C., in which a combined fleet of Carthaginian and Etruscan, especially Caeretan, vessels drove out the Phocaean Greek colonists in order to preserve their own spheres of influence in the Tyrrhenian. The Phocaeans were legendary sailors and merchants; their competition with the Etruscans in the west may have colored their accounts of the conflict. According to Herodotus (I.166.1–I.167.2), the Caeretans stoned to death some Phocaean prisoners after the engagement; this act precipitated divine retribution until the Caeretan citizenry made amends according to the terms of a Delphic oracle.

Greeks were thus expelled from Corsica, which was then left open to Etruscan cultural dominance; at the same time the Carthaginians consolidated their control over southern and eastern Sardinia. Sardinian trade with Etruria is suggested by sporadic finds of beautifully made native, nuragic bronze ornaments, for example, the boat models in tombs at Vetulonia and Vulci[89] (fig. III-5). Such a boat model shows that Pithekoussai, too, had early dealings with Sardinia.[90] At the beginning of the fifth century B.C., the Phocaean exile Dionysius settled navy crews in Sicily and staged pirate raids on Etruscan and Carthaginian shipping.[91]

Etruscan interests certainly must have clashed with those of the Greek colonists of Sicily and Magna Graecia (Map 3); in the battle of Cumae in 474 B.C. (Diodorus II.51.2), the Etruscans were defeated by Greeks led by Hieron of Syracuse. Some helmets then taken from the Etruscan marines were sent to the sanctuary of Zeus at Olympia with the dedication:

Hieron the Deinomenid and the Syracusans,
to Zeus, the Etruscan [spoils] from Cumae.[92]

Pindar (*Pythian* I.71–75) commemorated the victory of the Sicilian dynasty over both the Etruscans and the Carthaginians, implying that they were closely allied: "I beseech you to grant, son of Kronos, that the battle-cry of the Phoenicians and Etruscans will stay tamely at home, now that they have seen that their insolence was disastrous to them at Cumae. They suffered so much being vanquished by the ruler of the Syracusans, their strong men cast off from their swift ships into the sea, delivering Greece from harsh bondage." Even later, when the Etruscan cities were consolidating their forces to confront problems within Italy, Greek leaders engaged in their own pirate raids on the coastal towns in Etruria. Such an expedition, led by the tyrant Dionysius of Syracuse in 384 B.C., destroyed the sanctuary at Pyrgi. Perhaps this attack led to the burial (and eventual preservation) of the gold plaques found between two temples (figs. III-6; VII-12) discussed below.

ARCHAIC EXCHANGE WITH IBERIA AND GAUL

The wide-ranging Etruscan contacts of the sixth century B.C. also reached the western Mediterranean and Punic North Africa (Map 9). Bucchero ware was distributed to the Greek coastal cities of Spain and France and traveled inland, up the river valleys, to the Hallstatt princes of Gaul and to the societies of Spanish Tartessos, which were rich in silver and gold. Excavations at Ampurias, an ancient Emporion (north of Barcelona), show a varied trade, including bucchero cups, coarse amphorae presumably containing wine, and even an earlier

item, an Italic fibula of the so-called *navicella* type.[93] Other Spanish sites, native towns rather than Greek colonies, also show evidence of Etruscan commerce, particularly in the second and third quarters of the sixth century.[94] Even Etrusco-Corinthian pottery reached these towns, where real Corinthian ware does not appear in great quantity and local imitations of Etruscan wares were produced.[95] Interest continued in the Classical period. Etruscan bronzes have been identified at Ampurias: an engraved mirror and a fragmentary utensil decorated with a lion's head.[96] Reverse contacts with native Iberia (outside the Punic sphere) are suggested by sporadic finds in Etruria, such as the Iberian painted jars now in the Grosseto museum.[97] Precious metals must have made the trade worthwhile for the Etruscans; these are, of course, no longer identifiable in the archaeological record.

In Gaul, initial contacts seem to have occurred even before the Greek colonization of Marseille. Etruscan bronzes—fibulae, basins, and "Rhodian-type" oinochoai,[98] all of them prestige objects—were found mainly in tombs, and are contemporaneous with the imported seventh- to early sixth-century Greek ceramics at the site, such as "Ionian" cups, "Rhodian" skyphoi, and Early and Middle Corinthian wares. Such vases reflect the Greek custom of drinking wine, newly introduced in Etruria, and a concerted commercial effort on the part of Greek traders. Large Etruscan amphorae also appear in the sites of early contact in the Bouches du Rhône, Herault, Aude, and such towns as Marseille and La Liquière.[99] Celtic Gaul to the north, in what is now France and southwest Germany, likewise experienced Etruscan influence. Numerous bronzes, many of them small, from Villanovan razors and Italic fibulae to bronze vessels, were placed as prestige gifts in the tombs of Hallstatt princes.[100] Items of interest to Etruscans were probably such resources as Atlantic tin, local iron, and Baltic amber to be obtained through the interior of Gaul.

By 575 B.C. masses of bucchero kantharoi, oinochoai, and cups appear at Marseille and throughout southern Gaul in the Midi.[101] Whole cargoes of Etruscan amphorae were found at numerous sites in the interior and, as mentioned earlier, in wrecks off the coast from Cap d'Antibes to Ampurias. The most characteristic archaeological evidence for this stage of commerce are the shipwrecks, such as those at Bon Porte (two), Pointe du Dattier, and Cap d'Antibes.[102] The first three contained Etruscan amphorae associated with Ionian pottery, while the Antibes wreck held some Archaic Greek amphorae, about two hundred Etruscan amphorae neatly stacked in the hold, at least sixty-five bucchero kantharoi and oinochoai, vases of plain Etruscan and Etrusco-Corinthian fabrics, and a Punic lamp set.[103] It has been suggested that the cargo was loaded at Vulci and destined for the prosperous commercial city at Saint-Blaise. There the imports and their chronology show that most of the goods (including Greek products) must have been supplied by Etruscan shipping; Saint-Blaise declined and failed when Marseille, with her Greek trading partners, was founded in 600 B.C. and won over the old markets.[104]

Marseille entered the competition for Gallic markets when Greek and Etruscan goods were already penetrating far inland. Limited excavations at the port have revealed bucchero pottery, especially kantharoi, as well as the distinctive Etruscan micaceous-fabric amphorae. Soon after the establishment of the colony, Etruscan imports diminished, but until about 400 B.C., these imports, especially bronze vases for wine service, still reached the north, probably through the river valleys: goods crossed the Alps via the Po Valley, for example, perhaps to bypass Greek Marseille. Etruscan commerce was dealt several more blows: the battle of Cumae in 474 B.C. may have sealed its fate in the western Mediterranean as well as in the Tyrrhenian Sea by establishing Greek naval supremacy; at the same time French wine production may have driven out Etruscan imports. The Gallic invasions in Italy caused further setbacks for the Etruscan industries. After 400 B.C. Etruscan trade in Gaul and Greek-dominated Spain was, at best, sporadic.

CARTHAGE: PUNIC RELATIONS WITH ETRURIA

The other great power on the western Mediterranean, Carthage, QRTḤDŠT, one of the many

"New Cities" established by the Phoenicians, was ideally situated to dominate the commerce of North Africa, Italy, and the west (Map 9). By 800 B.C.[105] Carthage was functioning as a typical Phoenician *comptoir* engaged in the role of middleman for raw commodities and luxuries, as well as manufacturing its own small trade goods for local sales. By 600 B.C. Punic goods appeared in many parts of the Mediterranean, and secondary colonies had been established by Carthage itself, especially in Spain, the Balearic Islands, and Sardinia. Two early colonies were Mogador (off the Atlantic coast of Morocco) and the Balearic island of Ibiza. Neither site has produced evidence of direct Etruscan trade, for these and most of the western Punic colonies were dominated by a strict Carthaginian monop-

III-6. Plaque from Pyrgi with Phoenician (or Punic?) inscription. Gold. Ca. 500 B.C. (Pallottino, *Saggi di Antichità* 629–30, fig. 40.)

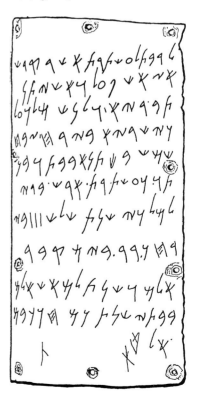

oly.[106] Few typically Punic products are found outside of Punic settlements, for the objects that appealed to their trading partners were Phoenician-
style luxuries, as well as raw commodities that have
left no traces.[107]

The most telling items of evidence of Punic involvement in Etruscan commerce are, of course, the
plaques from the sanctuary at Pyrgi (figs. III-6,
VII-12). These three gold plaques once decorated
an important offering in the seashore shrine of the
goddess Uni, attached to the port of Pyrgi, in Caeretan territory. Greek sources identify the shrine as
one famous in antiquity, sacred to Ino or Leukothea.[108] Excavation has uncovered a complex of two
temples, one a Greek-style peripheral construction
of the later sixth century, the other an Italic building
with triple cella erected in the fifth century B.C.
Both were elaborately decorated (see Ch. V).[109]
Evidently, after a Greek raid had destroyed the
sanctuary (probably in 384 B.C.), the three plaques
were collected from the ruins and carefully buried
to prevent further sacrilege. (They were discovered
by excavators in 1964.) One plaque has a Phoenician
inscription; the other two are engraved in Etruscan,
the longer one carrying a paraphrase of the Semitic
text.[110] The Phoenician version has lent itself to a
more complete translation than the Etruscan paraphrase:

> To the Lady Astarte this is the holy place
> which has made and given
> Tiberie Vel(ia)nas ruler over
> Kisry—in the month of the sacrifice
> of the sun as a gift in the temple and
> because Astarte has supported him by her hand[?]
> in the third year 3 of his reign in the month
> of Karar on the day of the burying
> of the god—and [may] the years of the statue of the
>   goddess
> in her temple be as many years as these
> stars.[111]

Some scholars maintain that the inscription represents a Punic or western Phoenician dialect, rather
than the Phoenician of the Levant. Historically, it
is tempting to interpret the inscription as evidence
of Punic, specifically Carthaginian, activity at Caere,
since there is little evidence of traditional Phoenician imports by this time, the early fifth century
B.C. The plaques appear to commemorate a dona-
tion made by the Etruscan ruler (*malik* in Phoenician, *zilac* to the Etruscans) of Kisry, that is, Caere.
The formula for the date seems Oriental in style,
as is the name of the goddess—called Astarte in the
Phoenician text and Uni/Astarte (Unialastres) in
Etruscan. The bilingual text may have been
intended as propaganda, to illustrate the gratitude
of the Caeretans for the presence of Punic or
Phoenician merchants on their shores as well as the
piety of the Phoenician travelers, famed for their
participation in the local cults when away from
home.[112] There is evidence of such cooperation at
Greek shrines in Cyprus;[113] an example nearer to
Etruria is the cult of Venus Erycina on Eryx, in the
Phoenician sector of Sicily.[114] According to some
scholars, a coup, assisted by a Carthaginian navy,
might have placed Thefarie Velianas in power: his
position could then be described as being "supported" by the hand of Astarte.[115] There is, however, no historical evidence of any Punic meddling
in Etruscan politics. On the other hand, the inscriptions serve as proof of the existence of a Semitic—
either Punic or Phoenician—commercial *comptoir* at
the port of Pyrgi, which would have called for a
bilingual Phoenician scribe. Such a scribe would
have been the engraver of the plaque. Excavations
might eventually uncover evidence for this type
of interaction at the nearby site of Punicum, known
to us only from literary sources. The date of the
plaques, about 500 B.C., shortly before the battle of
Cumae, shows the late Archaic period to have been
one of close involvement between Carthaginians
and Etruscans and of fierce competition (and piracy) with the Greeks.

These naval encounters highlight the problem of
our knowledge of the Carthaginian-Etruscan alliance: the lack of literary sources. The archaeological
record alone can never provide evidence of official
alliances. A few sources have survived. Aristotle
in the *Politics* (3.5.10–11) refers to treaties pledging
"mutual friendship" between Carthage and the
Etruscan cities made for the sake of commerce and
mutual assistance in emergencies:

A state is not set up merely for the sake of trade and commercial relations. For if that were so, the Etruscans and
Carthaginians and all those who have agreements [*symbola*]
with each other would be like the citizens of a single state.

At any rate, they have contracts concerning imports and agreements about not offending each other, and treaties concerning military alliance; but they do not have common officials appointed over all, but different ones for each, nor does either group concern itself with the quality of the other's citizens, whether anyone in the states under agreement is dishonest or behaves immorally, but only that the states do not wrong each other.

No Etruscan treaties, either of Aristotle's time or earlier, have survived, nor is it known which Etruscan cities signed them. Some circumstantial information is provided in the treaties recorded by Polybius (3.22.4–13) for Carthage and Rome. When Rome, having just overthrown the monarchy (about 510 B.C.), was in no position to bargain for terms, the military and commercial monopolies of Carthage covered almost all of the Mediterranean except for Latium.[116] Alliances between Carthage and the powerful Etruscan cities must have allowed a greater sphere for Etruscan trade; they need not have mentioned the military aggression feared by Rome.

Etruscan exports did not reach the Punic way stations of Ibiza in Spain and North Africa west of Utica; these were almost certainly Punic monopolies protected by the lost treaties. An early legendary clash between some Etruscan sailors and a Punic fleet (Diodorus Siculus 5.19–20 and Pseudo-Aristotle 84.3–5) ended in the diplomatic withdrawal of the Etruscans and the founding of a Punic colony, suggesting that some previous agreement, like the *symbola* of Aristotle, was in operation. The Etruscan-Carthaginian trade agreements evidently survived because they were mutually profitable; each side dealt in different commodities and markets or in materials which complemented each other, such as perhaps tin from Spain and copper from Italy. Etruscan imports found in Carthage itself include bucchero, bronzes, and Etrusco-Corinthian vases.[117] An enigmatic ivory plaque of unknown date with an Etruscan inscription suggests the presence of Etruscan metics, resident merchants, in the city: "Mi puinel karthazie . . . elsph . . . na" ("I belong to Puina of Carthage[?]").[118]

Other parts of the Punic commercial empire also received Etruscan cargoes.[119] Utica, a Phoenician colony older than neighboring Carthage but ultimately dependent upon it, has some bucchero

III-7. "Genucilia" plate from a Punic tomb, Malta. 500–400 B.C. Ashmolean Museum, Oxford, Acc. 1878.146. (Museum photo.)

vases.[120] From Gunugu, Algeria, comes an inscription, probably in the Etruscan language, on a bronze disc which reads: "gunigun . . . larthal."[121] Malta, the site of a strategic Punic colony, has provided an unusual assortment of Etruscan objects, among them three bronzes, one "Genucilia" plate, a simple painted plate of the fourth or third century B.C. (fig. III-7), and an Etruscan ivory, a thin plaque carved with a couchant boar, undoubtedly part of a small ivory-covered box.[122]

Other Punic colonies also acquired Etruscan goods. The Phoenician (later Punic) sphere of Sardinia traded with Etruria. The recently excavated city of Motya, a Phoenician foundation that came under Carthaginian domination, was a large and thriving commercial center, situated, in typical Punic fashion, on a small island off the Sicilian coast, where space problems were solved by "skyscraper" constructions of several stories. Also in Punic tradition, the town supported a tophet, a special cemetery for the burials of children and small animals sacrificed in religious ritual.

Phoenico-Punic religion differed radically from the cults of Greece and Italy, for it involved human sacrifice. The sacrifice of children was an extreme version of the concept of offering first fruits to a god, in this case Baal Hammon (Moloch to the ancient Israelites). At certain times, small animals could be substituted for firstborn children (a practice called *molchomor*). Frequently, offerings of simple Punic objects—ornaments, vases or figurines—were deposited with the remains.[123]

There are numerous examples, whole and fragmentary, of Etruscan bucchero pottery (often kantharoi) from the residential areas of Motya, as well as from the regular cemetery and the tophet.[124] An uncommon find from an overflow cemetery sited

on the mainland (Lilybaion) is a large, hollow terracotta head, molded with heavy features representing the face of a man with bobbed hair,[125] evidently
the cover of a cinerary urn like those from Chiusi.[126]
It is difficult to imagine why or how such a strictly
Etruscan object came to be imported and used for
its proper function in the Semitic settlement. Either
an Etruscan resident of Motya was buried in his
own peculiar fashion or a Punic citizen purchased
the unusual container from nearby Etruria.

Etruscans, Greeks, and Carthaginians fought
among themselves for their various commercial interests in the course of the fifth century, as commerce continued at a high level. The manufactured
goods that accompanied the exchange of essential
commodities now changed in character. Bucchero
and Corinthian and Ionian ceramics went out of
fashion and were superseded by bronze utensils
from Etruria and Attic vases from Greece. Punic
merchants found markets for their products in the
eastern Mediterranean as well as the west, as attested by recent finds of Punic amphorae in Olympia and Corinth.[127] The Levantine merchant became
a familiar figure in the classical world. He was often
satirized, as in an Etruscan class of comic vases, the
Bruschi Group of Tarquinia, molded in double-
headed caricatures, of which one side represents a
Semitic man's head (fourth century B.C.).[128]

ATTIC EXPORTS TO ETRURIA

Attic black-figure vases reached Etruria and other
areas by a trade route which ran from Reggio along
the Tyrrhenian coast to Marseille. These vase imports peaked about 525–500 B.C.,[129] while the number in Taranto peaked earlier, for they seem to have
arrived along a different route.

The most important evidence of a profound foreign influence on fifth- and fourth-century Etruscan
art was that of Attic red-figure vases. Great numbers were imported to Etruscan cities. Although
Greek imports declined in the fifth century, perhaps
indicating a decline in Etruscan shipping, there
was still much wealth in Etruria to be exchanged
for manufactured products.[130] Etruscan buyers also
seem to have had specific tastes in artists, judging
from the radically varying quantities of different

Attic workshops whose products were found in the
tombs of Vulci, Caere, and Tarquinia.[131] These were
obviously expensive vases, the best available. The
red-figure Attic crater signed by Euphronios may
have been placed in the tomb together with another
masterpiece by the same artist, a cup now in the
J. Paul Getty Museum. The crater's huge size presumably appealed to its ancient buyer as much as its
style does to us today.

Some transport amphorae actually have Attic
graffiti identifying their contents[132] as olive oil. So
great was the demand for Attic goods that an Adriatic port including Greek and Etruscan settlers
and Italic natives was opened, at the site of modern
Spina, apparently to deal with the trade with Athens. Huge quantities of fifth-century Attic red-
figure ware came from its cemeteries; more must
have been shipped overland through the river valleys to the interior, possibly as far as the Tyrrhenian
coast. There must have been close contact between
the suppliers in Athens and the merchants at Spina,
for the graves at Spina show a high proportion of
Attic stemmed plates and beaked jugs—shapes
known to be favorites of the native Italic fabrics.[133]
Adria, to the north of Spina, though less well
known, was also an important port. The site of
Marzabotto, which opened an iron foundry, must
have played a role in the distribution of commercial
goods, not only from the Adriatic, but also to the
north.[134]

Despite the politically turbulent times of the fifth
century B.C., vases decorated by the Meidias Painter
are also well represented among Greek imports into
Etruria. Vases have been found in two tombs at
Populonia; another, depicting the myth of Pelops
and Hippodameia, was buried at Arezzo. The influence of his style, characterized by windblown hair,
light drapery, and emotionally charged figures, can
be detected in subsequent Etruscan art, even in
monumental sculpture.[135] Moreover, local imitations of Greek wares were often the product of
schools inspired by immigrant Greek artists. Such
was the fifth-century group named for Arnth Prax-
ias.[136] Artists who emigrated from the Greek mainland about 400 B.C. seem to have been responsible
for the origin of several schools: the Falerii Group
of Dispater, in the Meidias tradition, and, at Cer-

veteri, the mid-fourth-century Group of Sokra.[137]
During the fourth century, Etruscan artists (and
probably merchants in general) looked to the colonies, especially Tarentum and Syracuse, rather than
the Greek homeland.[138] Schools of vase painting
dependent upon south Italian models or even artists
were formed at Vulci, Chiusi, Perugia, and Volterra, as well as in the Faliscan territory.

NORTHERN CONTACTS

Beginning with the late sixth century, the Etruscan
north developed into a commercially influential
area, for it was through this region that trade was
channeled into Illyria and central and eastern Europe (Map 3). The colony at Marzabotto was probably just one of many new foundations of the late
sixth and fifth centuries oriented toward the Cisal-
pine native trade. The material culture of the native
settlements north of Italy manifests Etruscan contacts through its imported pottery and bronzes.
The Po Valley, with its center at Bologna (Felsina),
was Etruscanized after its Villanovan phase. Livy
reports that twelve cities were founded here, as in
Etruria proper (5.33.9). Farther to the east, but in
frequent contact with Bologna, the culture of the
situla people—profoundly influenced by Etruscan
contacts—covered a large area, including northeast-
ern Italy (the Veneto and the Po Valley), the Alps,
and the Transalpine territory now included in modern Austria and Yugoslavia. Commerce took place
on a regular basis, perhaps organized by merchants
of the territory of Chiusi.[139] The principal object
of this trade was surely Baltic amber, found in huge
quantities in Etruscan tombs of the eighth century
and later.[140] Imports included the custom of wine
drinking with its paraphernalia, furniture for banqueting, sports, costumes, and the motifs used in
the bronze situlae which recorded such fashions in
reliefs of genre scenes.[141]

Etruscan elements in northern arms and armor
represented on situlae provide evidence of military
influence on the situla people.[142] Military traffic in
this northern corridor worked two ways, as Arruns,
the king of Chiusi, learned when he imported Gallic
mercenaries from the north. Although they out-

lived their usefulness to him, they were not willing
to leave the good life of Italy and so turned on their
Etruscan masters.[143]

The runic alphabet of northern Europe descends
from north Etruscan alphabets used in rural settlements and river valley trade routes.[144] A few Etruscan inscriptions are known from northern localities
such as Liguria, Genoa, and Nice. From Piacenza
comes an inscribed bronze model liver for use in
divination (see Ch. VII).

From Etruscan centers like Vulci and Chiusi
came small items of jewelry, pottery, and bronze
utensils: local imitations followed. But the bulk of
the trade goods seems to be missing from the archaeological record. Metals may have been
involved; another likely commodity is salt, shipped
through cities like Bologna and then along the Po
Valley.[145]

Etruscan culture had a great impact on its northern neighbors. The runic alphabets of Germany and
Scandinavia, certain styles of dress of Illyria and
beyond, and furniture, arms, and symbols of power
(e.g. the use of the *lituus*) originated with the
Etruscans. Even the German term for metal, *Erz,*
may well depend upon the original commerce of
the northern tribes with the Etruscan metallurgists
of Arezzo. Finally, the beginnings of the development of the city itself, and of an urban society, is
linked to the lessons learned by these peoples from
their prestigious Etruscan mentors.[146]

II. Fourth Century B.C. and Later

CONTACTS WITH GREEKS

Direct commercial dealings with Greece declined in
the fourth century: organized trade seems almost
to have been supplanted by the raids of Greek pirates or tyrants on the Tyrrhenian coast.[147] The for-
tunes of the Greek settlement and sanctuary at
Graviscae reflect the general climate for foreign
enterprise in Etruria during the fourth and third
centuries B.C. During that time, no dedications
seem to have been made by Greeks. The sanctuary
took on an Etruscan character, as the site became
integrated into the city plan. The few dedications

were poor and generally made by the lower classes, judging from the inscribed names. (One dedication is in Latin: "T. Gavio[s] c. f.")[148] In nearby Caere, however, there were still Greek residents, who in the third century made offerings to Uni/Hera in the old sanctuary. These third-century dedications seem to support the ancient tradition that Caere (known as Agylla to the Greeks) maintained a strong Philhellenic tradition. At Vulci, a fifth-century Attic kylix inscribed to Hera (in an Ionian dialect) may indicate a Greek cult in Etruria.[149] A few tokens of Etruscan trade in the fourth century, mainly bronze vessels and utensils,[150] are found in mainland Greece, at Dodona and Olympia.

While the Etruscans may have contributed some features to the *koine* of Hellenistic art, extensive borrowing from the Greeks also took place. Some classes of objects found in the tombs of Etruria, also occur at Cyprus, Macedonia, and further north.[151] Areas that were politically Greek during the Hellenistic period also seem to have received Etruscan curiosities: an Etruscan hand mirror[152] and the Zagreb mummy, whose linen shroud, inscribed with an Etruscan ritual text, is now in Zagreb, Yugoslavia.[153] The circumstances of the shroud's journey to Egypt in antiquity are not known; analysis of the textile might shed more light on the Etruscan linen industry.[154] Hellenized southern Russia also received a few Etruscan objects in the fourth and third centuries B.C.[155] When the various fabrics of Italian black-glaze ware are fully documented, they may offer interesting evidence on the range of later Etruscan commerce.[156]

PUNIC CONTACTS

Punic connections with Etruria seem to continue, though at a low level, throughout the fourth and third centuries. Trade goods are only now beginning to be identified, especially Punic amphorae (as at the site of Roselle[157]) and coins (both at the Caeretan port site of Punta della Vipera and at Sesto Fiorentino[158]). A most unusual find is a terracotta grotesque mask (cf. fig. III-8) found in a typically Etruscan burial of the third century B.C. at Spina.[159] Also in the tomb were terracotta masks or

III-8. Grotesque mask from Carthage, a typical Punic cult object. Terracotta. Sixth(?) century B.C.

protomes in the shape of Archaic female heads, of a type known in Etruria and east Greece, particularly Rhodes, and especially popular in Punic cemeteries and *tophets*. The clay is local, but the style of the grotesque mask, with its distorted and disproportionate features, is not Italic. It is similar to Punic grotesque masks from Iberian sites, such as Jerez, near Cadiz.[160] The mask from Spina remains an enigma. Its use in the burial might even suggest the presence of a foreign resident or of Punic merchants or prospectors with Spanish connections traveling the Adriatic during the beginning of hostilities between Carthage and Rome. The rare Etruscan goods in Punic contexts of the fourth and later centuries include a few Caeretan Genucilia plates from Carthage and Malta and some bronzes from Punic tombs in Malta.[161]

Relations between Carthage and Etruria are strikingly illustrated by three sarcophagi with almost identical effigies on their lids (cf. fig. III-9). Two were excavated in Carthaginian family tombs, the third in the large tomb of the Partiunu family outside Tarquinia.[162] All three are of Greek island marble. Each of the triangular, roof-shaped lids bears a portrait, in low relief, of a mature bearded man. One arm is raised in salute, a small covered dish is in his left hand. He wears a long, heavy robe with a ropelike stole over one shoulder, sandals with thick soles, and a large plain earring. This type of figure occurs elsewhere in Punic and Phoenician art: the venerable man is a priest or special votary, his hand raised in supplication.[163] In some represen-

III-9. Priest's sarcophagus from a tomb at Carthage. Marble. Fourth century B.C. Paris, Louvre, Inv. 71 En. 3794. (Museum photo.)

tations, the object held in his hand is not a dish, but a small child, about to be sacrificed according to Punic rites.

The sarcophagus in Tarquinia was originally decorated with painted scenes of Achilles sacrificing a prisoner and of an Amazonomachia; the name of the deceased, Laris Partiunu, was painted in Etruscan letters.[164] Though this "priest"'s sarcophagus had been disturbed by thieves when excavated in 1876, it still contained a human skeleton. The single tomb chamber contained fourteen sarcophagi and one urn in all; besides that of Laris Partiunu, only two were of white marble: one was carved with the effigy of the so-called Magnate, or "Official," rendered in flamboyant Etruscan style (fig. III-10).

Two other "priest" sarcophagi came from chamber tombs excavated in the Bordj-Djedid necropolis of Carthage in 1902.[165] One, in the Musée National at Carthage, contained a skeleton embalmed in resin and a wooden staff. This sarcophagus was associated with another fine marble effigy, of a "priestess," a young woman depicted in the vulture-wing costume typical of representations of the goddess Isis. The lower portion of the man's sarcophagus was decorated with simple black-and-red designs like those of Greek architectural terracottas. The tomb is dated by vases to the third century B.C. The third "priest"'s sarcophagus, now in the Louvre (fig. III-9), was found in another Carthaginian tomb. It, too, contained a resin-embalmed body, together with jewelry and coins of the third century B.C. The painted ornament on this sarcophagus was similar to that of the other Punic sarcophagus. The Bordj-Djedid cemetery, which held other burials of priests or "Rabs," was perhaps reserved for the use of these Punic political cult officials.

All three sarcophagi almost certainly were made of marble from the same Greek island source as that of a number of sarcophagi of the fifth through third centuries B.C., distributed across the Mediterranean.[166] Many, like these three, were carved by Greek or Greek-trained artisans, in formats related to the areas in which they were used, for example, anthropoid sarcophagi in Phoenico-Punic areas like Cadiz and Cyprus. Roughed-out sarcophagi, in different shapes but of the same material, reached the Black Sea, Cadiz, Malta, Sicily, Egypt, Cyprus, and the Levantine coast in the fifth and fourth cen-

III-10. Sarcophagus of Velthur Partunus, the "Magnate," Tarquinia. Marble. 300–270 B.C. (Alinari.)

turies B.C. There is evidence to suggest that specific orders were sent to the Greek quarries so that customers' local traditions of format could be provided and the goods shipped safely. It is tempting to assume that Punic intermediaries were responsible for this trade.

Why did the Etruscan magistrates select a Punic type of effigy? Did Laris Partiunu have some interest in Carthaginian ritual? Since Tarquinia was a mercantile center, Partiunu's family may have had commercial ties with, or have actually resided in, Punic territory. Possibly migrant artisans had left Punic employ to go to Etruria during the third century, during which the two Punic wars with Rome were waged.

In the later Classical period and the Hellenistic

era, trade relations and shipping slackened. Though the Etruscans were not restricted to their homeland, their later ventures were not particularly commercial. Etruscan nationals hired themselves out as mercenary soldiers, as we know from historical accounts. Thucydides (6.103.2) records the part played by Etruscan mercenaries in the disastrous Sicilian expedition sent from Athens in 415 (414–413) B.C. Etruscan mercenaries fought on both sides in the war between Carthage and the Sicilian Greeks.[167] A Sicilian coin type of the time of Timoleon (about 344–339 B.C.) overstruck with the legend Tyrrhe (TYPPH) might perhaps be a payment token for Etruscans in the employ of Carthage or of Dionysius of Syracuse.[168] An inscription in a tomb at Tarquinia mentions the participation of an Etruscan in the Punic wars in Italy: Felsnas Larth, who died at the age of 106, may have fought on the side of Hannibal (*hanipaluscle*), perhaps in 216 B.C.[169] These later mercenary associations were probably not official in the political sense, although they must have originated in and fostered a sense of international consciousness. At various times during the Second Punic War, Etruscan cities chose to rebel against Rome and side with Carthage, in hopes of acquiring their autonomy under Punic rule. As a result of the unsuccessful outcome of Roman political conflicts (see Ch. II), Etruscan colonists or exiles, perhaps from Chiusi, may have been forced to settle in the farming hinterland of Carthage in about 82 B.C. On three boundary markers from Bir Mcherga, Tunisia, the phrase "Tul. Dardanium," written in late Etruscan script, has been interpreted as designating their boundary (*tular*).[170] By the first century B.C., both Etruscan and Carthaginian autonomy was over. The new power of Rome had incorporated the cosmopolitan inquiring spirit of the Etruscans and their complex system of commerce and alliance.

Notes

1. A full account and the most recent bibliography can now be found in M. Cristofani, *Gli Etruschi del Mare* (Milan 1983).

2. See V. Tusa, "La statuetta fenicia del Museo Nazionale di Palermo," *RSF* 1 (1973) 173–79 for evidence of this primacy (the so-called Melkart of Sciacca). Greek historians claimed that Sicily was frequented by Phoenicians before the time of Greek colonization: see Thucydides VI.2; Diodorus Siculus V.35.5. On the background of Phoenician expansion in the West, see B.W. Truemann, "West-Phoenician Presence on the Iberian Peninsula," *The Ancient World* 1:1 (1978) 15–31.

3. B. Peckham, *Orientalia* 41 (1972) 457–68, with earlier references.

4. W. Culican, "Almuñecar, Assur and Phoenician Penetration of the Western Mediterranean," *Levant* 2 (1970) 28–36; P.G. Warden, "The Colline Metallifere: Prolegomenon to the Study of Mineral Exploitation in Central Italy," *Crossroads*. It will soon, we hope, be possible to chart Etruscan contacts in the Mediterranean, as Phoenician contacts are being charted (supra, Map 9); meanwhile, for the distribution of Etruscan bucchero and amphorae, see M. Cristofani and M. Gras, in *Gli Etruschi. Una nuova immagine* (Florence 1984) 91–93.

5. See Harden, *Phoenicians* 158ff. The Bible refers to Phoenicians as purveyors of silver, tin, iron, lead (from Tarshish), and gold, silver, ivory, and peacocks (perhaps from North Africa): *Ezekiel* 27.12. The Phoenicians of Ezekiel are Tyrians; traders described by Greeks are usually Sidonians. Homer characterizes them as kidnappers and traders in silver bowls: *Iliad* 23.741ff. and *Odyssey* 4.615 and 15.115, 14.288f. and 15.415ff.

6. On Phoenician bowls, see A. Rathje, "Oriental Imports in Etruria in the Eighth and Seventh Centuries B.C.: Their Origins and Implications," in *IBR* 145–83, esp. 152ff.; B. Grau-Zimmermann, "Phönikische Metallkannen in den Orientalisierenden Horizonten des Mittelmeerraumes," *MadrMitt* 19 (1978) 161–218; cf. M.G. Guzzo Amadasi, *Le iscrizioni fenicie e puniche delle colonie in Occidente* (Rome 1967) 157f.; P. Fronzaroli in *StEtr* 39 (1971) 313–31; D. Ridgway, *Archaeological Reports 1973–74*, 54f. fig. 18; P. Zancani Montuoro, *ASMG* 11–12 (1970–71) 9–33; and Culican, *Levant* 2 (1970) 28–36.

7. See Rathje, "Oriental Imports," 150–52 fig. II. On Egyptian material in Etruria, see G. Hölbl, "Beziehungen der ägyptischen Kultur zu Altitalien," *Mitt. der Österr. Arbeitsgemeinschaft für Ur- und Frühgeschichte* 28 (1978) 13–22; and *Etudes préliminaires aux religions orientales dans l'Empire Romain* 62:1 (Leiden 1979).

8. See S. Bosticco, *ParPass* 12 (1957) 218ff.; H. Hencken, *Tarquinia, Villanovans and Early Etruscans* (1968) 366f.; E. Schiapparelli, *MonAnt* 8 (1898) 89–99; E. Gabrici, *NSc* (1941) 284–85. On chronology for Bocchoris, see L. Byvanck-Quarles van Ufford, *BABesch* 39 (1964) 63–73.

9. Rathje, "Oriental Imports," 174, 176; Torelli, "Un uovo di struzzo dipinto conservato nel Museo di Tarquinia," *StEtr* 33 (1965) 329–65; M. Astruc, "Traditions funéraires de Carthage," *Cahiers de Byrsa* 6 (1956) 29–81; "Supplément aux fouilles de Gouraya," *Libyca* 2 (1954) 9–48; "Exotisme et localisme, études sur les coquilles d'oeufs d'autriche décorées d'Ibiza," *Archivo de Prehistoria Levantina* 6 (1957) 47–112; E. Acquaro, "Uova di struzzo dipinte da Bithia," *Oriens Antiquus* 20 (1981) 57–65.

10. On the incense trade, see G.W. van Beek, *BiblArch* 23 (1960) 70–95 and *JAOS* 78 (1958) 141–52; M. Passerini, *StEtr* 8 (1934) 329–30; CIBA *Medical Biology and Etruscan Origins* (1958) 71–72.

11. Ivory in the form of a tusk was found in a tomb at Vetulonia: see Y. Huls, *Ivoires d'Etrurie* (Brussels 1957) 208.

12. Rathje, "Oriental Imports" 166ff.

13. Cf. Steingräber, *Etruskische Möbel* 84ff. and *passim*; see review by J. MacIntosh Turfa, *Gnomon* 53 (1981) 717–19; C.B. Curri, *StEtr* 47 (1979) 263–80.

14. Brown, *Etruscan Lion* 20; S. Moscati, "Centri artigianali fenici in Italia," *RSF* 1 (1973) 37–52; M. Cristofani Martelli, "Documenti di arte orientalizzante da Chiusi," *StEtr* 41 (1973) 97–120, esp. 117–20.

15. Rathje, "Oriental Imports" 167.

16. See D.B. Harden, "Ancient Glass, I: Pre-Roman,"

ArchJ 125 (1969) 58–59; G. Caputo, in *Etudes Etrusco-Italiques* (1963) 13–17; and M. Bizzarri, in *Studi Banti* (Rome 1965) 57–61.

17. Strøm, *Etruscan Orientalizing,* with review by G. Colonna, *StEtr* 40 (1972) 565–69.

18. N. Hirschland Ramage, "Studies in Early Etruscan Bucchero," *BSA* 38 (1970) 1–60.

19. F. Prayon, "L'Oriente e la statuaria etrusca arcaica," *Colloquii del Sodalizio* 5 (1977) 165–72.

20. F.-W. von Hase, in *Hamburger Beiträge zur Archäologie* 2 (1975) 99–182.

21. Rathje, "Oriental Imports" 179.

22. Besides the Bernardini and Barberini tombs at Praeneste, such luxury goods have been found in northern Etruria at the Montagnola tumulus: ostrich eggs, tridacna shells, ivory and bone carvings, etc. See G. Caputo, "Gli athyrmata della Montagnola e la via dell'Arno e transappenninica," *Arte Antica e Moderna* 5 (1962) 58–72.

23. See J.M. Turfa, *AJA* 81 (1977) 369 no. 1. For parallels, see P. Deneauve, *Lampes de Carthage* (1969) 24–26, nos. 7, 8, 11, pl. 17; see also P. Cintas, *La céramique punique* (Tunis 1950) 520–29, pl. 40, type XL, 4. The Etruscans were not producing their own pottery lamps at this time.

24. See supra n. 10. For monkeys, see D. Rebuffat-Emmanuel, *StEtr* 34 (1967) 633–44; S. Bonacelli, *StEtr* 6 (1932) 341–82; W.C. McDermott, *The Ape in Antiquity* (1938) 33, 276–78. Agricultural products were included, as the Latin term for pomegranate, *malum punicum,* suggests; see Pliny, *NH* 13.9.34.112, 15.11.11.39, 15.28.34.112, etc. Also of interest is the "exceedingly white" *cera punica:* Pliny, *NH* 21.14.49.83; *LSJ,* s.v. *Poeni* (B). Perfumes and ointments may have come to Etruria in fine glass and faience vessels: cf. the Pseudo-Skylax 112 (fourth century B.C.). For the Phoenician slave trade, see Harden, *Phoenicians* 165 and Warmington, *Carthage* 151.

25. Two such beads have been identified in Italy: one (a sporadic find) from Populonia, the other from Capena, Tomb 86 (Villa Giulia inv. 30895, fourth–third century B.C.). See M. Torelli, *StEtr* 33 (1965) 358 n. 65; A. De Agostino, *Guida di Populonia* (1963) fig. 31. Examples are known from Punic territory, for example, G. Pesce, *Sardegna Punica* (1961) fig. 141 (opp. p. 137), as well as from Phoenicia and Carthage; M. Seefried, "Les premiers bijoux des verriers antiques," *Connaissance des Arts* 295 (1976) 44–48; B. Quillard, *Bijoux carthaginois* I; *Les colliers.* Aurifex 2 (Louvain 1979) *passim.*

26. Faience perfume vases, long thought to be Phoenician, seem to have been made in Rhodes. See A. Rathje, "Oriental Imports," 174; A. Rathje, "A Group of 'Phoenician' Faience Anthropomorphic Perfume Flasks," *Levant* 7 (1976) 96–106; J.M. Turfa, "Evidence for Etruscan-Punic Relations," *AJA* 81 (1977) 368–74, 369, no. 2; V. Webb, "'Phoenician' Anthropomorphic Flasks: A Reply," *Levant* 12 (1980) 77–89.

27. On the import of wine from Phoenicia and Chios at the end of the eighth century and throughout the seventh, see Cristofani, *Etruscans* 51; cf. Grant, *Etruscans* 267.

28. The earliest provenances of these local amphorae are from Latium; they also occur in small numbers in Vulci, Narce, and Populonia; see, for instance, *StEtr* 36 (1968) pl. 40; *Monumenti di antichità varie* 2 (1964) Tomb 173, no. 630; *MonAnt* 4 (1894); *StEtr* 47 (1979) 311; and *StEtr* 48 (1980) 372f. For the "Canaanite Jar," see V. Grace, "The Canaanite Jar," in *The Aegean and the Near East: Studies Presented to Hetty Goldman* (New York 1956) 80–87.

29. See J. MacIntosh, "Representations of Furniture on the Frieze Plaques from Poggio Civitate (Murlo)," *RömMitt* 81 (1974) 15–40. For the Near East, see M. Cool Root, *The King and Kingship in Achaemenid Art: Essays on the Creation of an Iconography of Empire.* Acta Iranica 19 (Leiden 1979).

30. P. Stary, "Foreign Elements in Etruscan Arms and Armour: 8th to 3rd Centuries B.C.," *ProcPS* 45 (1979) 79–206, esp. 179ff., 186ff.; Stary, "Orientalische und griechische Einflüsse in der etruskischen Bewaffnung und Kampfesweise," *Aufnahme* (1981) 25–40.

31. Stary (supra n. 30) 181, n. 20, 190; S. Paglieri, "Origine e diffusione delle navi etrusco-italiche," *StEtr* 28 (1960) 209–31; J.P. Oleson, "A Bucchero Boat-Shaped Dish and Globular Aryballos in the National Maritime Museum, Haifa," *Sefunim* 6 (1981) 27–33. Cf. M. Cristofani, "Nuovi spunti sul tema della talassocrazia etrusca," *Xenia* 8 (1984) 4.

32. Snodgrass, *Archaic Greece* 32, 220; reviewed by B.S. Ridgway, *ArchNews* 10 (1981) 30–31. See supra, Introduction n. 42.

33. See Warden (supra n. 4); see also the survey of Etruscan metal resources by J. Bodechtel in F.-W. von Hase, "Zum Fragment eines orientalischen Bronzeflügels aus Vetulonia," *RömMitt* 79 (1972) 155–65, esp. 162–65. For early periods of the eastern Mediterranean, see Madden, Wheeler, and Muhly, "Tin in the Ancient Near East: Old Questions and New Finds," *Expedition* 19:2 (1977) 35–47.

34. *Mostra dell'Etruria Padana* 152f., no. 535, pl. 28.

35. F.-W. von Hase, "Gürtelschliesse des 7. und 6. Jahrhunderts in Mittelitalien," *JdI* 86 (1971) 1; n. 1 refers to M. Rostoftzeff, "Notes d'archéologie orientale: 2, les agrafes de ceintures," *Syria* 13 (1932) 327–33 esp. 332, pls. 63.7–8.

36. For Monte Sirai, see F. Barreca in *Monte Sirai* IV (1967) 15, no. 6; for Bithia, see Turfa, "Evidence for Etruscan-Punic Relations," *AJA* 81 (1977) 371, no. 109; for Ras el Bassit, see P. Courbin, "Les premiers grecs à Ras el Bassit," in *Greece and Italy in the Classical World: Acta XI International Congress of Classical Archaeology,* London 1978 (1979) 198f.; *RA* 1974, 174ff.; *Archeologia* 116 (1978) 48ff. See also von Hase, *Seminar Marburg* 5 (1979) 85, n. 46.

37. For bucchero in Spain (Toscanos), see H.G. Niemeyer in *MadrMitt* 18 (1977) 91, n. 42; A. Arribas, O. Artega, *El yacimiento fenicio de la desembocadura del Rio Guad-*

alhorce (University of Granada 1975) 88–89, nos. 33–34, pl. 8. For bucchero from Kition in Cyprus, see F.-W. von Hase, *JdI* 26 (1971) 99, n. 64, no. 49. For Amathus, see K. Nikolaou, *AJA* 76 (1972) 312 (from a tomb). Cf. G. Camporeale, "Brocchetta cipriota dalla tomba del Duce di Vetulonia," *ArchCl* 14 (1962) 61–70. For Sicily, Sardinia, Carthage, and Utica, see infra nn. 117–22.

38. See L. Vagnetti, in "I micenei in Italia: la documentazione archeologica," *ParPass* 25 (1970) 359–80; E. Peruzzi, *Mycenaeans in Early Latium* (Rome 1980); A.M. Bietti Sestieri, "The Metal Industry of Continental Italy, 13th to 11th Centuries, and Its Aegean Connections," *ProcPS* 39 (1973) 383–424; G. Barker, "The Conditions of Cultural and Economic Growth in the Bronze Age of Central Italy," *ProcPS* 38 (1972) 170–208.

39. On Archaic Greek trade, see A. Mele, *Il commercio greco antico* (Naples 1979); O. Murray, *Early Greece* (London 1980) Ch. 5. For the site of Ras el Bassit, see supra n. 36; and P. Courbin, *Annales Archéologiques Arabes Syriennes* 22 (1972) 45ff.; 23 (1973) 25ff.; and 25 (1975) 59ff. For Tell Sukas, see Boardman, *Greeks Overseas* 45, 52. For Al Mina, see Boardman, *Greeks Overseas* 38–54. For the West, see B.B. Shefton, "Greeks and Greek Imports in the South of the Iberian Peninsula. The Archaeological Evidence," *Madrider Beiträge* 8: *Phönizier im Westen* (1982) 337–70.

40. For Naukratis, see Boardman, *Greeks Overseas* 117–33. For Chios, see Boardman, *Excavations in Chios 1952–1955: Greek Emporio, BSA* Suppl. 6 (1967).

41. See Boardman, *Greeks Overseas* 83–84. For Al Mina and Euboean history, see L. Jeffery, *Archaic Greece* (London 1976) 25–26 (alphabet) and 53–54, 63–70 (history).

42. See Rathje, "Oriental Imports" 179, and infra nn. 43–44.

43. Greek traders are probably to be credited with the distribution of painted pottery of the first half of the seventh century B.C. in Spain: see W. Culican, *Levant* 2 (1970) 29, and Shefton supra n. 39.

44. See G. Buchner and D. Ridgway, *Pithekoussai* I (forthcoming); D. Ridgway, "The First Western Greeks: Campanian Coasts and Southern Etruria," in *Greeks, Celts and Romans,* eds. C. and S. Hawkes (London 1973) 5–38; D. Ridgway, "Rapporti dell'Etruria meridionale con la Campania: prolegomena pithecusana," in *Aspetti e problemi dell'Etruria interna* 281–92 and *L'Alba della Magna Grecia* (Milan 1984).

45. G. Buchner, "Early Orientalizing: Aspects of the Euboean Connection," in *IBR* 129–44, with earlier bibliography on Pithekoussai.

46. K. Kilian, "Zwei italische Kammhelme aus Griechenland," *Études Delphiques, BCH* Suppl. 4 (1977) 429–42; F.-W. von Hase, *Seminar Marburg* 5 (1979) 69–99.

47. The story might actually refer to a slightly later date. See Steingräber, *Etruskische Möbel* 148–49; E. Kunze in *Studies Robinson* I, 742; G. Karo in *ArchEph* (1937) 316.

48. On the cups, see E. La Rocca, "Note sulle importazioni greche in territorio laziale nell'VIII sec. A.C.," *ParPass* 32 (1977) 375–97, and G. Bartoloni and F. Cordano, "Calcidesi ed Eretresi nell'Italia centrale e in Campania nel sec. VIII A.C.," *ParPass* 33 (1978) 321–30. See also J. Close-Brooks, "A Villanovan Belt from Euboea," *BICS* 14 (1967) 22–24.

49. See supra n. 45 and G. Buchner, *Cahiers Bérard* 2 (Naples 1975); Boardman, *Greeks Overseas* 168, n. 22, and F.-W. von Hase, *Hamburger Beiträge zur Archäologie* (1975) 99ff. (both *contra* Buchner). For trade, see Bartoloni and Cordano, *ParPass* 33 (1978) 321–30, esp. 324f. On Etruscan imitation of Greek painted vases, see also Boardman, *Greeks Overseas* 202–3; A. Giuliano, *Prospettiva* 3 (1975) 4ff.; J. Klein, "A Greek Metal-Working Quarter. Eighth Century Excavations on Ischia," *Expedition* 14 (1972) 34–39.

50. See Strøm, *Etruscan Orientalizing* 210ff., esp. 212; also F.-W. von Hase, *JdI* 86 (1971) 1–59.

51. G. Buchner and J. Boardman, "Seals from Ischia and the Lyre-Player Group," *JdI* 81 (1966) 1–62; K.M. Phillips, "Oriental Gemstones from Poggio Civitate," *ParPass* 33 (1978) 355–69. For a Phrygian fibula, see *Civiltà del Lazio primitivo* 95, 97, no. 21, pl. 10.

52. These will be published in the site report, forthcoming. The inscriptions have been discussed by P.K. McCarter, "A Phoenician Graffito from Pithekoussai," *AJA* 79 (1975) 140–41; G. Buchner, "Testimonianze epigrafiche semitiche dell'VIII° secolo A.C. a Pithekoussai," *ParPass* 33 (1978) 130–42; and G. Garbini, "Un'iscrizione aramaica a Ischia," *ParPass* 33 (1978) 143–50.

53. L. Jeffery, *LSAG* 236–37; J.A. Bundgaard, *Analecta Rom. Inst. Danici* 3 (1965) 12ff. See L. Bonfante, *Out of Etruria* (1981) 131, n. 1, 124 (discussion). See supra nn. 44–45.

54. See E. La Rocca, "Crateri . . . Aspetti della produzione di ceramica d'imitazione euboica nel Villanoviano avanzato," *MEFRA* 90 (1978) 465–514; F. Canciani, "Un biconico dipinto di Vulci," *DialAr* 8 (1975) 79–85; see also n. 44.

55. For one viewpoint, see M. Martelli, "Prime considerazioni sulla statistica delle importazioni greche in Etruria nel periodo arcaico," *StEtr* 47 (1979) 37–52, but the data on Corinthian exports are based on Payne's *Necrocorinthia* (1931). Corinthian imports more recently excavated in Italy and not as yet fully published need to be studied from this point of view: J.G. Szilágyi, *StEtr* 50 (1982) 17, n. 76. For the Laconian export of monumental bronze vessels, such as the Vix krater and Grachwyl hydria, see Boardman, *Greeks Overseas* 220–23, with references; and R.M. Cook, "Archaic Greek Trade: Three Conjectures," *JHS* 99 (1979) 152–55.

56. B.B. Shefton in Dunbabin et al., *Perachora* II (Oxford 1962) 386 and n. 1. For Italic fibulae at Perachora, see von Hase, *Seminar Marburg* 5; *Perachora* I (Oxford 1940) pls. 72.10–11, 84.18.

57. For Samos, see W. Technau, *AthMitt* 54 (1929) 26–

27; H.P. Isler, *AthMitt* 82 (1967) 77ff. and *Samos* IV (1978) 99–100, nos. 168–70 and 662–63. For Chios, see J. Boardman, *Excavations in Chios 1952–1955, Greek Emporio, BSA* Suppl. 6 (1967) 137, no. 480.

58. See Boardman, *Greeks Overseas* 198 and references. Johnston, *Trademarks* 49ff., notes that trademarks on vases do not record monetary prices until after 480 B.C. On Attic coinage in Etruria, see G. Colonna, "Ripostiglio di monete greche dal santuario etrusco di Pyrgi," *Atti del Congresso Internazionale di Numismatica 1961* (Rome 1965) 167–77. For Etruscan coinage, see Ch. VI.

59. M. Torelli, *ParPass* 32 (1977) 398–458.

60. Torelli (supra n. 59) 428ff.

61. Torelli (supra n. 59) 451.

62. M. Torelli, *ParPass* 26 (1971) 44ff.; A.W. Johnston, *ParPass* 27 (1972) 417ff.; P.A. Gianfrotta, *ParPass* 30 (1975) 311; C. Tronchetti, *ParPass* 30 (1975) 366ff.; F.D. Harvey, *ParPass* 31 (1976) 206ff.; Johnston, *Trademarks* 49.

63. Torelli, *ParPass* 26 (1971) 447ff., n. 82; *ArchNews* 5 (1976) 135.

64. Torelli, *ParPass* 26 (1971) 447.

65. Demaratus of Corinth is said to have established the coroplast's tradition in Italy; see, for instance, Pliny, *NH* XXV.152; Dion. Hal. 3.46; A. Blakeway, "Demaratus," *JRS* 25 (1935) 129–49; M. Torelli, "Greek Artisans and Etruria: A Problem Concerning the Relationship of Two Cultures," *ArchNews* 5 (1976) 134–38. Cf. N. Winter, "Architectural Terracottas Decorated with Human Heads," *RömMitt* 85 (1978) 27–58; C.K. Williams II, "Demaratus and Early Corinthian Roofs," *Stele. Festschrift Kontoleon* (Athens 1980) 345–50. See also Boardman, *Greeks Overseas* 207–10.

66. See J.G. Szilágyi, "Entwurf der Geschichte der etrusko-korinthischen Vasenmalerei," in A. Alföldi, *Römische Frühgeschichte* (1976) 183ff., *Etrusk-Korinthosi Vázafestészet* (Budapest 1975), to be published in translation, and *ArchCl* 20 (1968) 1ff. See also G. Colonna, *ArchCl* 13 (1961) 9–24; D.A. Amyx in *Studi Banti* (1965) 1–14.

67. B. Schweitzer, "Zum Krater des Aristonothos," *RömMitt* 62 (1955) 78–106.

68. See Torelli, *ArchNews* 5 (1976) 135, and "Beziehungen zwischen Griechen und Etruskern im 5. und 4. Jh. v.u.z.," in *Hellenische Poleis* II 823–40. G. Giuliano, "Il 'Pittore delle Rondini,'" *Prospettiva* 3 (1975) 4–8. For East Greek influence on Etruscan art, see Cristofani, *L'arte degli Etruschi* 77–84 and following sections.

69. J. Heurgon, *Kokalos* 18–19 (1972–73) = *Atti del III° Congresso Internazionale di Studi sulla Sicilia Antica* 70–74, esp. 71 and n. 13. Other Etruscan and Italic names also occur in Sicilian curse tablets (*defixiones*): Kailios, Matulaios, Pykelios.

70. R. Mengarelli, *StEtr* 10 (1931) 67–86; Banti, *Etruscan Cities* 39–41; M. Torelli, in *Hellenische Poleis* II 833, nn. 61–62. On an Athenian colony around 600 B.C. at Caere, see M. Guarducci, *ArchCl* 4 (1952) 241–44.

71. Torelli, *ParPass* 32 (1977) 407. For Ionian imports,

see M. Martelli, Torelli, F. Boitani Visentini, and Slaska, *Les céramiques de la Grèce de l'est et leur diffusion en Occident* (Paris and Naples 1978).

72. P. Stary, *ProcPS* 45 (1979) 180, 191ff.

73. M. Cristofani, "Il vaso François," *BdA* 62 s. spec. 1 (1980) 1–28, and *Materiali per servire alla storia del vaso François* (Florence 1981).

74. See T.B.L. Webster, *Potter and Patron* Ch. 20, esp. 289–95. The olive oil contained in the Panathenaic amphorae was also a precious commodity: see C.L. Albore-Livadie, *RSL* 33 (1967) 308. See also A.W. Johnston and R.E. Jones, "The 'SOS' Amphora," *BSA* 73 (1978) 103–41, esp. 140–41, and catalogue for the distribution of these amphorae.

75. Strabo V.2.3; V.1.7.

76. T.B. Rasmussen, "Etruscan Shapes in Attic Pottery," *Antike Kunst* 28 (1985) 33–39; M. Eisman, "Attic Kyathos Production," *Archaeology* 28 (1975) 76–83; Boardman, *Greeks Overseas* 200–207, 202, n. 151.

77. Webster, *Potter and Patron* 272; and M. Vickers, *Greek Vases* (Ashmolean Museum, Oxford, 1978) 30. Vases by the Michigan and Beaune painters carry a dipinto *SO*-inscription which is usually taken to indicate the name of a buyer in Athens. On the Etruscan market see now also W. Moon, "The Priam Painter," in *Ancient Greek Art and Iconography,* W. Moon, ed. (Madison, Wisconsin 1983) 97–118.

78. See M.A. Tiverios, *ArchEph* (1976) 44–57.

79. On bucchero exports to Greek sites, see von Hase, *Seminar Marburg* 5 (1979) 95–99 and 75 (map). For earlier catalogues and discussions, see G. Karo, "Etruskisches in Griechenland," *ArchEph* 1937, 316–20; B.B. Shefton, in *Perachora* II (1962) 385–86 n. 1; F. Villard, "Les canthares de bucchero et la chronologie du commerce étrusque d'exportation," in *Hommages Grenier* III (1962) 1625–35; G. Vallet and F. Villard, *Megara Hyblaea* II (Paris 1964) 131–32; A. Tusa Cutroni, *Kokalos* 12 (1966) 240–48. See J.M. Turfa, *Etruscan-Punic Relations* (forthcoming).

80. See E. Kunze, "Etruskische Bronzen in Griechenland," *Studies Robinson* I, 736–46; Savignoni, *MonAnt* 7 (1897) 277–376; P. Zancani Montuoro, "Un mito italiota in Etruria," *ASAtene* 24–26 (1946–48) 85–98. See also supra n. 47.

81. *The Athenian Agora: A Guide* (Princeton 1962) 154 (kantharos fragment). For the Acropolis, see Boehlau, *JdI* 15 (1900) 83, n. 74. For Kerameikos excavation reports, see *AA* (1940) 338ff., fig. 21; *JHS* 64 (1944) 80; and *AA* (1943) 343.

82. Kritias *apud* Athenaeus I.28b, and Pherekrates *apud* Athenaeus XV.700c. This may have been a new, rich industry practiced on a large scale, particularly in Vulci.

83. M. Cristofani, *L'arte degli Etruschi* 103ff. and 107, map, fig. 6. Also admired by Greeks were Etruscan sandals with hinged wooden soles: E. Touloupa, *Deltion* 28:1 (1973) 116–37; Bonfante, *Etruscan Dress* 59–60.

84. Amyklai: C. Stibbe in *Mededelingen Rom* 40 (1978) pl. 18,1. Vis: M. Gras, *Mélanges Heurgon* (1976) 344. Ithaca: M. Robertson, *BSA* 43 (1948) 103 no. 601, pl. 45. Corfu: P.G. Kalligas, *Deltion* 23 (1968) 314, pl. 255.

85. J. MacIntosh, "Etruscan Bucchero Pottery Imports in Corinth," *Hesperia* 43 (1974) 34–45; C.K. Williams, "Excavation at Corinth, 1973," *Hesperia* 43 (1974) 14–24.

86. MacIntosh, *Hesperia* 43 (1974), n. 112, 42. Camporeale suggested the use of "A" by a workshop: *La Collezione Alla Quercia* (Florence 1970) 69 and 196.

87. L. Aigner-Foresti, "'Tyrrhenoi' und 'Etrusci,'" *Grazer Beiträge* 6 (1977) 1–25; M.R. Torelli, "'Tyrranoi,'" *ParPass* 165 (1975) 417–33; M. Pallottino, "La Sicilia fra l'Africa e l'Etruria," *Kokalos* 18–19 (1972–73) 48ff.; J.P. Morel, "L'expansion phocéene en occident," *BCH* 99 (1975) 853–96; M. Gras, "La piraterie tyrrhénienne en Mer Egée: Mythe ou Réalité?" *Mélanges Heurgon* 341–70.

88. L. Casson, *Ships and Seamanship in the Ancient World* (Princeton 1971) 67–68 (krater in Palazzo dei Conservatori and vase from Vulci, now in British Museum, inv. H. 230). See also the Tomba della Nave, Casson's fig. 97; and an Attic black figure cup (now in the British Museum) depicting a battle between a pirate and a merchantman, (second half of the sixth century B.C.).

89. Camporeale, *Commerci di Vetulonia* 94–97; A. Taramelli, "Sardi ed Etruschi," *StEtr* 3 (1929) 43ff.; G. Lilliu, *La civiltà dei Sardi* (2nd ed., Turin, 1975) 173, 229ff., 282. On the battle over Alalia (Herodotus I 166) see J. Jehasse, *REA* 64 (1962) 241–86; J. Jehasse, "The Etruscans and Corsica," *IBR* 313–51.

90. G. Lilliu, *NSc* 1971, 289ff.

91. Herodotus VI.17.

92. L. Jeffery, *LSAG* (1961) 275 no. 7, pl. 51; *Olympia* V, 363f., no. 249, found in 1817, now in the British Museum. Another helmet, *BCH* 84 (1960) 721, fig. 12.

93. M. Almagro, *Las Necropolis de Ampuria* II (Barcelona 1955) 366, 392, 395, *RSL* 15 (1949) 88; *Ampurias* (guide, 1951) 158ff. (on the fibula) and "Los hallazgos de bucchero etrusco hacia occidente y su significación," *Boletín Arqueologico de la Sociedad Arqueologica Tarraconense* 49 (1949) 1ff.; E. Sanmarti and F. Marti, "Algunas observaciones sobre el comercio etrusco en Ampurias," *Simposio de Colonizaciones*, Barcelona-Ampurias, 1971 (Barcelona 1974) 53–59. See also infra n. 97.

94. B. Bouloumié, *Le bucchero nero étrusque et sa diffusion en Gaule méridionale*, Actes de la Table Ronde, *Coll. Latomus* 160 (Brussels 1979); review by G. Camporeale, *StEtr* 48 (1980) 594–600. See also the Etruscan bibliography, *Latomus* 33 (1974); J.M. Blázquez, *Tartessos y las origenes de la colonización fenicia en Occidente* (Salamanca 1975) Ch. VIII: "Influjo etrusco," 199–210.

95. Albacete, La Hoya de Santa Ana: P. Rouillard, "Le *bucchero nero* dans la peninsule ibérique," *Coll. Latomus* 160 (Brussels 1979) 167–68.

96. Ripoll-Perello, *Ampurias* (Guide 1972) pl. 23 (mirror); Garcia y Bellido, *Ampurias* 2 (1940) 76 pl. 4 (lion head). See supra n. 93.

97. These were made known to me by Ellen Macnamara. For Iberian contacts, see J.G. Szilágyi in *ActaAntHung* I (1953) 432–35, nn. 44, 51. See also infra, nn. 145, 155.

98. B. Bouloumié, *Recherches sur les importations étrusques en Gaule du VIIIe au IVe siècles av. J.-C.*, doctoral thesis, Université d'Aix-Marseille (1980). Professor Bouloumié very kindly supplied me with a copy of the abstract. On Hallstatt contacts with Italy (actual imports) see M. Egg, "Ein italischer Kammhelm aus Hallstatt," *Archäologisches Korrespondenzblatt* 8 (1978) 37–40.

99. Infra n. 103. B. Bouloumié and B. Liou, *RevArchNarb.* 9 (1976) 211–17; C. Albore-Livadie, *RSL* 33 (1967) 300–326; B. Liou, "Note provisoire sur deux gisements gréco-étrusques (Bon-Porté A et Pointe du Dattier)," *Cahiers d'Archéologie Subaquatique* 3 (1974) 7–19; F. and M. Py, "Les amphores étrusques de Vaunage et de Villevielle (Gard)," *MEFRA* 86 (1974) 141–254; B. Bouloumié, "Les amphores étrusques de Saint-Blaise (Fouilles H. Rolland)," *RevArchNarb.* 9 (1976) 23–43. G. Pruvot, "Navire étrusco-punique du Cap d'Antibes," *Archéologia* 48 (1972) 16–19.

100. For bronzes exported to Gaul, see B. Bouloumié in *RevArchNarb.* 10 (1977) 1–31 (basins); *Gallia* 36.2 (1978) 219–41 ("Rhodian" oinochoai at Pertuis); *Gallia* 31 (1973) 1–35 (*Schnabelkannen*); *Latomus* 37.1 (1978) 3–24 (stamnoi); *Gallia* 35.1 (1977) 3–38 (situlae); and *Gallia* 34.1 (1976) 1–30 (cistae). Also "Nouveaux jalons du commerce étrusque au nord des Alpes," *Cahiers de Mariemont* 2 (1971) 3–12.

101. Bouloumié, *Le bucchero nero étrusque*, review by G. Camporeale, *StEtr* 48 (1980) 594–600. F. Benoît, *Recherches sur l'hellénisation du Midi de la Gaule* (Aix-en-Provence 1965) 51ff.; B. Bouloumié, *Cahiers de Mariemont* 2 (1971) 9ff.

102. Supra n. 99.

103. C. Albore-Livadie, "L'épave étrusque du Cap d'Antibes," *RSL* 33, *Hommages Benoit* I (1967) 300–326; B. Bouloumié, *L'épave étrusque d'Antibes et le commerce en la Méditerranée occidentale au Ier siècle av. J.-C. = Seminar Marburg* 10 (Marburg 1982). For these amphorae see also B. Bouloumié and B. Liou, "Le colloque de Marseille sur les amphores étrusques et marseillaises archaïques," *RevArchNarb.* 9 (1976) 211–17. G. Buchner was perhaps the first to express the theory of the Oriental origins of the Etruscan amphora. E. Macnamara kindly helped me with references and discussions of these vessels. For the later phases of Etruscan commerce in France, see B. Bouloumié, infra n. 104.

104. See references supra n. 98. See also B. Bouloumié, "Saint-Blaise et Marseille au VIe siècle avant J.-C. L'hypothèse étrusque," *Latomus* 41 (1982) 74–91; and "Le vin étrusque et la première hellénisation du Midi de la Gaule,"

Revue Archéologique de l'Est et du Centre-Est 32 (1981) 75–81.

105. Cf. J.N. Coldstream, *BICS* 16 (1969) 1–8, and 18 (1971) 1–15. For Greek techniques in Carthage, see Boardman, *Greeks Overseas* 211–12. Although it is not necessary to conclude with E. Forrer that "Karthago wurde erst 673–663 gegründet" (*Festschrift Franz Dohrnseiff* [Leipzig 1953] 85–93), many scholars now prefer a date of about 725 B.C., following J.N. Coldstream, *Greek Geometric Pottery* (1968) 386–87, assuming that the Cintas deposit represents the earliest Phoenician activity at the site. For earlier opinions, see R. Carpenter, *AJA* 62 (1958) 35–53, and *AJA* 68 (1964) 178; R.E. Frézouls, *BCH* (1955) 153–76.

106. S. Moscati, *I Cartaginesi in Italia* (Milan 1977); Warmington, *Carthage;* A.M. Bisi, *La ceramica punica* (1970).

107. A Punic saucer lamp was found in a seventh-century tomb at Populonia: see A. Minto, *Populonia* (1943) 127f.; T. Szentléleky, *Ancient Lamps* (Budapest 1969) 25, n. 18.

108. For the sanctuary of Leukothea, see Aristotle, *Oecon.* 2.2; Diodorus Siculus 15.4; for Eilithyia, see Strabo 5.28; E.H. Richardson, "'Moonèd Ashteroth'?" *Brendel Essays* 21–24.

109. Pallottino et al., *ArchCl* 16 (1964) 49–117; *NSc* Suppl. (1970) II. Most recently, see *Die Göttin von Pyrgi;* G. Colonna, M. Cristofani, and G. Garbini, "Bibliografia delle publicazioni più recenti sulle scoperte di Pyrgi," *ArchCl* 18 (1966) 279–87; *Le lamine di Pyrgi* (Acc. Lincei, *Quaderno* 147, 1970); J. Ferron, "Un traité d'alliance entre Caere et Carthage . . . ," *ANRW* I¹ (1972) 189–216; J. Heurgon, "The Inscriptions of Pyrgi," *JRS* 56 (1966) 1ff.; G. Pugliese Carratelli, "Intorno alle lamine di Pyrgi," *StEtr* 33 (1965) 221ff.

110. For translations, see G. Garbini, *Oriens Antiquus* 4 (1965) 47; G. Levi della Vida *apud* Garbini; S. Moscati, *RStO* 39 (1964) 257–60; and A. Pfiffig, in *Uni-Hera-Astarte* (1965) 22. For the Etruscan inscriptions, see M. Pallottino, *ArchCl* 16 (1964) 79, 81; infra, Ch. VII. On religion, see E. Lipinski, "La fête de l'ensevelissment et de la résurrection de Melqart," in *Actes de la XVII Rencontre Assyriologique Internationale. Bruxelles, 1969* (1970) 30–58; S. Ribichini, "Melqart nell'iscrizione di Pyrgi?" *Saggi Fenici* I (Rome 1975) 41–47.

111. Based on translations listed supra n. 110. See also Bonfante, *Etruscan Language* 52–56.

112. Inscribed Phoenician dedications have been found in Greek ports. For Marseilles (fifth–fourth century B.C. stele, priests of Baal), see S. Bourlard-Collin, *Galerie des antiques* (Guide to Musée Borély) no. 44; G. Vasseur, "L'origine de l'inscription phénicienne de Marseille," in *Bulletin de la Société Archéologique de Provence* III, III, 180. For Piraeus stele of first century B.C. in an Attic temple portico, see A. Donner and W. Rollig, *Kanaanäische und aramäische Inschriften* no. 60, cited by Garbini, *Oriens*

Antiquus 4 (1965) 38. For more on bilingual inscriptions, see Harden, *Phoenicians* pl. 36 and note.

113. Cf. J. Heurgon, *JRS* 56 (1966) 11–12; O. Masson, "Cultes indigènes, cultes grecs et cultes orientaux à Chypre," in Eissfeldt, *Eléments orientaux dans la religion grecque ancienne* (1960) 129–42.

114. See S. Moscati, *Oriens Antiquus* 7 (1968) and references; *Die Göttin von Pyrgi*.

115. M. Pallottino, "Nuova luce sulla storia di Roma arcaica dalle lamine d'oro di Pyrgi," *StRom* 13 (1965) 1–13; Pallottino, *Etruscans* 90.

116. A. Toynbee, *Hannibal's Legacy* I (1965) 519–34; R.L. Beaumont, "The Date of the First Treaty between Rome and Carthage," *JRS* 29 (1939) 74–86; R.E. Mitchell, *Historia* 20 (1971) 633–55.

117. J.M. Turfa, *AJA* 81 (1977) 369, nos. 1–66, 67–86, 90–91; Rasmussen, *Bucchero* 71, 150–56. E. Colozier, *MEFRA* 64 (1952) 59–65.

118. E. Benveniste, *StEtr* 7 (1933) 245–49; M. Pallottino, *ArchCl* 16 (1964) 114, n. 110, *TLE* no. 724, and *Etruscologia* (1968) 122.

119. See Turfa, *AJA* 81 (1977); E. Boucher-Colozier, *Cahiers de Byrsa* 3 (1953) 11–38; E. Colozier, "Les Étrusques et Carthage," *MEFRA* 65 (1953) 63–68; J. Ferron, "Les relations de Carthage avec l'Étrurie," *Latomus* 25 (1966) 689–709.

120. See *BAC* 1906, cxcvii; and E. Colozier, *MEFRA* 65 (1953) 66.

121. Colozier, *MEFRA* 65 (1953) 66, with previous bibliography.

122. All are in the Roman Villa Museum, Rabat, Malta. See *Report on the Working of the Museum Department for the Year 1962* (Valletta, Malta) pl. 4 (to be published by W. Culican). Such bone and ivory relief plaques were evidently a popular export item: M.E. Aubet, *Studi Sardi* 23.1 (1973–74) 125–30; *Fouilles de Délos* XVIII, 237f., pl. 77; Cristofani, *L'arte degli Etruschi* 109–10, n. 103. See also Aubet, *RSF* 1 (1973) 59–68 (Ibiza); and Y. Huls, *Ivoires d'Etrurie* (1957) 193 (Rhodes, Cyprus).

123. J. Ferron, *Morts Dieux de Carthage ou les stèles funéraires de Carthage* (Paris 1976). For stele with baby as offering, see Harden, *Phoenicians* pl. 35; cf. pl. 43; 104f., n. 83 (sacrifice).

124. *Mozia* VII (1972) 16–17; VI (1970) 78; V (1969) 40–41; IV (1968) 50. Also *PBSR* 26 (1958) 14, 28.

125. Now in the Whitaker Museum, Mozia (inv. no. 750); Turfa, *AJA* 81 (1977) 371, no. 107.

126. See E. Gabrici, *NSc* (1941) 285–87. For other Etruscan imports, see Turfa, *AJA* 81 (1977) 371, nos. 108–66; M. Gras, *MEFRA* 86 (1974) 79–139; von Hase, *Seminar Marburg* 5 (1979), pp. 69–99, *passim;* G. Tore and M. Gras, *MEFRA* 88 (1976) 51–90, 85, for a bucchero kylix dated rather early at about 620 B.C. See also R. Zucca, "Ceramica etrusca in Sardegna," *RSF* 9 (Suppl. 1981) 31–37.

127. A study of Punic amphora types and their development is being undertaken by S. Wolff of the Oriental Institute. For finds in Greece, see W. Lauer in *Olympische Forschungen* VIII (1975) 67, 131f., pl. 22.3; and the Corinth excavation reports by C.K. Williams, *Hesperia* 45 (1976) 107; *Hesperia* 47 (1978) 15–20; and *Hesperia* 48 (1979) 107–24. Cf. Y. Solier, *Hommages Benoît* II (1972) 127–50 (contexts showing the association of Punic and Etruscan imports on the French coast).

128. Beazley, *EVP* 188–90.

129. C. Tronchetti, "Contributo al problema delle rotte commerciali arcaiche," *DialAr* 7 (1973) 5–16.

130. J. Boardman, *Expedition* 21 (1979) 33–39.

131. Johnston, *Trademarks* 51–52. On the limitations of painted pottery as evidence, see R.M. Cook, "Bedeutung der bemalten Keramik für den griechischen Handel," *JdI* 74 (1959) 114–23. For Athenian exports throughout the Mediterranean, see Boardman, *Expedition* 21 (1979) 33–39, esp. 37. On Etruscans tastes in Greek masters, see Cristofani, *L'arte degli Etruschi* 77ff. and *passim*.

132. For a thorough treatment of graffiti and dipinti on vases, see Johnston, *Trademarks* n. 164, and *AJA* 82 (1978) 222–26. See also M. Zuffa, "I commerci ateniesi nell'Adriatico e i metalli dell'Etruria," *Emilia Preromana* 7 (1971–74 = 1975) 151–79.

133. Webster, *Potter and Patron* 292.

134. Some of the buildings contained slag refuse: G.A. Mansuelli, *RömMitt* 70 (1963) 44ff.

135. For a recent study of artistic influences, see *Aufnahme* (1981), including I. Krauskopf, "Etruskische und Griechische Kannen der Form VI im 5. Jahrhundert" 146–55.

136. M. Torelli, in *Hellenische Poleis* II 832; J.G. Szilágyi, "Zur Praxias-Gruppe," *Archaeologia Polona* 14 (1973) 95ff. Another product of this workshop, in the Manchester Museum, is to be published by A.J.N.W. Prag.

137. Torelli, in *Hellenische Poleis* II 832.

138. Torelli, in *Hellenische Poleis* II 834–35. For statistics, compare Signe Isager-Mogens Herman, *Sources for the Trade Routes of Athens in the Fourth Century: Sites of Finds for Attic Red-Figure Vases of the Fourth Century B.C.* (Odense 1975).

139. Bonfante, *Out of Etruria* 37, 55, n. 36; M. Cristofani Martelli, *StEtr* 41 (1973) 97–120; R. Bianchi Bandinelli, "Osservazioni sulle statue acroteriali di Poggio Civitate (Murlo)," *DialAr* 6 (1972) 242–46.

140. Bonfante, *Out of Etruria* 46f., n. 100; W. Negroni Catacchio, "Le vie dell'ambra, i passi alpini orientali e l'alto Adriatico," *Aquileia* (1976) 21–59. D. Strong, *Catalogue of the Carved Amber in the Department of Greek and Roman Antiquities, the British Museum* (London 1966) 13–33.

141. O.-H. Frey, *Entstehung der Situlenkunst, Röm.Germ.Forsch.* 31 (Berlin 1960), and *Este e la civiltà paleoveneta a cento anni dalle prime scoperte = Atti del XI convegno di Studi Etruschi ed Italici, Este-Padova 1976* (Florence 1980). See also Bonfante, *Out of Etruria*. The aristocratic material culture that resulted from Etruscan interaction is illustrated by the recent discovery of a warrior's tomb near Heuneburg containing a bronze couch, leather and gold boots, etc.: see J. Biel, "Das frühkeltische Fürstengrab von Eberdingen-Hochdorf, Landkreis Ludwigsburg," *Denkmalspflege in Baden-Württemberg. Nachrichtenblatt des Landesdenkmalamtes* 7 (October–December 1978) 168–75.

142. Bonfante, *Out of Etruria* 21, n. 38; P. Stary, *ProcPS* 45 (1979) 180, table, and *passim*.

143. Livy 5.33.; *I Galli e l'Italia* (Rome 1978); M. Sordi, "La leggenda di Arunte Chiusino e la prima invasione gallica in Italia," *RivStorAnt* 6–7 (1976–77) 111–17.

144. C.F.C. Hawkes, "Runes and the 'caput Adriae,'" *Adriatica. Miscellanea G. Novak* (Zagreb 1970) 399–408; R.W.V. Elliot, *Runes* (Manchester 1959/80) 6–8. See G. Bonfante, "The Spread of the Alphabet in Europe: Arezzo, *Erz* and Runes," in Bonfante, *Out of Etruria* 124–34.

145. P.S. Wells: "Iron Age Central Europe," *Archaeology* 33 (1980) 6–11; "Late Hallstatt Interactions with the Mediterranean: One Suggestion," in *Ancient Europe and the Mediterranean. Studies Presented in Honor of Hugh Hencken* (Warminster 1977) 189–96; "West-Central Europe and the Mediterranean. The Decline in Trade in the Fifth Century B.C.," *Expedition* 21 (1979) 18–24; "Contact and Change: An Example on the Fringes of the Classical World," *World Archaeology* 12 (1980) 1–10; *Salt, the Study of an Ancient Industry*, eds. K.W. de Brisay and K.A. Evans (Colchester 1975).

146. Bonfante, *Out of Etruria* Ch. I, esp. 8 and 23–24.

147. E.g., the raid of Dionysius the Elder of Syracuse on Pyrgi in 384 B.C. (Diodorus 15.14.3). Dionysius the Phocaean, early fifth century B.C., according to Herodotus (6.17), preyed upon Carthaginian and Etruscan shipping from a base in Sicily.

148. Torelli, *ParPass* 32 (1977) 422, with references.

149. Torelli, in *Hellenische Poleis* II 833.

150. E. Kunze, *Studies Robinson*, I 736–46; and H.P. Isler, *Archelöos* (Bern 1970) 161, no. 234.

151. S. Boucher, "Trajets terrestres du commerce étrusque aux Ve et IVe siècles av. J.-C.," *RA* (1973) I, 79–96, esp. 85–95. A corpus of Etruscan bronze S-handled oinochoai is being prepared by Dr. I. Krauskopf of Heidelberg.

152. J.G. Szilágyi, *ActaAntHung* 10 (1962) 260, n. 35. A simple mirror with a four-person scene is said to have come from the Peloponnesos: see K.D. Mylonas, *ArchEph* 1883, 249–54; N. de Grummond, in *Guide to Etruscan Mirrors* 173, n. 42.

153. National Museum, Zagreb; Pallottino, *Etruscans* 198ff., 223ff., pl. 96, note; Bonfante, *Etruscan Language* 138.

154. Cf. D.L. Carroll, *AJA* 77 (1973) 334–36.

155. J.G. Szilágyi, *ActaAntHung* I (1953) 419–54; 432 n. 40.

156. As yet, most Etruscan fabrics have not been scientifically separated from the masses of black glaze found in the Mediterranean. For this kind of study, see A.J.N.W. Prag, F. Schweizer, and J.L.W. Williams, "Hellenistic Glazed Wares from Athens and Southern Italy: Analytical Techniques and Implications," *Archaeometry* 16 (1974) 153–87.

157. G. Maetzke et al., *Roselle: Gli scavi e la mostra* (Pisa 1975) 197, 94–97.

158. Torelli, *StEtr* 35 (1967) 337; N. Rilli, *Gli Etruschi a Sesto Fiorentino* (1964) 35–37, 88, pl. 15a.

159. *Mostra dell'Etruria Padana* I, 330, no. 1084, pl. 106; C.G. Picard, *Karthago* 13 (1967) 38–39.

160. R. Bloch, "Remarques sur un masque ibéro-punique découvert à Spina," *Arte Antica e Moderna* 17 (1962) 54–57; W. Culican, "Some Phoenician Masks and Other Terracottas," *Berytus* 24 (1975–76) 47–87. Earlier in this genre are the glass head-beads exported to Italy from Phoenician centers (supra n. 25).

161. Turfa, *AJA* 81 (1977) 371, nos. 97, 99, 100.

162. R. Herbig, *Die jüngeretruskischen Steinsarkophage* (1952) 63, no. 121, pl. 21a. For further discussion of dating, and evidence placing these sarcophagi in the fourth century (360–340 B.C.), see F. Matz, *MarbWPr* 1973 (1974) 13–36, esp. 32–36.

163. M. Pallottino, *Kokalos* 18–19 (1972–73) 63–68. Cf. supra n. 126.

164. *CIE* 5422.

165. H. de Villefosse, *MonPiot* 12 (1905) 79–111; Nichon *apud* Gauckler in *BAntFr* (1909) 293 (original comparison with Tarquinia example); J. Carcopino in *MemPontAcc* I, 2 (1924) 109–17. See references supra n. 119.

166. M. Martelli, "Un aspetto del commercio di manufatti artistici nel IV secolo a.C.: i sarcofagi in marmo," *Prospettiva* 3 (1975) 9–17.

167. See Diodorus Siculus 19.106.2; M. Torelli, *Elogia Tarquiniensia* 30–38, 56–66; and review by T.J. Cornell, *JRS* 68 (1978) 167–73. On another elogium that has been used to associate Tarquinia with the Punic Wars, see J. Heurgon, *ArchCl* 21 (1969) 88–91, pl. 34.

168. See B.V. Head, *Historia Nummorum* (1911) 190 (overstruck coin of Syracuse). J. Heurgon, *MEFRA* 63 (1951) 133, suggests their possible use by Carthaginians.

169. *TLE* 890. Bonfante, *Etruscan Language* 136; L. Cavagnaro Vanoni, *StEtr* 33 (1965) 473–74, pl. 104a; Pallottino, *StEtr* 34 (1966) 355–56, no. 1; Pfiffig, *StEtr* 35 (1967) 659–63, *Historia* 17 (1968) 118, and *Etruskische Sprache* 226.

170. Bonfante, *Etruscan Language* 138. For the stone object from the *tophet* at Carthage, see M. Pallottino, *ArchCl* 16 (1964) 14 = *Saggi di Antichità* I pls. 8, 2, similar to Caeretan cippi. Cf. J. and L. Jehasse, *La necropole préromaine d'Aléria* (1973) 26, 28 (discussion), pl. 167.

IV / Art

MARIE-FRANÇOISE BRIGUET

We must turn to the art produced in Italy under the aegis of Etruscan power from the seventh to the first century B.C. to understand something of the character of the people who created it, and to recognize aspects peculiar to their civilization. Without their art, this civilization would remain forever silent. In spite of over a century and a half of excavations and often passionate scholarly discussions, it is still difficult to explain the sudden emergence of art in Etruria or the reasons for its rise, development, and gradual decline. We remain perplexed at the surprising and complicated variety and contrasts of its monuments, which differ according to the periods and cities to which they belong, the social classes for which they were made, and the way they were produced. Controversial and often misunderstood, Etruscan art has nevertheless found its place among the arts of antiquity, as the first great art to develop in Italy.

If we consider Etruscan art only with reference to what preceded or was contemporary with it, especially the art of Greece, its constant and prestigious model, we run the risk of denying it any originality or creative power, of considering it merely a marginal, provincial aspect of a superlative art. Of course, Etruscan art could not have developed without constant recourse to Greek ideas and to the language of Greek art. Yet few comparisons with Greek art are valid, nor should second-rate works of Etruscan craftsmen be contrasted with the highest creations of Greek art. Etruscan originals are also often compared to copies of Greek monuments made in Roman times, but these "copies" are interpretations, by later artists, of works of art of times long past. The mistakes and misunderstandings of Greco-Roman copyists are thus often compounded by modern scholars.

What does emerge, as we learn more about the political, economic, religious, and cultural relations of the various regions of pre-Roman Italy and of the world outside, is an Italian cultural unity or *koine,* with distinctive regional features. In ancient Italy, if one discounts the monuments of Magna Graecia and Sicily as basically foreign creations transferred to Italy by Greek colonists who adapted the art of Greece to the tastes and necessities of their new homeland, the most important and original art was that of Etruria. Yet recent excavations and studies show that in spite of its predominance and autonomy it was not an isolated phenomenon in Italy. Reciprocal influences are many, though not always clearly understood.

A remarkable number of monuments of Etruscan art have survived. The loss or destruction of some of the most important, including wall paintings, large-scale bronze sculpture, and honorary portraits, has necessarily distorted our view of the overall quality of this art. On the other hand the scientific excavations being carried out under the supervision of the Italian government in necropoleis and also, for the first time, in some ancient Etruscan cities which have not been buried under medieval and modern buildings have greatly added to our knowledge. In the last fifteen years or so, "excavations" have also been carried out in museums housing older collections of Etruscan and Italic art. Scholars are now restoring famous works whose extensive nineteenth-century "restorations" falsified their true character. Examination of the recently restored Mars from Todi in the Vatican (fig. IV-1), of the Mater Matuta from Chiusi in the archaeological museum in Florence (fig. IV-2), or of a strange cinerary group from Chiusi in the Louvre (fig. IV-3) has brought up once more the question of a "Classical" phase of Etruscan art, which had once been dismissed. While recent progress in the study

IV-1. Statue of Mars from Todi (Umbria), after restoration. Bronze. Early fourth century B.C. Vatican, Museo Etrusco Gregoriano. (DAI.)

IV-2. Cinerary statue from Chiusi of seated mother with child, "Mater Matuta." Limestone.
460–440 B.C. Florence, Museo Archeologico. (Soprintendenza alle Antichità–Firenze.)

IV-3. Cinerary group from Chiusi, before and after restoration. Limestone. Early fourth century
B.C. Paris, Louvre, MA 2348. (M. Chuzeville, Louvre.) (Museum photo.)

IV-4. Villanovan vase from Benacci Tomb. Terracotta. Bologna, Museo Civico Archeologico. (Museum photo.)

of Greek art has not radically affected our knowl-edge of the Archaic and Classical phases of Etruscan art, the work being done on the chronology, schools, artists, and cosmopolitan features of Hel-lenistic Greek art does affect our understanding of this important phase. In the light of these new discoveries and research, any evaluation of Etruscan art is necessarily provisional. Yet it is possible to give a brief survey of the chronology and the types of Etruscan monuments which reflect the variety of

its technical abilities, its characteristic expressions, and the basic stages of its development.

Villanovan Preface

In the second millennium B.C. the civilization of the Bronze Age is attested in Italy, though it does not seem to be in any way remarkable. At the end of the prehistoric period, however, there developed in most of the peninsula a culture characterized by the spread of the technique of iron metallurgy, iron weapons, and a geometric style of decoration (Map 4). At the same time, the Hallstatt and Mediterranean cultures developed in western Europe. Greek Geometric art was also on the rise. This Iron Age phase in Italy was called Villanovan after the name of a site, Villanova, discovered in 1853 near Bologna. It was preceded in the tenth and ninth centuries B.C. by a "proto-Villanovan" phase, a period of transition between the Villanovan and the earlier, so-called Apenninic Bronze Age civilization, which included certain features of primitive art that persisted as deeply ingrained components of Italic and Etruscan art down to the historical period. The taste for abundant decoration and complex forms, for example, is evident in the dark brown or black vases of the Apenninic period, with their heavy, awkward shapes and added ornamentation complicating and transforming the original outline of the handles. A clay vase, or *askos,* from the Benacci necropolis of the Villanovan period is in the shape of a bird with the horned head of a bull (fig. IV-4), surmounted by the barely modeled form of a human rider, perhaps meant as a handle. Its surface is completely covered by incised geometrical designs. In this remarkable example, early artistic tendencies are restrained by the discipline and sense of form of Geometric art.

The abundant artistic production of this Villanovan Iron Age constitutes a kind of preface, a preparation for Etruscan art. Villanovan art developed between about 850 and 700 B.C., in a period more or less contemporary with that of Greek Geometric art in northern and central Italy, at sites where Etruscan art would soon flourish. All the known monuments of Villanovan art have been found in tombs, the so-called pozzo graves in the shape of pits or wells (fig. V-2). These were sealed above with stones, after having been filled with the furnishings with which the dead were provided, including ash urns or ossuaries to hold the ashes and bones of the deceased—since at that time cremation was the rule. These urns were made of rough brown, unpurified clay (impasto) in a biconical shape, with a small mouth and base and wide belly, like two cones with their bases touching. The lid

was usually a saucer placed upside down on the urn. Often, evidently marking a warrior's grave, a helmet of bronze or terracotta served as a lid instead (fig. IV-5). This type of biconical urn, very frequent in Tuscany, is also found in the Po Valley and various areas of southern Italy and Sicily. In southern Etruria and Latium, whose civilization was at the

IV-5. Biconical Villanovan urn with bronze helmet used as lid. Terracotta. Florence, Museo Archeologico, Inv. 83379. (Soprintendenza alle Antichità–Firenze.)

time very close to that of Tuscany, cinerary urns were made in the shape of huts (cf. fig. V-19). Such huts are the precursors of a funerary symbolism related to the shape of a house, a symbolism which was long-lasting on Italian soil, particularly in Etruria.

Villanovan art, in fact, concentrates on the form and decoration of furnishings meant either for the house (such as terracotta and bronze vases of various shapes, gourds, handled pails or situlas, flasks or water bottles, cups, and tripod bases) or for ceremonial use (bronze belt plaques, huge round shields, breastplates, helmets, swords, and fibulae to fasten robes and mantles). Shape and ornament often give evidence of the craftsmen's high standards. The shapes of clay vases, not yet wheel-made, have clearly defined profiles and a sober elegance. Ornamentation consists of geometric designs: straight lines, zigzags, triangles, dots, concentric circles, swastikas, occasional animal figures (horses, ducks, and birds), and, more rarely, human figures. Incised or hammered in repoussé relief, this decoration emphasizes the shape of the object whose function it underlines, while it neglects color (unless this was formerly provided by the inlay of per-ishable material such as wood, leather, or fabric). In spite of this stylization, the composition is harmonious and often lively, especially on the most successful Villanovan monuments, like a handsome cast bronze belt plaque decorated with incised designs from Tomb 543A of the Benacci necropolis of Bologna (fig. IV-6), or a bronze helmet from Tarquinia. The same object is often decorated both with abstract designs, engraved or incised, and with figures in the round, as on the vase or *askos* also from the Benacci necropolis (cf. fig. IV-4). It is only toward the end of the Villanovan period that the first faint signs of Italic sculpture appeared. Usually applied to objects, human figures were either stylized or roughly modeled but always exhibit a spontaneous, fresh and primitive gusto, like the figure settled at the banquet table on the lid of a seventh-century urn from Montescudaio (fig. IV-7), or the little men arranged in concentric circles, about to perform a magic dance on a bronze vase found in a tomb in the Olmo Bello necropolis at Bisenzio (fig. IV-8).

The problem of external influences on Villanovan art is complex; in later art of this period, features of the Orientalizing style can be clearly discerned. In

IV-6. Decorated Villanovan belt plaque from Benacci Tomb. Bologna, Museo Civico Archeologico. (Museum photo.)

IV-7. Urn from Montescudaio (Volterra) with representation of a funerary banquet on the lid. Terracotta. Middle of seventh century B.C. Florence, Museo Archeologico. (Soprintendenza alle Antichità–Firenze.)

any case, many of its tendencies, such as a lively, realistic style, and many specific motifs are to be found in the earlier phases of what is known as Etruscan art.

Character of Etruscan Art: Comparison with Greek Art

The urban civilization of the Etruscans began around 700 B.C., by which time their art had devel- oped into something quite different from that of the Villanovan tradition. Various foreign influences gave this first period of Etruscan art the character which set it apart, even within the wider context of the Mediterranean world to which it now belonged.

In the Orientalizing period, as in the following phases, the monuments of Etruscan art come from religious sanctuaries and, above all, from necropo- leis. Recent excavations of Archaic dwellings, how- ever—for example, at Acquarossa, near Viterbo (a modest-sized city during the seventh and sixth

IV-8. Vase from Bisenzio with representation of a hunt (or ritual dance?) on the lid, with details of
figures and animals. Bronze. End of eighth century B.C. Rome, Villa Giulia.

centuries B.C., abandoned around 500 B.C.; see fig. V-33)—reveal concerns of Etruscan art which are not purely religious, as do their tomb furnishings, designed for the daily use of private individuals. A basic feature and paradox of Etruscan art is that it served only private or religious purposes. The rich and powerful customers who commissioned splendid gold, silver, and amber jewelry, luxurious silver or bronze plate, and magnificently decorated vases were people with an aristocratic, sophisticated taste. Yet in contrast to other peoples of antiquity, they seem not to have been interested in recording or glorifying the historical events in which they took part or in publicizing their public virtues and merits.

The function of art in Etruria seems to have been primarily utilitarian, providing for the needs and luxuries of daily life and the afterlife. Because of the Etruscans' deep religious belief in a life beyond the present, their art serves to fulfill funerary necessities, as well as to realize their constant concern with satisfying the divine will of the gods and its commands. In Greece, too, religion provided artistic creation its primary impulse. In Etruria, it continued to do so until the end of Etruscan civilization: Etruscan art always seemed to aim more at the fulfillment of religious and funerary beliefs on a purely practical level than at extolling the glory of the gods and the cities they protected.

A number of peculiarly Etruscan features stemmed from this religious and practical purpose. Because the cities of Etruria did not spend time or money on public monuments to beautify their cities and sanctuaries and raise their prestige in the eyes of the world, we rarely distinguish the work of a great artist or the "hand" of a master. Though each period of Etruscan art reflects a variety of tendencies, fashions, currents, and ideas, we do not discern any competition between rival artistic personalities proud of their talents and recognized by the society in which they work, such as marked the art of Greece in the fifth and fourth century B.C. and influenced its later development. The originality and creative talents of Praxiteles, Skopas, or Lysippos left their mark throughout the Hellenistic period. Only one name of an Etruscan artist has come down to us, that of the sculptor Vulca of Veii, remem-

bered by the Romans as having contributed to the terracotta decoration of the great Temple of Jupiter Optimus Maximus, on the Capitoline Hill in Rome, at the end of the sixth century B.C.

Rather than schools of artists, there seem to have been workshops, whose members were apparently active mostly within their own cities. The most important of these workshops were probably responsible for major works of art as well as for smaller objects produced by craftsmen. In Cerveteri, for example, a workshop in the Archaic period almost certainly produced both architectural terracottas and cinerary urns, using the same motifs and even, in some cases, the same molds, for both. The same bronzeworkers who produced votive statuettes probably also made household utensils decorated with similar statuettes. Clearly the workshops produced objects for people of different social classes. Within the tombs, the range of workmanship is wide; the most amazing technical virtuosity, as in goldworking, contrasts, in the poorer tombs, with humbler and cheaper grave furnishings. Though "mass-produced," these cheaper wares are often charming. A popular vigor enlivens their decoration and often comes close to parody or caricature. Products of this art, essentially the creation of craftsmen, did not reach a high artistic level and seem to be somehow unfinished, for the workshops were not overly concerned with the technical perfection which generally would result from lively competition. Thus it is difficult to distinguish between the major and minor arts in Etruria. This lack of competition also explains the persistence of certain conservative forms and the lack of first-rate artists ready to renew or transform these forms. Powerful, rich cities developed their own styles, techniques, and forms more or less independently, and then suddenly abandoned them for no apparent reason. Vulci specialized in sculpture made from the local *nenfro* stone and in bronzework. In Cerveteri, many important workshops produced sacred, votive, and funerary terracotta objects. Chiusi is known for its vases of *bucchero pesante* and, in all periods, for a variety of interesting and original funerary monuments. Many of the features of Etruscan art which contrast with Greek art can be explained by the uses to which it was put and by

IV-9. Fibula decorated in repousssé and granulation from Regolini-Galassi Tomb, Cerveteri. Gold.
670–650 B.C. Vatican, Museo Etrusco Gregoriano, Acc. 77260. (DAI.)

the different status of its artists, hence its eclecticism and variety of motifs, themes, designs, techniques, and even styles, as well as the receptivity of its artists and craftsmen to outside influences.

Techniques and Forms of Art

JEWELRY

The technical accomplishment of Etruscan art is perhaps best seen in jewelry. From the beginning of that art, jewelers, particularly goldworkers, mastered the most sophisticated techniques, from hammered relief decoration (repoussé) to engraving, filigree, and granulation, using only rather simple tools. They did not invent these techniques, which go back to the third millennium B.C., but copied them, along with imported objects made by the goldworkers of the Near East. Nonetheless, they perfected the techniques that they borrowed and went on to create magnificent jewelry, which reached its peak in the seventh and sixth centuries B.C. Though often imitated, their jewelry has never been equaled.

In the rich tombs of this early period, an immense wealth of gold, silver, and amber jewelry reflects the taste of an aristocratic class, attracted by the barbaric splendor of an exorbitant luxury. In the north at Marsiliana d'Albegna and Vetulonia, in the south at Cerveteri in the Regolini-Galassi Tomb, and in the Latin city of Praeneste, in the Barberini and Bernardini tombs, extraordinary pieces of jewelry have been found. Some had no doubt been worn by their owners while they were still alive, but the fragility of many jewels shows that they were designed to be placed in a tomb. The earliest pieces of the seventh century exhibit Villanovan decorative motifs. Others are unique, almost unbelievable. A huge fibula from the Regolini-Galassi Tomb is adorned with tiny lions; an enormous plaque, 25 cm. long, is decorated in relief with linear animal and plant motifs and serried ranks of tiny animals of Eastern origin executed in the round— winged lions, chimaeras, and sphinxes (fig. IV-9). Filigree and granulation decorate the beard of a head of Acheloos, a river god from Greek mythology, used as a pendant (fig. IV-10). A filigree brace-

IV-10. Pendant representing the head of Acheloos, decorated with granulation. Gold. Sixth century B.C. Paris, Louvre, Bj 498. (M. Chuzeville, Louvre.)

let is made of minute golden threads (fig. IV-12; cf. fig. IV-11); this virtuosity also characterizes filigree or granulated necklaces with pendants, often embellished with amber beads, fasteners, fibulae, or pins. A special kind of earring in the shape of a cylinder or "little barrel" (*a baule*) (fig. IV-13), decorated with little balls and tiny figures of animals, seems to have been popular until the end of the sixth century B.C.

A decline followed these triumphal successes. Filigree and granulation gradually disappeared. Instead, repoussé (figs. IV-15–16) is used to decorate thin funerary bands, necklaces with heavy ball-shaped pendants, rings, and the lockets (bullae)

IV-11. Bracelet from Vetulonia. Gold. Seventh century B.C. Florence, Museo Archeologico.
(Soprintendenza alle Antichità–Firenze.)

IV-12. Bracelets from Vetulonia. Gold. Seventh century B.C. Paris, Louvre. (Museum photo.)

IV-13. Earrings in the shape of a cylinder, *a baule* (resembling a small bag or valise), an Etruscan creation composed of a rectangle of gold bent around, joined by a wire which passed through the ear. Sixth or fifth century B.C. Paris, Louvre.

IV-14. Fibula or safety pin decorated with *pulviscolo* decoration. The inscription reads: *mi arathia . . . tursikina* ("I belong to Arathia . . . the Etruscan"). Gold. Last quarter of seventh century B.C. Paris, Louvre, Bj 816. (M. Chuzeville, Louvre.)

IV-15. Earrings in the form of grape clusters. Gold. Fifth or fourth century B.C. Florence, Museo Archeologico. (Soprintendenza alle Antichità–Firenze.)

IV-16. Votive head wearing grape cluster earrings. Terracotta. Fourth century B.C. British Museum.
(Museum photo.)

which the Romans eventually took from the Etruscans and placed on their children's necks as good luck charms (figs. IV-47; VIII-27). A curious type of earring in the shape of a grape cluster or garlic cloves, which covered the whole ear and sometimes hung down to the neck (fig. IV-15), is also represented on a number of votive terracotta heads (fig. IV-16). During the later Classical and Hellenistic periods, technical decline and excessively complex shapes and decoration characterized the jewelry.

IVORY AND BONE

The Etruscan taste for luxury and exotic forms also informs delicate ivory objects, such as cups, toilet boxes (pyxides), combs, tiny human figures, and statuettes of wild animals. Their provenance is not always easy to identify. Some were no doubt imported from Cyprus or Syria. Some were made in Etruria, where foreign craftsmen must have taught local apprentices (just as the goldsmiths did) and provided them with techniques and models. The decoration in registers used on the handle of a fan (or perhaps a mirror) in the shape of an arm from the Barberini Tomb (fig. IV-17), dated about 670 B.C., and on a cup with caryatid supports from the same tomb, derives from the Orientalizing repertory with its lotus and palmettes and real and fantastic animals (fig. IV-18). Boxes of ivory or bone of the sixth century B.C. reflect the influences of the style and subjects of Ionian art (animals, charioteers, and banquets) (fig. IV-19). Around the middle of the sixth century B.C. carved ivory work suddenly disappears.

IV-17. Handle in the shape of a human arm, from the Barberini Tomb, Praeneste. Ivory. Second half of seventh century B.C. Rome, Villa Giulia. (Soprintendenza alle Antichità dell' Etruria Meridionale.)

STONE SCULPTURE

Stone was never favored by Etruscan artists. Though local stone—calcareous rock, travertine, and volcanic tufa such as the *nenfro* of the region around Vulci—is soft and rather easy to carve, it does not encourage sculptors to improve their techniques. Stone sculptures are often primitive, rough-hewn, and usually awkward, except for some made from the *pietra fetida* of Chiusi. Imperfections of material and of workmanship were in any case covered over by a painted decoration which emphasized the forms of the statues or brought out details of reliefs. Marble, which we think of as the sculptor's ideal material, was very rarely used; the marble quarries of Carrara, near Pisa, which the Romans knew as Luni, were not worked until the last century of the Roman Republic.

Large-scale stone sculpture was therefore never of major importance in Etruria. Since the use of stone in the Etruscan cities was tied to the tomb and thereby to the needs of the dead and of funerary ritual (fig. IV-20), the dimensions of this sculpture were always rather small; the stone statues from Vulci, for example, are all less than a meter high. In central and southern Etruria, funerary sculpture remains hidden and inaccessible deep within chamber tombs; in the northern cities, it serves as memorial, marker, or sign to remind the living of the dead. At Vulci, Orvieto, and Chiusi, the entrance of the tomb corridor (dromos), the door of the tomb, and the grave mound (tumulus) were decorated, guarded, and magically protected by a statue, a relief stele or grave marker (cippus) (figs. IV-21–22).

The subjects and motifs of large-scale sculpture were borrowed from the Greek or Near Eastern repertoire, known mostly through small decorated objects of ivory, wood, or metal, as well as through rugs and textiles imported to Etruria as early as the seventh century B.C. The influence of the minor arts is obvious in the larger sculptures. The elongated forms of the boy riding a fish, from Vulci (fig. IV-23), are linear rather than sculptured; the sculptor has carved out the flat, broad surfaces of the image in a kind of relief. The same is true of terracotta sculpture, for example, the two sarcophagi of the Bride and Groom from Cerveteri.

IV-18. Cup decorated with caryatids, female figures holding their braids, dressed in typical Etruscan fashion, from the Barberini Tomb, Praeneste. Ivory. Seventh century B.C. Rome, Villa Giulia. (Soprintendenza alle Antichità dell' Etruria Meridionale.)

IV-19. Three views of a pyxis or box from the Pania burial in Chiusi. Relief decoration in registers includes figures—a procession of women, Odysseus under the ram, a ship—as well as Orientalizing ornament with stylized plant motifs. Ivory. Seventh century B.C. Florence, Museo Archeologico. (Soprintendenza alle Antichità–Firenze.)

IV-20. Relief cippus from Fiesole. Limestone. Sixth century B.C. Florence, Museo Archeologico. (DAI.)

IV-21. Relief base of cippus from Chiusi, with scene of acrobat performing a handstand. Casuccini Collection. Stone. Ca. 475 B.C. Palermo, Museo Nazionale No. 5.

IV-22. Relief base of cippus from Chiusi, with scene of women at home. Stone. Ca. 475 B.C. Rome, Museo Barracco. (Alinari.)

IV-23. Statue of a boy riding on a fish, from Vulci. Limestone. Middle of sixth century B.C. Rome, Villa Giulia.
(DAI.)

IV-24. Sarcophagus of the Bride and Groom, Cerveteri.
Terracotta. Ca. 525 B.C. Rome, Villa Giulia. (DAI.)

IV-25. Sphinx and winged lion, statues from Ischia di Castro (near Vulci). Limestone. Ca. 550 B.C. (DAI.)

IV-26. Head of a warrior from Orvieto. Limestone. Ca. 525 B.C. Florence, Museo Archeologico. (Soprintendenza alle Antichità–Firenze.)

IV-27. Relief decoration of a base from Chiusi with runners competing in a race. Limestone. Ca. 500 B.C. Chiusi, Museo Civico. (DAI.)

IV-28. Stone cinerary urn from Chianciano (territory of Chiusi) in the form of a seated man, the so-called Plutus. 540–520 B.C. Palermo, Museo Archeologico.

On the sarcophagus in the Villa Giulia (fig. IV-24) and another in the Louvre, the faces of the figures in profile seem almost modeled in relief; from the front, they are very narrow.

Each city's specialization is very noticeable, not only in the choice of material, on the basis of whatever stone was most readily available, but also in the preference for a particular type of sculpture. Vulci and the neighboring region produced a remarkable group of "tomb guardians," influenced in subject and style by the art of the Syrians and Hittites, as well as of Rhodes and the Peloponnesus: the subjects include sphinxes and lions—either striding, seated, winged, or wingless—and a human rider on a sea monster. The excavations carried out some years ago at Ischia di Castro, near Vulci, by the Belgian Archaeological School—now unfortunately interrupted—brought forth ten statues (still unpublished) made out of *nenfro*. Representing lions, a sphinx, and rams, their rough-hewn, sober modeling is tempered by the softness of Ionian Greek sculpture (fig. IV-25). Somewhat later in the sixth century, around 525 B.C., a similarly soft, peaceful quality is seen in the smile on the broadly modeled face of the monumental head of a warrior from Orvieto (fig. IV-26).

In northern Etruria in this same period, at Volterra, Fiesole, and elsewhere, the custom arose of using stelae or quadrangular cippi as grave markers (cf. fig. IV-20). These were topped by palmettes or a floral motif in the Ionian manner, or, as in the cippus from Settimello, flanked by lions with their paws raised in heraldic fashion. The reliefs which decorate these monuments represent the deceased in profile, fully armed, or the banquets, hunts, or dances recalling his activities in real life. Despite their primitive appearance, these images were in fact made with more care and skill than is at first evident and have a serenity of balance and proportion. These "provincial" monuments are difficult to date, for they were somewhat isolated within the context of Archaic Etruscan art and often translated, with a lack of understanding and a peculiar awkwardness, the Greek or Near Eastern models they were following.

Chiusi was one of the very few cities where the arts of stone sculpture and terracotta were practiced throughout Etruscan civilization. From the sixth to the very end of the fifth century B.C., the sculptors of its workshops used the local *pietra fetida* (smelly stone), a kind of sulphurous calcareous rock whose fine-grained texture allowed them to carve and paint in precise detail the relief decoration of funerary urns, sarcophagi, and grave markers. The most frequent subjects are those of daily life: banquets, music and dancing, hunting, funerary games, and the laying out of the dead (figs. IV-21–22, IV-27). Some three hundred of these monuments have survived, though they are mostly fragmentary and in rather poor condition because the stone breaks easily. The style is homogeneous; the best period was around the turn of the sixth century and the fifth century B.C. Compositions are clearly designed and drawn; profiles are sometimes heavy, flattened out and massive, though at times there is a sharp but pleasing elegance of line. Always effective and expressive is the lively movement of the bodies and the hand gestures, which emphasize graceful contours.

These workshops were probably responsible for carving from the local stone half-length busts and full-length standing or seated figures like the so-called Plutus in the museum of Palermo (fig. IV-28). These figures are represented either alone or with a winged infernal divinity, as in a group from Chianciano (near Chiusi) (fig. IV-29). When cleaning and restoration remove the arbitrary restorations which were added in the nineteenth century, they recover their original calm and peaceful dignity and their austere simplicity, derived from the Classical Greek art of the fifth century B.C. (figs. IV-1–3).

The Etruscan city of Felsina (Bologna), in the Po Valley, concentrated on the production of funerary steles in fine sandstone, *grès,* from the fifth to the mid-fourth century B.C. Large stones were cut into imposing, heavy slabs, topped with a semicircular profile, and decorated in relief, in registers within a frame of wavy spirals (fig. IV-30). Above are represented animals and sea monsters as symbols of the underworld or as simple decorative motifs. Below appear representations of the deceased, sometimes in more complicated scenes, journeying to the underworld in a carriage (figs. IV-30–31), on horseback, or on foot, led by demons. Battles with Celts

IV-29. Stone statue group from Chianciano (territory of Chiusi). 460–440 B.C. (Soprintendenza alle Antichità–Firenze.)

IV-30. Funerary stele from Bologna with sea monsters, journey to the underworld, and battle against Gauls. Sandstone. Ca. 350 B.C. Bologna, Museo Civico Archeologico. (Museum photo.)

IV-31. Funerary stele from Bologna representing the voyage of the deceased to the underworld and a she-wolf nursing a boy. Sandstone. Early fourth century B.C. Bologna, Museo Civico Archeologico. (Museum photo.)

of Gauls (the earliest instance of this theme in Western art) also appear, not surprisingly, since the Gauls had by now invaded this region.

In the Hellenistic period, Etruscan sculptors, with some exceptions, turned to the carving of sarcophagi and funerary urns of stone or terracotta, most of which were "mass-produced" in specialized workshops. At first sight, these monuments, preserved in great quantities, are noticeable for the lack of skill with which they were made. Indeed, their chief interest for us resides in the subjects carved on the front and the effigy of the deceased shown reclining on the lid (figs. IV-32–38). The caskets, of stone or terracotta, are usually carved on only three sides. On the front are scenes from Greek myths, often taken from the tragedies of Euripides (figs. IV-34–37), and local legends whose meaning

is not always clear to us, scenes of daily life with a symbolic meaning—riders on horseback (fig. IV-38), journeys by carriage, and processions of magistrates led by musicians and accompanied by their following—or battles against Gauls (fig. IV-33; cf. fig. IV-30) or other enemies. (The presence of the Etruscan divinities of death—Charun, Vanth, and the Furies—shows that these scenes are symbolic, though their significance is not always apparent to our modern eye.) Three cities in particular specialized in the production of stone urns: Chiusi (which also produced terracotta urns), Perugia (where they were made of travertine), and Volterra (where alabaster was the norm). In contrast, the regions of Tarquinia and Viterbo, in southern Etruria, produced full-sized sarcophagi, of *peperino, nenfro,* or tufa.

IV-32. Funerary urns *in situ* in the Inghirami Tomb, Volterra. Hellenistic period. (Soprintendenza alle Antichità–Firenze.)

IV-33. Funerary urn from Volterra with portrait of deceased man reclining on the lid: on the front of the casket, a battle with Gauls. Terracotta. Second century B.C. Worcester Art Museum, Acc. 1926.19. (Museum photo.)

IV-34. Funerary urn with figure of woman reclining on lid: on the casket, mold-made representation of the duel between Eteocles and Polyneices. Painted terracotta. Second century B.C. Liverpool National Museums and Art Galleries on Merseyside. (Museum photo.)

IV-35. Cinerary urn from Volterra with portrait of the deceased reclining on lid; on front of casket, the death of Eriphyle. Marble. Second century B.C. Metropolitan Museum of Art, New York, Acc. 96.9.224, purchased by subscription, 1896. (Museum photo.)

IV-36. Cinerary urn from Volterra with the murder of Eriphyle. Alabaster. Second century B.C.
Florence, Museo Archeologico. (Soprintendenza alle Antichità–Firenze.)

IV 37. Cinerary urn from Volterra with the death of Oenomaus, who has fallen from the chariot. Pelops, brandishing the wheel with which he will kill him, wears strange detached sleeves. Alabaster. Second century B.C. Florence, Museo Archeologico. (Soprintendenza alle Antichità–Firenze.)

IV 38. Cinerary urn from Volterra representing a veiled rider's journey to the underworld accompanied by Charun. Alabaster. Second century B.C. Volterra, Museo Archeologico. (Soprintendenza alle Antichità–Firenze.)

IV-39. Statuette of a seated male figure from the Tomb of the Five Chairs. Cerveteri. Painted terracotta. Ca. 600 B.C. Rome, Museo dei Conservatori. (DAI.)

IV-40. Urn lid with reclining man (L. 28 inches), originally holding a patera. Perugia. Bronze. End of fifth century B.C. Leningrad Museum. (Museum photo.)

IV-41. Urn from Cerveteri with deceased woman on funeral couch. Terracotta. End of sixth century B.C. Paris, Louvre. (Museum photo.)

TERRACOTTA

Terracotta suited the techniques of Etruscan workshops as well as the tastes and purposes of their customers. The clay could be quickly and easily worked, successful models could be repeated because of the use of molds, and the brightly colored surfaces allowed a wide range of effects for decorative or expressive purposes. Not surprisingly, terracotta sculptures were in great demand among a people who commissioned quantities of funerary monuments, votive figures, and portraits, as well as extensive decoration for public and private buildings.

Before the appearance of the first large-scale terracotta sculpture in the beginning of the sixth century B.C., the Etruscans had produced many smaller funerary statuettes. In a tomb in Cerveteri in about 600 B.C. (fig. VIII-1) five statuettes of men and women were placed on seats carved out of the living rock. They were hand-modeled, with stocky proportions, their faces and bodies rounded, almost bloated, with their right hands held out in a ritual gesture (fig. IV-39). The two female bodies have

not been preserved. The three men were dressed in bright red garments of plaid-patterned wool, a shirt or tunic and a mantle fastened at the shoulder with a brooch which reproduced a type actually found in the Barberini Tomb. These statuettes are among the earliest Etruscan sculptures. Their heads, large in relation to their bodies, reflect the influence of the art of Greece and Asia Minor. We cannot yet speak of portraits, but the underlying realistic intentions of the artist are clear.

These works already reveal, at the beginning of Etruscan art, two basic tendencies which surfaced each time the Etruscan artist managed to free himself from foreign influence, especially that of Greek art. One is the desire to express the individuality of the human form by emphasizing what is most characteristic, the head. The second tendency, a natural result of the first, is a contempt for or indifference to the proper, harmonious proportions of the body.

The sculpture of Cerveteri is justly famous for the two terracotta sarcophagi in the Louvre and Villa Giulia (fig. IV-24). Less well known is a group

IV-42. Statuette of reclining youth, Cerveteri. Terracotta. Early fifth century B.C. Rome, Villa Giulia. (DAI.)

of similar, smaller urns, some of them recently discovered in the necropolis at Cerveteri (figs. IV-41–42). The custom of reclining on couches at banquets was borrowed from the Ionian Greeks of Asia Minor; from them the Etruscans also learned to represent this iconographic motif, popular in the minor arts (mostly reliefs) of both Greek and Etruscan art. In a workshop of Cerveteri an artist dared for the first time, between 520 and 500 B.C., to translate a two-dimensional design in miniature scale into a three-dimensional sculpture on a monumental scale, showing two couples reclining on their terracotta sarcophagi as though on their banquet couches (fig. IV-24). The lively, expressive hands, the slight smile which curves the thin lips, and the elongated faces modeled in the Ionian style lighten the serious dignity of the representation of death. Their faces are not meant to be portraits. (To reconstruct the physical appearance of the Etrus-

cans on the basis of what is simply the Etruscan-Ionic style of the period and use this physical type as an argument for the so-called Oriental origin of the Etruscans is implausible.) The remarkable restoration of the sarcophagus in the Louvre in 1979–80 by the Centro del Restauro in Florence has brought out its delicate polychrome decoration once again. (This color has disappeared from the sarcophagus in the Villa Giulia.) The subtle line of the crisp curves defines the bodies' stiff and massive forms, avoiding any surface modeling of the limbs and flattening the legs, which seem to have no flesh. The artist's interest is focused not on bodily forms but on the decorative effect of the drapery, whose folds flow in liquid waves over the bodies of husband and wife.

Later effigies of the deceased from Chiusi, Tarquinia, and especially Tuscania (fig. VIII-56), so often shown banquetng or sleeping on lids of terra-

IV-43. Sarcophagus of Seianti Thanunia Tlesnasa. Chiusi. Terracotta. Mid-second century B.C.
London, British Museum. (Museum photo.)

cotta urns and sarcophagi of Hellenistic times (figs.
IV-43–44), have no direct relation to these Archaic
funerary monuments from Cerveteri. Similar to
those carved out of stone, but more carefully executed because of the very nature of their material,
the great majority were made following workshop
models in the style of the great Classical Greek tradition (cf. the earlier, "Classical" bronze statue in
Leningrad, fig. IV-40). The heads, with their regular features, seem impassive and ageless, even in
the most successful examples, like the sarcophagi of
Seianti Thanunia Tlesnasa and Larthia Seianti from
Chiusi (figs. IV-43–44). In a few instances these
impersonal mold-made types have been reworked
on the surface, to hint at the vision of a young girl
in the bloom of youth, an elderly Etruscan weighed
down with age, or the moving image of a couple

with their sorrows etched on their faces (fig. IV-
45). Both stone and terracotta figures combine the
godlike dignity of those who have attained a hap-
pier life with the pose and attributes of the
deceased; only occasionally do they attempt to represent the individual features of the dead person.
Above all, these statues indicate the respect and
honor due the memory of the deceased, whose virtues and merits are thus commemorated. Wealth
and power are no doubt implied by the avoirdupois
of these distinguished gentlemen, whose heavy bel-
lies are carefully depicted, and by the luxury of the
women's dress and jewelry, shown in painstaking
detail.

In a much earlier period, a similar though less
individualized intent to commemorate the dead can
be seen in a peculiar type of ossuary, or funerary

IV-44. Sarcophagus of Larthia Seianti. Chiusi. Terracotta. Second century B.C. Florence, Museo
Archeologico. (Soprintendenza alle Antichità–Firenze.)

IV-45. Funerary urn with man and wife (or a female demon?). Volterra. Terracotta. Second century B.C. Florence, Museo Archeologico. (Soprintendenza
alle Antichità–Firenze.)

IV-46. "Canopic" urn representing female figure with earrings. Chiusi. Terracotta. Seventh century B.C. (Soprintendenza alle Antichità–Firenze.)

urn, a specialty of Chiusi, where cremation always continued to be practiced (fig. IV-46). Nineteenth-century scholars mistakenly called this type of urn "canopic," after a type of Egyptian jar used to hold the organs of the mummified dead. In these urns the desire to give a human form and a kind of life to the ovoid container for the ashes of the dead led to the representation of little arms modeled directly on the belly of the urn or added separately. The lid was modeled in the shape of a head, or, on earlier examples, a bronze mask was attached to a rounded, head-shaped lid. The features were always youthful and very stylized: low forehead, prominent cheekbones, wide, flat nose, and straight, thin lips. There are minor variations of this type, so that each urn is to some extent individualized, no one being exactly like any other. In this way, the actual appearance of the deceased was somehow symbolically and magically preserved. The dead person's new dignity was also frequently emphasized by placing the urn on a rounded armchair or "throne" of bronze or terracotta. Urn and chair were then

placed inside the huge vase (*dolium*, or *ziro*) which served for burials at Chiusi in the Archaic period. The chronological development of the one hundred and fifty or so urns which have come down to us is still not completely clear. It may have ranged from the seventh to the sixth century B.C.; toward the end, some of the heads seem to betray the influence of the Archaic Greek statues of kouroi.

For the gods, sculptors made cult statues of terracotta, all of which have been lost. They also modeled terracotta decorations for the gods' temples and votive images which the faithful left as gifts in their sanctuaries (figs. IV-47–49). These little clay offerings, generally of inferior quality, have not yet been fully studied: many still lie buried in museum storerooms. Somewhat better known are the numerous series of votive terracotta heads of human figures which flooded the great sanctuaries of Etruria at Cerveteri, at Veii, and at Tarquinia from the fifth century B.C. on. Their chief interest lies in the fact that they represent an attempt at portraiture.

Sculptured decoration on sacred buildings, in the Archaic period especially, represents one of the most typical and original features of Etruscan art (figs. IV-50–51; cf. fig. IV-99). It flourished in particular, though not exclusively, in the cities of southern and (in the Classical period) of central Etruria, but its influence directly affected the neighboring Faliscan and Latin regions, Falerii, Rome, Satricum, and Velletri. These friezes, antefixes, acroteria, revetment plaques, statues to be placed on the ridge of the roof, and pediment reliefs (figs. IV-50–61; cf. fig. V-38) were generally not meant—as in Greek art—to emphasize the forms of the building, accompanying the rhythm of its architectural design. They were exuberant, wildly colorful afterthoughts serving to protect and enliven the upper parts of the building (fig. V-38). Their independence and lack of structural logic derived from the nature of Etruscan architecture, which continued to be built of bricks and wood (see Ch. V).

Recent excavations seem to show that buildings other than temples—previously known only from their stone foundations or hard-to-interpret miniature models (cf. fig. IV-48)—also received such decoration, though no doubt their terracottas were of a less carefully made and less imposing type.

IV-47. Votive figures of swaddled babies with bullae. Veii. Terracotta. Fourth to first century B.C. Rome, Villa Giulia. (Soprintendenza alle Antichità dell'Etruria Meridionale.)

IV-49. Votive statuettes from Veii of mothers with children. Terracotta. Fourth to second century B.C. Rome, Villa Giulia. (Soprintendenza alle Antichità dell'Etruria Meridionale.)

IV-48. Votive figures from Vulci showing models of buildings in a sanctuary: portico, temple, and tower. Terracotta. First century B.C. Rome, Villa Giulia. (Soprintendenza alle Antichità dell'Etruria Meridionale.)

IV-50. Head of Hermes, from the group decorating the roof of the temple of the sanctuary of
Portonaccio at Veii. Painted terracotta. Lifesize. 510–490 B.C. Rome, Villa Giulia. (DAI.)

IV-51. Statue from Veii of a female divinity holding a little boy. Terracotta.
Lifesize. 500–490 B.C. Rome, Villa Giulia. (DAI.)

IV-52. Frieze decoration showing banquet scene, from a monumental building at Murlo (Poggio Civitate). Terracotta. Ca. 575 B.C. Siena. (DAI.)

IV-53. Frieze decoration from Murlo showing procession in a carriage with attendants (DAI.)

IV-54. Frieze decoration from Murlo showing horse race with trophy. (DAI.)

IV-55. Frieze decoration from Murlo showing seated personages with attendants (DAI.)

IV-56b. Antefix of Gorgon. Terracotta. Ca. 575 B.C. Murlo (Poggio Civitate). Siena, Palazzo Publico. (DAI.)

IV-56a. Antefix of Gorgon. Terracotta. Ca. 575 B.C. Veii. Rome, Villa Giulia. (DAI.)

Roofs of the aristocratic Archaic "houses" at Acquarossa were decorated with pierced acroteria or
roof finials and with continuous frieze plaques
whose painted or relief decoration showed subjects
borrowed from Orientalizing and Archaic Greek
iconography: floral motifs, processions of animals,
parades of carriages and horseback riders, banquets,
and so on. Some of these subjects also appear at
Murlo (Poggio Civitate, near Siena) (figs. IV-52–55)
in a building complex which may or may not be a
sanctuary (fig. V-33). Here the roof was apparently
decorated by a group of at least thirteen life-size
statues, found in fragments, whose style is striking
for its brutally primitive modeling (fig. IV-57).

The various forms of architectural decoration
were thus already set in their final form by the beginning of the sixth century B.C. They were not, of
course, all used on the same building at the same
time. They gradually changed with time but continued to reflect the motifs and figures of Greek iconography.

Several types of architectural decoration can be
distinguished. The earliest series consists of continuous friezes of terracotta, mold-made plaques
whose design unfolded beneath the cornice of the
temple; their prototypes are Corinthian and Ionian.
They have been found at Tuscania, Cerveteri, Velletri, and elsewhere (figs. IV-52–55). In the early period, rows of antefixes were placed on the two long
sides of the roof at the end of convex roof tiles (figs.
IV-56, IV-58–59) and finials or acroteria at the cor-
ners and along the slope of the pediment at the
ends of the building. Antefixes and acroteria became
more important and numerous and also more exu-
berantly ornamental in a second phase, which began
about the last quarter of the sixth century B.C. (fig.
V-38). The most famous and successful architectural
decoration known to us is the group of more or
less life-size statues—unfortunately fragmentary—
including Apollo, Hermes, and Herakles (figs. IV-
50–51, IV-99). Representing the gods' quarrel over
the sacred hind of Delphi in the presence of a female
figure carrying a child (perhaps Latona, mother of
Apollo and Artemis?), they loomed against the sky
on the ridge of the Temple of Portonaccio at Veii
(fig. V-38). A milestone in Etruscan art and a
unique monument, the group is obviously the work
of a great master, perhaps Vulca himself.

IV-57. Statue of a seated figure, the so-called Cowboy
from Murlo, wearing a large hat. Terracotta. Slightly under
lifesize. Ca. 575 B.C. Siena. (DAI.)

IV-58. Antefix from Satricum with satyr and maenad. Terracotta. Ca. 475 B.C. Rome, Villa Giulia. (Anderson.)

IV-59. Antefix from Veii of female head. Terracotta. Fifth century B.C. Rome, Villa Giulia. (Alinari.)

IV-60. Relief from Temple A, Pyrgi, showing Tydeus gnawing on the head of Melanippus in the presence of Capaneus, Athena, and Zeus. Terracotta. Ca. 460 B.C. Rome, Villa Giulia. (DAI.)

Many other beautiful though minor examples of temple decoration have been found, among them groups of dancing satyrs and maenads from Satricum (fig. IV-58), antefixes in the shape of heads of blacks or of women surrounded by great halo-like scalloped frames (fig. IV-59), reliefs and small pedimental statues from Cerveteri, and terracottas from Civita Castellana (Falerii) and Orvieto.

Terracotta decorations for temple pediments were used in Etruria from the end of the Archaic period to cover the projecting central beam. An example is a plaque found in the sanctuary at Pyrgi, one of the harbors of Cerveteri, dated about 460 B.C. (Temple A; fig. IV-60). As so often, it is based on Greek iconography. Modeled in extremely high relief, it represents an episode from the legend of

IV-61. Pediment sculpture from Civitalba, near Bologna, showing Dionysos' discovery of Ariadne. Terracotta. Second century B.C. Bologna, Museo Civico Archeologico. (Museum photo.)

Thebes: violently animated figures in battle contrast with the calm and enigmatic figure of the goddess Athena. By the Hellenistic period, the whole surface of the pediment was covered by the figured scene. In the second century B.C., two pediments of a temple at Civitalba, in the Etruscan Po Valley, were covered with a scene of a battle against Gauls and the mythological scene of Dionysos finding Ariadne asleep at Naxos (fig. IV-61). Though illogical from

the Greek point of view, such architectural decoration evidently suited the tastes and needs of the Etruscans. It protected the exposed wooden portions of the building from weathering, hid other sections, and kept dangerous evil spirits and influences away from the holy places by its apotropaic power. It was also artistically effective, with its contrasts of color, alternation of violent and peaceful scenes, and figures whose countenances, at times

IV-62. Chimaera of Arezzo, probably originally part of a group, with Bellerophon. Bronze. Lifesize. Fourth century B.C. Florence, Museo Archeologico. (Alinari.)

serene, at times wildly grimacing, served to excite the emotions and perhaps to satisfy the religious feelings of the faithful.

BRONZE

Well provided with the necessary raw materials, Etruscan smiths produced, from the seventh century B.C. on, great quantities of bronze statuettes and furnishings for both show and daily use. From this time on, bronze was a favorite material of Etruscan artists. Etruscan statuettes never attained the unparalleled perfection of Greek bronzes, but

these *Tyrrhena sigilla,* praised by the poet Horace in the first century B.C., did enjoy great success and were marketed along the coasts of the Mediterranean and even in Greece.

Etruscan craftsmen made use of all the varied techniques of bronzeworking: hammered plates, engraving, relief decoration, and casting by the *cire perdue* method. Few large-scale bronzes have come down to us, but those that have, for example, the statue of Mars from Todi (fig. IV-1), allow us to imagine the high technical and artistic quality of those that have been lost. Etruscan artists often used figures of animals as decorations for wooden and bronze furnishings. The most famous statues

IV-63. Statue of nursing she-wolf, so-called Capitoline Wolf, with twins, representing Romulus and Remus, added in Renaissance. Bronze. Fifth century B.C. Rome, Capitoline Museum. (Barbara Malter.)

are the Chimaera of Arezzo (fig. IV-62; fourth century B.C.) and the She-Wolf of the Capitol (fig. IV-63; early fifth century B.C.). The latter, adopted as the symbol of the Roman Republic, was an Etrusco-Latin creation full of aggressive vitality. In the Hellenistic period, Etruscan sculptors produced a series of striking portraits, starting with the so-called Brutus in the Capitoline museum (fig. IV-64; 300 B.C.). The latest important example of this type of art is the honorary (or votive and therefore religious?) statue of Aulus Metellus, the Arringatore (orator), dating to around 110–90 B.C. (fig. IV-65).

Throughout Etruscan history, the production of small bronzes, originally imitated from Greek models, was carried out with a freedom, originality, and flavor all its own. Statuettes represent male and female divinities (fig. IV-66), votive figures of men and women making offerings to the gods, warriors, athletes, and elegantly dressed ladies (fig. IV-67). There were bronze workshops in many cities of Etruria. In the Archaic period those of Cerveteri were responsible for the relief-decorated Loeb tripods (fig. IV-68). From Umbria came the Monteleone chariot (fig. IV-69), as well as fragments of a chariot and statuettes from San Mariano and San Valentino. Vulci produced great numbers of vases, tripods, lamp holders, and incense burners. A closer study of such furnishings for houses and tombs will

IV-64. "Brutus," bust of a man. Bronze. Lifesize. Ca. 300
B.C. Rome, Capitoline Museum. (Barbara Malter.)

placed on these triangular supports, made from
three arched triangular plates decorated with relief
figures hammered out in repoussé. The Greek-
Oriental repertoire of the figures includes the usual
animals and monsters, as well as Greek mythological
scenes. Similar motifs were used to decorate cast
bronze tripods and lamp holders apparently produced at Vulci (figs. IV-72–73). Relief figures and
statuettes in the round stand gracefully poised along
the upper borders and legs of the tripods, figurines
of athletes and dancers support the bases of the
lamp holders (figs. IV-74–75), while little animals
climb up on their slender stalks, often fluted like
columns. The most beautiful of these objects were
made between around 550 and 450 B.C. Lamp holders and incense burners were technically less competent but still decorated with considerable original-

eventually allow scholars to identify other centers
of production. At this time we still do not know
the origin of many bronze objects, particularly of
the Orientalizing period, when so many luxury
objects were imported. Scholars have long tried to
find out precisely where certain large cauldrons
were made. Decorated with repoussé reliefs and
figures in the round representing "sirens" (human-
headed birds) (fig. IV-70), so-called Assyrian at-
tachments or cast protomes, or busts of lions or
griffins, and often provided with a conical base (fig.
IV-71), they were found in such wealthy tombs of
Cerveteri as the Regolini-Galassi Tomb, as well
as at Praeneste, Vetulonia, and Marsiliana
d'Albegna. Most of the twenty or so examples
found are of Greek or Oriental workmanship; only
a few are local imitations.

Tripods, lamp stands, and incense burners were
among the specialties of Etruscan bronzeworkers.
The three Loeb tripods from the end of the sixth
century B.C. (fig. IV-68) are an original creation,
marking the triumph of the technique of working
bronze plaques so characteristic of the school of
Perugia. Cauldrons were provided with lids and

IV-66. Two statuettes, a pair of divinities. Bronze. Ca.
400 B.C. Paris, Louvre.

IV-65. Statue of Aulus Metellus, the "Orator" (*Arringatore*). Bronze. Lifesize. Ca. 90 B.C. Florence, Museo Archeologico. (DAI.)

IV-67. Statuette from Falterona of a striding woman. Bronze. Ca. 490 B.C. London, British Museum. (Museum photo.)

IV-68. Loeb tripod, decorated relief base showing winged panther and Peleus pursuing Thetis.
Bronze. 540–520 B.C. Munich, Staatliche Antikensammlungen und Glyptothek. (Museum photo.)

IV-69. Relief decoration of a chariot from Monteleone di Spoleto. Bronze. 550–540 B.C. New York, Metropolitan Museum of Art. (Drawing.)

IV-70. Basin on three feet, decorated in high relief and incision with six sirens whose legs rest on the head of a bull and whose wings look like arms. Barberini Tomb, Praeneste. Bronze, Seventh century B.C. Rome, Villa Giulia, Inv. 13131. (Soprintendenza alle Antichità dell'Etruria Meridionale.)

IV-71. Cauldron from Praeneste(?) decorated with griffin heads and stand with Orientalizing relief ornamentation. Bronze. Seventh century B.C. Rome, Villa Giulia. (Soprintendenza alle Antichità dell'Etruria Meridionale.)

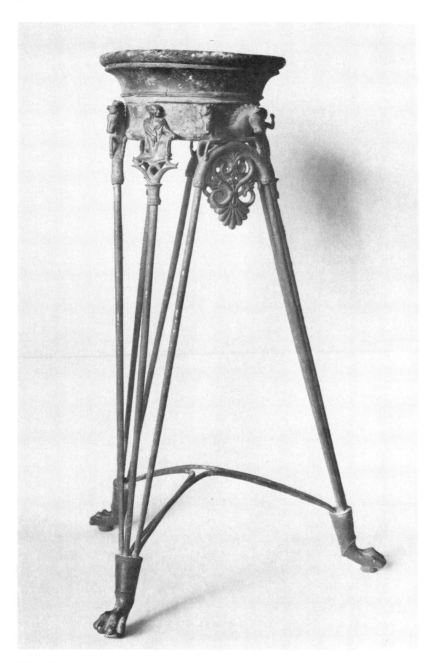

IV-72. Tripod stand from Vulci. Bronze. Fifth century B.C. City Art Museum of
Saint Louis, Acc. 37:26. (Museum photo.)

IV-73. Tripod stand from Vulci, detail. Bronze. Fifth century B.C. British Museum.
(Museum photo.)

ity. They were produced for homes and tombs down to the end of the Etruscan period, as were bronze vases, often with statuettes which served as decoration or handles.

Typically Etruscan are decorated mirrors and toilet boxes. The mirrors, of which over two thousand have come down to us, were made either with a bronze handle cast in one piece with the mirror disc (figs. I-19; VIII-36), or with a tang (figs. IV-76, IV-78; VIII-5–14) which was inserted into a separate handle, carved out of wood, ivory, or bone (fig. IV-77). Such handles have for the most part disappeared. The reflecting surface of the disc was

IV-75. Base of candelabrum or incense burner with dancer. Bronze. 470–450 B.C. Paris, Louvre, Br 3145. (M. Chuzeville, Louvre.)

IV-74. Base of candelabrum or incense burner supported by dancing caryatid figurine. Bronze. 470–450 B.C. London, British Museum. (Museum photo.)

IV-76. *Left,* mirror with relief decoration representing Herakles carrying off Mlacuch. Bronze. 460–450 B.C. London, British Museum. (Museum photo.)

IV-77. *Right,* mirror handle with relief decoration. Bone. Fourth century B.C. Liverpool, National Museums and Art Galleries on Merseyside. (Museum photo.)

slightly convex, the back was decorated with a variety of scenes, in the early period occasionally in relief (figs. IV-76, IV-78) but usually engraved (figs. VII-14–22; VIII-5–14, VIII-17–18, VIII-20, VIII-22–24). Illustrating the Etruscan taste for mythological subjects, both Greek and local, they provide, along with the urns and sarcophagi, a mine of information on mythology.

Praeneste seems to have had the monopoly on the production of the rounded, oval, or rectangular cistae used as toilet boxes by fashionable Etruscan and Latin ladies. The Ficoroni cista of the late fourth century B.C. is most famous for its decoration (fig. IV-79). The body, supported by feet cast in the shape of lions' paws stepping on frogs, is decorated with an engraved scene representing an episode from the Greek myth of the Argonauts. The engraved lid bears a hunting scene, in a landscape full of motion, evidently inspired by contemporary painting, and has a handle cast in the shape of a group of three statuettes representing Dionysos and two satyrs.

IV-78. Mirror with relief decoration showing Eos and Cephalos. Bronze. 470–460 B.C. Vatican, Museo Etrusco Gregoriano. (Museum photo.)

IV-79. Ficoroni cista, toilet box of Praenestine type with engraved decoration showing a scene from the legend of the Argonauts. Signed by Novios Plautios and made in Rome. Bronze. Second half of fourth century B.C. Rome, Villa Giulia. (DAI.)

IV-80. *A,* round-bellied amphora or amphoriskos with engraved decoration. Bucchero sottile. Seventh century B.C. Paris, Louvre. (Museum photo.) *B,* oinochoe or wine pitcher with engraved decoration. Bucchero sottile. Seventh century B.C. Paris, Louvre. (Museum photo.) *C,* kantharos or handled cup with engraved decoration and Etruscan inscription. Bucchero sottile. Seventh century B.C. New York, Metropolitan Museum of Art, Acc. 64.17. Gift of Mr. and Mrs. Jan Mitchell, 1964. (Museum photo.) *D,* amphora of Nicosthenic shape. Bucchero. Sixth century B.C. Paris, Louvre. (Museum photo.)

POTTERY

No doubt in order to produce a cheaper substitute for bronze vases, Etruscan potters developed their national fabric, the famous black bucchero (figs. IV-80–83). This dark fabric, which had perhaps resulted accidentally in the process of firing in the kiln, was made in various places in the Mediterranean basin from very early times. But the Etruscans, from the mid-seventh to the end of the fifth century B.C., brought this technique to its perfection, by methods not yet completely understood, with an enormous quantity of vases in an amazing variety of shapes and decoration. They had already previously improved the quality, color, shapes, and decoration of vases made from the rougher impasto (fig. IV-4) and had been using the potter's wheel ever since the eighth century B.C. Huge pots from Cerveteri dating from this earlier period were adorned with figures painted in white on a dark red background; tall supports with cut-out decorations served as bases for large pots.

There were two types of bucchero. Vases made from the lightweight *bucchero sottile,* with extremely thin walls, resemble metal vases in their elegant shapes, shiny surface, and engraved decoration. Many of these imitate the shapes of Greek painted pots: perfume vases, amphorae, pitchers, cups like

IV-81. Stand with molded decorations. Bucchero pesante. Seventh century B.C. London, British Museum. (Museum photo.)

IV-84. Red-figure vase or askos in the shape of a duck. Terracotta. End of fourth century B.C. Paris, Louvre, H 100. (M. Chuzeville, Louvre.)

IV-82. Cup with caryatid decoration imitating ivory models (cf. fig. IV-18). Bucchero. Seventh century B.C. London, British Museum. (Museum photo.)

IV-83. Pitcher and one-handled cup with stamped decoration. Bucchero. Seventh century B.C. London, British Museum. (Museum photo.)

IV-85. Etruscan black-figure vase. Terracotta. Sixth century B.C. Heidelberg, Archaeologisches Institut. (Institute photo.)

IV-86. Caeretan hydria showing Herakles and Busiris. Terracotta. Ca. 530 B.C. Vienna, Kunsthistorisches Museum. (Sindhöringer.)

the kantharos, the kylix with caryatid supports (figs. IV-80, IV-82). Their decoration too is inspired by that of Corinthian, Rhodian, Laconian, or Ionian vases. Around the end of the seventh century B.C., cylinders were used to stamp designs in relief on the sides of vases (fig. IV-83). In several places, especially Cerveteri, the development of such workshops was no doubt encouraged by the presence of immigrant Greek potters and the large-scale import of Greek vases. *Bucchero pesante* seems to have been made especially in the region of Chiusi from the sixth century B.C. on and to have lasted longer than *bucchero sottile*. Typical of *bucchero pesante* are its heavier weight, matte surface, and decoration, usually carried out in relief, by hand or with molds (fig. IV-81). The heavy, awkward, and often complicated shapes of these vases, which mostly came from Chiusi, are emphasized by their decoration, which covers every available surface: plant motifs and figures, heads of wild animals, or godroons.

In contrast to this native bucchero pottery, painted vases are the least successful feature of Etruscan art, as well as the least studied by modern scholars. Of course, Etruscan artists could not begin

to compete with the ambitious vases imported by the thousands from Greece. The fabric and glaze were poor; the shapes, whether local or imitated from the Greeks, were heavy, far different from the perfectly proportioned Greek vases. The decoration was often careless and ugly.

In the Archaic period, Etruscan potters produced great quantities of imitation Corinthian and Attic black-figure vases (fig. IV-85). Some vases produced in this period, the so-called Caeretan hydriae (figs. IV-86−87) and Pontic vases (figs. VIII-16, VIII-32), which are really quite good, were probably made in workshops directed by immigrant Greek artists (see Ch. III).

Of special interest, in spite of its frequently inferior quality, is the red-figure pottery of the fourth and early third century B.C. Produced in many different workshops, for example, at Cerveteri, Tarquinia, Volterra, Chiusi, and Falerii, this painted fabric is inspired by a type of pottery developed in the Greek colonies of southern Italy and adjacent Hellenized areas of southern Italy at this time. Many are quite handsome (fig. IV-84). Alongside a group of mass-produced ware (like the so-called

IV-87. Back of Caeretan hydria showing Egyptian servants of Busiris. Ca. 530 B.C. Vienna, Kunsthistorisches Museum. (Museum photo.)

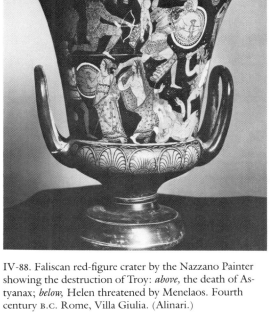

IV-88. Faliscan red-figure crater by the Nazzano Painter showing the destruction of Troy: *above,* the death of Astyanax; *below,* Helen threatened by Menelaos. Fourth century B.C. Rome, Villa Giulia. (Alinari.)

Genucilia Group, decorated with profiles of women), there are a few whose figured decoration is the work of real artists (perhaps Greek), as shown by the harmonious composition and careful execution of their mythological scenes and the fluidity of the drawing. Scenes chosen for their emotional power, with strange or cruel subject matter, are lively and striking (fig. IV-88). The calm and melancholy style of even the most dramatic scenes in Classical Greek art is very different from this striving for emotional effect. Often the scenes are lightened by a touch of humor. Humorous details and comical expressions, which are to be seen even on monsters or on demons of the Etruscan underworld, richly contrast with the horror of the scenes portrayed.

PAINTING

Modern methods of exploring the ground of Etruria in the last twenty years have enriched our

knowledge of Etruscan painting. It is hard to say precisely how many tomb paintings have been found; some recently discovered tombs at Tarquinia are still unpublished and remain closed to the public in order to preserve them (a great number of those which have survived are in a very poor state). A total of some one hundred painted tombs are now known in Etruria, from Chiusi, Orvieto, Cerveteri, Veii, Vulci, and Tarquinia. Tarquinia provides a kind of museum for Etruscan tomb painting, especially since, some twenty years ago, a civil engineer, Carlo Lerici, began to apply the methods of geophysical exploration to archaeology, and the use of a camera-equipped probe allowed excavators to identify and clear a number of previously unknown painted tombs.

It seems that Etruscan public buildings, which have disappeared, were originally decorated with wall paintings or, in the Archaic period, with painted terracotta plaques placed side by side, like the Boccanera and Campana plaques from tombs in

IV-89. "Boccanera plaques" from Cerveteri with the judgment of Paris and the toilette of Helen. Painted terracotta. Ca. 550–540 B.C. London, British Museum. (Museum photo.)

Cerveteri (figs. IV-89; V-44) or others found at the sanctuary of Portonaccio at Veii. The Boccanera and Campana plaques may have decorated a building in the city before being placed in a tomb. Even private houses may have been decorated in this manner. The sloping ceilings of some tombs and the walls of the Bartoccini Tomb of the third quarter of the sixth century (cf. the Tomb of the Hunter, fig. IV-90), with their gaily colored stripes, geometric patterns, and tiny multi-colored flowers, have often been taken to reflect the texture and patterns of textiles hung on the walls of wealthy houses, but they may reproduce the painted walls of these houses.

Tomb paintings were used in Etruria continuously from the seventh to the first century B.C., as can be seen from Tarquinia, which started to gain importance in this field as early as the sixth century B.C. We do not know the names of any of the artists who produced these paintings.

Etruscan tomb painting is important not only for its own sake, but also because it reflects, in a limited way, the great monuments of Archaic and Classical Greek painting which have almost completely perished. These paintings are thus not only works of art but also precious documents allowing us to reconstruct, in some cases, this type of Greek art.

The fresco technique and, more rarely, tempera over dry plaster were employed. The subjects were sometimes dictated by funerary ritual or belief and sometimes, in the early period, simply derived from the usual Orientalizing repertoire, with its processions of real or fantastic animals, lotus and palmettes, and horsemen and hunting scenes, as in the Campana Tomb at Veii. More often, however, funerary scenes seem to have been intended not as mere decoration nor as a sad memorial of the family of the deceased but as a way to commemorate the funerary meal served near the tomb and rites celebrated at the funeral and at the special holidays in honor of the dead. They signify the hopes of the living for the dead, in the form of religious and magic formulas; an affirmation of belief in an existence in the afterworld; and a kind of physi-

IV-90. Tomb of the Hunter, Tarquinia, representing an outdoor pavilion. 490–480 B.C. (DAI.)

cal communion between the living and the dead. On the walls appear scenes representing the pleasant or serious occupations of the family, the banquet and rites in honor of the deceased. Sharply drawn decorative motifs—black and red lines, attractive pomegranate friezes, stylized lotus and palmettes, garlands, ivy, and wave patterns—define such architectural forms as the pedimental area, plinths, and cornices and frame the attractive scenes: banquets and dances, as in the Tomb of the Leopards (fig. IV-91; cf. fig. IV-92), funeral games, as in the tombs of the Augurs (fig. IV-93) and of the Olympic Games, and ritual scenes like those in the Tomb of the Baron (fig. IV-94). Painted with a fine sense of decorative quality, these paintings attempt to recreate the appearance of actual living reality in all its immediacy and in its episodic, transitory, and sensuous quality. In dream gardens with delicate

IV-91. Tomb of the Leopards, Tarquinia, banquet scene. 480–470 B.C. (Alinari.)

IV-92. Tomb of the Triclinium, Tarquinia, dancers. 470–460 B.C. (DAI.)

blue leaves, dancers and musicians dance with light steps, turning happily; guests engage in animated conversation or exchange presents with refined gestures, reclining on banquet couches with splendid covers. There are serious touches and shrewd observation: a tired guest, a mouse clinging desperately to a branch. These scenes are always a living and lived reality; and always that of the aristocratic class. This relaxed and gay atmosphere reflects the noble Etruscans' taste for music, pleasure, luxury, and leisure.

Later, starting from the fourth century B.C., reality gives way to fantasy or merges with it. Belief in a strange, shadowy underworld and feelings of sadness and insecurity about this world of the Shades (fig. IV-95) take the place of the happy careless times of the Archaic period. The dead are shown journeying to Hades (in the Tomba del Convegno or the Tomb of the Meeting), taking part in a banquet in the world beyond before a veil of clouds (fig. IV-109), and in the presence of harsh and hor-

IV-93. Tomb of the Augurs, Tarquinia, Phersu directing a gladiatorial combat between a blindfolded man and a dog. Ca. 530 B.C. (DAI.)

IV-94. Tomb of the Baron, Tarquinia, end wall, ritual scene. Ca. 510 B.C. (DAI.)

IV-95. Tomb of Orcus, Tarquinia, head of a noble lady of the Velcha family, originally shown together with her husband (now lost). Second half of fourth century B.C. (DAI.)

IV-96. François Tomb, Vulci, sacrifice of the Trojan prisoners. 350–330 B.C. Original in Museo Torlonia, Rome; this copy in the Vatican Museum. (Museum photo.)

rible demons (in the tombs of Orcus and of Charun). At Vulci, in the François Tomb, blood flows freely in scenes of battle and of human sacrifice: the sacrifice of the Trojan prisoners (fig. IV-96), a battle with local chiefs, or condottieri, whose names are carefully recorded, the duel between Eteocles and Polyneices. Here Etruscan painting, near the end of its cycle, foreshadows Roman historical art, with its taste for narration and portraiture. This same tomb contains the image of Vel Saties, whom Massimo Pallottino calls "the first full-length standing [painted] portrait of European art" (fig. IV-97).

Geographical Variety

The geographical differences in Etruscan art constitute one of its most characteristic features. We can distinguish three major areas, defined by specific techniques, types, and styles: southern, northern, and central (inland) Etruria. Beyond this, there was the Etruscanized Po Valley to the north and, to the south, the Faliscan region, deeply influenced by Etruscan art, and Latium, where, in the Archaic period, Etruscan and Greek influences converged.

Artistic forms and styles varied from city to city, but there was a lively interchange between them as well as with other cities in Italy and elsewhere. A receptivity to the arts of other civilizations was shared by all the cities of Etruria, with greater or lesser enthusiasm. The coastal cities, the first to receive outside influences, responded almost immediately by imitation or adaptation. This was true of Cerveteri and Tarquinia in the south and also, in the north, of Vetulonia and Populonia. The delay before such influences reached the northern and inland cities was not as great as has been sometimes supposed by those who see their art as retarded,

IV-97. François Tomb, Vulci, portrait of Vel Saties. Fourth century B.C. Rome, Museo Torlonia. (DAI.)

Generally speaking, the periods are the Orientalizing and Archaic (about 725/700 to 460 B.C., sometimes later); the Classical (in Etruria, an intermediate period rather than a separate phase, about 460 to about 300 B.C.); and the Hellenistic (about 300 to the first century B.C.).

Etruscan art did not develop, as Greek art did, in a geographically and chronologically continuous sequence, but in spurts, as a series of responses to external stimuli. In the end it seems to express a kind of compromise between outside impulses and purely local tendencies, contrasting movements which existed in Etruscan art from its very beginnings. Indeed, the beginning of what we call Etruscan art, about 700 B.C., was sudden and remarkable. It developed in the context of Orientalizing art, a collection of tastes and tendencies, a common style, and a type of craftsmanship formed in the Orient, at the borders of Syria, Palestine, and Phoenicia. This style assimilated diverse elements from Semitic, Urartian, Iranian, and Anatolian art, and was spread to the cities of Greece and Etruria by the export of raw materials, like ivory and gold, and a variety of textiles and small luxury objects.

Etruscan craftsmen adopted certain sophisticated techniques of this unusual art, as well as its exotic "Orientalizing" iconographic repertoire. To this they added Greek mythology, with its powerful poetic attraction and organized composition, but this phase of Etruscan art does not exhibit the artistic creativity and national character so apparent in Greek art. Etruria's failure to develop a truly original style may stem from this period. She became rich too soon, and too quickly. Her need for material goods and greed for luxury items had grown before her own artists and artisans—without strong local artistic traditions, which develop over a long period of time—had learned to satisfy such cravings. Etruscan workshops were confronted too soon with a variety of fully realized foreign productions; overwhelmed, they resorted to a more or less successful imitation of these imported objects.

When Etruscan art entered the artistic sphere of Greece—both Greece proper and its colonies in southern Italy and Sicily—it succumbed to the fascination with the human body, the principal subject of Greek art. Greek artists, constantly perfecting or modifying the human form with all the gestures

preserving conventional, conservative motifs. To the contrary, it would seem that a city like Chiusi, with the remarkable variety and continuity of its art, was never isolated in the heart of central Etruria, but kept up with new fashions at a rapid and constant pace, no doubt through commercial relations with other cities by way of the Tiber and its tributaries.

Originality

The chronological development of Etruscan art runs more or less parallel to that of the various phases of Greek art. (At the beginning, however, there was a time lag, as the Etruscans continued to use styles which had run their course in Greece.)

and poses which represent man's nobility, were constantly renewing forms and types within the context of their extremely active intellectual and artistic tradition.

In its sculpture, Etruscan art of the Archaic period shares the Greek artists' concern with working out new forms, but it chooses models and transforms them, adapting them with strength and originality. The very appearance of carvings in stone in the first part of the sixth century B.C. was stimulated by the influence of seventh-century Greek Daedalic sculpture with its rigorously constructed geometric forms. Yet the centaur from Vulci (fig. IV-98) derives its peculiar power more from the brutal, blocklike construction of the body and the roughly idealized quality of the head than from any of the natural breath of life which animates even the earliest Greek kouroi of this period.

Toward the middle of the sixth century B.C., there appears in Etruscan art a taste for curved lines, a tendency to represent scenes and groups of figures in a lively style, full of movement, to show more rounded bodies, to soften planes and to decorate surfaces with delicate linear arabesques. Such a tendency, which originated in the Eastern regions of the Greek world, in the Ionian cities of the coast of Asia Minor and the islands, suited Etruscan art better than the rigorous abstractions of Daedalic art. The triumph of this art in Etruria marks the creation of an Etrusco-Ionian art, perhaps the highest point of the representational art of Etruria.

In the early fifth century B.C., the Severe Style of Attic art, with its sense of proportion and harmonious rendering of bodies, movements, gestures, and expressions, tempered the exaggerated tendencies of the Ionian style, particularly obvious in certain bronzes. Yet rather than the patient observation of the body and drapery evident in the Greek kouroi and korai, Etruscan sculpture can always be recognized by the uncertainty of its proportions. The body as model was used only reluctantly and awkwardly; the silence of the unmoving figure which dominates Archaic Greek art is noticeably absent in Etruscan sculpture. Figures are short and stocky, or puffed up, or elongated and almost threadlike. Also characteristic is the emphasis on expressive details of muscles, hair, or garments, which are

IV-98. Statue of a centaur, Vulci. Stone. Early sixth century B.C. Rome, Villa Giulia. (Soprintendenza alle Antichità dell'Etruria Meridionale.)

minutely rendered. (In contrast, other details are neglected or carelessly rendered.) Typical of this tendency is the incredible stylization of drapery: it is conceived of as decoration, rather than a covering through which the tightly modeled body forms are seen.

The Apollo of Veii, dated about 510–490 B.C. (fig. IV-99), exemplifies these tendencies and illustrates the Etruscans' love of life and their obsession with the divine will, as well as their ability to translate movement into art. Such a movement at its worst, in second- and third-rate work, degenerated into frantic gesticulation, ungraceful contortions or disproportioned, deformed shapes. But the "Master of the Apollo from Veii" knew how to combine the linear tradition of Archaic art with the features of the Ionian style, and to capitalize upon the possibilities of the medium of terracotta. The lunging movement of the god's stride, impetuous but stable and decisive, carries forward a body modeled with graceful, powerfully massive forms and muscles whose lines follow a rhythm of their own, from the calm contours of the shoulders to the crescendo of the folds of the mantle between his legs. The same nervous energy invests the locks of hair spread out

IV-99. Apollo from Veii, statue once decorating the roof of the temple of the sanctuary of Portonaccio, Veii, as part of a group with Apollo and Herakles fighting over the Ceryneian hind. Terracotta. Lifesize. 510–490 B.C. Rome, Villa Giulia. (DAI.)

IV-100. Polycleitus, statue of an athlete. Bronze. Roman copy of a Greek original of the fifth century B.C. Paris, Louvre, Br. 183. (M. Chuzeville, Louvre.)

over his shoulders and the fan-shaped muscles of the calves of his legs. The bright coloring of the Archaic period, the light ivory color of the fabric against the somber vigor of the reddish-brown face and flesh, accentuates the impression of a dark, implacable force, an irresistible power.

In spite of its earlier date, this masterpiece of the late sixth century can be compared to the great monuments of Classical art of Athens. These two visions of the world represent contrasting and almost incompatible artistic ideals, but they nevertheless derive from the same Greek source. The spearbearer of Polycleitus in the fifth century B.C. (fig. IV-100), teaches harmony, balance, sobriety, and

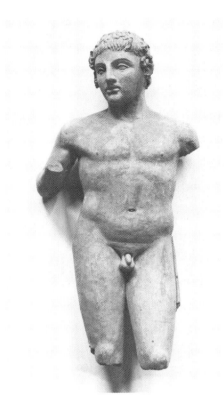 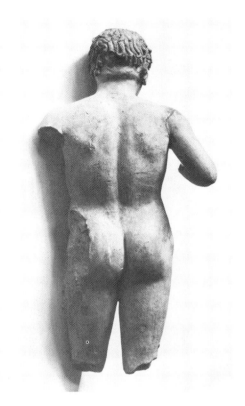

IV-101. Statue of a youth, sanctuary of Portonaccio, Veii, reflecting the influence of Polycleitus. Ca. 400 B.C. Rome, Villa Giulia. (DAI.)

self-control by means of the exact measurements of its parts. Based on a deep study of the human body, which the artist presents ritually naked, this piece expresses the Greeks' deep-seated need to express an ideal which is never fully realized but toward which they must strive in their daily lives in order to please the gods. The figure glorifies the perfection of the human body as a universal image of divine beauty, its regular features untroubled by any violent emotion, the purity of its lines unmoved by any irrational impulse, and the counterpoised rhythm of its limbs, carefully planned yet animated and alive, showing readiness for action, though not in action.

The essence of Classical Greek art was to remain for the most part alien from the spirit and traditions of the Etruscans, whose religious vision made them

conservative and whose artistic tendencies led them toward attention to detail and exuberant decoration. Yet the Greek Severe Style so warmly welcomed in Etruscan art had in some way paved the way for a Classical influence which gradually entered Etruria. During the fifth century B.C., Etruscan artists produced a number of monuments of sculpture and painting which were competent but cold imitations of Greek Classical art of the same period. These masterpieces clearly no longer stimulated the Etruscans' creative imagination. One cannot, however, speak of a simply conservative art, or of stagnation. Recent studies have shown Etruscan art of this period to be more influenced by current trends than was once thought (fig. IV-101). The heads of gods from Civita Castellana (Falerii) (fig. IV-102) and from the Belvedere of Orvieto (fig. IV-

IV-102. Head of Zeus(?) from the temple at Lo Scasato, Falerii. Terracotta. Late fifth century B.C. Rome, Villa Giulia. (DAI.)

IV-103. Antefix, Belvedere Temple, Orvieto. Terracotta. Fifth century B.C. Orvieto, Museo Civico. (DAI.)

IV-104. "Malavolta" head of a youth from Veii. Terracotta. 450–400 B.C. Rome, Villa Giulia. (DAI.)

103) and the beautiful *testa Malavolta* (fig. IV-104) prove that they appreciated the majesty of the works of Phidias and the more moving dignity of his successors, and were more than just passively inspired. This group of sculptures includes the Mars from Todi, funerary stone statues from Chiusi, and architectural terracottas from Orvieto.

We can see how Greek art and Greek models were transmitted in the early period; less clear is the way in which the influence of this later, Classical art entered Etruria. From the third century B.C., Etruria, by now under Roman power, was gradually integrated into the common Greek culture of the Hellenistic period, within which ideas and forms circulated with ease. Etruscan workshops probably used some sort of "artists' notebooks," or pattern books, perhaps made of terracotta, wood, cloth, or

IV-105. Decoration from the Temple of the Ara della Regina, Tarquinia, winged horses. Terracotta. Lifesize. Third century B.C. Tarquinia Museum. (Anderson.)

parchment. Artists must also have traveled to Magna Graecia: the influence of south Italian art is clearly visible in Etruscan art of the fourth century and later. The powerful influence of the sculpture of the great Altar of Pergamon can be seen in the style of many Hellenistic sculptured urns and sarcophagi and in the painting of Tarquinia, in the Tomb of the Typhon (fig. IV-106).

Etruscan originality can thus be understood by noting those of its features which are lacking in Greek art. Typically Etruscan is an interest in nature, a subject which apparently failed to inspire Greek artists (though the disappearance of monumental Greek painting may explain its absence). Tomb paintings show how the Etruscan painter's eye lovingly observed the different aspects of the world outside, while his hand transferred them to the wall with surprising speed and precision, despite their occasional awkwardness and the inevitable use of artistic conventions. People and nature occupy a light, limitless space extending far beyond the tomb chamber in graceful, sensuous waves. Men and women move gaily among small trees whose trunks prolong or interrupt the musical rhythm marked on the walls (figs. IV-91–94). There is a sense of spontaneous happiness, the joy of movement. In the Tomb of Hunting and Fishing (fig. IV-107), the Etruscan diving into the waves is only one of a number of figures moving in the middle of a col-

IV-106. Winged demon, Tomb of the Typhon, Tarquinia. Ca. 150 B.C. (DAI.)

ored landscape. In contrast, the Greek diver at Paestum, in the Tomb of the Diver in Greek Campania (fig. IV-108), remains isolated in an abstract, neutral space, frozen in a pose which emphasizes the forms of his body. In Etruria, the human figure is not, as in Greece, an end in itself. It expresses the passing moment: dancers, musicians, athletes, and guests at the banquet are rendered at different instants of the action, in an apparent realism which only seems to represent the real world. Greek depictions of banquets with their sober, pure lines satisfy us intellectually, but they do not move us as these sensuous Etruscan parties do. The daring stylization of the large hands, whose long fingers express all the shades of movement and feeling, poignantly reflect the Etruscan joy of life. The intense, occasionally garish colors, richly decorative, accentuate with their violent contrasts a certain popular flavor often present in these paintings.

More recent tombs reflect the new pictorial styles of the fourth century B.C. in Greece. (figs. IV-95–97). Linear designs still predominate, but the well-matched colors are more diluted and softer and often give an illusion of relief and three-dimensional

IV-108. Tomb of the Diver, Paestum. Ca. 475 B.C. Diver painted on roof of tomb. Paestum Museum. (Soprintendenza Archeologica–Salerno.)

IV-107. Tomb of Hunting and Fishing, Tarquinia, diver. Ca. 540–520 B.C. (DAI.)

space, while a delicate sfumato models the facial features (fig. IV-109).

From the third century B.C. on, the profound changes which have taken place in the art of the Hellenistic world are reflected in Etruscan art. The Hellenistic taste for the picturesque, for individual, emotional expression, theatrical scenes and effects (figs. IV-88, IV-110), and the depiction of an immediate reality was congenial to Etruscan art and temperament. This taste is best illustrated in funerary monuments such as urns, sarcophagi, and paintings. In contrast, an earlier style is used for bronzes, terracottas, and some types of luxury objects which not only continued to be manufactured but in many cases gained in popularity.

The poor quality of most of these monuments, especially the urns, does not affect their interest for us as evidence of the spread of Hellenistic culture. The relief decoration of the urns presents a combination of various themes and styles, only occasionally rising above the mediocre. Yet these subjects derived from daily life have a prosaic, familiar tone, an attractively earthy quality, expressed by the naive realism of certain details and the awkward depiction of space, in which side and frontal views are used together to represent stiff, jointed figures like marionettes in a bird's-eye view perspective (fig. IV–110).

While the figures reclining on the lids of urns from Chiusi tend to represent the deceased within the context of their daily lives, drawing their inspiration, often with some success, from Hellenistic motifs (cf. figs. IV-43–44), those from Volterra instead consciously deform the individual human figure in order to insist on the man's or woman's social position and heroic dignity (fig. IV-45). The body is schematized as a rigid, compact block, tightly enfolded by drapery whose curves are flattened and geometricized. The poses are frozen and ridiculous; the enormous head is usually expressionless, and the eyes stare straight ahead or turn upward. The deep-seated current of "popular" Italic art, already apparent, would reappear later in provincial Roman art in the time of the empire.

Portraits, which seem to be present on some of these funerary monuments, are the most striking feature of the last phase of Etruscan art (fig. IV-111). The final explosion of Etruscan Hellenistic art brings together all the anarchy of forms and violent creative imagination intermittently in evidence during the previous phases. In contrast to the Greek sculptor, who sacrificed detailed realism to an expressive and harmonious representation, the Etruscan artist based the "truth" of the portrait on actual observation of the model, representing external, surface aspects, such as the hair, wild and unkempt or neatly combed, or the boniness or fleshiness of

IV-109. Tomb of the Shields, Tarquinia, deceased couple at a banquet. Hellenistic. (Alinari.)

IV-110. Urn from Chiusi with relief decoration of the death of Hippolytus.
Stone. Second or first century B.C. Palermo, Museo Archeologico.

IV-111. Head of a man from the votive deposit of Manganello, Cerveteri. Painted terracotta. Ca. 100 B.C. Rome, Villa Giulia. (DAI.)

IV-112. Statuette of a soldier from Perugia. Bronze. Hellenistic. Florence, Museo Archeologico. (Soprintendenza alle Antichità–Firenze.)

IV-113. Statuette of a woman. Bronze. Hellenistic. Paris, Louvre. (Museum photo.)

the face. A specific individual is seen in a particular moment of his physical existence; these are not, as in Greece, portraits of character, or of a more general human or social type. This brutal, superficial analysis of the individual human being in Etruscan sculpture was developed further in Roman art and, eventually, in Renaissance and later portraiture.

On these isolated heads, originally belonging to statues whose bodies have been lost, the Etruscan artist's motivation is to produce a striking work of art: *épater les bourgeois,* as the French say. For Etruscan art is not a discipline, like Greek art; nor does it share the Greek ambition to attain a certain permanence or universality. Spontaneous and immediate, often modest in ambition and attainment, this art never isolated itself in a search for perfection. The beauty or ugliness of such works, both of which are frequently and unexpectedly present, their lack of sophistication, their sense of humor, and the daring stylization of forms all appeal directly to the viewer. This technical carelessness and extreme simplification aims at representing the fleeting moment, translating directly the movements of the heart—and perhaps also a certain selfish individualism—and appealing to the senses. The Greek form is an idea: the Etruscan form is an impression, deeply felt, even when represented in an incomplete, unfinished manner. This is perhaps the secret of its appeal to us today.

Bibliography

With the exception of Ducati and Giglioli, only recent books are listed.

GENERAL PUBLICATIONS

Banti, *Etruscan Cities.*
R. Bianchi Bandinelli, "Etrusca Arte," in *Enciclopedia dell'arte classica e orientale* (Rome 1961) 476–503.
———, and A. Giuliano, *Les Étrusques et L'Italie avant Rome* (Paris 1973).
R. Bloch, *L'Art et la civilisation étrusques* (Paris 1965).
———, *L'Art des Étrusques* (Paris 1965).
Brendel, *Etruscan Art.*
Cristofani, *L'arte degli Etruschi.*
———, *Etruschi. Cultura e società* (Novara 1979).

T. Dohrn, *Grundzüge etruskischer Kunst* (Baden-Baden 1958).
P. Ducati, *Storia dell'arte etrusca* (Florence 1927).
G.Q. Giglioli, *L'arte etrusca.*
G.A. Mansuelli, *Etruria and Early Rome* (London 1966).
H. Mühlestein, *Die Etrusker im Spiegel ihrer Kunst* (Berlin 1979).
M. Pallottino, *Civiltà artistica etrusco-italica* (Florence 1971).
P.J. Riis, *An Introduction to Etruscan Art* (Copenhagen 1953).
Sprenger-Bartoloni.
Strøm, *Etruscan Orientalizing.*
W. Zschietzschmann, *Etruskische Kunst* (Frankfurt-am-Main 1969).

EXHIBITION CATALOGUES

Arte e civiltà degli Etruschi (Turin 1967).
G. Colonna, *Nuovi Tesori dell'antica Tuscia* (Viterbo 1970).
Gli Etruschi e Cerveteri (Milan 1980).
G.A. Mansuelli, *Mostra dell'Etruria Padana e della città di Spina* (Berlin 1960).
Mostra dell'Arte e della Civiltà Etrusca (Milan 1955).
Nuove scoperte e acquisizioni nell'Etruria (Rome 1975).
Prima Italia. Arts italiques du premier millénaire av. J.C. (Brussels 1980–81).
R.S. Teitz, *Masterpieces of Etruscan Art* (Worcester, Massachusetts, 1967).

VILLANOVAN ART

Civiltà del Ferro (Bologna 1960).
H. Hencken, *Tarquinia, Villanovans and Early Etruscans* (Cambridge, Massachusetts, 1968).

PAINTING

M. Moretti, *New Monuments of Etruscan Painting* (University Park, Pennsylvania, 1970).
M. Pallottino, *Etruscan Painting* (Geneva 1952).
F. Roncalli, *Le lastre dipinte di Cerveteri* (Florence 1966).

SCULPTURE

A. Andrén, *Architectural Terracottas from Etrusco-Italic Temples* (Lund 1940).

R. Bianchi Bandinelli, *Storicità dell'arte classica* (Florence 1943).

M.-F. Briguet, "Urnes archaïques étrusques," *RA* (1968) 49–72.

———, "La sculpture en pierre fétide au Musée du Louvre," *MEFRA* 84 (1972) 847–77; *MEFRA* 87 (1975) 143–208.

———, "La sculpture en pierre fétide au Musée du Louvre," *Mélanges Boyancé* (Rome 1974) 103–39.

Brown, *Etruscan Lion*.

Caratteri dell'ellenismo.

G. Colonna, *Bronzi votivi umbro-sabellici a figurine umane. I. Periodo arcaico* (Florence 1970).

M. Cristofani, *Statue-cinerario chiusine di età classica* (Rome 1975).

CUE. Urne volterrane (Florence 1970).

Gempeler, *Etruskischen Kanopen*.

R. Herbig, *Die jüngeretruskische Steinsarkophage* (Berlin 1952).

A. Hus, *Recherches sur la statuaire en pierre étrusque archaïque* (Paris 1961).

———, *Les Bronzes étrusques* (Brusseles 1974).

F.H. Pairault, *Recherches sur quelques séries d'urnes de Volterra à représentations mythologiques* (Rome 1972).

P.J. Riis, *Tyrrhenika. An Archaeological Study of Etruscan Sculpture in the Archaic and Classical Periods* (Copenhagen 1941).

F. Roncalli, *Il "Marte" di Todi* (Città del Vaticano 1973).

M. Sprenger, *Die etruskische Plastik des V. Jahrhunderts und ihr Verhältnis zur griechischen Kunst* (Rome 1972).

N.A. Winter, "Architectural Terracottas Decorated with Human Heads," *RömMitt* 85 (1978) 27–58.

P. Zanker, "Zur Rezeption des hellenistischen Individualporträts," in *Hellenismus in Mittelitalien* (Göttingen 1976).

VASES

Beazley, *EVP*.

G. Camporeale, *Buccheri a cilindretto di fabrica orvietana* (Florence 1972).

M. Del Chiaro, *The Genucilia Group* (Berkeley and Los Angeles 1957).

———, *The Etruscan Funnel Group* (Florence 1974).

———, *Etruscan Red-Figured Vase Painting at Caere* (Berkeley and Los Angeles 1974).

L. Hannestad, *The Paris Painter* (Copenhagen 1974).

———, *The Followers of the Paris Painter* (Copenhagen 1976).

R. Harari, *Il Gruppo Clusium* (Bari 1980).

G. Pianu, *Materiali del Museo Archeologico Nazionale di Tarquinia—Ceramiche etrusche a figure rosse* (Rome 1980).

T.B. Rasmussen, *Bucchero Pottery from Southern Etruria* (Cambridge 1979).

F. Schippa, *Officine ceramiche falische* (Bari 1980).

JEWELRY

G. Becatti, *Oreficerie antiche, dalle minoiche alle barbariche* (Rome 1955).

Higgins, *Jewellery*.

MIRRORS AND CISTAE

Bordenache-Battaglia, *Ciste prenestine I*.

U. Fischer-Graf, *Spiegelwerkstätten in Vulci* (Berlin 1980).

G.A. Foerst, *Die Gravierungen der pränestinischen Cisten* (Rome 1978).

B. Gerhard, *Etruskische Spiegel* (Berlin 1839–97).

Guide to Etruscan Mirrors.

R. Lambrechts, *Les miroirs étrusques et prénestins des Musées Royaux d'Art et d'Histoire à Bruxelles* (Brussels 1978).

I. Mayer-Prokop, *Die gravierten etruskischen Griffspiegel archaischen Stils* (Heidelberg 1967).

Rebuffat-Emmanuel, *Le miroir étrusque*.

H. Salskov Roberts, *CSE*. Denmark 1, 1 (Odense 1981).

G. Sassatelli, *CSE*. Italia 1, *Bologna, Museo Civico 1–2* (Rome 1981).

L.B. van der Meer, *CSE*. Netherlands (Leiden 1983).

V / Architecture

FRIEDHELM PRAYON

Architecture is of special importance for our knowledge of the Etruscans, for it is primarily through their architecture, especially that of their tombs, that modern interest in them was awakened (see Ch. I). These tombs have kept their original, frequently splendid, appearance, particularly in southern Etruria where they were cut out of the soft volcanic stone called *tufa* (fig. V-1). They are also significant for other areas of Etruscan art because of their grave gifts, such as objects of precious metals and Greek vases, and their mural paintings. Moreover, these tombs yield information on Etruscan burial customs, attitudes toward death, and basic aspects of life, since the interiors of the tombs are often copies of actual houses. It is not surprising that interest in Etruscan art and culture was stimulated by these tombs, and that the understanding of house architecture was also advanced by way of the exploration of these tomb structures. The emphasis of the investigation has gradually shifted, however. Recently, the remains of settlements are also being systematically excavated, and scholars are studying town layouts as well as the forms of the single houses and sacred buildings.

In contrast to Greeks and Romans, the Etruscans made no use of marble either in architecture or sculpture, though important marble quarries, such as those of Carrara (Roman Luni), were conveniently situated within their region. Instead, the Etruscans preferred building materials which were easily workable, such as wood, clay, and tufa, and they became great masters of those mediums. Fortunately, the easily worked tufa hardens when it comes into direct contact with the air, allowing Etruscan architects and stonecutters to create a wide variety of architectural forms, which are preserved for us in excellent condition.

Tombs and Necropoleis

In the early seventh century B.C., an important change in burial custom took place in Etruria. In earlier centuries the single tomb was the only form of gravesite, whether as a simple urn grave for cremation burials (*a pozzo*) (fig. V-2) or as a burial of the corpse (*tomba a fossa*) (fig. V-3). Now people began to bury the dead collectively, or in family groups, and therefore to build bigger tombs in the form of chamber tombs (*tomba a camera*). This transformation from single to collective burial and from the fossa or "ditch" grave to the chamber tomb occurred slowly. At first, the simple casket form of the fossa was widened, and the number of burials was doubled (fig. V-3); later they became multiple graves. Yet the chamber tomb did not signify the end of the fossa burials. They were still used for some time, probably by poorer people.

That there was a continuous development of different forms of tombs is important for our knowledge of the Etruscans. Scholars have usually assumed that changes in burial customs, such as the changeover from single to collective burial in prehistoric cultures, signify ethnic changes. But this gradual transformation does not support such an assumption for Etruria. The Etruscans may have received inspiration for the formation of their tombs from outside sources, though such influence is hard to prove. Up to now, it has not been possible to determine the origin of certain tomb forms. Almost simultaneously with the earliest, simple chamber tombs, there also appear huge monumental tombs for which, in Etruria, there are no models nor precedents. In the north these tombs may have a round burial room and a long dromos, or entrance (fig. V-4, Nos. 2–5) which slightly resemble early

V-1. Drawing by James Byres, Tomb of the Cardinal, Tarquinia. The frescoes faintly visible on the walls have disintegrated since the eighteenth century, when this drawing was made. (DAI.)

V-2. Pozzo tomb from the Via Sacra, Rome. Early Iron Age. Rome, Antiquarium Forense. (Boethius fig. 7.)

V-3. Development of tomb types, Cerveteri necropolis. *Top to bottom:* fossa tomb to chamber tomb. (Prayon fig. 3.)

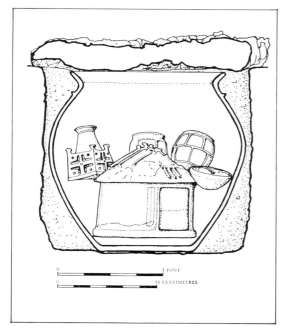

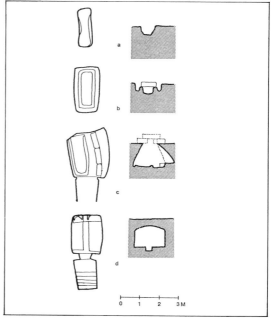

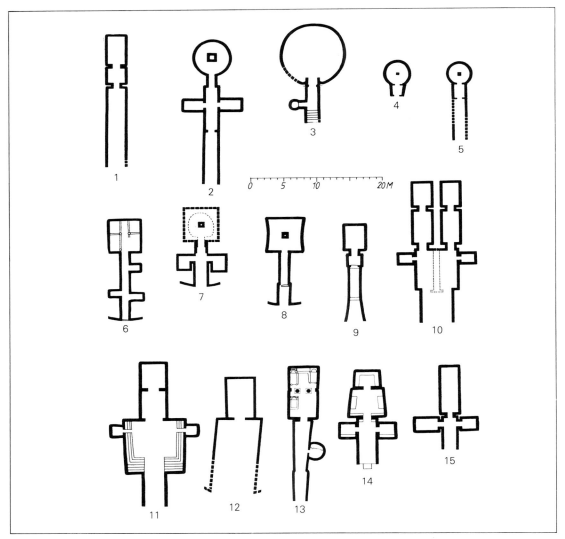

V-4. Early Etruscan chamber tombs. Ca. 650–550 B.C. *1*, Comeana, Montefortini; *2*, Florence, Montagnola; *3*, Florence, Mula; *4*, Casal Marittimo; *5*, Volterra, Casaglia Tomb; *6*, Populonia, Tomb of the Chariots; *7*, Vetulonia, Pietrera Tomb 1; *8*, Vetulonia, Pozzo all'Abate; *9*, Castellina in Chianti; *10*, Cortona, Melone dei Camucía; *11*, Vulci, Cuccumella; *12*, Tarquinia, Doganaccia Tomb 1; *13;* Blera, Valle Cappellana Tomb 1; *14*, Veii, Campana Tomb; *15*, Veii, Formello Tomb (reconstruction). (Prayon pls. 86, 87.)

Greek tholoi. In the south, the Regolini-Galassi Tomb in Cerveteri (Caere), with its overly long ground plan and upper structure and protruding stone blocks as roof cover (figs. V-5, No. 3; V-6), shows a remarkable similarity to tombs in Ugarit (Syria).

In the late seventh century B.C., such large tombs appeared throughout the Etruscan region. There are regional distinctions: tholoi are so far restricted to the region between Volterra and Florence (fig. V-4, Nos. 2–5); in Vetulonia and Populonia, the circular cupola rests on a square room (figs. V-4, Nos. 6–8; V-7). The tombs in Cortona are characterized by their many rooms (fig. V-4, No. 10),

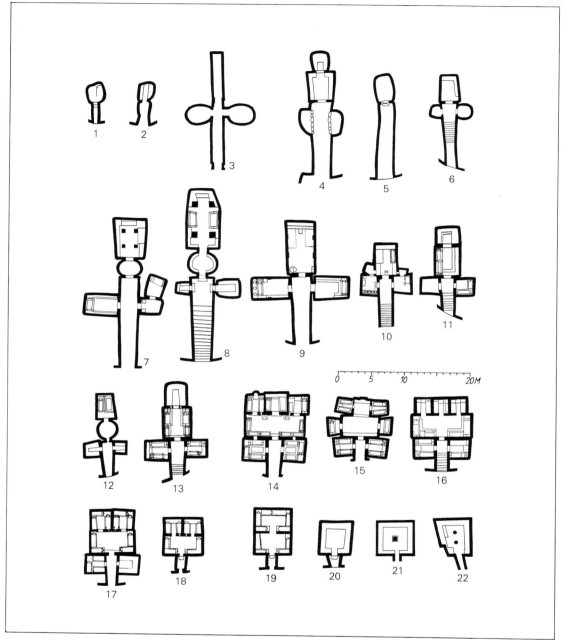

V-5. Archaic chamber tombs, Cerveteri. Ca. 700–500 B.C. *1*, Tomb 75; *2*, Tomb 176; *3*, Regolini-Galassi Tomb; *4*, Tomb of the Thatched Roof; *5*, Tomb of the Colonel 1; *6*, Tomb 2; *7*, Tomb of the Ship 1; *8*, Tomb of the Painted Animals 1; *9*, Campana Tomb 1; *10*, Tomb of the Five Chairs; *11*, Tomb 10 of the Jars and Fire Dogs (dei Dolii e degli Alari); *12*, Tomb 50; *13*, Tomb 8 of the Beds and Sarcophagi; *14*, Tomb of the Shields and Chairs; *15*, Tomba della Ripa (del Tablino); *16*, Tomb 9 of the Greek Vases; *17*, Tomb of the Potter's Clay (Argilla); *18*, Tomb 329; *19*, Tomb 386; *20*, Tomb 350; *21*, Canina Tomb 2; *22*, Tomb of the Doric Columns. (Prayon pl. 85.)

V-6. Regolini-Galassi tomb, Cerveteri. Seventh century B.C. (D. Anderson.)

V-7. Tomb of the Chariots, Populonia. (DAI.)

those in the south (Veii and Cerveteri) by their long
rectangular main chamber (figs. V-4, No. 14; V-5,
No. 3). They nonetheless all share certain characteristics, such as the preference for a long, narrow
dromos, with side chambers symmetrically branch-
ing off from it; a roof construction built from protruding stone blocks; and the outer appearance of
the tomb, which was covered by a huge mound and
bordered by stone slabs. Because of the tomb's
round shape, it is called a tumulus, or, in at least
one case, *a cuccumella*, or "melon." Often these tumuli contain only one tomb. One tumulus, near
Castellina in Chianti (fig. V-8), south of Florence,
holds four tombs, oriented approximately toward
the four points of the compass. All were apparently
built at the same time.

On the other hand, the great tumuli of Cerveteri,
the most impressive and best preserved necropolis

V-8. Tumulus of Monte Calvario, Castellina in Chianti.
The four tombs included are oriented North, South, East,
and West. (Prayon fig. 19.)

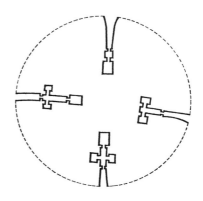

of the Etruscans (fig. V-9), normally contain several tombs. Each tumulus was in the possession of a family and served for several generations as the final resting place for its dead, as shown by the fact that the separate tombs were not built simultaneously but at definite intervals (fig. V-10). Between each of the four tombs of Tumulus II, for instance, there is an interval of about thirty to forty years, which probably marks a generational change. Tumulus II also illustrates the development of tomb architecture in Cerveteri. The earliest of its four burial sites, the Tomb of the Thatched Roof, in which both the burial chambers connected to the long dromos have been completely cut out of the tufa, is more advanced than the Regolini-Galassi Tomb, which was partly built with stone blocks. This development continued in the tombs of the following centuries in the tufa-rich south. Due to the lack of tufa in central and north Etruria, on the other hand, tombs there were always built of stone blocks.

The discovery that the desired architectural forms of the tombs could be carved out of the tufa allowed the tomb builders to imitate, quite spontaneously, the interior shape of a house, reproduced in all its detail. The inner chamber was now a more or less faithful copy of the dwelling-house. Behind the fashion for this tomb architecture lies the desire—earlier conceptualized by the inhabitants of the Villanovan period, who made cinerary urns in the shape of their own houses for the ashes of the dead (fig. V-ll), to leave the deceased within his usual environment, his home, and to furnish him with everything he liked that would be useful for him for his life after death. All kinds of furniture, implements, and weapons, as well as perishable things, such as food, were left for the dead, as we

V-9a. Plan of Banditaccia necropolis, Cerveteri. (Prayon fig. 2.)

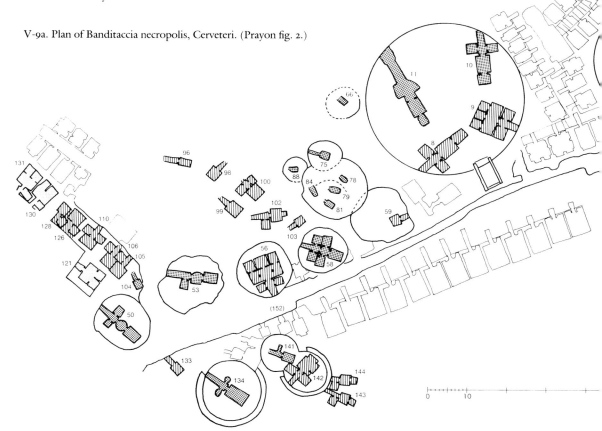

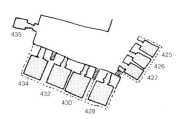

700–600 B.C.

600–530 B.C.

530–450 B.C.

450–100 B.C.

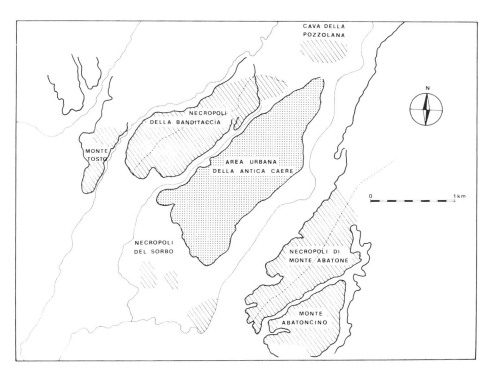

V-9b. Archaeological map of Cerveteri. (Prayon fig. 1.)

see in the earliest chamber tombs such as the Regolini-Galassi Tomb. A deliberate copy of a real house, the interior of the Tomb of the Thatched Roof is formed like a hut, with a narrow ridge beam and downward-sloping, "vaulted" roof (fig. V-12).

The later tombs of Tumulus II, the Tomb of the Jars and Fire Dogs, of the second half of the seventh century B.C. (figs. V-5, No.11; V-10, *detail*) and the Tomb of the Beds and Sarcophagi of the first half of the sixth century B.C. (figs. V-5, No. 13; V-10, *detail*) were modeled on massive larger houses, with plain roof beams and a broad ridge beam. The plan, which consists of two consecutive chambers, one opening on the other, was also imitated from the contemporary type of house. The latest tomb of Tumulus II, the Tomb of the Greek Vases, of the third quarter of the sixth century B.C. (figs. V-5, No. 16; V-10, *detail*), shows a different plan, consisting of a wide room with three chambers behind it. The details of construction, like the shape of the doors and windows, were again based on those

of contemporary houses. In the Tomb of the Thatched Roof, the furniture—for example, the beds—was still carried into the tomb and placed on a raised base of tufa or on river pebbles (fig. V-12). Soon thereafter, the deathbeds were carved out of the tufa (fig. V-13), as were other furnishings such as baskets, seats, chairs, and shields. Together with the very detailed imitations of wooden roof constructions and columns with sizeable capitals and profile bases (the so-called Etruscan column), these tombs give the impression of being real dwellings for the living (fig. V-14).

From the late sixth century B.C. onward, however, the tombs at Cerveteri no longer imitated real house forms. In contrast to house architecture, which became larger in ground plan, the reverse was true of tombs, which now consisted of fewer and fewer rooms (fig. V-5, Nos. 17–19). By about 500 B.C., the one-room chamber tomb appeared (fig. V-5, Nos. 20–22)—a type which in the following centuries became typical in this necropolis. In

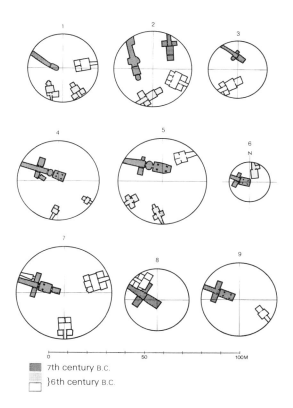

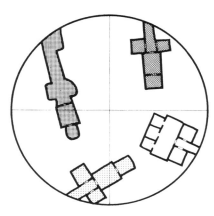

V-10. Orientation of chamber tombs in monumental tumuli, Cerveteri. Seventh and sixth centuries B.C. *1,* Tumulus of the Colonel; *2,* Tumulus II, of the Hut or Thatched Roof; *3,* Tumulus I, of the Sarcophagi; *4,* Tumulus of the Ship; *5,* Tumulus of the Painted Animals; *6,* Tumulus VII; *7,* Tumulus of the Shields and Chairs; *8,* Campana Tumulus; *9,* Tumulus III, of the Painted Tile. *Detail:* Tumulus II, Cerveteri (*clockwise*): Tomb of the Jars and Fire Dogs (dei Dolii e degli Alari); Tomb of the Greek Vases; Tomb of the Beds and Sarcophagi; Tomb of the Hut or Thatched Roof. (Prayon fig. 82.)

■ 7th century B.C.
▨ }6th century B.C.
□

V-11. Hut urn from Vulci. Terracotta. (Moretti, *Kunst und Land die Etrusker* fig. 97.)

V-12. Tomb 11 (Tomb of the Hut or Thatched Roof). Cerveteri. (DAI.)

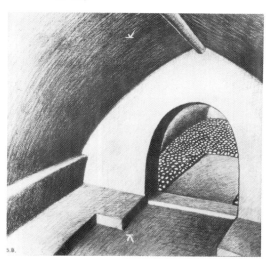

V-13. Tomb of the Beds and Sarcophagi (tomb 8), Cerveteri. (Prayon pl. 21.)

V-16. Tomba Torlonia, Cerveteri. (DAI.)

V-14. Tomba Giuseppe Moretti, Cerveteri. (Moretti, *Cerveteri* fig. 50.)

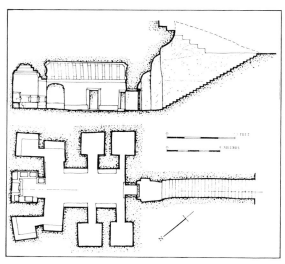

V-17. Tomb of the Volumnii, Perugia. (Boethius fig. 72.)

V-15. Tomba Campana 1, Cerveteri. (DAI.)

V-18. Porticus tombs, San Giuliano. (Moretti.)

V-19. Aedicula or house-shaped tomb, Populonia. (DAI.)

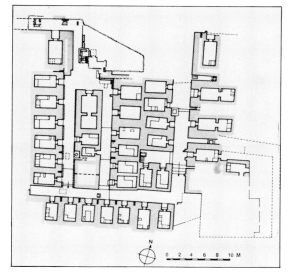

V-20. Crocifisso del Tufo necropolis, Orvieto. (Sprenger-Bartoloni fig. 6.)

V-21. Tumulus with ramp and *tomba a dado, scavi nuovi,* Cerveteri. (Moretti, *Cerveteri* fig. 27.)

some cases these one-room chamber tombs still reflect house architecture, at least in its central part. The impressive chamber tombs of some upper-class families, such as the richly decorated Tomb of Reliefs and the no less monumental Torlonia Tomb (fig. V-16), imitate in an abstract way the central part of contemporary dwellings (called atrium houses), while the smaller rooms (cubicula) in these tombs are reduced to simple niches (loculi) used for burial purposes only.

Outside Cerveteri, tomb architecture did not always develop in the direction of one-chamber tombs. In Chiusi and Vulci, for example, they often consisted of a group of single rooms, sometimes imitating real house architecture, as in the François Tomb in Vulci or, later on, in the Tomb of the Volumnii in Perugia (fig. V-17). Their structure, with a symmetrical layout of several chambers grouped around a T-shaped nucleus, resembles the above-mentioned atrium house type, which seems to be of Etrusco-Italic origin (see below).

It is not only the interior of the tomb which changed over time. The development of the outer shape is no less varied. In the seventh century B.C., large tumuli predominated (fig. V-10). In the sixth century B.C., smaller tomb structures became more frequent. At first, these retained the round shape of the tumulus, with the entrance to the tomb chamber cleverly concealed on the outside so that it was all but invisible to anyone who did not know where to find it. From the middle of the sixth century B.C., their orientation changed: while the tombs were at first usually oriented toward the west or the northwest—the netherworld region for the Etruscans (figs. V-9–10)—they were, from the middle of the sixth century B.C., simply planned according to the direction of the streets of the necropolis, and accessible directly from them. The entrance was recognizable and could be lavishly decorated. This tomb shape has variations, which have been given different names. In Cerveteri and in the rock-cut tomb necropoleis like Blera, San Giuliano (fig. V-18), and Norchia, it is called a cube tomb (*tomba a dado*) because of its square appearance (fig. V-21). The aedicula tombs in Populonia, named after their characteristic gabled roof (fig. V-19), or the tombs arranged like a row of houses in Orvieto and Cerveteri (*scavi nuovi*) (figs. V-20–21), have more dis-

V-22. Tomb PA 18, Castel d'Asso. (Colonna di Paolo and Colonna, *Norchia 1*, pl. 247.)

V-23. Sottofacciata tombs imitating temple façades, Norchia. (Colonna di Paolo fig. 66.)

tinct similarities with the dwelling house. In fact, as the concept of the house became less important in the interior, it became more decisive for the shaping of the exterior. In the late period (third to second century B.C.), this imitation of a house even inspired architects to provide the tomb with a projecting roof and porticus, as in the so-called *sottofacciata* (or "under the cornice") tombs in Norchia and Castel d'Asso (figs. V-22–23), or with a gable decorated with figures and columns in imitation of a temple, as at Norchia and Sovana (fig. V-37). The interiors of these tombs were now without the slightest trace of architectural form: something like a rough-hewn cave, the grave had no purpose other than to hold the largest possible number of burials.

This desire to decorate the exterior of the tombs lavishly is especially evident in the later period. It probably originated not from any cult or religious ritual but from the owner's wish to attract attention to the splendor of his tomb and to keep himself and his family alive in the memory of his descendants. The same purpose was served by the tomb inscriptions. Though rare in the early period (found at Orvieto), these were later on chiseled either on grave markers (cippi) in front of the tomb, as at Cerveteri, or on the structure itself, as on the façade of tombs at Norchia and Castel d'Asso (figs. V-22–23). The taste for showy design and decoration of the tomb's exterior could be indulged because many of the tombs lined the main thoroughfares outside Etruscan cities.

In rock-cut tomb necropoleis like Norchia, Castel d'Asso, San Giuliano, and Blera, with their steep and high rock walls, several graves could often be placed one above the other (figs. V-22–23). Then, too, the graves did not serve for burials alone. From the very beginning, they were conceived of as cult places, as monumental altars. By means of ramps (for mound tombs or tumuli [fig. V-21]) and stairs (for later tombs like the *sottofacciata* and cube and porticus tombs [fig. V-18]), the mounds and upper platforms were accessible for rites in honor of the deceased, including perhaps the annual memorial rites. Other rites, not yet exactly determined, were also held in the dromos (figs. V-4, V-10, V-12), or in front of it, as can be assumed from the benches that surrounded the façades of the *tombe a sottofacciata* (figs. V-22–23).

V-24. Barbarano Romano, overlooking San Giuliano necropolis. (Dorothee Jordens.)

These tombs and cities of the dead were thus closely allied with the cities of the living. The Etruscans were not in the habit of destroying old graves, of building on top of them, or—at least in the Archaic period—of using them over again, and since in the early period a generous amount of space was allowed for a single family, especially a wealthy one, the cities of the dead encompassed a large territory. In Cerveteri, for instance, the necropoleis spread over a larger area than that of the city itself. The necropoleis which encircled the town originally covered only the neighboring hills; later, when space became scarcer, the tombs crept up to the immediate vicinity of the town.

The necropolis also began to resemble a city (fig. V-21). Caeretan tumuli in the seventh and early sixth century B.C. were simply scattered over the ridges surrounding the settlement without any discernible system (fig. V-9). Apparently the main concern of the owners of these early tombs was that

they should be visible from the town. With the appearance of the cube tombs and other façade tombs, from the middle of the sixth century B.C. on, an orderly principle or city plan, in which tomb structures and tomb streets relate to each other, forming an orthogonal network of roads, took shape. Such a grid has been preserved in impressive condition in the Crocifisso del Tufo necropolis of Orvieto (fig. V-20).

In the so-called rock-cut tomb necropoleis near Viterbo, deep gorges separate the settlement of the living from the city of the dead. Here steep rock walls were used for construction of the tombs, with the result that façade tombs developed earlier and in greater variety, offering a striking view from the town, as at San Giuliano (Barbarano Romano: fig. V-24) or at Norchia, the "Etruscan Petra" (fig. V-23).

The different geological and geographical conditions of northern Etruria resulted in other forms of cemetery, as can be seen from the necropoleis of Populonia, which have been best preserved (fig. V-19). In contrast to those of the south, they are here situated on the plains directly by the seashore, far below the town area; neither the layout of the tombs nor the tomb streets show any governing principle of order.

Layout of Town and Houses

The prerequisites for the building of Etruscan towns and settlements were the vicinity of a river and sufficient possibilities for defense. The tufa landscape of the south offered natural, nearly ideal conditions. For thousands of years the river beds had sunk deeper and deeper into the soft stone, creating great numbers of isolated plateaus. Also ideal for settlements were sites surrounded on several sides by rivers, as long as it was still possible to reach the town from at least one side without excessive effort, as at Veii, Cerveteri, or in the rock-tomb necropoleis.

Access to the sea was also important. Most towns (Vulci, Tarquinia, and Cerveteri) were not situated immediately on the coast but several kilometers away, in order to be better protected against surprise attacks from the sea. Other cities, such as Fiesole on the Arno and Orvieto on the Tiber, profited from the navigability of the great rivers and were in this manner connected to the sea, despite being situated far inland. Confident in the security of their lofty and protected sites, most settlements seemed to have foregone a town wall; apparently in most cases they simply fortified weak or vulnerable spots. In Roselle, however, below a city wall made from polygonal stone blocks dating from the sixth century B.C., there was discovered a defense wall built in the seventh century B.C., with a foundation course of stones and an upper structure of sun-dried mud bricks. The possibility that similar mud brick walls originally protected other Etruscan towns, though these have now been lost, or are not yet discovered, cannot be excluded. In several cities we can also distinguish an inner section, or citadel, situated higher than the rest. In Volterra this acropolis was protected, during the late sixth or early

V-25. Porta dell'Arco, Volterra. (Prayon.)

fifth century B.C., by a surrounding wall (1.8 km. long), while a fortification wall around the settlement (7.2 km. long) was added during the fourth century B.C. This later wall still has the remains of two city gates of which the gate called Porta dell-'Arco is in remarkably good condition (fig. V-25). While the basic structure of the gate is part of the original Etruscan construction, the arch itself is partially due to a Roman restoration. Yet even it imitated an Etruscan model. Such arches, with the characteristic heads protruding from the wall, are not only preserved in Perugia (Porta Marzia) and in Falerii Novi but are also depicted on Hellenistic ash urns from Volterra (fig. V-26), whose city gates may have served as models for the sculptor's work.

Much less is known about the layout of the streets and the exteriors of the houses, squares, public buildings, and sacred shrines in Etruscan towns than about the necropoleis and their tombs.

One reason is the different state of preservation. The tombs were built completely from stone or hewn out of the rock. The houses normally had only a stone base, with an upper structure consisting of a perishable material, or a wooden framework and mud bricks. Another reason, and one which hinders excavation, is that the towns were inhabited over a longer period of time and that the houses were constantly built over or altered. Several Etruscan towns, especially in the interior, such as Perugia, Volterra, Chiusi, Cortona, and Orvieto, have been inhabited continuously up to the present. Furthermore, the lack of interest of earlier scholars also hinders our knowledge. Until recently, research was limited to exposing more "rewarding" objects, that is, the tombs and their rich finds, and to studying the often inaccurate, scanty literary tradition, and chamber tombs which copied houses.

Ancient tradition ascribes to the Etruscans the invention of an orthogonal town plan based on main streets intersecting each other at right angles: the *cardo,* oriented north-south, and the *decumanus,* running east-west. Such a system is known from Roman colonies like that of Ostia. Our knowledge of the layout of Etruscan towns is still too fragmentary to permit a definite judgment regarding this tradition, even though Pompeii, Capua (two Etruscan cities in Campania), and Veii seem to have had such a plan. The only Etruscan town which has been more thoroughly researched, Marzabotto,

V-27. Orthogonal town plan, Marzabotto, founded ca. 500 B.C. (Boethius fig. 62.)

near the modern city of Bologna, has an orthogonal network approximately oriented to the cardinal points of the heavens (fig. V-27), but the streets were simply laid out parallel to each other in a grid, without any emphasis on a central north-south and east-west axis. Marzabotto was founded relatively late, about 500 B.C.; Greek ideas, namely, the so-called Hippodamic system, characterized by the grid pattern, may have affected its layout.

No one, however, has so far found a rigorously orthogonal layout in any town of Etruria proper, the region between the Tiber and the Arno. In building streets, the principal consideration seems to have been to adapt the plan to the terrain, rather than to force it to fit a formal system, as probes made in the towns of Roselle and Acquarossa near Viterbo have shown. Domestic design also discouraged such a regular system of intersections. In the seventh century B.C., single houses had mainly oval plans. Whether in groups or alone, they conformed to terrain and weather conditions rather than to the direction of streets. These oval houses, of which the most impressive so far have been excavated in San Giovenale (fig. V-28), had foundations dug out of the tufa. The upper wall structure, built in a wattle and daub construction, was tied together by wooden posts which were driven into the

V-26. Cinerary urn from Volterra showing siege of a city. (H. Brunn and G. Körte, *I rilievi delle urne etrusche* II, pl. 21, 1.)

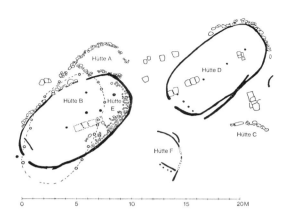

V-28. Early Etruscan hut foundations, San Giovenale. (Prayon fig. 27.)

ground (figs. V-29, V-32, Nos. 1–4). The entrance to the houses was on one of the narrow sides. The thatched overhanging roof was supported by the outer walls and by pillars in the middle of the room. Inside, these huts were sometimes divided by transverse walls into several rooms. Their exterior appearance is depicted on the house urns of the Villanovan period (fig. V-11); their interior has been copied in the Tomb of the Thatched Roof (fig. V-12).

After the middle of the seventh century B.C. oval houses were gradually displaced by rectangular structures (fig. V-30), also well preserved in San Giovenale (fig V-32, No. 5). A long house was first to develop. Then in the sixth century B.C., a wide

V-29. Reconstruction of early Iron Age hut on the Palatine, Rome. (Prayon fig. 28.)

type of house appeared, consisting of several adjoining chambers with one broad room in front (fig. V-32, Nos. 6, 8). Such wealthy Etruscan houses were often imitated in the tombs, which show that anteroom and rear chambers were connected by doors and windows (e.g., figs. V-4, No. 14; V-13–14). The excavated foundations of these two- or three-cella "broad" houses in Veii, Acquarossa, and Rome also show clearly that the wide front room was in many cases a vestibule, often supported by columns (cf. fig. V-14). The rooms behind it served as bedroom, kitchen, and storage room. The interior walls, made of framework and mud bricks and now and then of stone, were plastered and painted. The roof was sometimes covered with ornamental terracotta plaques decorated with reliefs, as at Acquarossa, making the house colorful on the outside as well as inside (fig. V-31). Apart from these luxurious homes, very simple dwellings were also built, even in the early period. At San Giovenale and Roselle, for example, small rooms leading one into the other without a fixed ground plan may have served as a living space or workrooms.

The wealthy, however, wanted larger rooms and more comfort. Since the Etruscans normally built one-story homes, dwellings grew bigger. In houses built in about 500 B.C. in Marzabotto (figs. V-27, V-32, Nos. 9–10), though little more than the foundations of the walls, made from river pebbles, has been preserved, the outlines and the interior divisions of the individual houses are still recognizable. A long entrance corridor, flanked by rooms, leads to a courtyard or space, again surrounded by rooms. The courtyard of some of these houses has the shape of a cross, formed by a transverse room which takes up the whole width of the house; another room opening into this transverse room is connected with the back wall as well.

We can understand this basic ground plan better if we recall the plan of the broad houses with three chambers (cf. fig. V-32, No. 6) and also look at the interior rooms of several chamber tombs (fig. V-5, Nos. 14, 16). This broad house type corresponds to the rear part of the Marzabotto house, in a development in which the middle room of the broad house was more or less opened to the anteroom. The transitional stage is strikingly illustrated by

V-30. House W, San Giovenale. (Prayon.)

V-31. Reconstruction of early house type at Acquarossa. (Östenberg pp. 206–207.)

two courtyard structures discovered by excavations at Murlo and Acquarossa (fig. V-33, *top* and *lower left*) and in the Tomba della Ripa in Cerveteri (fig. V-5, No. 15). This tomb and the two houses all date from the sixth century B.C. and thus are earlier than the Marzabotto houses. A false door on the rear side of the center room in the Tomba della Ripa (fig. V-34) represents a real door which originally led to a courtyard or garden behind the house. If we then look at the Marzabotto houses we find that their rear sections can in fact be traced back to the three-cella broad house with anteroom or porch. The courtyard, originally behind the house, has been moved farther to the front, a regrouping made necessary by the fact that the Marzabotto house, set within a block of houses, could only be lighted from the front (i.e., from the street) or from within. Only by putting the courtyard in the center could the several rooms be lighted satisfactorily.

The continued use of the courtyard house recognized at Marzabotto is indirectly proved by Etruscan tombs like the above-mentioned François Tomb in Vulci and the Tomb of the Volumnii in Perugia

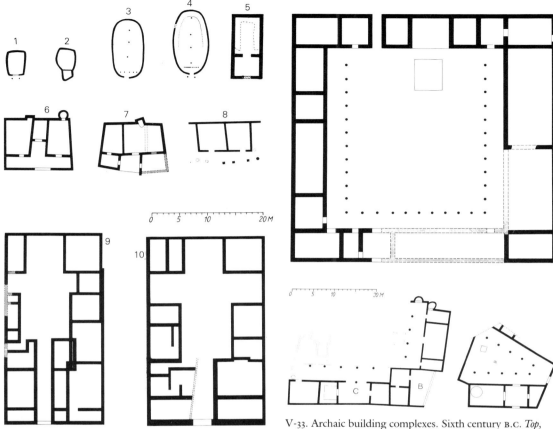

V-32. Archaic house plans, ca. 700–500 B.C. *1*, Rome, Hut A on the Palatine; *2*, Veii, Piazza d'Armi; *3, 4, 5,* San Giovenale; *6, 7,* Acquarossa; *8,* Veii, "Wooden building;" *9, 10,* Marzabotto, Reg. *IV,* Houses 2 and 6. (Prayon pl. 88.)

V-33. Archaic building complexes. Sixth century B.C. *Top,* Murlo, Poggio Civitate; *lower left,* Acquarossa, Complex A–C in Zone F; *lower right,* Rome, Regia of the Forum. (Prayon pl. 88.)

(fig. V-17). The courtyard house continued in the Roman atrium house. This atrium type, whose oldest examples can be traced back, in Pompeii, to the fourth century B.C. (fig. V-35), seems to have been based directly on such Etruscan (or Italic) courtyard houses. The typological development of the atrium house may have occurred as follows: the courtyard, enlarged, incorporated the central part of the anteroom, creating in this way the atrium, while the protruding ends of the wide anteroom became the alae and the former middle room the tablinum (eating room) which opened completely

to the atrium and partially to the peristyle (garden) behind.

More difficult to trace is the development of the upper structure. As mentioned above, the central part of the houses in Marzabotto were certainly open to the sky for lighting the small rooms and collecting rainwater. Rectangular openings in the protruding roof construction were reproduced on miniature houses in stone; these indeed are referred to in literature as *atrium tuscanicum* by the Roman architect Vitruvius.

In addition to this upper structure, there were other forms of roof constructions for the courtyard houses, especially the huge gable roof which cov-

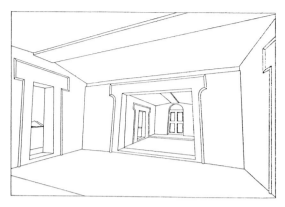

V-34. Tomba della Ripa (Tomb of the Tablinum), Cerveteri, reconstruction of interior. Fifth century B.C. (Prayon fig. 34.)

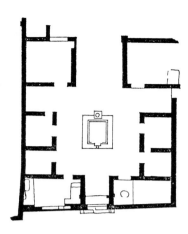

V-35. House of the Surgeon, Pompeii. Fourth or third century B.C. plan. (Boethius fig. 85.)

ered the whole complex of the building. The central part is called *atrium testudinatum* by Vitruvius (*De Architectura* III, 3), and often it was imitated in the interior of late Etruscan tombs (figs. V-34, V-37). Precious information about the exterior of such gable-roofed houses is also provided by small models of houses in stone, which had once served as urns for the ashes of the deceased (fig. V-36). From these we can deduce that late Etruscan upper-class family houses must have been richly decorated with pilasters, capitals, and ornaments and that they must often have had at least one upper story with a kind of outer loggia or gallery on all four sides of the building. The whole appearance is that of a palace; and indeed there is a striking resemblance between these models and the Renaissance palaces of the same region, in the Florence of the Medici, some fifteen hundred years later (fig. I-9).

Temples and Sanctuaries

There are different sources of information for the sacred architecture of the Etruscans. First, there is the archaeological record with its excavated monuments, which have fortunately multiplied in recent times. Second, there are the copies of temples and altars found in tombs, in the tomb façades in Norchia and Sovana (figs. V-37, V-23), and in miniature

V-36. Cinerary urn from Chiusi in the form of a house or palace with arched door. Hellenistic. Florence, Museo Archeologico. (DAI.)

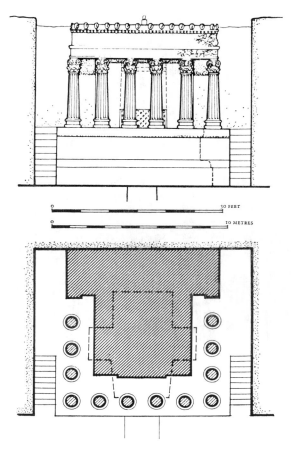

V-37. Tomba Ildebranda, Sovana, elevation and plan. Second century B.C. (Boethius fig. 29.)

form as votive gifts (fig. IV-48). Finally, there are the literary sources, especially Vitruvius (*De Architectura* IV, 7), who gives very detailed information about Etruscan temple construction. Nonetheless, his work, like that of other writers, has to be used with caution, since it was written at a time when most of the temples in question no longer existed. The increasing Greek influence on Etruscan religion and architecture, which can be noted as early as the sixth century B.C. (for instance, in the adoption of Greek names for native Etruscan gods), also has to be taken into account. Greek immigrants and craftsmen, at least near the coast, in Cerveteri (Temple of Hera), and in Graviscae, a port suburb

of Tarquinia, had their own temples and holy shrines. The close relations between Greece and Etruria are shown, among other things, by the treasure house built by the inhabitants of Cerveteri in the sanctuary of Apollo at Delphi in the sixth century B.C. (Strabo, *Geography* V, 220).

Yet the Etruscan temple or, as it is called today on the basis of its geographical occurrence, the Italo-Etruscan temple was from the very beginning non-Greek and remained so in essence into the Roman period. There are principally two reasons for this. First, in contrast to the self-contained Greek temple, the Etruscan temple opened out into an augural area, where the priest divined the will of the gods by observing the flight of birds and other signs in a space determined by the orientation of the temple. The second difference was in the construction material. We have mentioned that the Etruscans did not use marble and normally used stone only for foundations. So, while the Greek temple underwent a logical development and changed, around 600 B.C., from a wooden to a stone structure, the upper structure of the Etruscan temple remained of wood and therefore kept its Archaic, compact proportions. As a result, the few preserved remains of Etruscan temples consist mostly of the stone foundations and the terracottas, which were necessary to protect the wooden columns, beams, and other structures against the elements.

Until recently it was thought that the Etruscan temple, like the tomb and the house, had evolved from modest beginnings, and only relatively late. But recently in Murlo, near Siena, excavations have uncovered an ambitious building complex (fig. V-33, *top*), which forces us, at the very least, to reconsider this hypothesis and probably even to discard it. The Murlo complex has a central court, more than sixty meters wide by sixty meters long, surrounded by three rows of columns on the inside. On the fourth side, emphasized by a rectangular enclosure, we find the three-part room division seen in tomb and house plans. The room in the center opens out completely, facing a rectangular enclosure which can perhaps be interpreted as the remains of an altar. The decorative roof terracottas are extraordinarily luxurious and include large-scale statues originally set up on the ridge of the roof,

V-38. Reconstruction of Portonaccio temple, Veii, model. (Hanell fig. 50.)

like those of the temple at Veii (fig. V-38). It seems, therefore, that this monumental structure, or at least a part of it, had sacred functions.

As unusual as the dimensions, the ground plan, and the terracotta decoration is the dating of the complex at Murlo, which is extraordinarily early for such a monumental building: 575–550 B.C. It seems to be the oldest sacred Etruscan building found so far. Yet such sophisticated architecture can hardly have originated spontaneously from modest beginnings. Perhaps the architecture is not a native development but an imported type, most likely from

V-39. Portonaccio temple, Veii, plan of foundations. (Boethius fig. 27.)

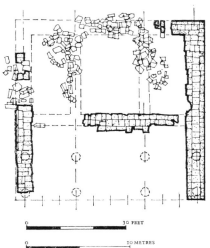

the Near East, where such building complexes with a central court had a long tradition. For the time being, however, the question about the origin or development of this building type must remain open. Beneath the walls of the foundation of the sixth-century building, the remains of the walls of a previous structure, dating from the seventh century B.C., have emerged, but it is not yet possible to determine the ground plan or the function of this older building.

In the second half of the sixth century B.C., the three-chambered nucleus of the building complex found at Murlo appears in two other remarkable buildings, in Acquarossa near Viterbo and in the Regia of the Forum in Rome (fig. V-33, *bottom*). While the function of the complex in Acquarossa is not yet clear, there is no doubt that the Regia was a sacred building, which served as an official priestly residence of the Pontifex Maximus, the high priest at Rome. As at Murlo, in Acquarossa and in Rome the center room opens onto the courtyard. Both complexes also have a kind of rectangular altar; in Acquarossa, it is situated in front of the center cella, in the Regia on the side of the inner yard, which is without columns. From these observations, it can be deduced that in the sixth century B.C. in Etruria the interior of the tomb, of the house, and of the sacred building were all apparently organized with a triple cella. This is important because the three-cella structure, which the Roman architect Vitruvius later termed characteristic of the Etruscan temple, is now confirmed by the archaeological evidence. There can be no doubt of the typological origin of the Roman temple on the Capitoline Hill, which also had three cellae (fig. V-40), or of those at Cosa, Segni, etc. When, about 570 B.C., Tarquinius Priscus, the Etruscan ruler of Rome, looked for a suitable temple form which could accommodate the Roman triad of gods, Jupiter, Juno, and Minerva, it was only natural that he should adopt this three-cella structure from the Etruscans, so that each of the three gods would receive his or her own cella. There is much evidence of Etruscan influence for the construction of the Temple of Jupiter on the Capitoline Hill. Etruscan artists were called in from Veii; the decision to build is said to have originated with Tarquinius Priscus, who was then ruling in Rome.

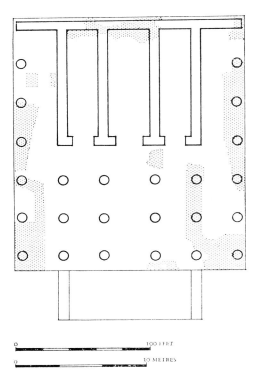

V-40. Temple of Jupiter Optimus Maximus Capitolinus, Rome, dedicated 509 B.C., plan by E. Gjerstad and B. Blomé. (Boethius fig. 34.)

Vitruvius again gives detailed information about the floor plan and the proportions of the three-cella type of Etruscan temple (*De Architectura* IV, 7), for which only modest archaeological remains have been preserved, as at Orvieto (fig. V-41) or at Pyrgi (Temple A) (fig. V-42). According to Vitruvius, the "Tuscan" temple had an unusual floor plan, with a proportion of width to length of 5:6. This layout, nearly square, was divided in two. The rear half was occupied by three cellae, the central one of which was wider. The other two, on the sides, opened toward the front, and could also function as alae or side chambers. In the front half were two rows of four columns, in line with the cella walls; the inter-columniation, or distance between the two middle columns, was therefore always greater than that of the two outer columns. Yet this Vitruvian temple

seems to be a theoretical model which did not necessarily correspond to reality; the columns in the temple at Orvieto, for example, were not placed in line with the cella walls (fig. V-41).

Besides the three-cella temple and the one-cella temple with two alae, there were still other temple forms in Etruria, due, no doubt, to the influence of Greece on Etruria. In the Roman Temple of Jupiter built on the Capitoline Hill in the late sixth century B.C. this Greek influence is unmistakeable (fig. V-40). Even the enormous size of the temple (53.5 m. × 62.25 m.), especially the front, has no parallels on Italian soil except the completely different structure in Murlo (fig. V-33, *top*). The only comparison would be the more or less contemporary giant temples of the Greek region in the Archaic period, in the east at Ephesus or Didyma, in the west at Agrigentum. It is similarly to be seen as an expression of the heightened self-assertion and strong desire to be noticed in the world which accompanies a rise to power.

Greek influence appears just as clearly in the floor plan. The Temple of Jupiter Capitoline consists of two different elements (fig. V-40): a specifically Etruscan nucleus with three cellae and columnar vestibule, to which the temple at Orvieto can be compared (fig. V-41), and a Greek peristyle, a three-sided ring of columns which excludes only the rear of the temple; the front, and the long sides, each have six columns. Strict frontality is thus partially eliminated, and a first step taken in adapting the Italo-Etruscan temple to the Greek temple.

The ring of columns on three sides is repeated in later temples in the Italian region; these, however, have only one cella instead of three. This special form, recognized by Vitruvius and called *peripteros sine postico* (*De Architectura* III, 2, 5), that is, "peristyle without porch," is preserved in Etruria, in southern Latium, and even in Paestum (fig. V-43, No. 3). Greek influence is thus illustrated by the occasionally exaggeratedly long proportions of the layout. Greek influence also determined changes in the structure and the decoration of the temple. The compact proportions resulting from the wide inter-columniations, one of the characteristics of the archaic Etruscan temple, were modified by high, closely placed columns. The terracotta architectural

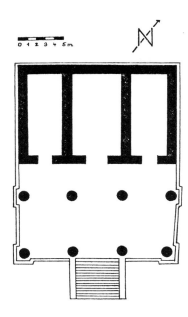

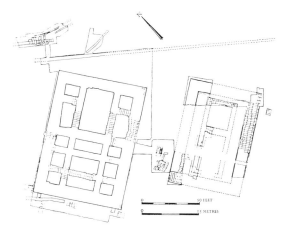

V-42. Pyrgi, Santa Severa, plan of foundations of temples A and B. The larger temple, 24.05 by 34.40 m., is tripartite. (Boethius fig. 28.)

V-41. Reconstruction of Belvedere Temple, Orvieto. Fifth century B.C. (Pfiffig, *Religio Etrusca* fig. 11.)

decorations, at first restricted to the cornices, the roof ridge, and the waterspouts of the open gable, began to take over more of the space of the originally empty gable or tympanun, until the latter was completely filled. In this way the spectator's eye, as in Greece, is drawn to this heretofore less important part of the temple, for instance, at Falerii Veteres or at Telamon. Even in this late period, the sculptured decoration was always of clay, and the entablature, or upper structure of the temple, of wood.

The temple was the most important but not the only type of sacred architecture for the Etruscans. It seldom stood alone. It formed part of a sacred area, as at Pyrgi or Graviscae, enclosed by a temenos wall. In conjunction with the temple, as at Pyrgi, or even in its absence, small, uncovered shrines or sacella also appear.

Of special interest are the outdoor altars. Apart from the large group of tomb altars—we have noted that the Etruscan tomb itself had the form of a monumental altar and was used as such—there existed a variety of other altar forms. These are partly known from the preserved originals, partly from

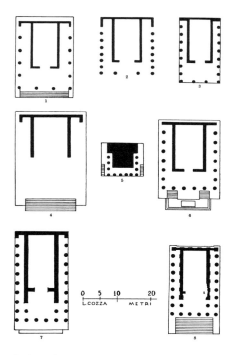

V-43. Peripteral temples *sine postico* (without columns in back) in central Italy. *1*, Largo Argentina; *2*, Ariccia; *3*, Paestum; *4*, Cascia; *5*, Sovana; *6*, Gabii; *7*, Jupiter Stator; *8*, Forum Holitorium. (F. Castagnoli, *RömMitt* 62 [1955] fig. on p. 140.)

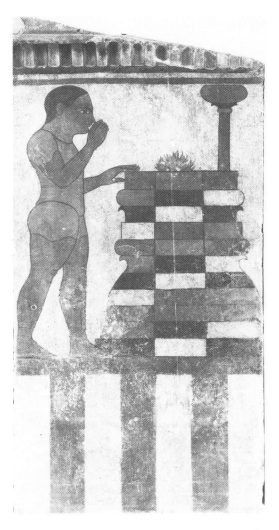

V-45. Altar D, Marzabotto. (W. Zschietzschmann, *Etruskische Kunst,* 1969, fig. 7.)

the liquid could be poured directly into the earth.

Libation sacrifices seem to have been quite common in Etruria. Indeed, recent excavations at Pyrgi and Santa Marinella seem to show that the Etruscans had a special cult with which they worshipped chthonic, that is, earth or underworld divinities. Even deities like Tinia/Jupiter, Uni/Juno, and Menrva/Minerva, in contrast to Greek and Roman belief, could exercise chthonic or funerary functions in relation to the dead.

Other Constructions

It is worth mentioning that the Etruscans are famous in ancient literature for their skill in the field of canalization, the drainage of marshes and irrigation. The picturesque Ponte Sodo in Veii, a water channel carved out of the rock, in part by the flowing river, in part by the Etruscans (fig. V-46), is one example; another is the extensive system of underground channels, frequently observed in the rocky plateaus under Etruscan cities like Cerveteri, Orvieto, or Veii, and serving, probably, as sewage channels: indeed, the most famous system of this kind in antiquity, the Cloaca Maxima in Rome, is

V-44. Campana plaque showing man before an altar, from the Banditaccia necropolis, Cerveteri. Painted terracotta. 530–520 B.C. Paris, Louvre, Cp 6626. (M. Chuzeville, Louvre.)

their representation on Etruscan vases, urns, and terracotta plaques (fig. V-44). The most common forms were steplike, round or square; their mouldings had a strong profile, often in the form of an hourglass, the so-called *gola etrusca* (fig. V-45). Their uses were varied: there were altars for burnt offerings or animal sacrifices, offering tables for bloodless gifts, and libation altars for drink offerings, the latter drilled with a hole through which

V-46. The Ponte Sodo, Veii, an eighty-meter stretch of an
Etruscan cuniculus, still diverts a part of the Formello
River. The conduit was built in the fifth century B.C. to
bypass a swampy horseshoe bend; the water flowing
through the tunnel has enlarged the passage since then.
(W. Zschietzschmann, *Etruskische Kunst*, 1969, fig. 4.)

said to be of Etruscan origin. Originally built for
the purpose of draining the marshy valleys of the
later market places (such as the Forum Romanum),
to collect all the sewage of the city, and to carry it
down to the Tiber, the Cloaca Maxima still fulfills
this function today as the last surviving relic of the
once splendid building activity of the Etruscan rulers of Rome. The later metropolis owed to these
Etruscan kings not only the first monumental
buildings, such as the Temple of Jupiter on the
Capitoline Hill, the Cloaca Maxima, and the Circus
Maximus (still existing today), but also the urbanization of the town. While the Roman emperor
Augustus later was able to boast that he had found
Rome a city of brick and left it a city of marble
(Suetonius, *Aug.* 28), the Etruscan kings of sixth-
century Rome could claim to have changed Rome
from a modest community into an urbanized
"modern" town.

Bibliography

GENERAL PUBLICATIONS

A. Boethius, *Etruscan and Early Roman Architecture* (Har-
mondsworth 1978; originally published as part of A.
Boethius and J.B. Ward-Perkins, *Etruscan and Roman
Architecture* [Harmondsworth 1970]).
———, "Of Tuscan Columns," *AJA* 66 (1962) 249–54.
F. Boitani, M. Cataldo and M. Pasquinucci, *Etruscan Cities*
(London 1978).
A. Ciasca, *Il capitello detto eolico in Etruria* (Florence 1962).
G. Dennis, *The Cities and Cemeteries of Etruria.*
J. Durm, *Die Baukunst der Etrusker und Römer* (Stuttgart
1905).
G. Patroni, *Architettura preistorica generale ed italica. Ar-
chitettura etrusca* (Bergamo 1946).
T.W. Potter, *The Changing Landscape of South Etruria.*
F. Prayon, *Frühetruskische Grab- und Hausarchitektur.*
L.T. Shoe, "Etruscan and Republican Roman Mouldings,"
MAAR 28 (1965).
S. Steingräber, *Etrurien. Städte, Heiligtümer, Nekropolen*
(Munich 1981).
M. Torelli, *Etruria.* Guide archeologiche Laterza (Rome
1980).

CITIES

See also the articles in *EAA* and in *The Princeton Encyclope-
dia of Classical Sites* (Princeton 1976).

Acquarossa: C.E. Östenberg, *Case etrusche di Acquarossa*
(Rome 1975). E. Rystedt, *Acquarossa* IV (Stockholm
1983).
Blera: H. Koch, E. von Mercklin, and C. Weickert,
"Bieda," *RömMitt* 30 (1915) 161–310; S. Quilici Gigli,
Blera (Mainz 1976).
Bolsena: F.T. Buchicchio, "Note di topografia antica sulla
Volsinii Romana," *RömMitt* 77 (1970) 19–45; R. Bloch,
*Recherches archéologiques en territoire Volsinien de la proto-
histoire à la civilisation étrusque* (Paris 1972).
Castel d'Asso: E. Colonna di Paolo and G. Colonna, *Castel
d'Asso I–II* (Rome 1970).
Cerveteri: L. Pareti, *La Tomba Regolini Galassi* (Vatican
1947); B. Pace, R. Vighi, G. Ricci, and M. Moretti,
"Caere," *MonAnt* 42 (1955); M. Pallottino, *La necropoli di
Cerveteri* (Rome 1960); M. Cristofani, *La Tomba delle
Iscrizioni a Cerveteri* (Florence 1965); I. Pohl, *The Iron
Age Necropolis of Sorbo at Cerveteri* (Stockholm 1972); F.
Prayon, "Das neugefundene Dämonengrab in Cerve-
teri," *Antike Welt* 3 (1975) 18–26; M. Moretti, *Cerveteri*
(Novara 1977).
Chiusi: R. Bianchi Bandinelli, "Clusium," *MonAnt* 30
(1925) 210–551.

Civita Castellana: E. Stefani, "Civita Castellana, Tempio di Giunone Curite," *NSc* 8, 1 (1947) 69–74; M. Moretti and A. Zanelli, *Civita Castellana* (Rome n.d.).

Cortona: A. Neppi Modona, *Cortona etrusca e romana nella storia e nell'arte* (Florence 1925: 2nd ed., 1977); M. Novelli, *Urbanismo italico a Cortona nel suo impianto umbro etrusco romano* (Milan 1973).

Cosa: F. Brown, *The Making of a Roman Town* (Ann Arbor 1979).

Ferento: P. Giannini, *Ferento, Città dai tre volti* (Viterbo 1971).

Ficana: R. Brandt, "L'architettura delle capanne nel Lazio e a Ficana nell'età del Ferro," *Ficana* (Rome 1980) 66–74; C. Pavolini and A. Rathje, "L'inizio dell'architettura domestica con fondamenta in pietra nel Lazio e a Ficana," in *Ficana* (Rome 1980) 75–87.

Fiesole: M. Lombardi, *Faesulae* (Rome 1941); G. Maetzke, "Il nuovo tempio tuscanico di Fiesole," *StEtr* 24 (1955/56) 227–53.

Ghiaccio Forte: M. del Chiaro, *Etruscan Ghiaccio Forte* (Santa Barbara 1976).

Graviscae: M. Torelli, "Il santuario greco di Gravisca," *ParPass* 32 (1977) 398–458.

Luni sul Mignone: C.E. Östenberg, *Luni sul Mignone e problemi della preistoria d'Italia* (Lund 1967), *Luni sul Mignone. Results of Excavations* . . . II, 1: T. Wieselgren, *The Iron Age Settlement of the Acropolis* (Lund 1969); II, 2: P. Hellström, *The Zone of the Large Iron Age Building* (Sockholm 1975).

Marzabotto: G.A. Mansuelli, "La casa etrusca di Marzabotto," *RömMitt* 70 (1963) 44–62; and *Guida alla città etrusca e al museo di Marzabotto* (Bologna 1966).

Murlo: *Poggio Civitate, Il santuario arcaico. Catalogo della mostra* (Florence, Siena 1970); E.O. Nielsen and K.M. Phillips, "Poggio Civitate (Siena). Gli scavi del Bryn Mawr College dal 1966 al 1974," *NSc* 30 (1976) 113–47; M. Cristofani, "Considerazioni su Poggio Civitate (Murlo)," *Prospettiva* 1 (1975) 9–17.

Norchia: E. Colonna di Paolo and G. Colonna, *Norchia I* (Rome 1978).

Orvieto: M. Bizzarri, "La necropoli di Crocifisso del Tufo in Orvieto," *StEtr* 30 (1962) 1–151; 34 (1966) 1–109; and *Orvieto etrusca, arte e storia* (Orvieto 1967); A. Andrén, "Il santuario della necropoli di Cannicella ad Orvieto," *StEtr* 35 (1967) 41–85.

Perugia: C. Shaw, *Etruscan Perugia* (Baltimore 1939); A. von Gerkan and F. Messerschmidt, "Das Grab der Volumnier bei Perugia," *RömMitt* 57 (1942) 122–235; M.A. Johnstone, *Estruscan Life in Perugia* (Florence 1964).

Populonia: A. Minto, *Populonia. La necropoli arcaica* (Florence 1922); and *Populonia* (Florence 1943); A. de Agostino, "La cinta fortificata di Populonia," *StEtr* 30 (1962) 275–82; and *Populonia. La città e la necropoli* (Rome 1965).

Pyrgi: G. Colonna et al., "Pyrgi. Scavi del santuario etrusco (1959/1967)," *NSc* 1970, Suppl. 2; Various authors, *Die Göttin von Pyrgi*.

Rome: E. Gjerstad, *Early Rome I–VI*, Lund 153–73; R.M. Ogilvie, *Early Rome and the Etruscans* (1976).

Roselle: A. Mazzolai, *Roselle e il suo territorio* (Grosseto 1960); V. Melani and M. Vergari, *Profilo di una città etrusca—Roselle* (Pistoia 1974).

San Giovenale: G. Hanell, in *Etruscan Culture, Land and People* (Malmö 1962) 279–340; S. Giovenale, *Results of Excavations* . . . I–VII (1967).

San Giuliano: A. Gargana, "La necropoli rupestre di San Giuliano," *MonAnt* 33 (1929–31) 297–467.

Sovana: R. Bianchi Bandinelli, *Sovana. Topografia ed arte* (Florence 1929); E. Baldini, *Sovana. La sua storia e i suoi monumenti* (Florence 1956).

Spina: N. Alfieri, P.-E. Arias, and M. Hirmer, *Spina* (Florence, Munich 1958).

Sutri: C. Morselli, *Sutrium* (Florence 1980).

Talamone: O.W. von Vacano, "Zum Grundriss des Tempels auf dem Talamonaccio," *Hommages à M. Renard III*, Brussels 1969, 675–94; "Telamon nach dem Brand des Tempels," *RömMitt* 87 (1980) 137–70; and *RömMitt* 88 (1981) 345–402.

Tarquinia: M. Pallottino, "Tarquinia," *MonAnt* 36 (1937); H. Hencken, *Tarquinia, Villanovans and Early Etruscans I–II* (Cambridge, Massachusetts 1968); M. Moretti, *Tarquinia* (Novara 1974).

Tuscania: S. Quilici Gigli, *Tuscana*. Forma Italiae VII, 2 (Rome 1970).

Veii: J.B. Ward-Perkins, "Veii—the Historical Topography of the Ancient City," *PBSR* 29 (1961); A. de Agostino, *Veio. La storia, i ruderi, le terrecotte* (Rome 1971); M. Torelli and I. Pohl, "Veio. Scoperta di un piccolo santuario etrusco in località Campetti," *NSc* 1973, 40–258.

Vetulonia: I. Falchi, *Vetulonia e la sua necropoli antichissima* (Florence 1891); C. Curri, *Vetulonia I* (Florence 1978).

Volterra: L. Consortini, *Volterra nell'antichità* (Volterra 1940); E. Fiumi, *Volterra etrusca e romana* (Pisa 1976).

Vulci: F. Messerschmidt and A. von Gerkan, *Nekropolen von Vulci* (Berlin 1930); R. Bartoccini, *Vulci. Storia, scavi, rinvenimenti* (Rome 1960); A. Hus, *Vulci étrusque et étrusco-romaine* (Paris 1971); and "La civiltà arcaica di Vulci e la sua espansione," in *Atti X Congresso di Studi Etruschi* (Florence 1977); G. Riccioni, "Vulci. A Topographical and Cultural Survey," in *IBR*, 240–76.

TEMPLES AND SANCTUARIES

A. Andrén, *Architectural Terracottas from Etrusco-Italic Temples* (Lund 1939).

————, "Origine e formazione dell'architettura templare etrusco-italica," *RendPontAcc* 32 (1959/60) 21ff.

A. Boethius, "Vitruvius e il 'Tempio Tuscanico,'" *StEtr* 24 (1955/56) 137–42.

F. Castagnoli, "Peripteros sine postico," *RömMitt* 62 (1955) 139–43.

————, "Sul tempio 'italico,'" *RömMitt* 73/74 (1966/67) 10–14.

T. Dohrn, "Frühzeit des 'Templum Tuscanicum,'" *RendPontAcc* 50 (1977/78) 91–106.

H. Drerup, "Zur Zeitstellung des Kapitolstempels in Rom," *MarbWPr* 1973, 1–12.

Pfiffig, *Religio etrusca* 49–90.

L. Polacco, *Tuscanicae Dispositiones* (Padova 1952).

R.A. Staccioli, "Due note sui frontoni del tempio etrusco-italico," *ArchCl* 20 (1968) 296–301.

————, *Modelli di edifici etrusco-italici. I modelli votivi* (Florence 1968).

E. Wistrand, "Das altrömische Haus und die literarischen Quellen," *Eranos* 68 (1970) 191–223.

————, "La protostoria della Regia," *RendPontAcc* 47 (1974/75) 15–36.

TOMBS AND NECROPOLEIS

A. Åkerström, *Studien über die etruskischen Gräber* (Uppsala 1934).

G. Caputo, "La Tomba della Montagnola a Quinto Fiorentino," *BdA* 47 (1962) 115–52.

F. Chiostri and M. Mannini, *Le tombe a tholos di Quinto* (Sesto Fiorentino 1969).

E. Colonna di Paolo, *Necropoli rupestri del Viterbese* (Novara 1978).

G. Colonna, "L'Etruria meridionale interna dal Villanoviano alle tombe rupestri," *StEtr* 35 (1967) 3–30.

M. Demus-Quatember, *Etruskische Grabarchitektur* (Baden-Baden 1958).

A. Minto, "Pseudocupole e pseudovolte nell'architettura etrusca delle origini," *Palladio* 3 (1939) 1–20.

H. Möbius, "Zeichnungen etruskischer Kammergräber und Einzelfunde von James Byres," *RömMitt* 73/74 (1966/67) 53–71.

F. Nicosia, *Il Tumulo di Montefortini e la Tomba dei Boschetti a Comeana* (Florence 1966).

J.P. Oleson, "The Galeotti Tomb at Chiusi; the Construction Techniques of the Etruscan Barrel-Vaulted Tombs," *StEtr* 44 (1976) 69–85.

————, "Regulatory Planning and Individual Site Development in Etruscan Necropoleis," *Journal of the American Society of Architectural Historians* 35, 3 (1976) 204–18.

————, "Technical Aspects of Etruscan Rock-Cut Tomb Architecture," *RömMitt* 85 (1978) 283–314.

G. Rosi, "Sepulchral Architecture as Illustrated by the Rock Façades of Central Etruria," *JRS* 15 (1925) 1–59; *JRS* 17 (1927) 59–96.

TOWNS AND HOUSES

F.E. Brown, "Of Huts and Houses," *Brendel Essays* 5–12.

F. Castagnoli, *Ippodamo di Mileto e l'urbanistica a pianta ortogonale* (Rome 1956).

P. Ducati, "La città etrusca," *Historia. Studi storici per l'antichità classica* 5 (1931) 3–26.

A. Gargana, "La casa etrusca," *Historia. Studi storici per l'antichità classica* 8 (1934) 204–36.

S. Judson and A. Kahane, "Underground Drainageways in Southern Etruria and Northern Latium," *PBSR* 31 (1963) 74–99.

R.E. Linington, F. Delpino, and M. Pallottino, "Alle origini di Tarquinia: scoperta di un abitato villanoviano sui Monterozzi," *StEtr* 46 (1978) 3–23.

G.A. Mansuelli, "La necropoli orvietana del Tufo: un documento di urbanistica etrusca," *StEtr* 38 (1970) 3–12.

————, "The Etruscan City," in *IBR,* 353–71.

M. Pallottino, "La città etrusco-italica come premessa alla città romana," *Atti Convegno Internazionale sulla città antica in Italia* (Milan 1971) 11–22.

R.A. Staccioli, "Considerazioni sui complessi monumentali di Murlo e di Acquarossa," *Mélanges Heurgon* 961–72.

————, "L'urna etrusca 'a palazzetto' del Museo Archeologico di Firenze," *ArchCl* 19 (1967) 293–305.

————, "Urbanistica etrusca," *ArchCl* 20 (1968) 141–50.

Studi sulla città antica. Atti del convegno di studi sulla città etrusca e italica preromana (Bologna 1970).

J.B. Ward-Perkins, "Etruscan and Roman Roads in Southern Etruria," *JRS* 47 (1957) 139–43.

VI / Coinage

DAVID ENDERS TRIPP

Interest in Etruscan coinage goes back to the sixteenth-century Renaissance, two millennia after the coins were minted. Yet until recently methodical collection and study of the coins lagged behind other scientific archaeological investigations in Etruria. It was in the nineteenth century that people first became aware that Etruscan coins were burdened with more problems of mint, date, and iconography than most other ancient coinages. Mrs. Hamilton Gray in 1839 may have realized the importance of coin hoards (see Glossary at end of chapter for this and other special terms): she comments briefly on one found in Populonia, which she regrets not having been able to see. Ten years later, George Dennis noted the various coin types of virtually all the cities and made some valuable attributions, though many others were admittedly speculative. In 1873, the first volume of the *Catalogue of Greek Coins in the British Museum* included Etruscan coins and offered many tentative conclusions about the collection. Since then the museum's holdings have grown considerably, particularly with the addition in 1946 of the Lloyd collection, published as the second volume of the *Sylloge Nummorum Graecorum*. B.V. Head's *Historia Numorum* is being revised, but until that appears, the study by Arthur Sambon in 1903 is still the most authoritative. Sambon compiled a corpus of all the Etruscan coin types known at that time. Fortunately, it was up to date in approach and method and underscored problems that still need to be resolved.

The recent emphasis on the so-called lesser or peripheral coinages resulted in an international congress on Etruscan coinage in 1975 in Naples. At this important meeting some facts about Etruscan coins were clarified. First, the number of Etruscan coins is not as small as had been previously thought: at the Congress, two thousand casts were exhibited.

F. Panvini Rosati presented a comprehensive introduction to the study of Etruscan coins, while the overview by Tony Hackens, in which he dates and groups the coins, is the clearest exegesis of this kind to date. With the other articles included in the *Contributi*, we have a scholarly commentary on the uncertain history of Etruscan coinage. It is hoped that a clearer understanding will emerge with the precise recording of coins found in hoards and in archaeological contexts, and most important, with a methodical collection of all known types and examples, which may even produce additions to issues which are now known from a single example.

Etruscan coins, in gold, silver, and bronze, were in most cases struck by dies (as coins are today) and at times cast in molds. Only a few issues bear legends or other symbols to identify their origin. Those without any identifying clues are the source of the uncertainty; some of these are occasionally ascribed to Etruria only on the flimsy grounds that they were found there.

Coins were introduced comparatively late into Etruria, in the first quarter of the fifth century B.C., as a result of the influence of Western Greeks. (Much later, the Romans were to adopt the Etruscan weight standards.) The Greeks in Italy themselves did not adopt the practice of coining money until over two centuries after their immigration there. The Carthaginians began even later, in the last decades of the fifth century B.C., when the hiring of soldiers for campaigns in Sicily forced them to mint coins. After the introduction of their own coinage, the Etruscans made no attempt to maintain it on a regular basis. The sporadic nature of the coinage is evident from the dates given to the various series: the first in the fifth century B.C., the second after 345 B.C., and the third about 300 B.C.; then three separate groups in the third century B.C., ending in a final group during the Second Punic War. Coinage was introduced in a time of political and economic decadence, and the different coinages of the various periods coincide with specific historical periods or events, such as participation in maritime commerce in the south, the shipment of mercenaries to Sicily, involvement in the war against Rome, and aid in the Punic War, when Etruscan cities helped Rome against Hannibal. The difference in metal, size, and style of the early coinage indicates little interest in establishing a permanent, recognizable, widely acceptable coinage. Important cities like Caere, Vulci, and Veii did not mint any coins at all, and only a few can be attributed to Tarquinia. It may be significant that, generally speaking, gold and silver coins were found in coastal Etruria, bronze in the interior. Evidently the Etruscans had no need for a continuous supply of coins. Rather, wealthy Etruscans, especially those engaged in sea trade, used the system of barter and exchange, trading Etruscan minerals, wood, and worked bronze for foreign luxury goods.

The uniface issues of Etruria, i.e., those with a plain surface or with no engraving on the reverse (figs. VI-5–8, VI-11, VI-18) attracted the attention of scholars, who recognized immediately that their only parallel was Cypriot coins (especially at Salamis), which followed the same convention. Archaeological research continues to supply evidence of the close connection between Cyprus and Etruria in all periods: the influence of Cypriot coins on those of Etruria may fit in this context. It should be noted that the lack of reverse design does not signify technical incompetence, since the earliest coins with the running Gorgon and wheel do have engraved reverses (fig. VI-2).

Many Etruscan coins, unlike the Greek but like the Roman, bear signs of value:

$$)|(= 100 \qquad \uparrow = 50 \qquad XXX = 30$$

$$XX = 20 \qquad \wedge XX = 25 \qquad)||X = 12\frac{1}{2}$$

$$X = 10 \qquad \wedge = 5 \qquad \text{or} \quad <|| = 2 \qquad 1 = 1$$

The marks on gold coins indicate their equivalent in silver at the ratio of 15:1; those on silver coins indicate their value in bronze at the ratio of 150:1. It is therefore apparent that the decimal system was in use in both gold and silver.

The prototypes of the designs of many issues are Greek, but not all are from Magna Graecia. Hoard evidence gives striking proof that Ionian influence on Etruria, specifically in Populonia in the earliest period, came (perhaps via southern France?) from Phocaea. This is seen in the coin type with hippocamp (a kind of sea horse) (fig. VI-4), and in another with the Gorgon.

Just as some Etruscan coins can be traced to Cypriot and Greek models, so others owe their iconography to the Romans. The major bronze coins are very large and date to the period of Rome's domination. None appear to be earlier than 350 B.C. In fact, the cast pieces of the *aes grave* class (fig. VI-19) look more Roman than Etruscan. Chronology of the bronze depends on the still-disputed dates of the Roman silver coins. Problems concerning the chronology of Etruscan coinage are unlikely to be solved until there is full agreement on the dating of Roman silver as well as of the Roman *aes signatum* and *aes grave*. (For Etruscan *aes signatum*, see fig. VI-17).

New methodology is proving effective: Rudi Thomsen, using comparisons, dates certain Populonian silver coins to the same time as the Roman denarius (Second Punic War). He also attempts to date the Etruscan gold lion types (fig. VI-6) to the same period as the Roman Mars and eagle gold type. Even when Etruscan coins carry legends, they present problems. Some clearly refer to cities: Volsinii (gold), Volterra, Tarquinia (*aes grave*). The difficulty lies in identifying letters or words. For example, the identification of Peithesa as Pisa is incorrect. The legend Thezi or Thezle (figs. VI-2–3; *TLE* 786) makes up the largest question mark, together with the chronology of the mint—if it was a mint.

The coins of Populonia (figs. VI-5–10, VI-12–13) have come down to us in great numbers, in bronze and silver and, in a very few instances, in gold (figs. VI-6–7). The most popular obverse type was the Gorgoneion (fig. VI-7), while reverses were either blank (figs. VI-7–8) or engraved with squids or

sepias, with opposing caducei or with an astral motif of stars and crescent (fig. VI-10). The time span
of the stars and crescent issues is comparatively
long; it furnishes a fine opportunity to study the
changes in the style of the astral motif as well as in
weight standards.

Two designs are illuminated by a comparison
with the Populonia Gorgoneion coins. The first
design is that of silver didrachms of the third century B.C. with Herakles and lionskin, one didrachm
with blank reverse, another with club (fig. VI-9).
The didrachms carry no ethnic, but there is no
doubt about their mint because they have the same
weight, fabric, style, and "heavy" execution as the
Populonian coins. The second didrachm, with the
legend Pupluna, presents a facing head of Athena in
three-quarter profile, wearing a triple-crested helmet, with star and crescent, similar to a reverse
motif of the Gorgoneion series (fig. VI-10). The
obverse resembles the well-known head at Syracuse
signed by the die-maker Eukleidas (fig. VI-20) and
undoubtedly copied on Lycian coins. It was one
of the favorite themes which, despite its difficulty,
was rendered with ease at Populonia. In contrast,
the number of facing heads on early Greek coins as
a whole is limited. Although it has no legend, the
unique gold coin mentioned above (fig. VI-7) has
the same fabric and type as the other Gorgoneion
issues with blank reverse. The prolific production
of the mint proves Populonia's importance as a
commercial city, as does perhaps one interesting
bronze triens which represents Hephaestus with his
hammer and tongs (fig. VI-13). Populonia depended
in large measure on the iron reserves of nearby
Elba: the representations of the metalworking god
of the forge and his tools were a perfect hallmark of
the city.

An intriguing historical question is raised by a
series of coins from the valley of the Clanis (Chiana)
River, dominated by Chiusi (fig. VI-16). On the
obverse is the head of a Negro whose race, as Frank
Snowden puts it, "is vividly delineated by his broad
nose, thick lips, and kinky hair." On the reverse is
an elephant. E. Babelon in 1885 conjectured that the
people of north Italy were impressed by the Negro
mahouts they saw on Hannibal's elephants at the
time of the Second Punic War at the end of the
third century B.C. and were thus inspired to issue
the coins. We know that the Ethiopians were skilled

in handling these animals. The playwright Plautus,
who was active at the time of the Second Punic
War, gives the impression (in the *Poenulus*) that
African blacks were living in Italy in his day. Some
of the black mahouts could have survived the rigors
of the Alps when Hannibal descended into Italy
(Livy 21.56). Although we have evidence that a
number of Etruscan cities sent aid to Rome, an
inscription recently found at Tarquinia suggests
that a Larth Felsna may have fought in Hannibal's
army. There was Etruscan support for this Carthaginian general: it is reasonable to suppose that these
coins were struck in a north Etruscan city by Hannibal's allies in Italy in order to pay his soldiers.

Vetulonia is another city whose coins can be
identified. Exclusively bronze, they are of several
types, some of which were also popular with other
Etruscan die-makers. A marine motif found in this
area is interpreted as alluding to Etruscan seafaring
prowess. The most common Vetulonian type represents a marine god wearing what looks like a
dolphin-skin headdress (fig. VI-14). The reverse,
with its tridentlike anchor flanked by two diving
dolphins, is particularly interesting. It turns up
approximately three hundred years later on denarii
of Domitian. It also has an afterlife that extends
right up to the present: we find it used as an em-
blem by navies today.

Volsinii gives us two fascinating gold types. The
first, represented by a unique example in the British
Museum, is of unrivaled beauty (fig. VI-1). The
obverse type, a young man's laureate head right,
has been identified as either Apollo or Eros; the
reverse represents a bull advancing left, above which
is a dove in flight. The second bears a young female
head, perhaps Artemis, on the obverse, and a leap-
ing dog on the reverse. The legends read *Velznani*
and *Velsu,* respectively. Among the gold series of
Etruria, these are the only examples which can be
stylistically dated to the late fourth or early third
century B.C.; the majority of gold coins have usually
been considered to be the earliest coins minted by
the Etruscans. The stater (fig. VI-1) is in typical
Hellenistic style, the only Etruscan coin to display
such rich die-cutting. In addition to the similarity
of the legends, the two coins share another feature:
they are struck on so-called dished flans, a most
unusual feature.

Etruscan coins also provide source material for

the religious, political, and commercial life of Etruscan cities. Hephaestus (fig. VI-13) may have appeared on a coin simply as a symbol for a commercial city or may have been adopted by the Etruscans as a sacred symbol. Herakles (figs. VI-9, VI-12) may have been adopted because he appeared on Greek coins, or he may have appealed to the Etruscans because he resembled a local deity or even a Phoenician god. He was usually equated with Melqart in the Punic world, and we know that the Etruscans accepted a Punic sanctuary at Pyrgi in the fifth century B.C. An exciting opportunity of comparing the literary and archaeological evidence with that of the coins awaits the historian when the basic numismatic work is done. Someday the *raison d'être* may prove to be much more than just the utilitarian purposes thus far attributed to these precious miniatures in metal.

Appendix: Glossary

Aes grave: cast circular bronze coin

Aes signatum: cast bronze bar with designs

As: bronze coin, originally cast, of one Roman pound (12 unciae)

Coin hoards: groups of coins uncovered (or discovered) in a common context, important in determining dates of specific coins or series

Didrachm: coin of two drachms weight (also called a stater)

Die: engraved striking implement for producing coins

Die-cutting: engraving (in negative) die with design to be used in striking a coin

Dished flans: concave/convex-shaped coin module (usually formed by impact of similarly shaped dies in striking process)

Drachm: coin of usual Greek weight unit (actual weight can vary from mint to mint)

Electrum: usually (but not exclusively) natural alloy of gold and silver

Ethnic: symbol or letter identifying place of minting

Fabric: physical characteristics of flan (size, shape, and thickness)

Flan: blank piece of metal upon which dies are struck (also generically used to describe physical characteristics of coin)

Incuse: sunken design, struck intaglio into flan

Legends: letters or words incorporated in coin's design to identify minting authority or place of manufacture

Litra, half litra: weight used as denomination for heavy Greek bronze coins, also for their equivalent in silver

Marks of value: numerals or symbols used to denote coin's denomination

Mint: place of coin's manufacture

Romano-Campanian standard: earliest weight standard utilized by Rome, borrowed from silver coinage of Campania

Sextans: denomination equal to one-sixth of an as (mark of value :)

Triens: denomination equal to one-third of an as (mark of value · · · ·)

Type: design on coin: obverse type, design on side of coin impressed by fixed die ("heads"); reverse type, design on side of coin impressed by movable die ("tails"); blank or no reverse type; struck with unengraved, usually moveable die

Uncia: denomination equal to one-twelfth of as

Weight standard: theoretical metallic weight-value relationship upon which coinage of an area is based

Bibliography

BOOKS

E. Babelon, *Description historique et chronologique des monnaies de la république romaine* (Paris 1885–86).

S.L. Cesano, *Tipi monetali etruschi* (Rome 1926).

Contributi introduttivi allo studio della monetazione etrusca. Atti del V Convegno del Centro Internazionale di Studi Numismatici 1975 (Naples 1976).

M.J. Crawford, *Roman Republican Coin Hoards* (London 1969).

————, *Roman Republican Coinage* (Cambridge 1974).

G. Dennis, *Cities and Cemeteries of Etruria.*

R. Garrucci, *Le monete dell' Italia antica* (Rome 1885) 18ff.

W. Giesecke, *Italia Numismatica* (Leipzig 1928) 20ff.

M. Grant, *The Etruscans.*

E.J. Haeberlin, *Aes Grave. Das Schwergeld Roms und Mittelitaliens* (Frankfurt 1910).

B.V. Head, *Historia Numorum* (Oxford 1911).

C.M. Kraay and M. Hirmer, *Greek Coins* (London 1966).

Milani, *Mus. Arch.,* 39ff.

Mueller-Deecke I, Beilage I, "Die Etruskischen Münzen," 379–434.

R.S. Poole, *British Museum Catalogue of Greek Coins. Italy* (London 1873).

A. Sambon, *Les monnaies antiques de l'Italie* (Paris 1903).

I. Scandaliato Ciciani and F. Panvini Rosati, *La letteratura numismatica nei secoli XVI–XVIII* (Rome 1980).

A. Stazio, "Storia monetaria dell'Italia preromana," *Popoli e civiltà* 7 (1978) 113–93, esp. 143–44.

Sylloge Nummorum Graecorum. American Numismatic Society, vol. I (1969) nos. 1–100.

R. Thomsen, *Early Roman Coinage: A Study of the Chronology* (Copenhagen 1957–61).

ARTICLES

C. Ampolo, "*Servius rex signavit aes,*" *Parola del Passato* 28 (1974) 382–88. Against this early date, see A. Burnett and P. Craddock, "Early Italian Currency Bars," in *Aspects of Italic Culture*. On the Bitalemi (Gela) *ramo secco* bar: "it seems desirable to resist the temptation to associate the Bitulemi bar with [. . .] Pliny's statement, 'Servius rex primus signavit aes.'" According to the authors, there is no connection between these bars and Rome.

M.P. Baglione, "Su alcune serie parallele di bronzo coniato," *Contributi* 153–80.

L. Breglia, "L'oro con la testa di leone," *Contributi* 75–86. The author holds for a sixth-century date (550–500 B.C.), against others who believe in a fifth- or fourth-century date. See also discussion, pp. 131–39, 211–15.

———, "A proposito dell'*aes signatum,*" *Annali dell'Istituto Numismatico* 12–14 (1965–67) 269–75.

J.-P. Callu, "Eléphants et cochon: sur une représentation monétaire d'époque républicaine," *Mélanges Heurgon* 89–100.

L. Camilli, "Le monete a leggenda Vatl (Vetulonia)," *Contributi* 181–97.

R. Catalli, "La zecca di Volterra," *Contributi* 141–52. To Haeberlin's 483 examples she adds 150 pieces.

G. Colonna, discussion on Populonia coinage, *Contributi* 345–48; and discussion on Gorgon representations, 369–70.

M. Cristofani, "Problemi iconografici ed epigrafico-linguistici della monetazione in bronzo," *Contributi* 349–58; discussion, 359–61.

T. Hackens, "La métrologie des monnaies étrusques les plus anciennes," *Contributi* 221–72.

J. Heurgon, "Les contremarques sur les revers des didrachmes de Populonia," *Congresso Internazionale di Numismatica, Roma 1961, Atti* II (Rome 1965) 159–66.

———, "Les types monétaires étrusques et le bestiaire orientalisant," *Contributi* 311–18.

Ingrid Krauskopf, "Gorgonendarstellung auf etruskischen Münzen und in der etruskischen Kunst," *Contributi* 319–43.

P. Marchetti, "La métrologie des monnaies étrusques avec marques de valeur," *Contributi* 296.

Marina Cristofani Martelli, "Il ripostiglio di Volterra," *Contributi* 87–104. The author reconstructs a hoard found near the walls of Volterra in 1868, containing 65 silver coins without legends, silver bars weighing two pounds or more, and a statuette of a lion, since dispersed. Along with a nucleus of coins from Phocaea, imports and imitations (probably from Southern France), she distinguishes a group of local coins.

Francesco Roncalli, "Il gorgoneion tipo 'Belvedere' a Orvieto," *Annali della Fondazione per il Museo Claudio Faina* I (Orvieto 1980) 79–98.

P. Petrillo Serafin, "Le serie monetarie di Populonia," *Contributi* 105–30.

Robert F. Sutton, Jr. "The Populonia Coinage and the Second Punic War," *Contributi* 199–211.

ETRUSCAN NUMISMATICS

G.B. Passeri, *In Thomae Dempsteri Libros de Etruria regali paralipomena* (Lucca 1767) 153ff., "De re nummaria Etruscorum dissertatio." Cited by Scandalia to Ciciani and Panvini Rosati, *Contributi* 25.

F. Panvini Rosati, "Gli studi e la problematica attuale sulla monetazione etrusca," *Contributi* 25 (a survey of the history of the study of Etruscan coinage from the eighteenth century).

Luigi Tondo, "Per una storia della numismatica etrusca. Studiosi dei secolo XVI–XIX," *Rivista Italiana di Numismatica* 81 (1979) 143–54 (the history of Etruscan numismatics and the role of Italian scholars of the sixteenth through the nineteenth centuries).

HANNIBAL COINAGE WITH ELEPHANTS

Grant, *Etruscans* 176, 285.

G.K. Jenkins, "Greek Coins Recently Acquired by the British Museum," *Numismatic Chronicle* (1955) 131–56, esp. 154–56; on the Hannibal issue, see "Carthaginians in Spain."

———, "Recent Acquisitions of Greek Coins by the British Museum," *Numismatic Chronicle* (1959) 23–25.

E.S.G. Robinson, "Greek Coins Acquired by the British Museum in 1930–31," *Numismatic Chronicle* (1932) 200–14.

———, "Coinages of the Second Punic War," *Numismatic Chronicle* (1964) 46–48, cf. 37.

H.H. Scullard, *The Elephant in the Greek and Roman World* (London 1974) 72.

———, "Hannibal's Elephants," *Numismatic Chronicle* (1948) 162–68.

———, and Gowers, "Hannibal's Elephants Again," *Numismatic Chronicle* (1950) 271–83.

F.M. Snowden, *Blacks in Antiquity* (Cambridge, Massachusetts, 1970) 130–31.

Illustrations

Note: unless otherwise indicated, all coins shown are in the British Museum collection and were photographed by the author.

VI-1. Gold stater, *Velznani* (probably Volsinii). Unique. 4.67 gms. Ca. 300 B.C. *Obverse:* laureate young male head facing left; *below, on either side,* mark of value: X X. *Reverse:* bull advancing left, dove flying above, star in field left.

VI-2. Silver stater, *Thezi,* uncertain mint. 11.12 gms. 425–400 B.C. (per F. Panvini Rosati). *Obverse:* winged Gorgon running left. *Reverse:* inscription within archaic wheel.

VI-3. Silver stater, *Thezle,* uncertain mint. Unique. 9.26 gms. Fourth century B.C. *Obverse:* three-quarter head of bull facing right, inscription around. *Reverse:* hippocamp swimming right.

VI-4. Silver drachm, uncertain mint. Unique. 5.36 gms. Fourth century B.C. *Obverse:* hippocamp swimming right, circled by dolphins. *Reverse:* Cerberus standing right, within square.

VI-5. Silver double stater, uncertain mint, possibly Populonia. 22.66 gms. End of fifth century B.C. *Obverse:* octopus emerging from amphora, with uncertain object behind; below, mark of value: X X. No reverse type.

VI-7. Gold fifty litrae, uncertain mint, probably Populonia. Unique. 2.77 gms. Late fourth century B.C. *Obverse:* facing Gorgon's head with protruding tongue, mark of value below: ↑ . No reverse type.

VI-6. Gold twenty-five litrae, uncertain mint, probably Populonia. 1.37 gms. Fourth century B.C. *Obverse:* lion's head with protruding tongue facing right; to left and below, mark of value: ↑ . No reverse type.

VI-8. Silver hemidrachm, uncertain mint, possibly Populonia. 1.61 gms. Third century B.C. *Obverse:* head of Hermes facing right, wearing winged petasos; mark of value to left: ∧ . No reverse type.

VI-9. Silver didrachm, Populonia. 8.45 gms. Third century
B.C. *Obverse:* facing head of Herakles wearing lionskin
headdress with mark of value to either side: X X. *Reverse:*
club.

VI-10. Silver didrachm, *Pupluna*, Populonia. 7.88 gms.
Third century B.C. *Obverse:* three-quarter facing head of
Athena wearing triple-crested helmet with mark of value
to either side: X X. *Reverse:* inscription around star and
crescent.

VI-11. Silver tetradrachm, uncertain mint. 16.35 gms. Fifth century B.C. (per T. Hackens). *Obverse:* boar walking right on rocky ground. No reverse type.

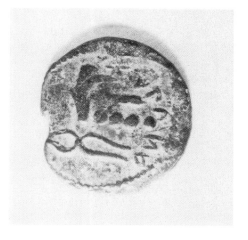

VI-13. Bronze reduced triens, *Pupluna,* Populonia. 7.08 gms. Third century B.C. *Obverse:* head of Hephaestus facing right wearing pileus with X behind. *Reverse:* hammer and tongs with inscription at right, mark of value between hammer and tongs: four pellets.

VI-12. Bronze sextans, *Pupluna,* Populonia. 12.40 gms. Third century B.C. *Obverse:* head of Herakles facing right. *Reverse:* bow, arrow, and club with inscription below and, between arrow and club, mark of value: two pellets.

VI-14. Bronze sextans, Vetulonia, *Vatl.* 9.95 gms. Third
century B.C. *Obverse:* head of marine deity facing right,
with mark of value behind: two pellets, inscription below.
Reverse: trident between two diving dolphins and mark
of value at left and right: two pellets.

VI-15. Bronze fifty units, uncertain mint. 24.76 gms.
Fourth century B.C. (per T. Hackens). *Obverse:* bearded
head facing right wearing dolphin headdress, mark of
value behind: ↑   *Reverse:* incuse hippocamp swimming right.

VI-16. Bronze, Clanis Valley. 5.33 gms. Late third century B.C. *Obverse:* head of Negro facing right, with behind. *Reverse:* elephant facing right wearing bell around neck, below.

VI-17. Bronze *aes signatum,* uncertain mint in northern Etruria. 1167 gms. Sixth to fourth century B.C. *Obverse:* dry branches. *Reverse:* dry branches. (Courtesy Estate of Jane Brand Allen.)

VI-18. Silver tetradrachm, uncertain mint. 16.67 gms. Fifth century B.C. (per T. Hackens). *Obverse:* lion with tail terminating in serpent's head (Chimaera?) stalking left. No reverse type.

VI-19. Bronze as, uncertain mint. Ca. 190 gms. Third century B.C. *Obverse:* facing head of augur wearing conical hat. *Reverse:* ritual implements. (Courtesy The Johns Hopkins University.)

VI-20. Silver tetradrachm, Syracuse. 17.21 gms. Ca. 410 B.C. *Reverse:* three-quarter facing head of Athena wearing crested helmet and necklace, with swimming dolphins and inscription around and, on bowl of helmet, engraver's signature: *Eukleida.*

VII / An Archaeological Introduction to the Etruscan Language

EMELINE RICHARDSON

The study of the Etruscan language is based on archaeological finds, almost all of them inscriptions on stone, terracotta, or metal. Some are scratched on pots or potsherds; some are painted on the walls of tombs. One fragmentary book is preserved, a linen scroll like the books of the magistrates kept in the Temple of Juno Moneta on the Arx at Rome (Livy 4.7.12; 4.20.8; 4.23.2), though the Etruscan scroll is a book of rituals and therefore more like the *vetus liber linteus* from which the Samnites read the rites of sacrifice before the battle of Aquilonia (Livy 10.38.6).

Etruscan was the only non-Indo-European language written, and possibly spoken, in Italy in historic times (Maps 5, 8). Etruscan inscriptions have been found in Etruria proper, between the Tiber and the Arno, the Apennines and the Tyrrhenian Sea, as well as in the Po Valley and in Campania, that is, in those parts of Italy to which Etruscan civilization spread. It was the same language from Mantua to Nola, without sharp dialectical distinctions. From this, the distinguished Etruscan scholar Ambros Pfiffig concludes that the language spread from a single center in Italy and that it had not been introduced there much before it was first written down.[1] The earliest preserved inscriptions date from about 700 B.C. If Pfiffig is right, the language was not that of a very ancient, autochthonous people, as Dionysius of Halicarnassus believed,[2] nor that spoken in Lydia in the Bronze Age, as Herodotus's story of the coming of the Tyrrhenoi to Italy would imply,[3] nor yet that of the Villanovans, the first Iron Age settlers of Etruria,[4] as Professor Pallottino

and I would like to think, but a language introduced to Etruscan territory some time in the eighth century B.C. How it came, and where it came from, remain unexplained. On the Aegean island of Lemnos off the coast of the Troad, where, according to Thucydides (4.109.4), there were Tyrsenoi living before Miltiades annexed the island for Athens, inscriptions have been found dating from the sixth century written in an unknown non-Indo-European language (fig. VII-5) but in an archaic Greek alphabet. The language has many resemblances to Etruscan[5] but probably is only one of the pre-Indo-European languages of the Aegean. The Etruscans, wherever they came from and whoever they were, learned to read and write from the Greeks, probably from the largely Euboean colony of Pithekoussai (Ischia),[6] the oldest Greek colony in the west and the nearest to Etruria. Cumae was settled by 760 B.C. and began to trade with the people living in Etruria almost at once; Etruscan was written by the end of the century.

The Alphabet

The earliest alphabet so far found in Etruria is scratched on the margin of a miniature ivory writing tablet found in a tomb at Marsiliana d'Albegna (fig. VII-1).[7] It is a perfectly good archaic Greek alphabet of twenty-six letters: alpha, beta, gamma, delta, epsilon, digamma, zeta, eta, theta, iota, kappa, lambda, mu, nu, xi, omicron, pi, san, koppa, rho, sigma, tau, upsilon, chi, phi, and psi (fig. VII-2). It has some special characteristics, noted here:

> gamma was, or came to be, pronounced like hard *C* (*K*), as at Rome and sometimes in our own alphabet;

ꟻ digamma was pronounced *V* as in Greece (before the Greeks dropped it), Rome gave it the sound of *F*, and we inherited that;

ᗺꟼO beta, delta, and omicron, though they appear in this and other early Etruscan alphabets, are not used in Etruscan inscriptions, though the Romans (and we) kept them all;

ᗷ eta has the value of *H* as it did in Rome and does in English;

⊙ theta is used frequently in Etruscan, but Rome did not take it over since the sound appears in Latin only in loan words, like *theatron,* and as a result, we, who use the sound constantly, have no symbol for it and must write *TH* instead;

⊞ ksi, **M** san, and **X** chi are all forms of *S* in Etruscan; **M** san is often used: it is transcribed as *ś* in English; the other two appear only in archaic inscriptions;

ꟼ koppa and **Φ** phi only appear in archaic inscriptions;

Y psi has the value of **X** chi in the Attic alphabet;

88 *F* was added to the Etruscan alphabet in the sixth century.

Reading Etruscan is not difficult. The problem is to understand what is being read. Three archaic inscriptions, one each in Greek, Latin, and the non-Indo-European language of Lemnos, are illustrated here to show how much their alphabets are like the Etruscan. The Greek (fig. VII-3) reads "Apolonos Aiginata emi. Sostratos epoiese ho—" ("I belong to Aiginetan Apollo. Sostratos had me made"). This dedication was found in the early Greek trading post (emporium) at Graviscae on the coast near Tarquinia.[8] The wealthy trader Sostratos is mentioned by Herodotus (4.152). The Latin (fig. VII-4) "Castorei Podlouqueique qurois" ("To Castor and Polydeuces, sons [of Zeus]") is inscribed on a bronze plaque of the sixth century, found at Lavinium south of Rome.[9] The Lemnian stele (fig. VII-5) is a grave marker for a warrior, and most likely

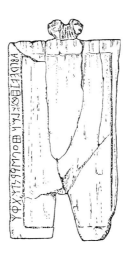

VII-1. Miniature writing tablet from Marsiliana d'Albegna with model alphabet. 8.8 cm. × 5 cm. Ivory (the back was originally covered with gold leaf). Ca. 650 B.C. Florence, Museo Archeologico, Inv. 93480. (Soprintendenza alle Antichità–Firenze.) (Drawing from Sprenger-Bartoloni, fig. 1.)

gives his name and his titles, and perhaps something of his history.

The Inscriptions

More than ten thousand Etruscan inscriptions are known: unfortunately, most of them are only a few words long, and many are aggravatingly fragmentary. The longest piece of Etruscan prose we have, the text of the Zagreb mummy (*TLE* 1), has preserved about twelve hundred words that can be read more or less clearly and one hundred more that can be guessed at. With its many duplications, the total vocabulary is only about five hundred words.[10]

Another obstacle to translation is that too many words appear only once. Take, for instance, the inscription scratched on a bucchero cup from the Tomba del Duce at Vetulonia,[11] of the mid-seventh century, one of our earliest Etruscan inscriptions (*TLE* 366; fig. VII-6): "naceme uru ithal thilen ithal icheme mesna mertanśina mulu" (the separation of the words here is pure conjecture). *Mulu* is the only

Model	Archaic	Transitional	Late	Special Forms	Pronunciation
					a
					b
					c (= k)
					d
					e
					v
					z
					h
					ϑ (= th)
					i
					k
					l
					m
					n
					ś
					o
					p
					ś
					q (= k)
					r
					s
					t
					u
					ś
					φ (= ph)
					χ (= kh)
					f

VII-2. Forms of the Etruscan alphabet. Column one shows the model alphabet. The earliest inscriptions, those that date from the mid-seventh to the mid-fifth century, are written in an archaic alphabet shown in column two. A classical alphabet, which drops a number of letters found in the archaic, was used in the later fifth and early fourth centuries (column three). Column four shows the latest alphabet, which is not very different from the second; it was used in the later fourth century, and thereafter as long as the Etruscan language was used for inscriptions. Column five illustrates some special forms; and column six gives an approximate pronunciation. Pfiffig, *Etruskische Sprache* 20.)

VII-3. Greek votive inscription from Graviscae in the form of an anchor, with dedication to Apollo by Sostratos. Stone. Ca. 500 B.C. (Courtesy Mario Torelli.)

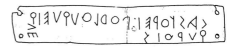

VII-4. Latin votive inscription from Lavinium dedicated to Castor and Pollux. Bronze. Ca. 500 B.C. (Pfiffig, *Religio Etrusca* fig. 135.)

VII-5. Funerary stele from Lemnos with inscription in a language akin to Etruscan. Stone. Sixth century B.C. Athens, National Museum. (Pallottino, *Etruscans* fig. 9.)

VII-6. Inscription on the foot of a bucchero cup from the Tomba del Duce, Vetulonia. Seventh century B.C. Florence, Museo Archeologico. (*TLE* 366.) (Camporeale, *Tomba del Duce* fig. 15.)

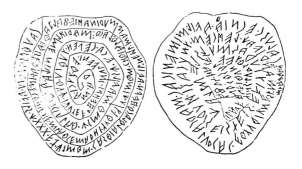

VII-7. Lead plaque from Magliano (Heba), inscribed on both sides, spirally inward from the outer borders. Fifth or fourth century B.C. (*TLE* 359.)

word that appears elsewhere; it is quite common on votive inscriptions and seems to mean "offering."

The preserved inscriptions are of five kinds: ritual (lists of sacrifices, calendars of offerings, lists of divinities, etc.); legal (these are all boundary stones, and they all contain the word *tular,* which must mean "boundary" or "boundaries"[12]); funerary (inscriptions on tombs, sarcophagi, ash urns, etc.); votive (dedications of some object to some divinity, in which the dedicator's name is sometimes given, sometimes the divinity's, and occasionally the object is named); and mythological (which include the huge number of inscribed mirrors, some tomb paintings, and many of the Hellenistic ash urns from Volterra and Chiusi). The six longest inscriptions are listed below.

1. The Zagreb text.[13] This is the only surviving sacred book on cloth. It was re-used in the Hellenistic period to wrap an Egyptian mummy. It is a book of rituals devoted to certain gods: Aisera, Crapsti, Nethuns, Thanr, Thesan, Tins, Tius, and Uslan.

2. The Capua tile (*TLE* 2).[14] Almost 300 legible words are preserved; this is another ritual text mentioning the gods Calus, Laruns, Lethams, Tinian, and Uni.

3. The Perugia cippus (*TLE* 570),[15] a boundary stone of 46 lines and 130 words. It is one of the handsomest inscriptions from Etruria.

4. A lead strip from the sanctuary of Minerva at Punta della Vipera near Santa Marinella (*TLE* 878).[16] There are traces of at least 80 words, only half of which are legible; it is a calendar of offerings.

5. A lead plaque from Magliano in the valley of the Albegna (*TLE* 359; fig. VII-7).[17] At least 70 words are written in a spiral on each side of the plaque; it is another calendar of offerings, mentioning the gods Aisera, Calus, Cautha, Maris, Thanr, and Tin.

6. The sarcophagus of Lars Pulena at Tarquinia (*TLE* 131).[18] The effigy of Lars Pulena carries a scroll containing nine lines with 59 words. It begins: "L'ris Pulenas Larces clan Larthal papacs Velthurus nefts—" ("Lars Pulena son of Larce grandson of Larth great-grandson of Velthur"). It lists his honors and offices and the names of two gods, of whom he was probably the priest: Catha and Pacha.

Funerary Inscriptions

The inscription on the scroll of Lars Pulena is the longest. Inscriptions on sarcophagi and ash urns are usually quite short. An urn from Chiusi (fig. VII-8)[19] is inscribed only with the gentleman's name: Larth Sentinates Caesa. One from Volterra (fig. VII-9)[20] gives the name, A (Avle) Cecni, and his age at his death: *ril* ("aged") ↑ ||| (53) *leine* ("died"). A painted inscription from the Tomb of the Hill at Chiusi (*TLE* 460)[21] reads "Tiuza Tius Vetusal clan Thanas Tlesnal avils XIII" ("Tiuza Tius, son of Vetus and of Thana Tlesna, 13 years").

Such inscriptions, short as they are, provide a great deal of information about the Etruscan language and society. A gentleman is apt to have three names, corresponding to the Roman praenomen, nomen, and cognomen: Larth Sentinates Caesa (cf. Caius Julius Caesar) (fig. VII-8), or two, praenomen and nomen, for example, A. Cecni (cf. Sex. Propertius, T. Livius) (fig. VII-9). The mother's name (unlike Roman custom) may be included in the pedigree along with the father's: Tiuza Tius is the son of Vetus and of Thana Tlesna, and the mother has a name of her own, not just a gentilitial adjective (like the Latin Julia, Livia, Octavia). The words *ril, leine, clan,* and *avils,* which reappear on numberless funerary inscriptions, can be translated with considerable assurance as "aged," "died," "son," and "years," respectively. A certain modicum of grammar can be extracted even from these short inscriptions: a genitive in -*l* (-*al*), Vetusal, Tlesnal; and one in -*s*, Thanas; a past tense of the verb in -*e,* *leine.*

Dedicatory Inscriptions

These can be written on almost any kind of object. I have chosen three little bronzes as examples. *TLE* 640 (fig. VII-10) is a janiform divinity whose image was found at Cortona.[22] The inscription reads "V Cvinti Arntiaś Culśanśl alpan turce" ("V [Velthur] Cvinti son of Arnth dedicated this to Culsans").

VII-8. Ash urn of Larth Sentinates Caesa from the Tomba della Pellegrina, Chiusi. Second or first century B.C. Chiusi, Museo Etrusco. (Felbermeyer.)

This translation leaves out *alpan,* the meaning of which is debated: according to some scholars it means "gift," acording to others it is an adverb, "gladly." This example gives the name of the dedicator and of the divinity. *TLE* 736 (fig. VIII-33) represents a priest.[23] "In turce Vel Sveitus" ("Vel Sveitus dedicated it"); here, only the name of the dedicator is given. *TLE* 737 (fig. VII-11) is the figure of a young god, probably Apollo.[24] In the statement "mi fleres svulare Aritimi Fasti Ruifris trce clen cecha," *mi* stands for "I am"; and *fleres* must be related to the word *fler,* known elsewhere, which has something to do with "offering." Some scholars translate *fleres* as "god," others translate it as "statue." My guess would be that it meant "votive offering": "I am a votive offering. Fasti Ruifris (*svulare?*) dedicated me to Artemis"—*clen* is genitive of *clan,* "son"; *cecha* seems to mean "rite" or "right"— "the right offering for a son"? Here the object, the dedicator, and the divinity are all mentioned, as well as the reason for the dedication. The word *turce* (*trce*), which appears in all three inscriptions,

had been translated conjecturally as "gave." This meaning has now been confirmed by the inscriptions found at Pyrgi in 1964.

These gold tablets are the most beautiful dedicatory inscriptions yet found. Two are in Etruscan; the third is Phoenician (Carthaginian?). Though they do not, unfortunately, provide a Rosetta Stone, they add a number of possibles to our knowledge of word meanings. *Turce* (*turuce*) is translated in the Punic inscription "gave" (*TLE* 874, 875, figs. VII-12, III-6).[25] The tablets record the dedication of something by a certain Thefarie Veliinas, king of Caere, to the goddess Uni, who is identified with the Phoenician Astarte. These, our longest votive inscriptions, date from about 500 B.C. (see Ch. III).

Ritual Inscriptions

Of the six longest Etruscan inscriptions, four are ritual: the Zagreb mummy wrapping (*TLE* 1), the

VII-9. Ash urn of A. Cecni from Volterra. Hellenistic. (Felbermeyer.)

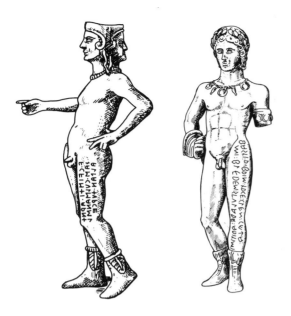

VII-13a. Model of a sheep's liver, from the vicinity of Piacenza, inscribed with the names of Etruscan gods. Bronze. Hellenistic period. Piacenza, Museo Civico. (*TLE* 719.) (DAI.)

(*Left*) VII-10. Votive statuette from Cortona of a double-faced divinity, Culśanś. Bronze. Fourth or third century B.C. (*TLE* 640.) (Pfiffig, *Religio Etrusca* fig. 108.)

(*Right*) VII-11. Votive statuette from Ferrara of a young man, Apollo?, wearing laurel wreath, jewelry, and boots. Bronze. Fourth century B.C. Paris, Bibliothèque Nationale. (*TLE* 737.) (Pfiffig, *Religio Etrusca* fig. 110.)

VII-12. Plaques from Pyrgi with Etruscan inscriptions, dedicated by Thefarie Veliiunas, king of Caere, to Uni-Astarte (Juno-Astarte). Gold. Ca. 500 B.C. (Pallottino, *Saggi di Antichità* 629–30, fig. 40.)

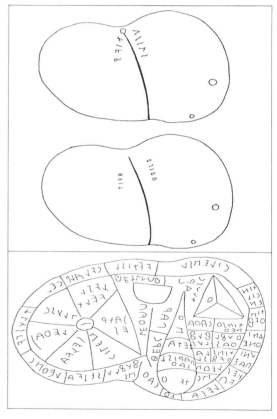

VII-13b. Drawing of the underside of the liver, showing the names incised on the upper and lower surfaces. (L.B. van der Meer, *BABesch* 54 [1979] 59–60.)

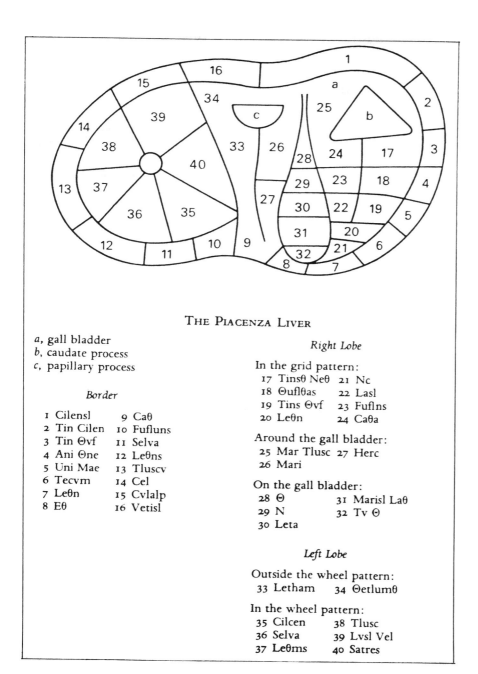

THE PIACENZA LIVER

a, gall bladder
b, caudate process
c, papillary process

Border

1 Cilensl	9 Caθ
2 Tin Cilen	10 Fufluns
3 Tin Θvf	11 Selva
4 Ani Θne	12 Leθns
5 Uni Mae	13 Tluscv
6 Tecvm	14 Cel
7 Leθn	15 Cvlalp
8 Eθ	16 Vetisl

Right Lobe

In the grid pattern:

17 Tinsθ Neθ	21 Nc
18 Θuflθas	22 Lasl
19 Tins Θvf	23 Fuflns
20 Leθn	24 Caθa

Around the gall bladder:

25 Mar Tlusc 27 Herc
26 Mari

On the gall bladder:

28 Θ	31 Marisl Laθ
29 N	32 Tv Θ
30 Leta	

Left Lobe

Outside the wheel pattern:

33 Letham   34 Θetlumθ

In the wheel pattern:

35 Cilcen	38 Tlusc
36 Selva	39 Lvsl Vel
37 Leθms	40 Satres

VII-13c. Diagram of the upper side of the liver, showing
the names of the divinities. (Du Mésil, *Archaic Roman
Religion,* p. 653.)

VII-15. Engraved mirror from Praeneste with Tinia giving birth to Menrva, assisted by Ethauśva and Thanr. Bronze. Fourth century B.C. London, British Museum. (*ES* 5.6.)

VII-14. Engraved mirror with Apulu and Artumes. Bronze. Ca. 470 B.C. Berlin, Staatliche Museen, Antikenmuseum. (*ES* 293.)

Capua tile (*TLE* 2), the lead strip from Santa Marinella (*TLE* 878), and the lead plaque from Magliano (*TLE* 359; fig. VII-7). A bronze model of a sheep's liver, found near Piacenza in the Po Valley (*TLE* 719; fig. VII-13),[26] may also be counted among the ritual inscriptions, since it gives us our longest list of divinities. The liver of the sacrificial animal was considered to be a microcosm of the heavens; by studying its appearance, the priest (whom the Romans called a haruspex) could tell which divinity or divinities were involved in the undertaking in hand, and whether the involvement was favorable or the reverse. This bronze liver was obviously an annotated guide for the haruspex. Its upper face is divided into forty-four "houses," each assigned to a divinity. Several gods have more than one house. The lower face is divided between the territories of two more gods, the Sun, USILS, cf. the mirror (fig. VII-20), and TIVR, who is presumably the Moon.

VII-16. Engraved mirror from Tarquinia with Sethlans freeing Uni from the throne he made to imprison her; Tretu works with hammer and chisel as Sethlans' assistant. Bronze. Fourth century B.C. Dresden. (*ES* 5.49.)

VII-17. Engraved mirror from Vulci with Apulu, Semla, and Fufluns. Bronze. Ca. 350 B.C. Berlin, Antiquarium. (*ES* 83.)

VII-18. Engraved mirror with Turms, Tinia, and Apulu. Bronze. Fourth century B.C. (*ES* 74.)

Altogether, the names of twenty-eight divinities are inscribed on the liver.

CATH, CATHA (twice), cf. the CAUTHA of the Magliano plaque (*TLE* 359) and the Catha of Lars Pulena's scroll (*TLE* 131)

ETH, perhaps an abbreviation for the ETHAUSVA on the mirror (fig. VII-15)

LETHN, LETHNS, LETHAM (five times); cf. the LETHAMS of the Capua tile (*TLE* 2)

TECUM

UNI; cf. the UNI of the Pyrgi plaques (*TLE* 874, 875) and the mirror (fig. VII-16)

ANI

TIN, TINSTH (three times); cf. TINS on the Liber Linteus (*TLE* 1), TINIAN on the Capua tile (*TLE* 2), TIN on the Magliano plaque (*TLE* 359), and TINIA or TINA on the mirrors (figs. VII-15, VII-18, VII-22)

CILENS (twice)

VETIS

CVL

CEL

TLUSCV (twice)

SELVA (twice)

VII-19. Engraved mirror with Turan embracing Atuns in the presence of Menrva, Apollo, Lasa, and Amuce. Bronze Fourth century B.C. (*ES* 5.23.)

FUFLUNS (twice); cf. the mirror (fig. VII-17)
THUFLTHAS
LAS; cf. LASA on the mirror (fig. VII-19)
NC (?)
TVETH
MARIS, MARI (twice); cf. MARIS on the Magliano
    plaque (*TLE* 359)
LETA
NP (?)
TH (?)
HERC
THETLUMTH
SATRES
LUSL
USILS; cf. USLAN on the Liber Linteus (*TLE* 1) and
    USIL on the mirror (fig. VII-20)
TIVR

Some of these names have obvious Latin equivalents: Uni-Juno, Ani-Janus, Selva-Silvanus, Satres-
Saturnus. One is a Greek name, Herc-Herakles.
Maris seems not to be the equivalent of the Roman
Mars.[27] All the others have Etruscan names and we
know nothing whatever about most of them,
whether they are singular or plural, masculine or
feminine, or what the god's function may have
been. But some can be identified by their images on
Etruscan mirrors. During the later Classical and
Hellenistic periods the Etruscans had a taste for
engraving scenes from Greek myths on the backs of
hand mirrors, and they often inscribed the names of
the characters beside the figures, as the Attic vase
painters of the sixth and fifth centuries B.C. had
done.

Mythological Inscriptions

Not all the characters named on the mirrors were
necessarily cult figures in Etruria. If a name does
not appear on a ritual or dedicatory inscription,
one may assume that the name merely designates a
character borrowed from Greek myth. But there are
surprisingly few names of gods in the mythological
inscriptions that do not find a place somewhere
among the dedications or ritual texts. Apulu and
Artumes on fig. VII-14 are clearly a young Apollo
and Artemis; they sit together affectionately while
she entertains him by playing a lyre.[28] Neither name
appears on any of our lists of Etruscan gods, but
the bronze statue (*TLE* 737; fig. VII-11) was dedi-

VII-20. Engraved mirror with Nethuns, Uśil, and Thesan.
Bronze. Fourth century B.C. (*ES* 76.)

cated to Aritimi, Artemis under another spelling.
More often the Etruscan names turn out to be the
equivalents of well-known Greek divinities. On fig.
VII-15, Ethausva and Thanr (the Eth of the bronze
liver[?] and the Thanr of the Zagreb text and the
Magliano plaque) are winged ladies in the act of
helping Tinia (who turns out to be no less a divinity
than Zeus himself) give birth to Menerva (another
Latin name), who appears in the guise of a winged
Pallas Athene.[29] On another mirror Tina is again
giving birth to Menerva (not named or winged this
time) with the help of Thanr and of Thalna, another
midwife (who turns up on several other mirrors),
in the presence of Sethlans, Hephaistos, whose
hammer (here an axe) split Zeus's head and set
Athene free (fig. VII-22).[30] Sethlans is on none of
our lists of divinities, and there is no extant dedication to him, but the fact that he has an Etruscan
name leads one to suppose that he was a genuine

VII-21a. Engraved mirror with Lasa, Aivas, and Hamphiare. Bronze. Fourth century B.C. London, British Museum. (Museum photo.)

VII-21b. Drawing of the mirror. (Rallo, *Lasa*, pl. 1.)

Etruscan god, not just a borrowing from Greek myth. He appears on another mirror (fig. VII-16), setting free his mother Uni from the magic throne—in which he imprisoned her as a retribution for her treatment of him when he was a baby—with the help of an otherwise unknown workman named Tretu.[31] From this mirror we learn that to the Etruscans Uni was not only the equivalent of the Roman Juno and the Phoenician Astarte but also of the Greek Hera.

The young god Fufluns appears with Apulu and Semla on a mirror (fig. VII-17).[32] Apulu we have met. Semla is Semele, the mother of Dionysos, and Fufluns is Dionysos himself, an important god in Etruria, with two houses on the bronze liver. He gave his name to the city of Populonia (Fufluna, Pupluna), and he is almost certainly the Pacha (Bacchus) on the scroll in the hands of Lars Pulena (*TLE* 131). On fig. VII-18, Turms (identified as

Hermes by his winged petasos) and Apulu flank a youthful Tinia, ivy-crowned and carrying scepter and thunderbolt.[33] On fig. VII-19 Menrva and Lasa, with Apollo unnamed but identified by a laurel branch, flank two embracing lovers, Atuns (Adonis) and Turan, who must be Aphrodite.[34] Lasa often appears with Aphrodite, as if she were an Etruscan equivalent of Eros, but she was an important divinity with her own house on the liver of Piacenza, and she had a more serious function than mere attendance, as we shall see.

Three divinities whose names are all mentioned on the text of the Zagreb mummy are conversing on another mirror (fig. VII-20).[35] Nethuns, the Latin Neptunus whose trident also proclaims him the Greek Poseidon, talks to a young god whose nimbus is like that of Helios and whose bow is Apollo's. He must be an (or the?) Etruscan sun god. His name, Usil, appears on the linen scroll as Uslan, and on the bronze liver as Usils (a genitive of possession?). Leaning on his shoulder is Thesan, a handsomely dressed goddess who is identified on another mirror as Eos, the Dawn who flies before the chariot of the Sun.[36] (What these divinities had in common is a puzzle; the Etruscans of Italy never saw the dawn break over the sea nor the sun rise out of it; to do so, one must live on an eastern coast.)

The Usil mirror illustrates a curious Etruscan triad of gods. One last example (fig. VII-21) illustrates the Etruscan use of Greek myth as a sort of allegory. Here Lasa, a stately winged lady with a scroll in her hands, stands between two Greek heroes, Aivas, Ajax, and Hamphiare, Amphiaraos.[37] She is clearly the messenger of ill tidings. A scroll as a sort of account book, summing up a person's life and dignities as he departs for the underworld, is illustrated on the sarcophagus of Lars Pulena (*TLE* 131) and on other Etruscan funerary monuments. Ajax and Amphiaraos are both doomed to die, though not, in Greek legend, in the same story: Ajax belongs to the Tale of Troy, Amphiaraos to the Seven against Thebes. But both died betrayed, Amphiaraos by his wife, Ajax by Athena. Their fate must have linked them in the Etruscan mind. This connection also casts some light on the character of the goddess Lasa. On one mirror (fig. VII-19) she is a sweet little attendant on Turan, Aphrodite; here, she is a major divinity, as on the liver of Piacenza, and a goddess of fate. Some scholars have even seen her as the Etruscan equivalent of the Latin Fortuna Primigenia.[38]

VII-22. Engraved mirror with Tinia (here "Tina") giving birth to Menrva, attended by Thanr, Thalna, and Sethlans. Bronze. 350–325 B.C. Bologna, Museo Civico. (*CSE* Italia 1.1.13.)

Vocabulary

Names of divinities on the mirrors are translated, one might say, by their images; Tinia is Zeus, Uni is Hera, Sethlans is Hephaistos, Fufluns is Dionysos, Turan is Aphrodite, etc. Men's names can be recognized on their tombs or sarcophagi by their form, like the Roman Larth Sentinates Caesa; compare Caius Julius Caesar, Marcus Tullius Cicero.

We know the meanings of some Etruscan words from glosses—that is, words with Greek or Latin translations found in the texts of classical authors.[39] A few of these are *Aclus*, the month of June; *aesar,* god; *Andas,* the North Wind; *arimos,* monkey; *(h)ister,* actor; *lanista,* gladiator; *lucumo,* king; *Rasenna,* Etruscans; and *subulo,* flute player. Unfortunately, few of these ever appear in the surviving inscriptions. *Hister* (as *histrio*), *lanista,* and *subulo* were taken over by Rome: "(h)ister Tusco verbo ludio vocabatur, "*(h)ister* was the word for actor in the Tuscan language" (Livy 7.2.6); "lanista, gladiator, id est carnifex, Tusca lingua appellatus," "a gladiator, that is, an executioner, was called *lanista* in the Tuscan language" (Isidore x.159); and "subulo Tusce tibicen dicitur," "in Tuscan, the word for flute player is *subulo*" (Festus p. 403). Similarly, the word Phersu, which we find painted beside the image of a masked dancer in the Tomb of the Augurs at Tarquinia (fig. IV-93),[40] was borrowed by the Romans. It became persona, "mask," in Latin. This gives the English language at least two words of ultimately Etruscan derivation: "histrionics" and "person."

Three glosses are particularly interesting. Suetonius (*Aug.* 97) says "quod aesar . . . Etrusca lingua deus vocaretur" ("because the word for god in the Etruscan language is *aesar*"), which justifies our translation of *Ais-, aiser* as "god," *aisera* as "goddess," and *aisiu, aisna* as "god-like," "belonging to the god," which are all frequently used Etruscan words. According to Servius (*Aen.* ii.278), "Lucumones reges sunt lingua Tuscorum," "kings, in the language of the Tuscans, are *lucumones.*" The stem *luc-, lauc-* is therefore translated with confidence as something to do with "king," "royal," the verb *lucair-* as "to rule" or "to be great," and *lucairce* (past tense, third person singular) "he ruled." Rasenna, which Dionysius of Halicarnassus says was the name the Etruscans had for themselves (I.30) ("they, however, call themselves Rasenna"), appears in the stem *rasna-, rasnes-,* and *rasna-l* and can be translated as "Etruscan."

A few words have been explained by bilingual inscriptions, like the *turce* of the Pyrgi tablets. A funerary bilingual inscription from Pesaro (*TLE* 697) reads: "L. Cafatius L.F. Ste[—] haruspex fulguriator. Cafates lr. lr. netśvis trutnvt frontac," i.e., "Lucius Cafatius son of Lucius—diviner and lightning-interpreter." Next to divination by the observation of the liver of the sacrificial animal, the observation and explanation of lightning bolts was Etruria's chief form of divination; L. Cafatius apparently was expert in both. In the Etruscan form of the inscription, *netśvis trutnvt* ought to correspond to haruspex[41] and *frontac* to the Latin *fulguriator* (diviner of lightning) unless, perhaps, it is an adjective derived from the name of a city—Ferentum?[42]

The Etruscans were fond of games of chance, and a pair (or several pairs) of dice was often included among their grave goods. The dice are marked with dots ranging in number from one to six, like ours, except for a pair said to have been found at Tuscania, on which the numbers are written out: *mach, zal, thu, huth, ci, śa* (*TLE* 197).[43] The word *ci* appears on the longer Etruscan inscription from Pyrgi (*ci avil*) and is translated in the Punic inscription as "three years." If the arrangement of dots on Etruscan dice is the same as on ours, the numbers one to six are *thu, zal, ci, śa, mach,* and *huth.*

As we have seen, many words and phrases can be translated by plain common sense: *clan,* "son"; *sec,* "daughter"; *puia,* "wife"; *avil,* "year"; *ril,* "aged"; and *leine,* "he died." Other words, titles of magistracies or priesthoods, are more uncertain, for example, *zilath, purth,* and *maru* are official titles, but

their exact meanings are elusive. The *zilath* seems to have had considerable distinction and is usually translated as "praetor."

Sometimes the general meaning of a stem can be grasped, but not the specific translation of a word built on that stem. *Sac-* has something to do with a sacred action or condition; *śacnicleri* may perhaps mean "temple." *Spur-* has something to do with "city." We have seen the difficulties presented by *fler* and *fleres*.

Despite the fact that many words are still waiting to be translated, the Etruscan language is not entirely unexplained. Any inscription that is not hopelessly fragmentary can at least be assigned to a specific category: ritual, legal, votive, or mythological. There are no other categories, no scraps of history, no speeches, no letters, no stories, and no poems. Etruscan art is full of vigor, motion, color, emotion—sometimes jocular, often gloomy; unfortunately, the words expressing those feelings have not come down to us.

Appendix A: Grammar

What we know about Etruscan grammar comes from the funerary, ritual, and votive inscriptions.

NOUNS

There is no characteristic ending for the nominative case, and no way of telling whether a word is masculine, feminine, or neuter unless it is a proper name.

The accusative has the same form as the nominative unless the direct object of the verb is particularly stressed, when it has the suffix *-ni.*

The genitive is formed by adding *-s* or *-l* to the stem, often inserting a vowel between stem and ending: Vetus, Vetusal; Velthur, Velthurus. The genitive in *-l* is used for feminine names ending in *-i,* like Uni, Unial; Ati, Atial, and for masculine names ending in a dental or *-s,* like Arnth, Arnthal; Laris, Larisal.

The genitive is used to express possession ("Arnthal clan," "son of Arnth"), time ("avils X lupu," "he died at ten years"), and dedication, taking the place of the Latin dative ("Culśanśl turce," "he gave this to Culsans").

There is no certain dative.

The plural is formed by adding -r (-ar, -er, -ur); apparently it is indeclinable. An uncommon shift of the stem vowel in the plural occurs in *clan, clenar,* "son," "sons."

PRONOUNS

The personal pronouns I, he/she, and it are known, but not those for you, we, and they. *Mi* is "I," *mini* is "me," *an* is "he/she," and *enaś* (genitive singular and plural, *in*) is "it." The demonstrative pronoun *ca, eca,* is common.

ADJECTIVES

There are very few adjectives in the extant texts. Unless they are used as substantives, adjectives are not declined, as shown by the following: *aisiu* (from *ais,* "god"), "god-like"; *rasna* (plural *rasnal*), "Etruscan"; *ril,* "aged"; *rumach,* "Roman"; *spurana* (from *spur-,* "city"), "belonging to the city"; and *suthina* (from *suthi,* "grave"), "belonging to the grave," "grave offering." Adjectives indicating "belonging" end in *-na* and are often used as nouns.

ADVERBS, PREPOSITIONS, AND CONJUNCTIONS

Adverbs are very rare. There are no prepositions identified with certainty. The conjunction *-c* is equivalent to the Latin *-que* and was not introduced until the fifth century.

VERBS

The stems of many verbs can be recognized. The third person singular past (aorist)—"he lived," "he gave," "he died"—is well known: *sval-,* "to live," *svalce,* "he lived"; *tur-,* "to give," *turce,* "he gave"; and *lupu,* "to die," *lupuce,* "he died."

Appendix B: Glossary

ais: god; *aisiu,* god-like
am: to be; *ama,* he is; *amce,* he was
an: he/she; *enaś* (genitive)
avil: year
-c: and (Latin *-que*)
ca: this
ci: three
clan: son; *clenar,* sons; *clens* (genitive)
eca: this (intensive form of *ca*)
zal: two
zil: to rule
zilath: praetor
hinthial: ghost, image in a mirror
huth: six
thu: one
lein-: to die; *leine,* he died
luc-: to rule; *lucairce,* he ruled
lupu: to die; *lupuce,* he died
malstria: mirror (?)
mach: five
men-: to give; *menache,* he gave
mi: I
mini-: me
mul-: offer; *mulu,* offering(?)
nefts: grandson (Latin *nepos*)
netśvis: haruspex
puia: wife
rasna: Etruscan (plural *rasnal*)
ril: aged
rumach: Roman
śa: four
sec: daughter
sval-: to live; *svalce,* he lived
spur-: city
suthi: grave; *suthina,* grave offering
tular: boundary, boundaries
tur-: to give; *turce (turuce, trce,)* he gave
fler: offering; *flereś,* god(?), statue(?), votive offering(?)
frontac: Latin *fulguriator(?),* diviner of lightning; or the man from Ferentum(?)

Notes

1. Pfiffig, *Etruskische Sprache* 7.
2. *D.H.* I.30.1–2; Pallottino, *Etruscans* 64.
3. Herodotus I.94.
4. Pfiffig, *Etruskische Sprache* 7, n. 11.
5. Buonamici, *Epigrafia etrusca* pl. 58, fig. 99; Pallottino, *Etruscans* 72–73, 194; pl.9.
6. Jeffery, *LSAG* 236, pl. 48; Pallottino, *Etruscans* 209.

7. A. Minto, *Marsiliana d'Albegna* (Florence 1921) 122, 236–39, fig. 20, pl. 20; Buonamici, *Epigrafia etrusca* 101–3, pl. 1, fig. 1; Jeffery, *LSAG* 236–37, pl. 48, fig. 18; Pallottino, *Etruscans* 209, pl. 93.

8. M. Torelli, *ParPass* 26 (1971) 55–60, fig. 7 on p. 56; Pallottino, *Etruscans* 112, pl. 11; Pfiffig, *Religio Etrusca* 253, fig. 109.

9. F. Castagnoli, *Lavinium* II. *Le tredici are* (Rome 1975) 441–43, L I, fig. 507; Pfiffig, *Religio Etrusca* 339, fig. 135.

10. Buonamici, *Epigrafia etrusca* 353–56, pl. 36, fig. 64; Pallottino, *Etruscans* 142–43, pl. 96; Pfiffig, *Religio Etrusca* 103–9.

11. Milani, *Mus. Arch.* I, 214, II, pl. 61; Buonamici, *Epigrafia etrusca* 385–86, pl. 45; Camporeale, *Tomba del Duce* 115–20, fig. 15, pls. 25a and b.

12. Buonamici, *Epigrafia etrusca* 374–76; R. Lambrechts, *Les inscriptions avec le mot "tular"* (1970).

13. Supra n. 10.

14. Buonamici, *Epigrafia etrusca* 356–59, pls. 37–38; Pallottino, *Etruscans* 222, pl. 97.

15. Buonamici, *Epigrafia etrusca* 378–79, pl. 44, fig. 77. Lambrechts (supra n. 12) 42–49, no. 11, pls. 15–16; Pallottino, *Etruscans* 200, pl. 98.

16. M. Torelli, *StEtr* 35 (1967) 347–52, pls. 60–61; Pallottino, *Etruscans* 221, pl. 101.

17. Buonamici, *Epigrafia etrusca* 358–59, pl. 39; Pallottino, *Etruscans* 221–22.

18. Buonamici, *Epigrafia etrusca* 336, 444, pl. 25; Giglioli, *L'Arte etrusca* pls. 351–52, fig. 1; Pallottino, *Etruscans* 200, 219.

19. From the Tomba della Pellegrina. Chiusi, Museo Etrusco; von Matt, Moretti, and Maetzke 116, pl. 134.

20. Volterra, Museo Etrusco Guarnacci.

21. Buonamici, *Epigrafia Etrusca* 444, pl. 15.

22. A. Neppi Modona, *Cortona etrusca e romana nella storia e nell'arte* (Florence 1925) 143–44, pl. 20d; Buonamici, *Epigrafia etrusca* 367; Pfiffig, *Etruskische Sprache* 246–47, fig. 108.

23. Giglioli, *L'Arte etrusca* pl. 261, fig. 2; Pfiffig, *Religio Etrusca*. 48, fig. 6.

24. Paris, Bibl. Nat.; Babelon-Blanchet 46–47, no. 101; Giglioli, *L'Arte etrusca* pl. 367, fig. 1; Buonamici, *Epigrafia etrusca* 368; Pfiffig, *Religio Etrusca* 253–54, fig. 110.

25. M. Pallottino, G. Colonna, et al., *ArchCl* 16 (1964) 49–117; J. Heurgon, "The Inscriptions of Pyrgi," *JRS* 56 (1966) 1–15, pl. 1; Pallottino, *Etruscans* 221, pls. 12–14.

26. C. Thulin, *Die Götter des Martianus Capella und der*

Bronzeleber von Piacenza, Religionsgeschichtliche Versuche und Vorarbeiten 3 (1907) 1–92; Buonamici, *Epigrafia etrusca* 359–61, pl. 41; Pallottino, *Etruscans* 145–46, pl. 38.; Pfiffig, *Religio Etrusca* 121–27, figs. 51–53.

27. Pfiffig, *Religio Etrusca* 249.

28. *ES* 4, pl. 293; Herbig, *Götter und Dämonen* 4, fig. 1.

29. *ES* 5, pl. 6; Herbig, *Götter und Dämonen* pl. 3.

30. *ES* 1, pl. 66; J. D. Beazley, *JRS* 69 (1949) 10, fig. 10; Pfiffig, *Religio Etrusca* 258, fig. 112.

31. *ES* 5, pl. 49.

32. *ES* 1, pl. 83; Beazley, *JRS* 69 (1949) 6, fig. 7 and pl. 6; Herbig, *Götter und Dämonen* 6, fig. 2.

33. *ES* 1, pl. 74.

34. *ES* 5, pl. 23.

35. *ES* 1, pl. 76. Herbig, *Götter und Dämonen* pl. 4; Pfiffig, *Religio Etrusca* pls. 244–46, fig. 107.

36. *ES* 4, pl. 290; Pfiffig, *Religio Etrusca* 259.

37. *ES* 4, pl. 359; R. Enking, "Lasa," *RömMitt* 57 (1942) pl. 1; Herbig, *Götter und Dämonen* 28, fig. 10.

38. Enking, "Lasa," 13–15.

39. Pallottino, *TLE*, Part III.

40. *TLE* 80; G. Becatti and F. Magi, *Le pitture delle Tombe degli Auguri e del Pulcinella* (Rome 1955) 9, 11, figs. 10–11, pls. VIII, XI.

41. Pfiffig, *Etruskische Sprache* 297, 305; Pallottino, *Etruscans* 146, 230, 233.

42. Pallottino, *Etruscans* 200, 234, 261–62, pl. 100.

43. Buonamici, *Epigrafia etrusca* 406–7, fig. 107b; pl. 61, fig. 97; Pallottino, *Etruscans* 216, 292, pl. 95.

Bibliography

Bonfante, *Etruscan Language*.

Buonamici, *Epigrafia Etrusca*.

CIE (1893; 1970; 1980).

ES.

A. Fabretti, ed., *Corpus Incriptionum Italicarum* (Turin 1867).

Guide to Etruscan Mirrors.

Jeffery, *LSAG*.

Pallottino, *Etruscans*, Part 3, "The Etruscan Language," 187–234.

Pfiffig, *Etruskische Sprache*.

REE.

TLE.

VIII / Daily Life and Afterlife

L A R I S S A   B O N F A N T E

More is known about the private life of the Etruscans than about their public life. We have details of the way they lived, their houses, their furniture, their clothes, and their religious rituals. We know that many were very rich and that they had skilled technicians. We can assume something about their society (about the role of women, for example) from what they have left behind and what Greeks and Romans have written about them. A remarkable feature of Etruscan society, the fact that it remained an aristocracy long after the Romans had their Republic and the Greeks their democracies, no doubt accounts for much of the Greek and Roman attitude toward them, portraying them as tyrants, lustful, and luxury-loving.

Archaeological finds have the most to tell us of how the Etruscans lived. The cities of the dead allow us to reconstruct the houses and, at least in part, the layout of the cities of the living (see Ch. V). Recent excavations at Acquarossa and Murlo (figs. V-31–33), show how luxurious and highly decorated the "palaces" of the wealthy were in the seventh and the sixth centuries B.C., that is, in early times, when the residential center, temple, sanctuary, and political center were not yet separate.[1]

The rock-cut walls of Tarquinia and other great Etruscan cities still dominate the surrounding countryside, allowing us to imagine what the ancient landscapes looked like. The fields were once fertile, though Tiberius Gracchus saw them lying desolate and untilled as early as the second century B.C., and the declining power of the Roman Empire left them empty and malaria-ridden until fairly recent times. Forests where rich nobles hunted boars are growing back, now that urbanization is causing much land to lie uncultivated. The rich mines which, along with agriculture, formed the wealth of the Etruscans are of course long since exhausted.

Roads and rivers allowed trade and communications between north and south, opening up the interior so that cities like Chiusi developed splendid local cultures and artistic styles. Some of these roads underlie the later Roman roads which connected the cities of Italy from the third century B.C. and which are still being used today. The Etruscans, who were great engineers, taught the Romans how to build houses, temples, and tombs, as well as roads, bridges, and sewers. In Rome, the Tarquins built the Cloaca Maxima, the great sewer which runs from the Forum into the Tiber; its mouth (often rebuilt) can still be seen today. Livy describes these building programs, which wearied Roman workers willing to be ditch-diggers as well as soldiers in times of war, but not to be used in that way for civilian projects, as was the Etruscan habit.[2] In fact, many of the stories about the Tarquins of Rome put details of daily life, Etruscan banquets, ambitious building projects, expensive clothes, and elaborate entertainments (illustrated in the decoration and furnishings of Etruscan tombs of the Archaic period) into a historical, urban context and explain the primitive Romans' hostile reaction to the wealth and luxury of the Etruscan aristocrats whose influence indelibly marked Rome's first two centuries as a city.

Perhaps no feature of Etruscan society differed so much from the Roman as the position of women.[3] Stories of the Etruscan queens seem to preserve genuine elements of Etruscan local color. Livy emphasizes the role played by the wives of the Tarquins—for example, Tanaquil, the wife of the first Tarquin—in acquiring the kingly power for their husbands. Married to Lucumo Tarquinius, son of a Greek émigré, Tanaquil urged her husband to leave Tarquinia and seek his fortune in Rome. As she saw it, an expanding city would afford his talents larger scope. At his side in the carriage approaching Rome she foresaw his royal destiny—in the tradition of the *etrusca disciplina* of augury and bird lore—when an eagle plummeted down from the sky, flew off with his hat, and then as suddenly returned it. In Rome, he changed his Etruscan name to a Roman one, Lucius, and Tanaquil and he worked together toward his election as king. In time she also chose the heir to the throne, Servius Tullius, her son-in-law.

The story of Tullia, younger daughter of Servius Tullius, reveals that the energetic Tanaquil was the rule rather than the exception. Married and mismatched to the less ambitious of the two younger Tarquins, Tullia decided to take as her partner Lucius Tarquinius, her brother-in-law. She despised her less forceful sister for her lack of *muliebris audacia* ("the daring proper to a woman"), a term which made sense in an Etruscan context, but which was foreign to the Roman mentality. The double murder of the weaker pair allowed her to achieve her goal: with sister and husband out of the way, she married Lucius Tarquin and pushed him into taking over the throne. To do this, she went so far as to drive her chariot over the body of her father, King Servius Tullius, spattering herself with his blood, an act of unthinkable horror to the mind of the Romans, to whom the head of the household, the paterfamilias, was sacred. The crime was commemorated forever in Rome by the name of the street in which it was perpetrated, the Sceleratus Vicus or Street of Horrors.

Elsewhere in Livy's pages, the indulgence of Etruscan fathers toward their sons is contrasted with the strict, heroic role of the Roman paterfamilias. In Roman eyes the Tarquins were diminished as men. Their permissiveness is featured in the story of the famous rape of Lucretia, told in masterly fashion by Livy. During a lull in the fighting at the time of the siege of a neighboring city the young Etruscan princes, idle and bored, were drinking

together in their camp and boasting of their wives. Excited by the late hour and the wine, they made a bet, each boasting his own wife was the best. They ride out to find Lucretia. Quite unlike the king's daughters-in-law, whom they had seen at a luxurious dinner party, passing the time with others of their set, Lucretia is hard at work at her spinning, surrounded by her servants, all of them working late into the night. Sextus Tarquinius, the son of a tyrant, is typically lustful: he lays a trap for Lucretia as her house guest and, having failed to seduce her, rapes her. Lucretia summons her father and husband, informs them of her dishonor, and then kills herself, while they avenge her and precipitate the fall of the Tarquins, who are banished. Rome becomes a republic.

The story contrasts the classical Greek and Roman picture of the seated matron working the wool, surrounded, like a good materfamilias, by her household servants, with the picture (well known now from Archaic Etruscan paintings from Tarquinia) of elegant Etruscan ladies reclining with the men on banquet couches, amid musicians, dancers, and servants bringing food and drink (figs. I-3; IV-91–92). From a Roman point of view, Lucretia clearly won. Yet later verdicts disagree: D.H. Lawrence, who also portrays the conflict between the Roman and the Etruscan ways of life, clearly favors the Etruscan.

What interests us here is the accuracy of the description. Banquets are represented in Etruscan art from earliest times. The funerary banquet held in honor of the dead was in all respects like the banquet of the living. In seventh-century tombs in Cerveteri and Chiusi the deceased were shown seated in chairs before tables laden with food and wine (the image of the deceased on a vase from Montescudaio bears the earliest representation of an Etruscan banquet [fig. IV-5]). In the Tomb of the Five Chairs at Cerveteri, men as well as women were portrayed thus seated (figs. VIII-1; IV-39). Ovid reminds his readers (*Fasti* 6.305) of the old days, when Romans used to sit by the fire: "ante focos olim scamnis considere longis mos erat." Reclining at table was a custom brought in by the Greeks. The earliest representation of banqueters reclining on couches comes from Murlo and ap-

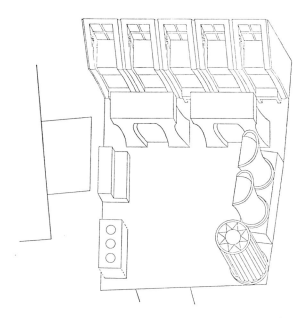

VIII-1. Tomb of the Five Chairs, Cerveteri, reconstruction of cult room. Seventh century B.C. (Prayon, *RömMitt* 82, 1975, 166, fig. 1.)

pears on some of the terracotta plaques which once decorated a luxurious building dating from about 575 B.C. (fig. IV-52). In the north (Murlo) the banqueters were men, according to Greek custom, while in the south, at Tarquinia, men and women attended banquets together (fig. IV-91). This custom of reclining contrasts sharply with the practice of both Greek and Roman women. In Roman religious ritual even goddesses or their statues sat in the ritual banquet or sellisternium, while their male colleagues reclined on couches in the lectisternium. The art of the south Etruscan cities in fact seems to show a world of married couples. In contrast to the male world of the Greek democracy and of the Roman paterfamilias, the Etruscan world, long ruled by noble families, included the women of these families in its public life. While it is normal in Archaic Etruscan art to see women reclining together with men on banquet couches, in the contemporary Greek vase paintings of drinking parties or symposia which served as models for pictures of Etruscan banquets wives are absent. Instead, men

recline with men or with pretty flute girls whose nakedness shows them to be slave girls. A remarkable recent find, the Tomb of the Diver from Paestum, painted in imitation of Etruscan technique but with Greek subject matter, is a clear contrast (fig. VIII-2).[4] The south Italian scene shows men courting a handsome young boy with bright red lips and cheeks. No women appear, not even as dancers or attendants.

Over one hundred years ago, J.J. Bachofen interpreted the stories in Livy and the archaeological evidence as indicating that Etruscan society was matriarchal.[5] The case was overstated; such a tyranny of women never existed, and Bachofen's claim of "matriarchy" must be carefully distinguished from the fact (as he himself points out) that Etruscan women occupied a high position. The status of Etruscan women in the Archaic period, from the seventh to the fifth century B.C., was surprisingly high when compared with that of contemporary Greek and Roman women. Bachofen describes the difference between the early Roman system of the paterfamilias with legal powers of life and death over his family and the type of society implied by tales of the Etruscan queens. In truth, Rome's confrontation with the civilization across the Tiber must have represented her first cultural shock, foreshadowing the later clash with the Hellenistic culture.

To learn what an outsider felt about the Etruscans of the Archaic period, we have to turn to Theopompus, a Greek historian of the fourth century B.C. He collected earlier Greek accounts to form a picture which is in part a literary cliché about the luxurious living of the barbarians, including the Etruscans, but which is perhaps also based on eyewitness accounts of Greek travelers in Etruria. This passage was cited by Athenaeus, a Greek writer of around A.D. 200, in a book whose title can be translated as *Brilliant Dinner Party Conversation,* or *Clever Men at Dinner:*

> Among the Etruscans, who were extraordinarily pleasure-loving, Timaeus says . . . that the slave girls wait on the men naked. Theopompos, in the forty-third book of his *Histories,* also says that it is normal for the Etruscans to share their women in common. These women take great care of their bodies and exercise bare, exposing their bodies even before men, and among themselves: for it is not

shameful for them to appear almost naked. He also says they dine not with their husbands, but with any man who happens to be present; and they toast anyone they want to.

And the Etruscans raise all the children that are born, not knowing who the father is of each one. The children also eventually live like those who brought them up, and have many drinking parties, and they too make love with all the women.

It is no shame for Etruscans to be seen having sexual experiences . . . for this too is normal: it is the local custom there. And so far are they from considering it shameful that they even say, when the master of the house is making love, and someone asks for him, that he is "involved in such and such," shamelessly calling out the thing by name.

When they come together in parties with their relations, this is what they do: first, when they stop drinking and are ready to go to bed, the servants bring in to them— with the lights left on!—either *hetairai,* party girls, or very beautiful boys, or even their wives.

When they have enjoyed these, they then bring in young boys in bloom, who in turn consort with them themselves. And they make love sometimes within sight of each other, but mostly with screens set up around the beds; these screens are made of woven reeds, and they throw blankets over them. And indeed they like to keep company with women: but they enjoy the company of boys and young men even more.

And their own appearance is also very good-looking, because they live luxuriously and smooth their bodies; for all the barbarians living in the West shave their bodies smooth. . . . They have many barber shops.[6]

Athenaeus furthermore quotes Aristotle's remark that the Etruscans eat with their wives, reclining at table with them under the same blanket. It was also said that their house servants, who were very beautiful, dressed better than is the custom of slaves.

So much for the Greek sources. All the standard charges of luxurious living (Greek *truphe*) are present: the lust, the luxury, the nudity, the homosexuality, the parties, and the fancy barbers. How much of this was true? Perhaps only the extraordinary freedom of the women, emphasized by the implied contrast with the Greek women of the time. The distaste that a Greek of Theopompus's time felt for this mingling of the sexes in a respectable context is evident. The fourth century B.C. was a puritanical time. Seeing husbands and wives so unexpectedly together was such a serious breach of Greek culture and good taste that it seems to have led Theopompus to imagine that women joined men in another traditionally male place, the gymnasium, where Greek men, as the name itself proclaims, exercised naked (Greek *gymnos,* "naked"). Plato and other Athenians were impressed that Spartan women exercised like men, for eugenic reasons. But Etruscan women were not particularly fond of such strenuous physical exercise as Spartan women practised—like their husbands, they much preferred spectator sports. Nor were they ever shown naked: Etruscan male and female athletes probably wore shorts, though they were sometimes represented naked, in the Greek artistic fashion. "Athletic nudity" was a purely Greek invention in

VIII-2. Tomb of the Diver, Paestum, wall with symposium scene. Ca. 480 B.C. Paestum Museum. (Soprintendenza alle Antichità–Salerno.)

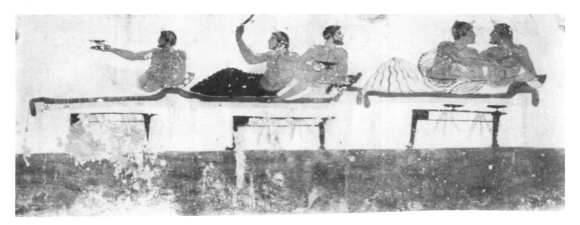

VIII-3. Achilles waiting in ambush for Troilus; wall above with erotic groups. Tomb of the Bulls, Tarquinia. Ca. 540 B.C.

the ancient Mediterranean world; it was practiced by Greeks alone after Homeric times and constituted, as much as language did, the chief distinction between Greeks and non-Greeks (or "barbarians") like the Etruscans.[7]

Other observations of Theopompus are indeed supported by archaeological evidence. Etruscan women did attend games, as we see in paintings and reliefs from Chiusi from the fifth century B.C. In this they differed from Athenian women, who did not attend the theater or the games at Delphi— but were like Ionian women, who, according to Thucydides, attended the festivals at Ephesus.

Later Etruscan funerary inscriptions, which occasionally identify the dead person by means of the mother's name in addition to the father's, show the legal and social importance of Etruscan women, though they refute, at the same time, Bachofen's claim that a real matriarchy existed. We know the word for wife, "*puia,*" because a woman is fre-

quently identified as someone's wife, but we do not know the word for "husband," for no man is ever identified as some woman's husband.

The individual names of Etruscan women indicate a different legal and social status from that of Roman women. Etruscan inscriptions confirm Livy's simple use of the name Tanaquil without reference to father or husband. In contrast, a Roman woman had no name of her own: she was known first as her father's daughter—Lucretia was the daughter of Lucretius—and later as her husband's wife, when she came into his legal power. Etruscan noblewomen were evidently more independent legally than contemporary Athenian women. Inscriptions on some tomb façades at the necropolis of Orvieto identify the tombs as belonging to women, implying that they could legally own property. Furthermore, Theopompus's statement that the Etruscans generally raised all their children, if correct, might mean that they depended less than usual on infanticide or child exposure as a means of population control, perhaps because of their greater wealth, unlike the Greeks, who were constantly threatened by overpopulation and poverty. It might also mean that an Etruscan woman, unlike Greek women, had the right to raise her own children without her husband's formal recognition. Perhaps she could even raise the children she had by a slave. Theopompos would certainly translate either situation, in terms of Greek law, as equivalent to the child's illegitimacy.

The high status of Etruscan women is also reflected by their literacy, witnessed by the many decorated bronze mirrors inscribed with names of divinities and mythological figures. Such toilet articles, along with the fine clothes and expensive jewels represented on women in art and buried with them in their graves, illustrate something more important than feminine vanity or a taste for frivolity: they symbolize a woman's rank and status. This is clear from the relief of the sarcophagus of Ramtha Viśnai in Boston (fig. VIII-4), about 300 B.C., showing the husband, Arnth Tetnie, followed by young men holding his insignia of office (the curule chair, lituus, and war trumpet). The lady's attributes, carried by her attendants (parasol, fan, toilet articles, and jewels), symbolize her rank and status. The statement of the Roman tribune L. Valerius, who in 195 B.C. championed women's right to display marks of honor, strikingly confirms such an interpretation: "No offices, no priesthoods, no triumphs, no honorary insignia, no gifts or spoils from war can come to [women]; elegance and adornment and apparel—these are the insignia of women" (Livy 34.7.8–9).[8] Even for Etruscan women, who lived a more public life, these signs of private wealth reflected their place in society.

Both the character of Etruscan art and this social context account for the detailed picture of Etruscan daily life engraved on the backs of Etruscan and Praenestine mirrors. The private, intimate context of the bronze mirror provided a perfect opportunity for the artist to emphasize scenes and details which showed off the wealth and luxurious way of life of the upper classes. Here the artist could indulge his fondness for representing jewels, shoes, hats, clothes, furnishings, and accessories—the "local color" which gives much of Etruscan art its peculiar character and charm.

VIII-4. Sarcophagus of Ramtha Viśnai from Vulci, with married couple in bed; the couple, with their attendants, also appear in relief on the front of the casket. Limestone. Ca. 300 B.C. Museum of Fine Arts, Boston. Gift of Mr. and Mrs. Cornelius Vermeule III 1975.799.

VIII-6. Engraved mirror with couple standing before a double bed. Bronze. 510–500 B.C. Berlin, Staatliche Museen, Antikensammlung. (*ES* 4.421.)

VIII-5. Engraved mirror with couple at home. Bronze. Ca. 300 B.C. Copenhagen, Ny Carlsberg Glyptothek. (*CSE* Denmark 1.26.)

The type of scene represented often reflects the importance of the family and of family prosperity.[9] In the Archaic period, husband and wife were represented attending banquets and symposia, but they also appeared as couples at home (fig. VIII-5). One mirror shows a large bed behind a beautifully groomed couple, similar to the bed in the Tomb of the Funeral Couch at Tarquinia (fig. VIII-6).[10] As in banquet scenes in frescoes at Tarquinia, there is much dancing.[11] Castanet players are dressed in their special costume, a heavy wool plaid jerkin or *ependytes* worn over a thin chiton, as in tomb paintings and bronze statuettes (fig. VIII-8).[12] The importance of music in Etruscan life, shown in many scenes in the Archaic period and later, is confirmed by the literary evidence.[13]

The family conference is a motif popular in Etruscan iconography as well. On a third-century mirror Leda, her husband Tyndareus, and other members of this famous mythological family, including her children Castor and Pollux, discuss the egg of Helen (fig. VIII-9).[14] Elsewhere Helen and Alexander (Paris) are shown together with the newborn Hermione as a family, in the intimacy of the bedroom (fig. VIII-10).[15] As often, the iconography of the Greek myth has been modified by the Etruscan artist to fit local tastes.

Another Archaic picture of baby Hermione snuggled up beside Helen,[16] whose breast is bared in order to nurse her, emphasizes a related theme, much more evident in Etruscan than in Greek art: that of mother and child. In the fourth century B.C., this interest in children is also evident. Divine children[17] like Dionysos[18] (fig. VIII-11) or the mysterious Maris (fig. VIII-12)[19] or Epiur[20] appear frequently. A red-figure cup shows Pasiphae with the baby Minotaur on her lap: "The absurdity of the

VIII-7. Engraved mirror with couple playing a game: the inscriptions, in Latin, record their conversation. Bronze, from Praeneste. Third century B.C. London, British Museum. (*ES* 5.146.)

VIII-8. Engraved mirror with dancers with castanets. Bronze. Ca. 475 B.C.

VIII-9. Engraved mirror from Orvieto with Leda and Tyndareus, Castor and Pollux, Turan, and Helen's egg. Bronze. Third century B.C. Perugia, Museo Civico. (*TLE* 219.)

VIII-10. Engraved mirror from Praeneste with Helen, Hermione, Alexander (Paris), and Turan (Aphrodite). Bronze. Ca. 450 B.C. Rome, Villa Giulia. (*ES* 379.)

VIII-11. Engraved mirror with birth of Dionysos. Bronze. Ca. 400 B.C. Naples, Museum. (*ES* 82.)

maternal idyll serves as a reminder: even the monster was once a dear child."[21] Birth scenes are popular: the birth of Athena, a favorite Greek myth in Etruria (fig. VII-15), and the birth of Helen from the egg which is being lovingly handled by her assembled family in the mirror mentioned above. Another baby, not yet visible but already affecting the action represented, is probably Adonis, hidden in a chest, the object of an intense struggle between Venus and Proserpina.[22] The nursing theme also surfaces in the striking representations of the full-grown Herakles at the breast of Uni (figs. VIII-13–14);[23] it evidently had some special, ritual meaning in Etruria which was applied to the local concept of Herakles. The importance of the *kourotrophos*—the figure of the mother or nurse holding the baby (fig. VIII-15) and the woman actually nursing the baby at the breast—in the art of early Italy was surely related to religious cult and ritual.[24]

The popularity of the group of the three goddesses, Hera, Aphrodite, and Athena, in Etruscan art can perhaps be connected to close relations with the Phoenician world at the end of the sixth century. They frequently appear together in scenes of the Judgment of Paris (figs. IV-89; VIII-32). On a Pontic amphora by the Paris Painter, three elegant ladies recline together, probably at the wedding of Peleus and Thetis, together with a fourth woman, perhaps Eris (with flyaway hair like a man's) (fig. VIII-16). One of them holds a bird, perhaps a dove, the bird that Astarte-Aphrodite loved. Uni is "syncretized" with Ishtar on the Pyrgi tablets, about 500 B.C.; and Athena can also apparently be identified with this Phoenician goddess. Herakles is clearly related to Melqart. Further study of Etruscan iconography may result in surprising conclusions as to the relationship between the Etruscan and Phoenician religions.[25]

The scenes on the mirrors place a remarkable emphasis on groups made up of older women and younger men. Sometimes they are lovers, as in the case of Turan and Atunis (Venus and Adonis) (fig. VII-19) or Thesan and Thinthun (Eos and Tithonos; Eos is represented as aggressively carrying off her young lover). Labels proclaim similar images to represent mother and son, as in the case of Semla and Fufluns (fig. VII-17).[26]

Scenes of the toilette appear frequently, showing young men and women bathing or dressing and adorning themselves (figs. I-14; IV-89). Domestic scenes of women engaged in a variety of activities among their female attendants often occur on Greek vases of the fifth and fourth centuries; many have been interpreted as preparations for a wedding. In particular, South Italian, especially Campanian, vases represent numerous toilette scenes with women holding mirrors—a motif also seen on Etruscan mirrors.[27] The servants waiting on their mistresses in these scenes again signify wealth and status.[28] But the range of subjects designed to appeal to women on Etruscan mirrors is much wider than the Greek domestic scenes of the toilette or of women working wool. T.B.L. Webster has pointed out that the Etruscans imported relatively fewer Greek vases with scenes of women alone.[29] Perhaps such representations made less sense in Etruria,

VIII-12. Engraved mirror with Menrva and other divinities with babies: Mariś Isminthians, Mariś Husrnana, Mariś Halna. Bronze. 275–250 B.C. London, British Museum. (*ES* 257B.)

VIII-13. Engraved mirror with Uni (Hera) nursing the full-grown Herakles (Hercle). Bronze. Ca. 300 B.C. Bologna, Museo Civico. (*CSE* Italia I.1.15.)

where women did not lead the separate, secluded lives of women in Classical Athens. In Italy, mirrors and cistae show scenes of aristocratic hunts, athletes,[30] and battles, as well as the numerous scenes with couples banqueting and dancing which imply broader social activities. Women athletes are represented on the lids of Praenestine cistae;[31] a woman and a man wrestling together on a beautiful mirror in the Vatican are labeled Pele and Atlnta (fig. VIII-18).[32] Athletic women were dressed in short bikini pants like those worn by women acrobats and entertainers in Greece and Rome. But here in Etruria we see representations of skilled and refined athletes, not vulgar professional entertainers, little better than prostitutes.[33] The hunt of Meleager, for example, in which Atalanta played a leading role, is often portrayed on later mirrors, and the mood is aristocratic.

The Etruscans and their neighbors in Italy, like

Homer's Phaeacians, preferred spectator sports and calmer, urbane amusements. A Praenestine mirror depicts a young man and young woman seated at a game table, or *tabula lusoria,* inscribed with a dialogue: "I'm going to beat you," she says, and he replies, "I do believe you are" (fig. VIII-7).[34] This seems to be a true genre scene, with no mythological overtones. Another mirror in Milan with Achilles and Ajax playing, a theme familiar in Greek vase painting, shows the *tabula lusoria* in detail.[35] (A similar gaming board was represented, in relief, hanging on the wall in the Tomb of the Reliefs at Cerveteri.) Once again, an entertainment that may have been reserved for men in Greek society was shared by upper-class men and women in Italy.

There is certainly an emphasis on the theater and literacy in Etruscan mirrors and urns; inscriptions often identify the figures depicted as characters from Greek and Roman tragedy.[36] Representations

VIII-14. Engraved mirror from Volterra with Uni (Hera) nursing the full-grown Herakles in the presence of other divinities. Ca. 300 B.C. Florence, Museo Archeologico. (Soprintendenza alle Antichità–Firenze.)

VIII-16. Pontic amphora by the Paris Painter, four divinities reclining. Ca. 540 B.C. New York, Metropolitan Museum. (Museum photo.)

VIII-15. *Kourotrophos Maffei* from Volterra, statue of woman holding a baby. Stone. Third century B.C. Volterra, Museo Guarnacci. (Felbermeyer.)

VIII-17. Engraved mirror with Minerva, Fufluns (Bacchus), and Artemis carrying a soul. Ca. 460 B.C. Musées Royaux d'Art et d'Histoire, Brussels.

VIII-18. Engraved mirror with Peleus and Atalanta wrestling. Bronze. Ca. 400 B.C. Vatican, Museo Etrusco Gregoriano. (Alinari.)

VIII-19. "Portrait" figure of the deceased reclining on the lid of an urn, holding an inscribed dip-
tych. Alabaster. Second or first century B.C. Volterra, Museo Guarnacci. (Felbermeyer.)

VIII-21. Lid of a Praenestine cista: consulting the oracle(?). Third century B.C. Rome, Villa Giulia.

VIII-20. Engraved mirror from Bolsena with Cacu, Artile, and the two brothers Caile and Avle Vibenna. Bronze. Third century B.C. London, British Museum. (*ES* 5.127.)

VIII-22. Engraved mirror from Tuscania with Pava Tarchies as haruspex reading the omens in the presence of Tarchunus and others. Bronze. Third century B.C. Florence, Museo Archeologico. (Pfiffig, *Religio Etrusca* fig. 3.)

of people reading, writing, or holding writing tablets or scrolls (fig. VIII-19) must have had a religious or ritual connotation in Etruscan art of the fifth century, different from the genre scenes of Greek vases on which such activities are depicted.[37] These connotations seem to be confirmed on a number of monuments of the fourth century and the Hellenistic period, especially funerary urns and mirrors, on which portraits of the deceased as well as mythological figures display scrolls or tablets (figs. VIII-20; VII-21).

Most interesting to scholars have been the historical scenes, like those of the François Tomb at Vulci. Aside from such specific historical references, several illustrations of rituals and the study of omens fit the context of *etrusca disciplina*. We have seen Vel Saties reading the bird omens in the Fran-

çois Tomb. On a rectangular Praenestine cista a boy reads from a tablet while a line of visitors await their turn (fig. VIII-21).[38] Is it a reading of the Praenestine *sortes*? On a mirror in the British Museum an Apollo-like Cacu plays the lyre, while the boy Artile reads an open-hinged writing tablet; the two are being stalked by Caile and Avle Vipinas, the Vibenna brothers known to us from Roman history and from the paintings in the François Tomb (fig. VIII-20).[39] Another mirror, from Tuscania, illustrates a haruspex reading the omens from a liver to an attentive audience (fig. VIII-22).[40] The dress and

VIII-23. Engraved mirror with Chalchas reading the omens. Ca. 400 B.C. Vatican, Museo Etrusco Gregoriano.

VIII-24. Engraved mirror from Perugia with Athrpa (Atropos) hammering the nail of Fate. Bronze. Ca. 320 B.C. Berlin, Antiquarium. (*ES* 176, 5.121.)

the names of the characters (Tarchon and Pava Tarchies) make this a more genuinely Etruscan scene than the one showing a heroically draped Chalchas reading the liver of a freshly slaughtered animal (the victim's windpipe and lungs are lying on the table) (fig. VIII-23).[41] A scene on a mirror in Berlin showing Athrpa (Atropos), the Etruscan version of the Greek Fate, is related to these ritual scenes. She is carrying out a ritual act known to us from literary sources; she hammers into place a ceremonial nail, while other figures witness the event (fig. VIII-24).[42]

Even more than the scenes chosen for the mirrors, their details provide us with a wealth of information about daily life. Etruscan artists always enjoyed adding local color to scenes of Greek or Etruscan mythology. In the manner of many craftsmen, they also liked to "advertise their own wares," in this case not only mirrors but cistae and other bronze implements and toilet articles probably made in the same workshops.[43] The proud craftsman often showed a mirror carefully drawn in all its parts, including its convex shape and other details of its manufacture (fig. I-14). The reflection of the face of the onlooker is occasionally included.[44]

Handsome boxes or cistae are placed on the ground or hung up beside their owners, indoors or outside,[45] sometimes displaying their contents, including perfume bottles and dippers. Expensive metal symposium ware made by these craftsmen or their colleagues is prominently displayed, advertising their makers' skills and their owners' taste and wealth.[46]

Furniture, too, was represented with gusto,[47] ranging from the simple folding stool (*diphros okladias*) to Helen's splendid sphinx-decorated stool (fig. VIII-10); tables, beds, fountains, and thrones on which gods, goddesses, heroes, and heroines sit in majesty. Ladies protect themselves from the sun with elegant parasols.[48] Architecture is hinted at: the Aeolic capital is common.[49] Statues are represented; one is labeled *flere*, perhaps meaning "statue."[50] There are altars and herms.[51]

Given the Etruscans' wealth and luxurious tastes, it is not surprising that their craftsmen concen-

VIII-25. Bust of a woman, from Ariccia. Terracotta. Third century B.C. Rome, Museo delle Terme, Antiquarium. (Courtesy F. Coarelli).

VIII-26. Amber relief sculpture of reclining couple. Sixth century B.C. New York, Metropolitan Museum of Art, Acc. 17.190.2067. Gift of J. Pierpont Morgan, 1917. (Museum photo.)

trated, from earliest times, on the making of beautiful, and often impressive, jewelry. As we have seen, these jewels, worn by the women in their lifetime and often placed in their graves after death, visually symbolized the social position of their owners (fig. VIII-25).

In the Orientalizing period of the seventh century, a time of wealth and active commerce, when the southern cities imported luxury goods in quantity, the Etruscans learned to make the gold jewelry which became one of their specialties,[52] the large golden brooches, earrings, and bracelets found in great quantities in the rich tombs of this period. In the south a special technique was developed for working designs onto the surface with tiny granules of gold. This granulation technique was known elsewhere, for example, at Rhodes, but nowhere was it so ambitiously used as in Etruria. Modern craftsmen have made various attempts to reproduce the technique, whose difficulty lies in soldering the tiny granules onto the surface without melting them down to a shapeless mass. Such jewelry, made in

the southern cities in this period, tends to be gaudy, while that of the north is more sober and refined (though no less expensive). Pieces from Vetulonia, for example, are decorated with minute particles known as *pulviscolo* (gold dust).

Amber is found in Italy, mostly in the form of jewelry, dating from Mycenaean times to the fourth century B.C. Particularly impressive are some carved pieces of the sixth century B.C., where the craftsman considers the shape of the original piece in carving human faces or figures in various poses (fig. VIII-26). One of the earliest centers for the import of amber in the late Bronze Age (twelfth to tenth century B.C.) is Frattesina, in northeast Italy. Not coincidentally, this is also one of the largest early glass factories found so far, for amber and glass beads are regularly found together.[53]

Around 400 B.C., in this as in other aspects of Etruscan art, a "Renaissance" took place. Lovingly represented on mirrors and cistae are necklaces and bracelets with large hanging bullae and pendants worn by men and women alike. Bullae in particular are well known to us from tomb finds (figs. IV-105; VII-15, VII-17, VII-19; VIII-27) This is a typically Italian, not just an Etruscan, decoration, represented on a great variety of monuments, from the warrior of Capestrano to the Ficoroni cista. Its peak was in the fifth and fourth century. The story of Tarpeia, who betrayed the Capitol to the Sabines, asking in return for what the Sabine soldiers had on their left arms ("quod vulgo Sabini aureas armillas

VIII-27. Bulla with relief decoration, this side showing Daedalus with his saw and adze, flying. Icarus is shown on the other side. The lower view shows the inscription on the top of the bulla identifying the two figures. Gold. Fifth century B.C. Baltimore, Walters Art Gallery, Acc. 57.371. (Museum photo.)

magni ponderis brachio laevo . . . habuerint" [Livy I. 11]), may well be connected with these gold bracelets with pendant bullae; these were worn chiefly by men on the left arm as prizes for victory. The rings with bullae worn on the arms by grown men may also have been worn as necklaces when they were boys.[54] A representation of Amphiaraos with Tydeus holding out a bracelet with hanging bullae exemplifies the local color used to enliven and explain a myth (fig. VIII-35).[55]

The fourth century, with its preference for large, majestic, and brooding figures, favors women heavily adorned with jewelry: large diadems, tied in back; bracelets and circlets, spiral-shaped or with hanging bullae. Certain huge pendants, also worn by both men and women, were the fashion around 300 B.C. (figs. VII-11, VII-16, VII-18, VII-20; VIII-14).[56] Heavy earrings, in the typically stylized grape cluster form known from actual gold earrings in tombs of this period, were worn throughout the fifth and fourth centuries (figs. IV-15–16).[57] Necklaces made up of beads were often worn with longer necklaces from which hung bullae or other elaborate pendants. Bullae, much in favor in this period, were worn by men, women, and children. Earrings with a long oval pendant and a smaller, teardrop pendant below were also typical. Pointed pendant drops, hinged and attached to a disc fastened to the ear lobe, which appear on late fourth- and early third-century mirrors (fig. VIII-24), also characterize the sculpture of Tarentum and Latium in the fourth and third centuries.[58] In the early third century, bead necklaces and bullae remain popular, as do torques (figs. IV-40; VIII-25)[59] and smaller pendants (fig. VIII-12). "Body jewelry" of one or two strands crossing the breast (either covered or bare), a third-century fashion, was popular throughout the Hellenistic and Roman periods.[60]

Another sign of wealth and technical skill are the false teeth fastened with gold wires found in the jaws of some of the bodies in the tombs.[61] Neither Egyptian nor Greek dentistry has left traces of such prosthetic or restorative dentistry, the art of applying artificial substitutes for lost teeth. Examples of Phoenician dental art of the fifth century B.C. from tombs near Sidon, skillfully contrived from human teeth attached to the mandible with thin gold wire, have amazed a modern dentist by their delicacy and ingenuity, yet he notes, these do not by any means measure up to the achievements of Etruscan dentists.[62] The art of dentistry in antiquity was first developed to a high level in Etruria in the seventh century B.C., as can be seen from specimens preserved in museums and collections around the world.[63] An appliance from a seventh-century B.C. burial is one of the finest specimens (fig. VIII-28).[64] Gold bands were fitted over the remaining natural teeth; lost teeth were partially replaced by other human teeth and in one case by the tooth of an ox.

This sophisticated dental care was extended to

the Romans, who, during the seventh and sixth century B.C., learned a great deal from the Etruscans, particularly techniques. Around 500 B.C., when the Romans passed their anti-luxury laws, they specifically excluded the gold from the false teeth of the dead: "But him whose teeth shall have been fastened together with gold, if a person shall bury or burn him along with that gold, it shall be with impunity." Yet these laws forbade just the kind of elaborate funerals and displays of luxury familiar to us from Etruscan tomb paintings: "Anointing by slaves is abolished, and every kind of drinking bout. Let there be no costly sprinkling . . . no long garlands . . . no incense boxes."[65]

According to the Greeks, a people could be recognized by its language, dress, and customs (the word, custom, related to costume, like habit, can refer to either dress or mental predisposition). Etruscan dress is interesting for its own sake as well as for the light it sheds on Etruscan art and history, including the history of its international relations. While the study of Etruscan language and religion is difficult because Etruscan literature, unlike Greek

VIII-28. Etruscan false teeth with gold bridge bands. Ca. 600 B.C. Liverpool, National Museums and Art Galleries on Merseyside. (Museum photo.)

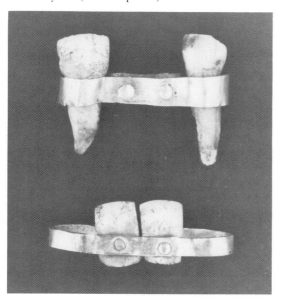

and Roman literature, has not survived, many monuments remain to illustrate Etruscan dress.

How did the Etruscans portray themselves? How could you tell an Etruscan from a Greek? How could you distinguish priest or priestess, magistrate, laborer, god or goddess? In most periods of their history, the clothes of the Etruscans were similar to those of the Greeks, with whom they were always in more or less close contact. But at all times a special look distinguished the Etruscans. Recognizing Etruscan clothes of various periods represented in art can help in dating the monuments, as well as in documenting and tracing foreign influence in Etruria and Etruscan influence outside Etruria.

It is hard to tell much about the dress of the Villanovan period, for representations of human figures were rare and rendered in a primitive, schematic manner.[66] But there is evidence that active men wore short pants or loincloths (*perizomas*) and broad, willow-shaped belts like those found in tombs and represented on figures of the eighth and seventh centuries B.C. (figs. IV-6; VIII-29).[67] Older men no doubt wore the wide mantles common throughout the Mediterranean: we see these heavy, square woolen cloaks, often decorated with a plaid pattern, worn by mourners on burial urns from Chiusi and seated "ancestors" from Cerveteri (fig. IV-39). Their complicated patterns, rendered by a variety of artistic devices, emphasize the importance of textiles, both as local manufactures and as luxury items of trade from the east and the north. Much has been lost, but recent attempts to preserve traces of textiles (on the surface of bronzes, etc.) and spectacular finds like the amber and silver robe of a lady at Decima, in Latium, on the border of Etruscan territory, are providing more information.[68] The wide woolen mantles were wrapped around the body and fastened at the right shoulder with a brooch, allowing the right arm to move; actual miniature metal brooches were originally attached to the figures on the Chiusi urns at the shoulder.

While men's fashions were like those worn all over the Mediterranean at this time, certain women's fashions differed from dress worn anywhere else. Etruscan women wore the normal chitons or robes, belted at the waist as usual. But over these

VIII-29. Vase from Cerveteri with loving couple. Terracotta. Ca. 650 B.C. Cerveteri, Museo Archeologico. (Bonfante, *Etruscan Dress* fig. 41.)

they wore long back mantles fastened at both shoulders with buttons or stitching; their long braided hair was often fastened with a circular clasp below and fell down the back of these cloaks to their feet.

A mythological couple wearing such standard seventh-century fashions (fig. VIII-29) appears on a vase from Cerveteri. The youth wears the short trunks of the Orientalizing hero, plaid-patterned like the mantles we saw before, while the lady touching him affectionately on the chin wears the belted robe and the long Etruscan braid. The youth also wears, above his plaid-patterned trunks, the typically early Etruscan or Villanovan type of belt. Wider in front than at the sides, the belt was made of bronze plates sewn onto a leather backing. Many such metal plates have been found in Etruria in Villanovan graves of the eighth and seventh centuries B.C. (fig. IV-6); the type was also imitated farther north.[69]

VIII-30. "Tintinnabulum" or pendant from Bologna with relief decoration showing women at work carding, spinning, and weaving. Bronze. Ca. 600 B.C. Bologna, Museo Civico Archeologico. (Museum photo.)

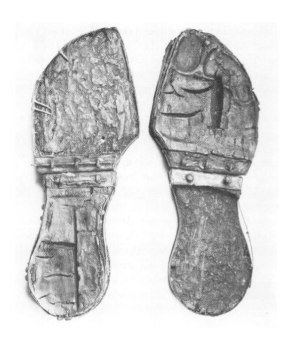

VIII-32. Pontic amphora by the Paris Painter with the Judgment of Paris. Ca. 540 B.C. Munich, Staatliche Antikensammlungen und Glyptothek, Inv. 837. (Museum photo.)

VIII-31. Sandals from Bisenzio. Wood and bronze. Sixth century B.C. Rome, Villa Giulia. (Soprintendenza alle Antichità dell'Etruria Meridionale.)

A design engraved on a bronze from Bologna, beyond the northern frontier of Etruria but reflecting Etruscan costume, shows women busily at work cleaning, carding, spinning, and weaving (fig. VIII-30).[70] Heavy woolen plaid-patterned fabrics were extremely popular in Etruria and long remained a specialty in northern Italy and Gaul, as we read in Pliny and other later Roman authors.

The Etruscans were famous for their shoes. In the early period they wore special hinged high-soled sandals, many of which have been found in tombs of the seventh century and later (fig. VIII-31). In the fifth century, Attic authors name Etruscan sandals with gold laces as one of the luxuries which Athenian ladies felt they must own.[71]

A new wave of fashion came to both Etruria and Greece from the Ionian cities of Asia Minor in about 550 B.C. The same fashion, however, expressed itself quite differently in the Etruscan cities and in mainland Greece. It seems clear that the Etruscans adopted the new styles directly from

the Ionians who, as we now know, were in Graviscae as early as 600 B.C., or from their colonies in south Italy,[72] and not from Athens. Etruscans and mainland Greeks wore their Ionian robes and mantles, the chiton and himation, in different ways. Etruscan youths, like Ionian kouroi, were often shown draped.[73] While a typical Ionian-style kore (a female statue from the Acropolis) wore a square himation in a diagonal drape which inspired the artists of the time to represent its folds in stylized swallow-tail pleats,[74] Etruscan ladies never followed this particular fashion of wearing the mantle. Another difference was that, though they wore a thin linen chiton, it was never as long as the Ionian garment (fig. IV-67), so that the refined gesture of holding it up and out of the way is an affectation that Etruscan artists adopted from Greek art. We see this, for instance, in the Judgment of Paris on a Pontic amphora painted in Etruria (fig. VIII-32). Hermes is shown leading the three divine beauty contestants, Hera, Athena, and Aphrodite, each characterized by her dress: Aphrodite looks coquettish as she lifts her skirt to show off her handsome red shoes. (The sense of humor one sees on Pontic vases and elsewhere in Etruscan art is one more indication of their closeness to the Ionian spirit.) On terracotta plaques from Cerveteri with the same subject, Aphrodite (second from the left) again

VIII-33. Statuette of haruspex, dressed in characteristic pointed hat and pinned mantle. Bronze. Fourth century B.C. Vatican, Museo Etrusco Gregoriano. (Museum photo.)

lifts up her skirt very high, showing off her red laced pointed shoes, the latest Etruscan style (fig. IV-89).[75]

Shoe and hat fashions, taken over by the Etruscans in this period directly from Ionia, are represented with loving care, especially the pointed-toe boots which were so popular in Etruria for both men and women from the mid-sixth to the mid-fifth century B.C. (fig. IV-94). Perhaps because they went outside and led a more public life than Athenian women, Etruscan women wore shoes and hats more often: a variety of melon-shaped hats is represented. An elongated, upswept hairdo called the *tutulus* gave them a Nefertiti-like profile. Their mantles were usually simply thrown over their shoulders, with the ends in front.

Clothes were carefully depicted by the artists who engraved the mirrors.[76] As usual in art, these mirrors represent both actual fashions and artistic stylizations. They span three periods: late Archaic, Classical, and Hellenistic. Early fifth-century mirrors illustrate most of the characteristic fashions of the late Archaic. Male figures appear dressed more often than they do in Greek art of this period. As in Greece, they often wore the rectangular himation, but in this period there was also a rounded local mantle, the Etruscan *tebenna,* which eventually developed into the Roman toga. These mantles were draped in a variety of ways: in the Greek heroic manner, leaving the torso bare, with the ends pulled over the right arm, or with the ends thrown back over the shoulder, in a manner particularly popular in Etruria in this period. Men are often shown wearing chitons. While satyrs and athletes regularly appear naked, generally speaking, Etruscans are reluctant to show men or gods completely naked before the Hellenistic period. Even if their sex is uncovered, they wear something: a short mantle, shoes, jewelry (figs. VII-8, VII-10−11, VII-17−19). This is usually true even in the Hellenistic period, when a fashionable nudity for both men and women prevailed.

Herakles, who is shown nude in Greek art, in Etruria frequently has a garment, often his lion skin, draped about his waist. As he bends down to nurse at Uni's breast on the famous Volterra mirror (fig. VIII-14) he modestly hides his nakedness, as does Usil, on another mirror (fig. VII-20).

VIII-34. Statuette of haruspex. Bronze. Hellenistic. Rome, Villa Giulia. (Alinari.)

VIII-35. Engraved mirror with Amphiaraos, Tydeus, and Adrastus. Ca. 300 B.C. Presently lost. (*ES* 178.)

In the Archaic period women usually wore a mantle over their long Ionic chitons. Sometimes the mantle is shown fastened diagonally over one shoulder, in the contemporary Greek fashion (Etruscan women probably did not, in fact, adopt this fashion). More often it is worn with the ends slung over both shoulders in front, sometimes over the head. Forms are pointed: the folds of the garment, the gestures of the figure, and the laced shoes (*calcei repandi*) typical of late Archaic Etruscan fashion. Decorative patterns enliven the garments of both men and women, now and throughout Etruscan art. Hair is worn in long ringlets (fig. VIII-32), as shown in the Apollo from Veii (fig. IV-99), or else bound up, with a diadem, kerchief, or *mitra*.[77]

In the fifth and fourth centuries B.C. new fashions appear. Shoes, sandals, or boots are often represented, especially a type of shoe with crosspieces. Shoes lose their point, except for the *calcei repandi* of the earlier period, still represented on goddesses or mythological female figures such as Uni or Leda. An important sign of rank for women in this period, and a local fashion found nowhere else, is

VIII-36. Engraved mirror with the release of Prometheus by Herakles in the presence of Athena and Asklepios. Bronze. Third century B.C. New York, Metropolitan Museum of Art. Rogers Fund, 1903. (Museum photo.)

a braided tassel which hung down from the shoulder seam of the chiton. Only goddesses, nymphs, or great ladies are shown wearing this symbol of status (figs. VIII-4, VIII-37). Hair is often worn short (figs. IV-30; VIII-5), fastened around the head in a bun, or *krobylos* (fig. VIII-27), hidden under a kerchief or *mitra* (Helen, figs. VII-14; VIII-10); a wide wreath or diadem is very popular (figs. IV-66; VII-15–20; VIII-11, VIII-37). Toward the end of this period, special costumes appear more frequently: Phrygian dress, the special hat and pinned mantle of the Etruscan haruspex (figs. VIII-33–34), and Perseus's traveling costume.

The fashions of the third century represented in art contrast with the heavily clothed look of the previous century. Figures wear fewer and fewer clothes, until we see groups of beautiful (if slightly vapid) young figures standing around in attractive nudity on mirrors of the Hellenistic period (fig. VIII-36). The third century still favors accessories,

VIII-37. Engraved mirror with Turan and Atunis (Venus and Adonis). Ca. 350–325 B.C. (*ES* 112.)

VIII-38. Engraved mirror from Perugia with Peleus, Neleus, and their mother. Third century B.C. Naples, Museo Nazionale. (*ES* 170.)

however. Jewelry and shoes are worn as much by naked as by dressed figures of both sexes; countless Lasas wear only slippers and a torque or necklace. Heavy necklaces with pendants are now replaced by strands of beads and torques; bullae are still worn. Women's chitons are high-waisted, Empire style (figs. IV-34–35, IV-43–44), often worn with body jewelry in single or double straps. The Dioskouroi also wear a high-waisted chiton, knee-length, complemented by boots, laced or plain, and a Phrygian cap or the simpler Greek pointed *pilos*.[78] Long, loose hair, much in vogue for both men and women, is often represented in stylized concentric circles or semicircles framing the face (figs. VIII-9, VIII-20, VIII-38). Women wear the hair loosely pulled back and tied in a topknot or bound up with a diadem or kerchief.

On many artistic representations of the Hellenistic period, especially engraved mirrors, nudity pre-

VIII-39. Praenestine bronze cista, triumphal procession and rite (parody?). Fourth century B.C. Berlin, Antikenmuseum, Staatliche Museen Preussischer Kulturbesitz, Berlin (West), Acc. 6238. (Jutta Tietz-Glagow.)

vailed. The decorated relief panels of funerary urns, on the other hand, show a different style of dressing. The figures pictured in these scenes are rarely naked.[79] In fact, they are dressed in heavy draped garments (figs. IV-35–36) whose style was clearly influenced by the full, belted garments with overfolds represented on the frieze of the Altar of Pergamon, with the epic battle of the Gods and Giants. Another influence—the stage—accounts for the long-sleeved, full robe worn by the figure of Oedipus,[80] who is dressed as a tragic hero, as well as for the Phrygian hats of a number of figures, and for the "plaid" pants or leggings of archers and

other active men. Such decorated leggings are also worn by the "triumphing general" represented on a Praenestine cista in Berlin whose scene has been interpreted as stage parody or comedy (fig. VIII-39).[81] A very peculiar costume, consisting of separate sleeves (fig. IV-37), may also be connected with theater dress. Here, and elsewhere, Vanth looks like a Fury, the south Italian Lyssa, with wings, bared breasts, boots, and cross straps, or baldric, above the characteristic double *kolpos* of her skirt.[82]

We see only real clothes represented on the portraits of the dead placed on top of their funeral urns and sarcophagi, and even on stylized bronze statuettes. There are richly bejeweled women's empire-waisted thin linen robes with rectangular mantles, and men's mantles, worn either alone or over shirts or tunics (figs. IV-3, IV-33–35, IV-40; VII-8–9; VIII-56).

During the fourth century B.C., Rome was replacing the Etruscan cities as the leading power in Italy and was on her way to becoming the chief power in the Mediterranean. It is difficult, in this period, to distinguish Etruscan from Roman symbolism of costumes represented in art. The Etruscan figure of Vel Saties in the François Tomb at Vulci, for example, wears a mantle decorated like the Roman *toga picta* which Roman generals wore at the triumph (fig. IV-97). Vel Saties may be wearing a Roman costume or perhaps an Etruscan costume adopted by Rome.

The Arringatore, a bronze life-size statue from near Perugia, is another interesting monument made at a moment of transition (fig. IV-65). Aulus Metellus had himself represented with all the insignia of a Roman citizen of the equestrian rank (as a gentleman outside the Senate), wearing the laced shoes of the Roman citizen (in contrast to Greek sandals), the gold ring, the tunic with stripes (inlaid in a darker bronze color), and the magistrate's bordered *toga praetexta*. All this was by now honorary, symbolic Roman costume. Yet his titles were written in Etruscan on the border of his toga. He was evidently a native Etruscan and a magistrate in his own Etruscan city. Scholars considered the date of the statue to be about 150 B.C. because after this time the Romans no longer wore such a short toga. But the Etruscans continued to wear their rounded mantles short, and if the statue is viewed in an Etruscan rather than a Roman context, it can perfectly well be dated around 100 B.C.

We have surveyed in some detail the history of dress of the Etruscans from the eighth to the first centuries B.C. as an example of what can be learned from the evidence of their "material culture." The picture we get of the Etruscans is not of an isolated people, but of one whose contacts with the world outside were reflected in various aspects of their daily life. Their dress, for instance, shows a variety of foreign influences as well as local styles. Near Eastern influence of the latter part of the seventh century B.C. is evident in fashions such as hats and knee-length chitons. The Greek Daedalic style, lasting longer in Etruscan dress fashions (as it did in art), gave way to the exuberant Ionian style of the sixth century (which may reflect a relationship with the Greeks of southern Italy) and brought many features of costume which became part of an "Etruscan style": pointed hats and shoes, long, full chitons, and diagonal mantles. In fashion as in art, an Etruscan character generally prevailed. Such special styles as the tassel on important women's chitons, the costume of the haruspex, and the triumphal mantle (it is not a rounded toga) of the triumphator of the François Tomb were developed in the fourth century. A common piece of jewelry such as the torque, ubiquitous in this period, marks a closer relationship with the Etruscans' northern neighbors, the Celts. In the Hellenistic period, certain artistic stylizations clearly belong to what we might call an "international style" of this phase of art; but they do not obscure the realistic representation of actual clothes on the "portraits" of the dead.

Certain characteristics tended to remain constant throughout the history of Etruscan dress. The special place women held in society is reflected in their dress. In the Archaic period women wore more outdoor clothes than Greek women, including hats and sturdy shoes; that is, they wore clothes which were elsewhere reserved for men. The greater use of mantles, hats, and coverings for men in turn contrasts with the Greek simplicity of clothing and heroic nudity; a barbarian expresses respect for a figure by dressing it with many splendid garments. Etruscan reluctance to represent heroic nudity was, indeed, a barbarian habit, shared by all non-Greeks, including the later Romans.

A recent survey of Etruscan armor shows how this, like their dress, reflects the history of the Etruscan cities and the influences at work, from Greek to Celtic, and distinguishes between the adoption of individual features (such as parts of Greek armor) and the more basic ideas, techniques, or systems connected with it (e.g., the hoplite reform).[83]

Etruscan wealth and luxury are constantly referred to or implied in Greek and Roman literature. Their reputation as a pleasure-loving people and their fondness for games and shows figure in Herodotus's tale of the Etruscans' migration from Asia

Minor, which attributes to them the invention of
many games. He writes:

> In the reign of Atys son of Menes there was a great scarcity
> of food in all Lydia. For a while the Lydians bore this
> with patience; but soon, when the famine continued, they
> looked for remedies, and various plans were suggested. It
> was then that they invented the games of dice, knuckle-
> bones, and ball, and all the other games of pastime, except
> for checkers, which the Lydians do not claim to have in-
> vented. Then, using their discovery to forget all about the
> famine, they would play every other day, all day, so that
> they would not have to eat. . . . This was their way of life
> for eighteen years. Since the famine still did not end, how-
> ever, but grew worse, the king at last divided the people
> into two groups and made them draw lots, so that one
> should stay and the other leave the country.[84]

That, according to the Lydians, who told the story,
is how the king's son Tyrrhenus came to emigrate

VIII-41. Oinochoe from Tragliatella (Cerveteri), decorated
in imitation of Corinthian pots, with mythological figures.
625–600 B.C. Rome, Museo dei Conservatori. (Drawing
from G.Q. Giglioli, *StEtr* 3, 1929, pl. 26.)

to Italy; there his people called themselves Tyrrhenians, or Etruscans.

Sports and games do indeed figure prominently
in Etruscan art (figs VIII-18, VIII-40; IV-21, IV-
27). Hunting scenes appear from the very earliest
times on the Villanovan urns which first represent
human figures, and later in the Archaic tomb paintings of Tarquinia, such as the beautiful and strange
Tomb of Hunting and Fishing (fig. IV-107), and
the recently discovered Tomb of the Hunter (fig.
IV-90). Contests very like those of Homeric funeral
games are also represented: wrestlers fight for a
trophy while judges stand by watching. But the
Etruscans, as we saw, were particularly fond of
spectator sports. In the Tomb of the Augurs a
bloody gladiatorial game of the type which was
taken over later in Rome and became a favorite
spectacle in the circus (fig. IV-93) is shown. According to tradition, the Tarquins built the Circus
Maximus in Rome, where horse races took place;
and scenes of horse racing and chariot racing can be
seen in friezes and in tomb paintings. A contest on
horseback labeled *Truia,* illustrated on a seventh-
century vase from Cerveteri, may be related to what
the Romans later called the Trojan Games (fig.
VIII-41). A particularly good representation of a
horse race appears on terracotta plaques from
Murlo (fig. IV-54), while other scenes show jockeys
and charioteers tying their reins about their waists
to give them extra power at the turns—a dangerous
trick the Romans and north Italians learned from
the Etruscans.

We can only guess at the possible existence of
Etruscan plays, from such meager linguistic evidence as the adoption in Latin of the Etruscan
words *histrio* for "actor," and of persona (from
Etruscan *Phersu*) for "mask" or "character." It is

VIII-40. "Pilgrim bottle" from Cerveteri with two wrestlers, wearing wide belts, fighting before a crater. Terracotta. Ca. 600 B.C. Berlin, Antikenmuseum, Staatliche
Museen Preussischer Kulturbesitz, Berlin (West), Acc.
31.270. (Jutta Tietz-Glagow.)

true that artists from Volterra in the Hellenistic period portrayed many scenes from the Greek plays of Euripides on their alabaster urns, particularly scenes showing their bloody endings, such as the duel between the sons of Oedipus, Eteocles and Polyneices (fig. IV-34), the death of Actaeon, and the murder of Eriphyle (figs. IV-35–36). But it is not clear whether they had actually seen these on a stage, or whether they were copying models such as drawings. In any case these urns appear quite late in Etruscan history, and could refer to plays performed in Greek in south Italy or in Latin translations in Roman theaters.[85] There is no evidence of any theaters in Etruria before the Roman presence, though in a tomb in Tarquinia, there is a very clear picture of wooden bleachers for spectators, where women as well as men are watching a performance.[86]

That theatrical performances, juggling, music, and dancing were part of Etruscan life is clear from many beautiful representations in Archaic tomb paintings, mirrors, reliefs, and bronze statuettes.[87] Women clacking castanets are often accompanied by musicians playing the pipes or the lyre. The Etruscans, it was said, did everything to the sound of music: they fought battles, beat their slaves, hunted, and even cooked to the sound of music. The effect of their music on the game they hunted is described by the Roman writer Aelian, in the third century B.C.:

It is said that in Etruria wild boars and stags are caught with nets and dogs in the usual manner but that hunters are even more successful when they use music. Nets are stretched out, and all kinds of traps are set in position in a circle. A skilled flutist then plays the sweetest tunes the double flute can produce, avoiding the shriller notes. The quiet and the stillness carry the sounds, and the music floats up into all the lairs and resting places of the animals. At first the animals are terrified. But later they are irresistibly overcome by the enjoyment of the music. Spellbound, they are gradually attracted by the powerful music and, forgetting their young and their homes, they draw near, bewitched by the sounds, until they fall, overpowered by the melody, into the snares.[88]

Cooking to music is illustrated by a painting in a tomb near Orvieto, dated to the fourth century B.C. (cf. fig. VIII-42), which gives us a rare glimpse into the servants' quarters.[89] The flurry of activity is regulated by the sound of a flute played as the others work.

Livy gives us a description of some Etruscan ballets. In the fourth century B.C., the Romans hired dancers and musicians from Etruria, along with soothsayers, to help placate the gods and put down a plague. Such performers "danced to the sound of the flute in the most graceful way imaginable, in the Etruscan fashion, their movements unaccompanied by either singing or dramatic action."[90]

The war dance by armed warriors holding shields and lances depicted on the decorated mantle of the triumphing general from the François Tomb in

VIII-42. Kitchen scenes and dialogue of cooks on an engraved cista from Praeneste. Fourth century B.C. Brussels, Musées Royaux d'Art et d'Histoire. (G. Bordenache Battaglia, *Le ciste prenestine* I, 12a.)

Vulci (fig. IV-97) would seem to be related to much earlier war dances represented on Villanovan monuments (fig. IV-8), as well as to the dance traditionally performed by the Salii, the warrior priests of Rome.[91] We know that the influence of Etruscan victory celebrations transformed Roman ritual in the late sixth century; the Romans borrowed the concept of military organization and techniques, including war trumpets,[92] from the Etruscans and celebrated their military triumphs with Etruscan dress and music, marching to the three-beat rhythm they called the *tripudium* or *triumphus*.[93]

But what impressed the Romans most was the Etruscans' skill at reading omens and at performing rituals which insured the *pax deorum,* or good relations with the divinities. This *etrusca disciplina,* a body of knowledge which was used to interpret bird omens and prodigies and to learn the will of the gods from the signs in the entrails of sacrificial animals, was, like the art of writing with the alphabet, taken over by the Romans and changed to meet their own needs. Ambros Pfiffig, in his recent study of the religion of the Etruscans, points out that the *etrusca disciplina* must not be confused with religious theory. It comprises, rather, a set of rules for interpreting certain rigidly defined portentous events, to be applied in various circumstances. Much of it, too, is probably based on Roman needs, rather than reflecting a peculiarly Etruscan frame of mind.

The Romans, for their part, characterized the Etruscans as a most religious or "superstitious" people: "The difference between us and the Etruscans . . . is the following: while we believe that lightning is released as a result of the collision of clouds, they believe that clouds collide so as to cause lightning. For since they attribute everything to the gods' will, they believe, not that things have a meaning insofar as they occur, but rather that they happen because they must have a meaning." So writes Seneca, Nero's tutor, in the first century A.D. (Seneca, *Quaestiones Naturales* 32.2). The role of fate was certainly important in Etruscan religious belief, affecting their concept of history as regulated by the great ages (saecula) set out by destiny. The belief in saecula or phases of history which have been allotted to a people may even have made an impres-

sion on Roman ideas at the end of Etruscan history, if Marta Sordi is right.[94]

Other aspects of Etruscan religion and ritual were far from agreeing with classical models or ideals, and in fact emphasized the distance that separated Etruscan culture from the "classical" tradition of Greece. The emphasis on blood in such funerary art as that of the François Tomb seems to have been an Etruscan peculiarity related to sacrifices in honor of the dead. The custom continued in the gladiatorial games represented in Etruscan tombs (fig. IV-93). Other scenes of sacrifice, cruelty, and dismemberment (figs. VIII-43–44), together with the Etruscans' readiness, at least beginning in the fourth century B.C., to adopt the artistic motif of severed heads, most likely from their neighbors the Celts, lead us to believe that the Etruscans practiced human sacrifice. There are historical allusions to such sacrifices. Two famous cases are recorded in the fourth century, in the course of the fierce struggle between the Etruscan cities and Rome. In 356 B.C. some 300 captured Roman soldiers were sacrificed by the men of Tarquinia (Livy 7.15.9–10). The following year, the Romans retaliated, killing 358 noble Tarquinian prisoners. Both slaughters were carried out as "sacrifices," as public rituals, in the forum of each city. It was probably according to an Etruscan ritual that the Romans, just after the battle of Cannae, in 216 B.C., sacrificed two couples, *Gallus et Galla, Graecus et Graeca,* burying them alive in the Forum Boarium, a desperate measure which Livy (22.57) found shockingly un-Roman. A representation of this sacrifice may appear on a sarcophagus from Tuscania (fig. VIII-43). (The emphasis on the couples, as well as the fact that Greeks and Gauls were enemies not of Rome but of the Etruscans, make Etruscan influence likely in this single, and most uncharacteristic, instance.) It was probably because of their ritual connotations that the bloody scenes of the killing of the Trojan prisoners and the deaths of Eteocles and Polyneices were so frequently represented in Etruscan art in the fourth century and later. Not surprisingly, the Homeric scene of Achilles's slaughter was not popular in Greece, where cruelty to prisoners was casual rather than ritual. Etruscans, Carthaginians, and Celts were all "barbarians," not because they were not

VIII-43. Sarcophagus from Tuscania with scene of human sacrifice. Hellenistic. Rome, Villa Giulia. (Soprintendenza alle Antichità dell'Etruria Meridionale.)

"civilized"—the Etruscans and the Carthaginians certainly participated in a "culture of cities" and were thus civilized in this sense—but because they practiced that human sacrifice which so offended Greeks, Romans, and Jews.[95]

According to Ambros Pfiffig, Etruscan religion must also be compared to the ancient religions of the Mediterranean because of the importance of their mother-goddesses. Certainly, as we have seen, female divinities were greatly honored and frequently represented not only in Etruscan but in Italic religion. (Rome is an exception: George Dumézil's concept of Rome as continuing the tradition of ancient Indo-European language and religion seems to be confirmed by evident contrasts between Etruscan and Roman beliefs.) Nursing mothers, absent in Greek art of the Classical period (the motif enters the art of Greece, along with a variety of other genre scenes, only during the Hellenistic period), were always present in art in Italy, though for a long time the theme was overwhelmed by the prestige of Greek art. Representations of nude goddesses, too, disappeared in Italy, as in Greece, after the Orientalizing period, during which time statuettes were imported or imitated from the Near East.

Some monuments of Etruscan art, however, seem to reflect, in particular instances, an attempt to resolve the conflict existing between Etruscan religious belief, custom, and ritual and the pressure of

VIII-44. Engraved mirror with Menrva threatening the giant Akrathe with his own severed arm. Bronze. Ca. 300 B.C. (*ES* 68.)

Greek art and culture. One of the most striking examples is the so-called Venus of Cannicella, excavated in a sanctuary at Orvieto a century ago but only recently re-examined (fig. VIII-45). This large statuette (though under life-size) represents a nude goddess and is thus unique in Etruscan art. It exhibits further surprising features: the head looks like that of a Greek male kouros, and the body was restored in antiquity, when one of the breasts was re-attached (the other is lost). Breast and leg are made of different marble. For cult purposes, a naked image of the goddess was necessary, but Greek art had only a male kouros to offer as a model, since female figures were regularly shown wearing drapery at this time. What we have is the result of a change or adaptation of a Greek model carried out by the artist to serve the needs of the local cult. (Similarly, to seated or standing female figures taken from Greek models, Italic artists added images of children.)[96]

For all the importance of Etruscan culture in Italy, however, Etruscan religious influence at Rome was surprisingly external and superficial. Just as the Romans retained their Latin language almost untouched by Etruscan influence, the *etrusca disciplina* that the Romans borrowed left Roman religious beliefs untouched. In the early Republic, members of the Roman aristocracy sent their sons to Etruria (Livy 9.36) to learn the Etruscan language and to study omen-reading, a useful technical skill for a general and a member of the government. It was part of the duty of a Roman magistrate to carry out the necessary sacrifices before every battle, every election, and every public action, and to make decisions based on the will of the gods manifested after these sacrifices. The twenty books of Etruscan lore which the learned Emperor Claudius wrote in the middle of the first century A.D., if only they had survived, would probably consist in large part of this material (though he obviously had studied Etruscan histories as well, as shown by his statement that the Etruscan name for Servius Tullius was Mastarna [Macstrna]; see Ch. I above).

Some of the rites included in the *etrusca disciplina* we know from Roman literature. The system of marking off the boundaries of a city by ploughing a sacred furrow, which seems to be Etruscan,[97] is apparently illustrated by the bronze statuette of the

VIII-45. "Cannicella Venus" from Orvieto. Greek marble, restored in antiquity. Ca. 500 B.C. Orvieto Museum. (DAI.)

ploughman from Arezzo, whose hat, according to Emeline Richardson, marks him out as a priest, rather than a farmer shielding his head from the sun (fig. VIII-46).

Two kinds of priests were adept in the art of augury. One, called in Latin the haruspex, read the entrails of sacrificed animals, especially the liver. Another, the *fulguriator,* knew how to read the sky, interpreting the divine will from thunder and lightning. Their Etruscan names were, respectively, *netsvis* and *trutnt frontac.*

The method used by the haruspex is known from several representations of such a priest in action, on bronze mirrors and statuettes. He is shown wearing the special priestly costume, a mantle fastened in front with a large brooch and a tall hat (figs. VIII-33–34).[98] An actual teaching tool once used by a haruspex to show pupils how to read the different parts of the sacrificial sheep's liver (fig. VII-13), a bronze model of a liver, found in 1877 in the northern Italian city of Piacenza, just south of Milan, has been carefully divided by means of engraved lines into sections which match the parts of the sky.[99] In each section is written the name of the divinity which rules over that area. On the border are also inscribed the sixteen sections of the universe, used not only in divination but also in the planning of cities and orientation of temples. The inauguration of Numa, the second king of Rome and the most religious, is described by Livy (5.43) as taking place in accordance with these ancient rules. The bird omens which Vel Saties (fig. IV-97), Romulus and Remus, and Tanaquil read were all likewise based on this Etruscan science, as were numerous other recorded instances of augury and omens.[100]

The gods named on the liver, and those invoked in the prayers and rituals written in Etruscan on the linen bandages of the mummy in Zagreb, were the native Etruscan gods. Some of these were identified with the Italic divinities of their neighbors and with the Greek gods which, from the sixth century B.C. on, began to be adopted in Italy. So Tinia, the god of thunder, was identified with the Roman Jupiter and the Greek Zeus; Sethlans, the god of the forge, with Vulcan or Hephaestus (figs. I-19; VII-16); and Turms with Mercury or Hermes. Uni was identified with the Italic Juno and the Greek Hera. The

VIII-46. Statuette of a ploughman from Arezzo. Bronze. Fourth century B.C. Rome, Villa Giulia. (DAI.)

gold tablets from Pyrgi, dating from about 500 B.C. (figs III-6; VII-12), reveal that Uni was further identified with the Phoenician Ishtar or Astarte: the Etruscan inscription clearly says Unialastres. The Etruscan Hercle, Hercules or Herakles in Latin and Greek, respectively, is often shown with a female companion; on some mirrors she is labeled Mnerva, which would be Minerva or Athena in Latin or Greek. On the famous mirror from Volterra, dating from about 300 B.C., Herakles appears as a full-grown man, nursing at the breast of Uni in what looks like an adoption ceremony (fig. VIII-14). Several gods witness the scene, and above Uni a placard proclaims: "This shows how Herakles, Hera's son, drank milk." Representations of Hera nursing Herakles, which occur only in Italy (figs. VIII-13–14), may be connected with the special place still held by the mother goddess (fig. VIII-15). Greek mythology, in contrast, emphasized the jealous anger of Hera against Herakles, whom the mortal Alcmena had borne to her husband Zeus. Fufluns, Bacchus or Dionysos, another god who was particularly important in Etruria, had Populonia (Pupluna or Fufluna) named after him.

Etruscan mirrors and paintings often also label figures from Greek mythology with their names transcribed into Etruscan. Uthuze, or Odysseus, calls up the ghost of Teiresias ("hinthial Terasiaś") from Hades; accompanying him is Turmś Aitaś, "Hermes of Hades," or Hermes Psychopompos,

VIII-47. Tomb of Orcus, Tarquinia, ghosts of Agamemnon and Teiresias. Fourth century B.C. (Soprintendenza alle Antichità–Firenze.)

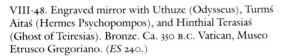

VIII-48. Engraved mirror with Uthuze (Odysseus), Turmś Aitaś (Hermes Psychopompos), and Hinthial Terasiaś (Ghost of Teiresias). Bronze. Ca. 350 B.C. Vatican, Museo Etrusco Gregoriano. (*ES* 240.)

VIII-49. Engraved mirror with Lasa, after cleaning. Bronze. Hellenistic. Courtesy of the Royal Ontario Museum, Toronto, Canada. (Museum photo.)

"leader of souls," as he is called in Greek (fig. VIII-48; cf. fig. VIII-47). Apollo becomes Aplu (or Apulu: figs. VII-14, VII-17); Artemis, Artimi or Artumes; Adonis, Atunis; Hades, Aita; Persephone, Phersipnai; and so on (figs. VIII-35–38, VIII-44; VII-14–21). The words may have undergone this radical transformation by being pronounced in Etruscan, having been transmitted orally in plays or performances rather than in writing.[101]

Next to the major deities, whose form and attributes were paralleled in Greek mythology, there were also many native divinities, less clearly defined.

Gods were often referred to as a group. Ancient
writers speak of Dii Superiores ("high gods"), Dii
Involuti ("covered" or "wrapped in shadows"),
whom Jove consulted before hurling his thunder-
bolts, and Dii Consentes, who were Jupiter's advi-
sors. Then there were the Penates, the Lares and
the Manes. Some gods come in pairs: the twins
Castor and Pollux and a number of gods who appear as couples, such as Aita and Phersipnai. In
Etruscan iconography, as distinct from that of the
Greeks, attributes were not always fixed. Sometimes
a god will appear in either female or male form.
The figure of Lasa (fig. VIII-49) seems to be an
attendant divinity in various contexts or else one of
a group, something like a Greek nymph (fig. VII-
19). A particular Lasa is often specified, such as Lasa
Racuneta, Lasa Vecu, etc. Lasa Vecu may be identified with the nymph Vegoia, whose prophecy was
famous in Roman times.

   Figures of Lasae, of the Etruscan Fury called
Vanth, of Charun (the god who led the dead to the
underworld), and of *Tuchulcha* only appeared in the
fourth century (figs. I-7; IV-96; VII-21; VIII-50).
Many scenes of this period or later are framed by
the two demons Vanth and Charun. The dress and
attributes of Vanth are easily recognizable: short
chiton, crossed straps or baldric, hunting boots,
and (often) a torch. Deriving from the Greek Fury
Lyssa by way of south Italian vase painting, Vanth
enters Roman art as Allecto in Vergil's *Aeneid,* as
well as in the decoration of the Villa of the Mysteries at Pompeii. Like the Valkyrie, Vanths are present
at but not involved in death.[102] Her companion,
Charun, a horrifying figure armed with a hammer,
is a terrifying deformation of the Greek ferryman of
souls, the boatman Charon (fig. VIII-50). His
hooked nose and menacing appearance was still
terrifying to the inhabitants of Tuscany in the
Middle Ages, when contemporary artists made use
of his figure. In fact, the medieval idea of angels
and devils seems to have its antecedents in these
Etruscan demons. Another of these, Tuchulcha,
even more monstrous, with the face of a vulture,
the ears of a donkey, wings, and snaky locks, shakes
his open-jawed serpents in the Tomb of Orcus in
Tarquinia, near the melancholy seated figure of
Theseus, labeled These. The Greek hero is shown
during his sojourn in the underworld, where he

VIII-50. Statue of Charun from Cerveteri. Stone. Ca. 300
B.C. Cerveteri, Museo Archeologico. (DAI.)

had been fastened to his chair after trying to abduct the queen of the underworld, Persephone.

Life after death meant much to the Etruscans. Even in the early period in the north, when cremation was practiced, the spirits of the dead were kept "alive" or given a human form for their trip to the underworld by being placed in urns which had human features (fig. IV-46).[103] Tombs were furnished for life after death. Yet Etruscan concepts of the afterworld are not clear. In the early days it is not often represented. There are allusions to it, for example, in the Tomb of the Augurs, where men dressed in dark clothes greet the departure of a dead man beyond the painted door which opens into the world beyond (fig. VIII-51) with the traditional gesture of mourning. Elsewhere, a huge crater, or an empty bed, refers to the dead (fig. I-3).[104] But scenes in the tombs and on funerary monuments up to the end of the fifth century B.C. are all of the world of the living, including some very physical aspects of the banquet theme (fig. VIII-52).

The decorated patterns on some of the walls and ceilings of tombs at Tarquinia were meant to recreate the brightly colored tents or outdoor pavilions where banquets were held (fig. IV-90).[105] More frequently, the interiors of Etruscan houses may be reconstructed from the rock-cut tombs which imitated them, and which were prepared for the dead like the houses they lived in (Ch. V). Much of the furniture, made of wood or wicker, has deteriorated, but objects made of bronze or terracotta have survived and show how kitchens, dining rooms,

VIII-51. Tomb of the Augurs, Tarquinia, mourners by the door of the Other World. Ca. 510 B.C. (Anderson.)

VIII-52. Tomb of the Jugglers, Tarquinia, man defecating behind a tree; an inscription gives his name, Aranth Heracanasa. Ca. 520 B.C. (DAI.)

and bedrooms were furnished in various periods. Bronze stands of many kinds once stood in these rooms: some held lights to illuminate banquets; some supported handled cups or utensils.[106] Still others, provided with a little dish, served for the popular after-dinner game of *kottabos,* borrowed from Greek drinking parties, in which each guest took a turn at splashing drops of his wine into the cups from a distance[107] (figs. IV-68, IV-74–75). Jugglers often balance such stands during their acts (figs. VIII-52, VIII-59). The early tombs are provided with large portable bronze or terracotta cauldrons and stands used for cooking in the houses of the wealthy (figs. IV-70–73), bucchero trays with dishes and cups (figs. IV-80–83), and bronze serving carts, beds, tables, and chairs, of which the grandest is the "throne" in the Regolini-Galassi Tomb, originally made of wood covered with bronze plates with an embossed relief decoration.[108] In the seventh century, when the invention of writing was still fresh, the alphabet was often used to decorate objects, and craftsmen made up fancy writing sets, like one which included the rooster-shaped bucchero inkstand with an alphabet on it that is now in the Metropolitan Museum in New

York (fig. VIII-53). From Marsiliana d'Albegna, near Vetulonia, comes one of the best preserved alphabets, on a miniature "wax tablet" found together with other writing implements, styluses, and ivory erasers. (fig. VII-1).[109]

Some of the dishes found in the tombs still hold the remains of the meal, such as olives, grain, and fruit. Most important at all times was the set of pitchers, mixing bowls, cups, and mugs for the drinking parties the aristocrats held in conjunction with their dinner parties (figs. IV-80, IV-82–88).[110] Each family tried to have as fine a set as possible, which was handed down as an heirloom or placed as a gift in the grave of its owner. Those who could not afford expensive imported pitchers and mixing bowls made do with local imitations or native, local ware, but bucchero cups were used by everyone.

In the chamber tombs of Cerveteri, which copy the designs of the houses of the living, the decoration is sculptured, with beds, chairs, and shields carved out of the rocks (figs. I-18; VIII-1; see Ch. V). A late tomb, the famous Tomb of the Reliefs, reproduces in relief all the furnishings of a home:

VIII-53. Ink stand from Viterbo in the shape of a rooster, incised with Etruscan alphabet. Bucchero. Seventh century B.C. The Metropolitan Museum of Art, New York, Fletcher Fund, 1924. (Museum photo.)

VIII-54. Grave markers, male and female. Stone. Cerveteri. Fourth century B.C. (M. Moretti, *Cerveteri*, 1977, fig. 3.)

pots, pans, and pets; perhaps even a "book" of linen, shown with its envelope, carefully folded on a chest.[111] Funerary beds at Cerveteri were distinguished by sex. Those for men represent couches with turned legs and special headrests; those for women are the same, but encased in a gabled sarcophagus or house-shaped casket (figs. V-3–5, V–13, V-15).[112] In the fourth century and later, women's graves were marked with small stone pillars shaped like boxes or houses, in contrast to the phallus-shaped pillars of the men (fig. VIII-54).

Grave furnishings were often dedicated to the dead by inscriptions scratched on them. *Suthina*, meaning grave gift, was often followed by the name of the dead person in the genitive or dative case (fig. I-19). Sometimes vases were broken before putting them in the grave to make them unfit for use by the living.[113] Miniature scale models could serve the dead just as well as the original objects, as could objects less solidly made. In the ancient world, objects were sometimes especially made up to be used as grave gifts, ephemeral in material or decoration, like gold wreaths of paper-thin gold

leaf in Etruria, or, in Greece, *lekythoi* or oil pitchers decorated with colors which faded rapidly.

In the fourth century, in paintings at Tarquinia and Orvieto the world of the dead replaced the cheerful world of the living, for example, in the Tomb of Orcus and the Golini Tomb, where Hades and Persephone reign.[114] The style of the paintings also changed. A brooding and melancholy quality appeared for the first time (figs. IV-95, IV-102; VIII-47). Yet the customs of the living still continued beyond death: clothes, jewelry, household furniture, and whole household staffs, which were now represented for the first time in public.

The reasons for this change are not yet clear. Was it psychological, a premonition of impending disaster which followed the political chaos and economic crisis of the fifth century? Or the influence of ideas about the afterworld from south Italy, where they had long been current? Certainly the recovery of the end of the fifth century B.C. marks a moment when Greek ideas, artistic motifs, and influence were imported into Etruria from south Italy.

The changed society of the period also accounts for the popularity of sanctuaries where gods of healing and fertility were worshiped by the simple people, and gifts were left as thank offerings for favors divinely granted (figs. IV-16, IV-47–49). Terracotta models of uteri or sexual organs, of cattle, of feet or legs miraculously healed, or of the divinity have been found where they were buried in votive pits near such shrines.[115]

What is becoming quite clear is the existence of an Italian *koine*, or common culture, of the fourth century B.C., in which the Etruscans were participants rather than leaders. Terracotta votive figurines of the same type are found in Etruria, Latium, and Campania, for example. The role of Campania in this *koine* needs to be studied further.[116] Recent excavations and publications are at least beginning to give us a picture of the art and the society of the fourth century B.C., both in Italy and in Greece. The focus is moving away from the great centers; the art is at the same time international and regional, extraordinarily sophisticated and local or provincial. Central Italian monuments illustrate traditional motifs like the barren tree, the *arbor infelix,* to which, on a Praenestine mirror now in Toledo, Amycos is being tied (fig. VIII-55). Peoples

VIII-55. Engraved mirror from Praeneste with Castor, Pollux, and Amycos. Third century B.C.
Toledo Museum of Art, Gift of Edward Drummond Libbey. (Museum photo.)

VIII-56. Terracotta sarcophagus from Tuscania, lid figure of woman. Second century B.C. New York, Institute of Fine Arts. (Philip Evola.)

VIII-57. Cinerary urn from Monteriggioni (Volterra) with image of dead child on lid. Terracotta. Second–first century B.C. Volterra, Museo Etrusco Guarnacci. (Museum photo; *CUE* I 252.)

like the Scythians, the Celts, and the Lucanians appear on the scene for the first time. Important discoveries are defining a period which had long been considered little more than a hiatus between the Classical and the Hellenistic ages, between Athens and Macedonia in Greece, Etruria and Rome in Italy.[117]

During the latest period of Etruscan culture, the second and first centuries B.C., a last flurry of local craftsmanship, for example, terracotta sarcophagi from Tuscania (fig. VIII-56), took place. Cinerary urns made to contain the ashes of the dead (cremation persisted in the northern cities) at Volterra, Chiusi, and Perugia, once scorned as mass-produced objects of the Hellenistic period, are today eagerly studied from a variety of aspects: the typology of the "portrait" figures reclining on the lids, the scenes carved on the front of their caskets, and the organization of the workshops where they were made. Last but not least, they constitute the single most important source material for a study of the Romanization of these cities (figs. I-22–23; IV-32–38; VIII-57–58).[118] Craftsmen copied the designs of their relief decoration—scenes from Greek mythology, battle scenes, or such typically Etruscan themes as the voyage to the underworld—from books of models. At Chiusi a favorite theme was a battle scene in which a figure whom some have identified with the Greek hero Echetlos wields a huge plough; reminding us of the statuette of the ploughman from Arezzo (fig. VIII-46) and also of the story of Romulus, who ploughs a furrow as a boundary for Rome according to an Etruscan ritual. Other strange scenes, and details, such as those on an urn representing two severed heads (fig. VIII-58), show the continuing originality of Clusine artists and patrons.[119] Vanth and Charun continue to appear on the urns (cf. fig. VIII-50), and Lasae populate many of the later mirrors (fig. VIII-49), as purely Etruscan characters alongside scenes and figures taken from Greek mythology.

These funerary urns testify to the gradual Romanization of Etruria during the period they were being made through the appearance of Roman hairstyles on the women represented on the lids and the gradual changeover from Etruscan epitaphs to Latin ones.[120] This language shift from Etruscan

VIII-58. Ash urn from Chiusi with scene of impending sacrifice (from Euripides' *Iphigenia in Tauris*) foreshadowed by the severed heads above the altar. Alabaster. Ca. 100 B.C. New York University, Classics Department, (Department photo.) (Philip Evola.)

to Latin took longer at Chiusi than elsewhere: many examples show that the progress of Latinization covered two or three generations. (There are even married couples, and brothers, one of whom has an epitaph in Latin, another in Etruscan.) Chiusi and Perugia together account for some 90 percent of

VIII-59. Engraved mirror, juggler with balls and candelabra. Bronze. Ca. 520 B.C. The Nasli and Alice Heeramaneck Collection, on loan to the Brooklyn Museum No. L78.17.47. (Drawing by Jo Goldberg.)

the inscriptions written in Latin characters which still show Etruscan features. Perugia was Umbrian, and, therefore, more Etruscanized than actually Etruscan. In the linguistic area, as in its art, Chiusi was conservative, keeping alive older features along with the new.

Arezzo is one of the few Etruscan cities to have yielded nonfunerary inscriptions. In the mid-first century B.C., Arezzo became famous in Italy and Europe for her shiny red, mold-decorated Arretine ware, with which the city reflected its earlier tradition of metalworking. This pottery, as well as the later *terra sigillata,* so called because of its stamped decoration, provides epigraphic evidence for the end of Etruscan: stamps were inscribed with letters, monograms, names, or abbreviations, all in Latin.

In the south at Tarquinia, the end of the Etruscan language and the beginning of Latin is marked by the Latin inscriptions of wall paintings. The Tomb of the Typhon, of the second or first century B.C., whose wall paintings were decorated in late Hellenistic style (fig. IV-106), had funerary inscriptions in both Etruscan and Latin. Here, as at Cerveteri, the language shift from Etruscan to Latin seems to have taken place around 100 B.C., as shown by several hundred grave markers, or cippi, with inscribed epitaphs in Etruscan and Latin (some are bilingual). A peaceful process of Romanization is reflected by such inscriptions, as these Etruscan cities became Roman in language and in law. By the time of Augustus, Italy had once more been united (Map 7). But this time it was a Roman Italy which claimed her place as the center of the Mediterranean.

Notes

1. Chapter V provides the relevant bibliography. For the controversy on the sixth-century "palace" or "sanctuary" of Murlo, see M. Cristofani, *Prospettiva* 1 (1975) 9–17. For the lack of distinction between domestic and sacred buildings in early Greece, see H. Drerup, *Griechische Baukunst in geometrischer Zeit. Archaeologia Homerica* II O (cited by Rathje, below). For a survey of Etruscan communications and urban planning, see G. Colonna, "La cultura dell'Etruria meridionale interna con particolare riguardo alle necropoli rupestri," *Aspetti e Problemi dell-'Etruria Interna* (Florence 1974) 253–63.

The difference between the isolated building complex at

Murlo and the habitation site of Acquarossa, where "normal" undecorated houses have been uncovered, has been emphasized by Ingrid Strøm (unpublished lecture, Day School on the Etruscans, Manchester Museum, December 4, 1982). For these houses, see C. Nylander, in D. Ridgway's "Archaeology in Sardinia and Etruria," *ArchReports 1974–79* 64. A complex building has recently been excavated at Castelnuovo Berardenga, near Siena: see A. Talocchini, *StEtr* 48 (1980) 550–54.

Recent excavations in Latium have also concentrated on habitation sites rather than tombs (Ficana, Satricum) in an attempt to understand the process of urbanization in a wider context, in relation to other peoples of Italy, especially the Greeks and Etruscans. See *Ficana* (1981); and Rathje, "Banquet Service," with bibliography, on which some of the following account of the banquet is based. See also C. Fayer, *Aspetti di vita quotidiana nella Roma arcaica* (Rome 1982).

2. Livy 1.38, 1.56; and Ogilvie, *Commentary* 156, 213–15.

3. Heurgon, *Daily Life*, is basic (he discusses *muliebris audacia*). See also L. Bonfante [Warren], "The Women of Etruria," *Arethusa* 6 (1973) 91–101, now reprinted in J. Peradotto and J.P. Sullivan, eds., *Women in the Ancient World. The Arethusa Papers* (Albany, New York, 1984) 229–39. On the prominence of married couples in Etruscan art, ancient references to the *truphe* or luxury of the Etruscans, and the aristocratic character of Etruscan society, see L. Bonfante, "Etruscan Couples and Their Aristocratic Society," in *Reflections of Women in Antiquity,* ed. H. Foley (New York and London 1981) 323–41; M. Nielsen, "Women in the Late Etruscan Society. Practices of Commemoration and Social Stress," *Fromhed og Verdslighed i Middelalder og Renaissance. Festskrift til Thelma Jexlev* (Odense 1985) 191–202; cf. Cristofani, *L'arte degli Etruschi* 129, 136, and *passim;* Cristofani, *The Etruscans* 27–29; and D. Musti, *Atti XVI Convegno Magna Grecia* (Naples 1977) 23ff. For the Tarquins, see G. Dumézil, "Pères et fils dans la légende de Tarquin le Superbe," in *Hommages Bidez et Cumont* (Brussels 1949) 77–84.

4. M. Napoli, *La Tomba del Tuffatore* (Bari 1970). For Etruscan banquets, see S. De Marinis, *La tipologia del banchetto nell'arte etrusca arcaica* (Rome 1961); S. Stopponi, *La tomba della Scrofa Nera* (Rome 1983) 42–65, esp. 59–65.

5. J.J. Bachofen, *Myth, Religion, and Mother Right.* Bollingen Series 84 (Princeton 1967); *Das Mutterrecht* (Basel 1948, orig. publ. 1861); *Die Sage von Tanaquil* (Heidelberg 1870).

6. Theopompus, in Athenaeus, *Deipnosophistae* 12, 517D–18B.

7. On nudity, see Bonfante, *Etruscan Dress,* Ch. 2. On the language taboo, see G. Bonfante, "La parola nudo e la nudità sacrale per gl'Indoeuropei," *AGI* (1981) 89–94. For erotic scenes in Etruscan art, see J. de Wit, "Die Vorritzungen der Etruskischen Grabmalerei," *JdI* 44 (1929)

31–85, esp. fig. 6 (homosexual couple in the Tomb of the Bulls, Tarquinia); fig. 8 (man with woman on top of another man, in the same tomb); fig. 7 (man with woman in the presence of another woman, on a gravestone from Tarquinia in Florence). Cf. N.T. de Grummond, in *Guide to Etruscan Mirrors* 184–85; L. Bonfante, *Out of Etruria* 40–41, 59–60, figs. 56, 63–64, 66.

8. N.T. de Grummond, in *Guide to Etruscan Mirrors* 180. The following account is taken from my chapter, "Daily Life," pp. 79–89. For summaries and ancient references, see Heurgon, *Daily Life,* and Macnamara, *Everyday Life.*

9. See R. De Puma, "A Praenestine Mirror with Telephos and Orestes," *RömMitt* 87 (1980) 11, n. 3; genre scenes include symposia, bathing scenes, athletes: "Were it not for accompanying inscriptions identifying the figures as divine, some mirrors would be interpreted as ordinary genre scenes."

10. Mirror in Berlin, Staatliche Museen. See Mayer-Prokop 95–96, S 43, pl. 38. Cf. Tarquinia, Tomb of the Funeral Couch, in Brendel, *Etruscan Art* 264, fig. 177 (470–450 B.C.).

11. M. Johnstone, *The Dance in Etruria* (Florence 1956); Brendel, *Etruscan Art* 270, figs. 270–71.

12. *ES* 98–99, 312; Bonfante, *Etruscan Dress* 38, 120, fig. 81.

13. Heurgon, *Daily Life* 195–99; Macnamara, *Everyday Life* 175, 179–81; J.R. Jannot, *AntCl* 47 (1978) 469–507; Bo Lawergren, "The Cylinder Kithara in Etruria, Greece, and Anatolia," *Imago Musicae* 1 (1984) 147–74; and "The Cylinder Kithara, a Lyre Common to Etruria, Greece, and Anatolia," *Acta Musicologica* 57 (1985) 25–33.

14. See *ES* 5, 77, for mirror from Orvieto, Perugia Museum; and see L. Bonfante Warren, "Etruscan Dress as Historical Source," *AJA* 75 (1971) 281, fig. 15. A red-figure cup from Chiusi in Florence, dating from about 350 B.C., shows Hermes delivering to Leda and Tyndareus the egg from which Helen will be born: see Brendel, *Etruscan Art* 349–50, fig. 272; Beazley, *EVP* 115, pl. 27.4. Beazley (115–16) lists vases and mirrors with this subject.

15. Mirror from Praeneste, Rome, Villa Giulia No. 16691. See Bonfante, *Etruscan Dress* fig. 149.

16. *ES* 125.

17. *ES* 165; Pfiffig, *Religio Etrusca* 349–52, fig. 138. For a child (perhaps Caeculus, the founder of Praeneste) nursing from a lioness on a type of Praenestine bronze cista foot of the late fifth century B.C., see F. Jurgeit, "Aussetzung des Caeculus. Entrückung der Ariadne," in *Tainia. Roland Hampe zum 70. Geburtstag dargebracht* (Mainz 1980) 269–75. The child wears a bulla, as does the baby Dionysos on the mirror in *ES* 82.

18. Rallo, *Lasa* 5, pl. 33.2; de Simone 20 (7).

19. E. Simon, "Il dio Marte nell'arte dell'Italia centrale," *StEtr* 46 (1978) 135–47; G. Hermansen, "Mares, Maris, Mars, and the Archaic Gods," *StEtr* 53 (1985).

20. *ES* 181, mirror from Vulci, Paris, Bibliothèque Nationale; Brendel, *Etruscan Art* 369–70, fig. 286. For Epiur, see Rebuffat-Emmanuel, *Le miroir étrusque* 521–28; Pfiffig, *Religio Etrusca* 349–52.

21. Brendel, *Etruscan Art* 344.

22. Paris, Louvre. Pfister-Roesgen, S 60, pl. 65.

23. Bologna, Museo Civico, Sassatelli, *CSE* Italia I.1.15. Cf. *ES* 5.60; M. Renard, in *Hommages Bayet* (Paris 1964) 611–18, fig. 3.

24. See Brendel, *Etruscan Art* 240, on the *kourotrophos* accompanying the Veii Apollo and "the multifarious list of mythical mothers and nurses who were so popular, and often venerated, in early Italy. . . . An unnamed *kourotrophos* occurs quite frequently among the artless statuettes which worshippers deposited as ex-votos, to please the sacred spirits of the place." See also T.H. Price, *Kourotrophos. Cults and Representations of the Greek Nursing Deities* (Leiden 1978), an informative but all-inclusive catalog of the Greek *kourotrophos* type; V. Tran Tam Tinh, *Isis Lactans* (Leiden 1973), with review by L. Bonfante, *AJA* 80 (1976) 104–15.

25. On Ishtar, Hera, Aphrodite, and the dove, see B.L. Trell, "The World of the Phoenicians, East and West. The Numismatic Evidence," in *Proceedings of the 9th International Congress of Numismatics, Berne 1979* (Louvain-Luxembourg 1982) 421–43. For Athena and the Phoenician goddess, see R. Stieglitz, in *Actes du II Congrès de l'Histoire et de la Civilization du Magreb, Tunis 1980* (forthcoming). For the Judgment of Paris in Etruria, and the figure of Paris as a shepherd, wearing the costume later used to identify the haruspex who reads the omens, see F. Roncalli, "Die Tracht des etruskischen Haruspex als frühgeschichtliches Relikt in historischer Zeit," *Aufnahme* 124–32. See also S. Haynes, *RömMitt* 83 (1976) 227–31.

26. For older women and younger men, see *ES* 112; Bonfante, *Etruscan Dress* fig. 83; *ES* 5.23; Rallo, *Lasa* pl. 17, 1. Cf. Rallo pl. 7; Pfiffig, *Religio Etrusca* 284, fig. 121; Brendel, *Etruscan Art* fig. 203; de Grummond, in *Guide to Etruscan Mirrors* 184–85. For Semele and Fufluns see *ES* 299. Cf. an Archaic mirror, *ES* 87; Pfister Roesgen, pl. 10.

27. L. Bonfante, *StEtr* 45 (1977) 160, n. 60, 164, n. 75; S. Hiller, *Antike Kunst* 19 (1976) 30–40, pl. 7.

28. On the scenes of servants in the fourth-century Golini Tomb in Orvieto, see Heurgon, *Daily Life* 186–89. For a cista with a kitchen scene, see Bordenache-Battaglia, *Ciste prenestine I* no. 12. Work scenes are rare on the mirrors.

29. Webster, *Potter and Patron* 228.

30. For the Calydonian boar hunt with Meleager and Atalanta, see the mirror in Paris, Louvre Museum, *ES* 175; Bonfante, *Etruscan Dress* fig. 91; G. Daltrop, *Die Kalydonische Jagd in der Antike* (Hamburg and Berlin 1966) 26; G. Camporeale, *La caccia in Etruria* (Rome 1984) 88–89, 99, 175–76. Meleager and Atalanta are a popular couple in

Etruscan art. See also boxing scenes, with Castor and Pollux, on the Ficoroni cista, and a mirror now in Toledo: T. Dohrn, *Die Ficoronische Ciste* (1972) 50, fig. 7; and review by E. Simon, *Gymnasium* 80 (1973) 404ff. Scenes with fountain, strigil, etc., indicate a palaestra as background: Rebuffat-Emmanuel, *Le miroir étrusque* 515–19; Mayer-Prokop 96.

31. Bordenache-Battaglia, *Ciste prenestine I* pls. 5, 95, 131, 142, 185, etc.

32. *ES* 224; *Guide to Etruscan Mirrors* fig. 88. See also Cruisie ("Croesus") and Talitha on a mirror from Bologna, G. Colonna, *StEtr* 43 (1975) 215ff.; G. Sassatelli, *CSE,* Italia I, Bologna, Museo Civico I, No. 41; *Guide to Etruscan Mirrors* 70. For Peleus and Atalanta in Greek art, see L. Roller, *AJA* 85 (1981) 111–12.

33. In Greece, certain pictures of Atalanta were described as "pornographic": Bonfante, *Etruscan Dress* 26.

34. Mirror from Praeneste, London, British Museum, third century B.C.; *ES* 5, 146; *Guide to Etruscan Mirrors* 75.

35. *ES* 5, 109. See Greek examples listed in A. Stenico, *StEtr* 23 (1955) 201–6, fig. 2; and D. Thompson, "Exekias and the Brettspieler," *ArchCl* 28 (1976) 30–40.

36. Bonfante, *Etruscan Dress* 212, n. 43, with bibliography; *Getty Museum Journal* 8 (1981) 147–54; *Guide to Etruscan Mirrors* 159; L.B. van der Meer, "Etruscan Urns from Volterra. Studies on Mythological Representations," *BABesch* 52–53 (1977–78) 57–98; J.P. Small, *Studies Related to the Theban Cycle on Late Etruscan Urns* (Rome 1981) 77, 95 and *passim*.

37. G. Colonna, "Scriba cum rege sedens," *Mélanges Heurgon* 187–95; Rallo, *Lasa* 51, nn. 3–5; Dumézil, *Archaic Roman Religion* 695. For the *libri lintei* as official and priestly attributes, see F. Roncalli, "Carbasinis voluminibus implicati libri: Osservazioni sul *liber linteus* di Zagabria," *JdI* 95 (1980) 227–64; and "Osservazioni sui *libri lintei* etruschi," *RendPontAcc* 51–52 (1978–79, 1979–80) 3–21.

38. Rome, Villa Giulia: O.J. Brendel, *AJA* 64 (1960) pl. 8, fig. 1; L. Bonfante, "Historical Art: Etruscan and Early Roman," *AJAH* 3 (1978) 145, fig. 6.

39. For Cacu and the Vibenna brothers, see J. Penny Small, *Cacus and Marsyas in Etrusco-Roman Legend* (Princeton 1982), with bibliography.

40. Pallottino, *Etruscans* fig. 37; Pfiffig, *Religio Etrusca* 37–38; L. Bonfante, *AJAH* 3 (1978) 148–51, fig. 5.

41. Brendel, *Etruscan Art* 362, fig. 280. On the techniques of hepatoscopy and *haruspicina,* see L.B. van der Meer, *BABesch* 54 (1979) 49–64; Dumézil, *Archaic Roman Religion* 625–96.

42. See Brendel 367, fig. 284; L. Aigner Foresti, "Zur Zeremonie der Nagelschlagung in Rom und in Etrurien," *AJAH* 4 (1979) 144–58.

43. See *Guide to Etruscan Mirrors* 179, nn. 76–80; Webster, *Potter and Patron* 128. For examples of Greek vase

painters "advertising their own wares" see also J.V. Noble, *The Techniques of Painted Attic Pottery* (New York 1965) *passim*, for scenes of potters working, and fig. 252, showing a broken pot on the ground, which has broken exactly where it was pieced together by the potter. See also C.G. Koehler, "Amphoras on Amphoras," *Hesperia* 51 (1982) 284ff.

44. *ES* 2, pls. 122–23; Pfister-Roesgen pl. 59; G. Mansuelli, *Ricerche sulla pittura ellenistica* (Bologna 1950) 38–41, fig. 42, with discussion on the motif.

45. Cf. *ES* 5, pl. 18; and Tomb of Hunting and Fishing, Tarquinia, in Cristofani, *Etruscans*, pl. on pp. 38–39.

46. *ES* 5, pl. 43; Rebuffat-Emmanuel, *Le miroir étrusque* pl. 88 (a platter imitating silver dishes from Tarentum). According to Webster (215), if one was rich enough, one had metal symposium ware instead of decorated terracotta pots.

47. Steingräber, *Etruskische Möbel* 257–79 (nos. 317–97, mirrors); 270–71 (nos. 398–401, cistae).

48. *ES* 4, pls. 384, 404; Bianchi Bandinelli-Giuliano, *Etruschi e Italici* 305, fig. 353. A lady with a parasol is watching the funeral games in the Tomb of the Monkey at Chiusi, 480–470 B.C. (Brendel, *Etruscan Art* 272, fig. 191).

49. A. Ciasca, *Il capitello detto eolico in Etruria* (Florence 1962).

50. *ES* 170. See Bonfante, in *Guide to Etruscan Mirrors* 85, n. 50.

51. *ES* 147. For stepped altars of Phoenician style represented on the relief decoration of *bucchero pesante* vases, see L. Donati, *StEtr* 45 (1977) 99–104, pl. 16.

52. Higgins, *Jewellery* 135–48, 219–22, with bibliography; G. Buchner, "Early Orientalizing: Aspects of the Euboean Connection," *IBR* 129–44; Strøm, *Etruscan Orientalizing*; F.-W. von Hase, *Hamburger Beiträge zur Archäologie* 5 (1975), and "Die goldene Prunkfibel aus Vulci, Ponte Sodo," *Jahrbuch des Röm.-Germ. Zentral-Museums* 31 (1984) 247–304.

53. Higgins, *Jewellery* 20–22, 141–42, on granulation and amber. Benvenuto Cellini describes the process of granulation in *I trattati dell'oreficeria e della scultura* (Florence 1857; English trans., London 1898) Ch. 3. For amber, see N. Negroni Catacchio, "L'ambra nella protostoria italiana," *Ambra Oro del Nord* (Venice 1978) 83–87; and L. Bonfante, "Amber, Women and Situla Art," *Journal of Baltic Studies* (1985) (forthcoming), with references.

54. A. Rumpf, "Armillae," *JHS* 7 (1951) 168–71; Bonfante, *Etruscan Dress* 143–44; *ANRW* II⁴ (1973) 605; Higgins, *Jewellery* 141–42; Rallo, *Lasa* 30, pl. 17. For a Roman child wearing a large bulla, see D.E.E. Kleiner and F.S. Kleiner, *ArchNews* 10 (1981) 3–8. For the Walters Art Gallery bulla, G.M.A. Hanfmann, *AJA* 39 (1935) 189–94; Richardson, *Etruscans* 152, pl. 40a. See also P.G. Warden, "Bullae, Roman Custom and Italic Tradition," *Opuscuola Romana* 14 (1983) 69–75.

55. *ES* 2, pl. 178 (lost); G. Ronzitti Orsolini, *Il mito dei Sette a Tebe nelle urne volterrane* (Florence 1971) 13.

56. D. Rebuffat-Emmanuel, "La Collection Dutuit," *MonPiot* 60 (1976) 53–67, no. 48, figs. 12–14, 27, 3 (*ES* 5, pl. 22); G.A. Mansuelli, *StEtr* 19 (1946–47) 105; L. Bonfante, *StEtr* 45 (1977) pl. 25b. For terracotta figures from Latium wearing such large necklaces see *Enea nel Lazio, Archeologia e Mito* (Rome 1981) 221–48 *passim* (for bullae, see, e.g., 225, D241); M. Torelli, *Lavinio e Roma* (Rome 1984) *passim*.

57. M.F. Briguet, *La Revue du Louvre* 24 (1974) 247–52; Bonfante, *Etruscan Dress* 144–45.

58. For pointed-pendant earrings from Tarentum, see R. Higgins, *British Museum Catalogue of Terracottas* I (London 1954), "Taras," nos. 1329–30, 1360, mid-fourth century B.C.; M. Kilmer, *The Shoulder Bust in Sicily and South and Central Italy* (Göteborg 1977) nos. 87–88, figs. 147–50, busts from Ariccia; nos. 89–90, 92, figs. 156, 159–61, busts from Palestrina. See also A.Z. Gallina, in *Roma Medio Repubblicana* (Rome 1973) 321–27, nos. 473–74, pls. 42–43, on the busts from Ariccia: "All'Italia meridionale e alla Sicilia richiamano altresí i tipi dei gioielli, specialmente gli orecchini, esemplari ben noti di oreficeria greca di IV secolo, documentati anche nella glittica e nelle monete" (323). Cf. F. Coarelli, in *Roma Medio Repubblicana* 303–4, nos. 447–49, pl. 100–102; Rallo, *Lasa* 36: "Gli orecchini piramidati . . . sono particolarmente diffusi nel IV–III secolo su monete, su specchi e nell'oreficeria"; K. Hadaczek, *Der Ohrschmuck der Griechen und Etrusker* (Vienna 1903) 69.

59. On torques, see L. Bonfante, *ANRW* I⁴ (1973) 613.

60. Bonfante, *Etruscan Dress* fig. 92. For this adornment on ladies on Volterran urns, see C. Gambetti, *I coperchi di urne con figurazioni femminili nel Museo Archeologico di Volterra* (Milan 1974) *passim*.

61. For the need to preserve and study the enamel of excavated teeth, see G.T. Craig and D. Fine, "Dental Care for the Dead," *Antiquity* (1981) 138–39.

62. D. Clawson, "Phoenician Dental Art," *Berytus* 1 (1934) 22–31, pl. III; A.W. Lufkin, *A History of Dentistry* (Philadelphia 1948); J. Woodforde, *False Teeth* (London 1962).

63. Rome, Villa Giulia 13213, Helbig⁴ 2957; Lufkin, *History of Dentistry* 58–59, figs. 17–20; I. Edlund, "A Tomb Group from Bisenzio in the Barrett Collection, Buffalo, N.Y.," *AJA* 85 (1981) 81–83, about 500 B.C.

64. Merseyside County Museums, Liverpool. Macnamara, *Everyday Life* 170, fig. 104 (drawing); Grant, *Etruscans*, fig. pp. 240–41.

65. The Twelve Tables: N. Lewis and M. Reinhold, *Roman Civilization Sourcebook I. The Republic* (New York 1966) 108–9.

66. Brendel, *Etruscan Art* 37–41; Gempeler, *Etruskische Kanopen*; F. Delpino, "Elementi antropomorfi in corredi villanoviani," *Atti X Convegno di Studi Etruschi* (Florence

1977) 173–82; Aigner Foresti, *Ostalpenraum und Italien;* L. Quilici, *Roma primitiva e le origini della civiltà laziale* (Rome 1979).

67. Bonfante, *Etruscan Dress* 19–29. The following account is taken from this book: relevant bibliography will be found there.

68. Bonfante, *Etruscan Dress* 11–17. Jeanine Stage is presently at work on a study of Etruscan textiles, using the evidence of actual finds. Recently developed techniques of excavation and conservation are making it possible to preserve more fragments of actual textiles once placed in the tombs, like the robes found in the Greek tomb at Lefkandi: see Introduction, n. 68.

69. Bonfante, *Etruscan Dress* figs. 35–37, 41, 43; *Out of Etruria* figs. 42–44.

70. Bonfante, *Out of Etruria* 16–17, figs. 5–6.

71. For shoes and sandals, see Mueller-Deecke I 254ff.; Heurgon, *Daily Life* 177–79; V. Ehrenburg, *The People of Aristophanes* (Oxford 1948) 105, 278; Bonfante, *Etruscan Dress* 59–66.

72. On Etruscan and Ionian artistic connections, see B.S. Ridgway, *The Archaic Style in Greek Art* (Princeton 1977) 67, 254–55, etc.

73. For draped Ionian *kouroi,* see Boardman, *Greeks Overseas* 247, fig. 287; J. Charbonneaux, *Archaic Greek Art* (Paris, New York 1971) figs. 288, 290; cf. 169.

74. Ridgway, *Archaic Style* figs. 18, 20, and *passim.*

75. Bonfante, *Etruscan Dress* figs. 146, 74. On Ionian humor, see Charbonneaux, *Archaic Greek Art* 93.

76. The following section is taken from my chapter, "Daily Life," in *Guide to Etruscan Mirrors* 87–88.

77. For male figures wearing the *mitra,* see Bonfante, *Etruscan Dress* 142 (n. 85); Tölle-Kastenbein, *RA* (1977) 23–36; H.A. Shapiro, *AJA* 85 (1981) 139.

78. R.D. De Puma, "The Dioskouroi on Four Etruscan Mirrors in Midwestern Collections," *StEtr* 41 (1973) 159–70, pls. 51–54.

79. Such nudity, on female figures, often implies vulnerability: see J.P. Small, *Cacus and Marsyas in Etrusco-Roman Legend* (Princeton 1982) 52 (quoting Bonfante). It may also imply divinity.

80. For Oedipus's stage dress, see *Talamone. Il mito dei Sette a Tebe* (Florence 1982) pl. 4. Cf. J.P. Small, *AJA* 78 (1974) 49–54. See also a mirror with the aged King Oeneus: Bonfante, *Etruscan Dress* fig. 91. See also supra n. 36.

81. Long pants (their checked patterns represented either an actual colored pattern or a rough texture) signify "barbarian" dress; they appear on cistae as well as urns: see L. Bonfante [Warren], *AJA* 68 (1964) 35–42. For the Berlin cista, see Bordenache-Battaglia, *Ciste prenestine I,* 56–61, no. 7, esp. p. 60; in this interpretation of the scene as taken from comedy, Bordenache follows H. Kähler, *Rom und seine Welt* (Munich 1960) 50–51, fig. 23.

82. Bonfante, *Etruscan Dress* fig. 90; Small, *Studies* 35. For long sleeves, see K. Knauer, *ANRW* II¹² (1982); *Expedition* 21 (1978) 18–36.

83. P.F. Stary, "Foreign Elements in Etruscan Arms and Armour, Eighth-Third Centuries B.C.," *ProcPS* 45 (1979) 179–206.

84. Herodotus 1.94.2.

85. L.B. van der Meer, *BABesch* 52–53 (1977–78) 57–98.

86. Tarquinia, Tomb of the Chariots: see Brendel, *Etruscan Art* fig. 181; cf. cippus from Chiusi, fig. 196; R. Bronson, "Chariot Racing in Etruria," *Studi Banti* (Rome 1965) 89–106.

87. S. Haynes, "Ludiones Etruriae," *Festschrift H. Keller* (Darmstadt 1963) 13–21; J.G. Szilágyi, "Impletae modis saturae," *Prospettiva* 24 (1981) 2–23. Jugglers were particularly popular in the art of the sixth and fifth centuries B.C. For musical instruments, see supra n. 13.

88. Aelian, *de natura animalium* 12.46 (third century A.D., but drawing on earlier sources); cf. Varro, *RR* 3.12.1; Macnamara, *Everyday Life* 175.

89. Tomba Golini I: Brendel, *Etruscan Art* figs. 263–64. For the Praenestine cista of this period with a kitchen scene, see Bordenache-Battaglia, *Ciste prenestine I* 12. The mirror with the couple playing a game (supra n. 34) may be by the same hand; the dialogue in both cases is in the Praenestine dialect. On the kitchen scene of the Golini Tomb in Orvieto the names are in Etruscan: see A.E. Feruglio, ed., *Pittura Etrusca a Orvieto* (Rome 1982) 49–52, 58–62, figs. 20–23, 29–37. On the importance of the cook and the butcher in Roman comedy, see the remarks by M. Frederiksen in *Hellenische Poleis* 364, who cites E. Fraenkel, *Elementi Plautini in Plauto* (Florence 1960, revised translation, orig. publ. as *Plautinisches im Plautus,* 1922) 124ff., 239, 408ff.

90. Livy 7.2 (364 B.C.).

91. For the dance, see J.C. Poursat, *BCH* 92 (1968) 550–615. For the Salii, see L. Bonfante, *ANRW* I⁴ (1973) 588–89, with references.

92. For the use of the war trumpet to give signals in battle, see Stary (supra n. 83) 193–96.

93. L. Bonfante, "Etruscan Influence in Early Rome: The Latin Word *Triumphus,*" *Out of Etruria* (1981; orig. publ. 1970) 93–110; *JRS* 60 (1970) 49–66.

94. For M. Sordi, see Introduction n. 80. See also Pfiffig, *Religio Etrusca,* from which much of the following account derives and specific references can be found, and Dumézil, *Archaic Roman Religion* 625–96.

95. For human sacrifice, see L. Bonfante, *AJAH* (1978) 136–62; "Un'urna chiusina con *têtes coupées* à New York," *Studi di Antichità in onore di G. Maetzke* (Rome 1984) 143–50; and "Human Sacrifice on an Etruscan Urn in New York," *AJA* 88 (1984) 531–39.

96. For the Cannicella "Venus" from Orvieto, see A. Andrèn, *Antike Plastik* 7 (1967) 10–24; Pfiffig, *Religio*

Etrusca 65–81, 265–66. For the baby added to the nursing mother or *kourotrophos,* see R. Bianchi Bandinelli, "La *kourotrophos* Maffei del Museo di Volterra," *RA* (1968) 225–40, figs. 5–6: the large (1.65 m.) statue was modeled after a fourth-century Greek type of standing female figure, but the baby and the hand holding it were added by the Etruscan sculptor. See also L. Bonfante, "Votive Terracotta Figures of Mothers and Children," *Aspects of Italic Culture* (forthcoming); and supra n. 24.

97. J. Rykwert, *The Idea of a Town: The Anthropology of Urban Form in Rome, Italy, and the Ancient World* (Princeton 1976).

98. Pallottino, *Etruscans* pl. 37. For the origin of his costume, see F. Roncalli, *Aufnahme* 124–32.

99. *TLE* 719; van der Meer, *BABesch* 54 (1979) 49–64; Dumézil, *Archaic Roman Religion* 653; Pfiffig, *Religio Etrusca* 121–27.

100. R. Bloch, *Les prodiges dans l'antiquité classique* (Paris 1963); Dumézil, *Archaic Roman Religion* 625–95.

101. Heurgon, *Daily Life* 245–46.

102. O.J. Brendel, *JdI* 81 (1969); Richardson, *Etruscans* 243; Rallo, *Lasa* 50–53.

103. Gempeler, *Etruskische Kanopen.*

104. Brendel, *Etruscan Art* figs. 110, 177; J.-R. Jannot, "Une représentation symbolique des défunts," *MEFRA* 89 (1977) 579–88.

105. S. Stopponi, "Parapetasmata Etruschi," *BdA* 53 (1968) 60–62; R. Holloway, *AJA* 65 (1965) 341–47.

106. Macnamara, *Everyday Life* 21–24, 109–18; *Aspects of Italic Culture,* forthcoming.

107. For the kottabos, see Pallottino, *Etruscans* fig. 46; Macnamara, *Everyday Life* 115, 178. Banti, *Etruscan Cities* pl. 83.

108. Supra n. 47. Some doubts have been expressed about the antiquity of parts of the tripod in St. Louis, fig. IV-72.

109. For writing equipment, see Macnamara, *Everyday Life* 186–87; J.G. Szilágyi, *Bull. Mus. Hongrois des Beaux-Arts* 54 (1980) 13–27; Bonfante, *Etruscan Language* 106–9.

110. On the banquet, see Rathje, supra n. 1.

111. F. Roncalli (on Etruscan linen books), supra n. 37.

112. Heurgon, *Daily Life* 93–94.

113. L. Bonfante and N.T. de Grummond, in *Guide to Etruscan Mirrors* 76, 184. For similar funerary customs in Greece, see D. Kurtz and J. Boardman, *Greek Burial Customs* (Ithaca 1971) 204, 215–17; A. Snodgrass, *Arms and Armour of the Greeks* (1967) 93; A. Jackson, *LCM* 8 (February 1983) 22–27.

114. Brendel, *Etruscan Art* 337–39.

115. For the rich bibliography on these terracotta figures, long ignored, see Bonfante, in *Aspects of Italic Culture* (forthcoming); "Dedicated Mothers," in *Visible Religion* III (Leiden 1984) 1–17 (on p. 5, cut "Indo-European"; fig. 8 is a Roman relief).

116. M. Frederiksen, "The Etruscans in Campania," in *IBR* 277–311; and "Campanian Cavalry: A Question of Origin," *DialAr* 2 (1968) 3–31. The colloquium "Aspects of Italic Culture," held in memory of Martin Frederiksen at the British Museum in December 1982, included a number of contributions dealing with this question.

117. Two exhibition catalogues mark this drastic change and provide further bibliography: *The Search for Alexander* (Washington, D.C., 1980); and *Roma Medio Repubblicana* (Rome 1976).

118. M. Cristofani Martelli, *Le tombe di Tuscania nel Mus. Arch. di Firenze* (Florence 1977). For Hellenistic urns, see *Caratteri dell'ellenismo* with preceding bibliography; M. Cristofani et al., *CUE* I. *Urne volterrane* I.

119. Supra n. 95.

120. J. Kaimio, "The Ousting of Etruscan by Latin in Etruria," in *Studies in the Romanization of Etruria.* Acta Istituti Romani Finlandiae V (Rome 1972) 85–245; Harris, *Rome in Etruria and Umbria.*

Selected Readings

Note. Readers will now be able to consult the various catalogues prepared for the exhibitions of the "Progetto Etruschi" held in Tuscany and Perugia in 1985. The catalogue of the principal exhibition, *Civiltà degli Etruschi,* held in Florence, features monuments and information of general interest. The other catalogues are more specialized. *La Fortuna degli Etruschi* (Florence) and *L'Accademia Etrusca* (Cortona) are important for our Chapter I, "Rediscovery." *La Romanizzazione dell'Etruria: Il Territorio di Vulci* (Orbetello) is relevant for the later history of the Etruscan cities: see Chapter II, "History." *Artigianato Artistico in Etruria* deals with the alabaster, tufa, and terracotta urns of the Hellenistic period from Volterra, Chiusi, and Perugia—the exhibition was divided between Volterra and Chiusi—some types of pottery, and sculpture in marble and bronze, of interest in the context of Chapter IV, "Art." Sections on coins in this catalogue and in *L'Etruria Mineraria* can be read in connection with our Chapter VI on coinage, while *Santuari d'Etruria* (Arezzo) and *Case e Palazzi d'Etruria* (Siena) are relevant for Chapter V on architecture. *Scrivere Etrusco* documents the exhibition of the three longest Etruscan inscriptions, the mummy wrappings in Zagreb (newly restored and studied), the Capua tile from the museum in Berlin, and the stone cippus from Perugia—appropriately enough, on view in Perugia (see Chapter VII on Etruscan inscriptions). In 1986 other exhibitions and catalogues are forthcoming, for example, *La Formazione della Città in Emilia Romagna dalle Origini all' Età Romana* (Bologna 1986). Other important publications have appeared too late to be included. To the numismatic bibliography for Chapter VI can now be added P. Visonà, "Foreign Currency in Etruria, circa 400–200 B.C.: Distribution Patterns," in *Ancient Coins of the Graeco-Roman World,* The Nickle Numismatic Papers, eds. W. Heckel and R. Sullivan (Waterloo, Ontario, 1984) 221–40; and "The Coinage of Populonia and Other Etruscan Centers," unpublished thesis, University of California at Santa Barbara, 1980. Etruscan painting (see Chapter IV) is receiving attention: *Catalogo ragionato della pittura etrusca,* edited by S. Steingräber (1984), will soon appear in English; see also *Pittura etrusca a Orvieto,* edited by A. Feruglio (1982). The history of the Archaeological Museum in Bologna, of Etruscan discoveries and

their results, as told in *Dalla Stanza delle Antichità al Museo Civico,* edited by C. Morigi Govi and G. Sassatelli (1984), makes interesting reading in connection with sections of our Introduction as well as Chapter I, "Rediscovery." For later Etruria, see A. Carandini, *Settefinestre, una villa schiavistica nell' Etruria romana,* 3 vols. (Modena 1985).

Aspetti e problemi dell'Etruria interna. Atti dell'VIII Congresso di Studi Etruschi e Italici, Orvieto 1972 (Florence 1974).

L. Banti, *The Etruscan Cities and Their Culture* (Berkeley and Los Angeles 1973). Translation of *Il mondo degli Etruschi,* 2nd ed. (Rome 1969).

J.D. Beazley, *Etruscan Vase Painting* (Oxford 1947).

R. Bianchi Bandinelli, *L'arte etrusca* (Rome 1984). Collection of articles on Etruscan art.

R. Bianchi Bandinelli and A. Giuliano, *Etruschi e Italici prima del dominio di Roma* (Milan, 1974).

R. Bianchi Bandinelli and M. Torelli, *L'arte dell'antichità classica. I. Etruria, Roma* (Turin 1976).

A. Boethius, *Etruscan and Early Roman Architecture* (Harmondsworth 1978).

F. Boitani, M. Cataldi, M. Pasquinucci, M. Torelli, and F. Coarelli (ed.), *Etruscan Cities* (Milan, 1974).

G. Bonfante and L. Bonfante, *The Etruscan Language: An Introduction* (Manchester and New York 1983; revised translation, *Lingua e cultura degli Etruschi,* Rome 1985).

L. Bonfante, *Etruscan Dress* (Baltimore and London 1975).

———, *Out of Etruria. Etruscan Influence North and South.* BAR International Series 103 (1981), with two chapters on language by G. Bonfante.

——— [Warren], "Roman Triumphs and Etruscan Kings: The Changing Face of the Triumph," *JRS* 60 (1970) 49–66.

O.J. Brendel, *Etruscan Art,* edited by E.H. Richardson (Harmondsworth 1978).

G. Colonna, "Basi conoscitive per una storia economica dell'Etruria," *Supplemento. Annali 22 dell'Istituto Italiano di Numismatica* (1975) 3–23.

———, "Scriba cum rege sedens," *Mélanges Heurgon* (Rome 1976) 187–95.

M. Cristofani, *L'arte degli Etruschi. Produzione e consumo* (Turin 1978).

————, "Contatti fra Lazio ed Etruria in età arcaica: documentazione archeologica e testimonianze epigrafiche," *Alle origini del latino*. Atti del Convegno della Società Italiana di Glottologia, Pisa 1980. Testi raccolti a cura di E. Vineis (Pisa 1982) 27–42.

————, "Il 'dono' nell'Etruria arcaica," *ParPass* 30 (1975) 132–52.

————, *The Etruscans* (New York, London 1979).

P. Defosse, "Chronique d'étruscologie" I-III, *Latomus* 32 (1973) 96–129; 33 (1974) 128–66; 34 (1975) 465–98.

G. Dennis, *The Cities and Cemeteries of Etruria*[3] (London 1883).

G. Dumézil, "Appendix. Etruscan Religion," *Archaic Roman Religion* (Chicago 1970) 623–96.

Enea nel Lazio. Archeologia e mito (Rome 1981).

Die Göttin von Pyrgi. Akten des Kolloquiums zum Thema. Archäologische, linguistische und religionsgeschichtliche Aspekte, Tübingen 1979. (Florence 1981). With contributions by M. Pallottino, G. Colonna, F. Prayon, M. Cristofani, C. de Simone, H. Rix, A. Tovar, R. Bloch, I. Krauskopf, O.-W. von Vacano.

M. Grant, *The Etruscans* (New York 1980).

————, *Roman Myths*[3] (Harmondsworth 1973).

The Greek Renaissance of the Eighth Century B.C.: Tradition and Innovation. Proceedings of the Second International Symposium at the Swedish Institute in Athens. June 1–5, 1981.

N. T. de Grummond, *A Guide to Etruscan Mirrors* (Tallahassee, Florida 1982).

W.V. Harris, *Rome in Etruria and Umbria* (Oxford 1971).

J. Heurgon, *The Daily Life of the Etruscans* (New York 1964). Translation of *La vie quotidienne chez les Etrusques* (Paris 1961).

————, *The Rise of Rome to 264 B.C.* (London 1973). Translation of *Rome et la Méditerranée occidentale jusqu'aux guerres puniques* (Paris 1969).

————, "The Date of Vegoia's Prophecy," *JRS* 49 (1959) 41–45.

R.A. Higgins, *Greek and Roman Jewellery* (London 1961; 2nd ed. 1980).

A. Hus, *Les Etrusques et leur destin* (Paris 1980).

Italian Iron Age Artefacts in the British Museum: Papers of the Colloquium, edited by J. Swaddling. Official publication of the papers given at the colloquium on early Italian cultures in December 1982 (London 1985).

Le lamine di Pirgi. Tavola rotonda internazionale, Rome 1968. Accademia Nazionale dei Lincei, Quaderno No. 147 (Rome 1970).

E. Macnamara, *Everyday Life of the Etruscans* (London and New York 1973).

G. Mansuelli, *The Art of Etruria and Early Rome* (New York 1967).

S. Mazzarino, "Sociologia del mondo etrusco e problemi della tarda etruscità," *Historia* 6 (1957) 63–97, 98–112.

L.B. van der Meer, "*Iecur Placentinum* and the Orientation of the Etruscan Haruspex," *BABesch* 54 (1979) 49–64.

K.O. Mueller and W. Deecke, *Die Etrusker*. Revised by A.J. Pfiffig (Graz 1965; original publication, Stuttgart 1877).

La Naissance de Rome. Exhibition Catalogue. Paris, Petit Palais (Paris 1977).

R.M. Ogilvie, *A Commentary on Livy, Books 1–5* (Oxford (1965).

————, *Early Rome and the Etruscans*. Fontana History of the Ancient World (London and Atlantic Highlands, New Jersey 1976).

M. Pallottino, "Documenti per la storia della civiltà etrusca," *Saggi di Antichità II* (Rome 1979) 475–863.

————, *Etruscan Painting* (Geneva 1951).

————, *The Etruscans* (Harmondsworth 1978).

————, *TLE*[2] (Florence 1968).

————, with the collaboration of G. Colonna, L. Vlad Borelli and G. Garbini, "Scavi nel santuario etrusco di Pyrgi," *ArchCl* 16 (1964) 49–117.

E. Peruzzi, "Appendix I. Mycenaeans and Etruscans," *Mycenaeans in Early Latium* (Rome 1980) 173–49.

A.J. Pfiffig, *Einführung in die Etruskologie —Probleme, Methoden, Ergebnisse* (Darmstadt 1972).

————, *Die etruskische Sprache* (Graz 1969).

————, *Religio Etrusca* (Graz 1975).

Popoli e civiltà dell'Italia antica, 7 vols. (1974–78).

T.W. Potter, *The Changing Landscape of South Etruria* (London 1979).

F. Prayon, *Frühetruskische Grab- und Hausarchitektur* (Heidelberg 1975).

E.H. Richardson, *The Etruscans* (Chicago 1964).

————, *Etruscan Votive Bronzes* (Mainz 1983).

D. Ridgway, *L'alba della Magna Grecia* (Milan 1984).

————, "Archaeology in Central Italy and Etruria 1968–73," *Archaeological Reports* 1973–74, 42–59.

————, ed., "Aspects of the Etruscans," *IBR* 239–412.

————, *The Etruscans*. University of Edinburgh, Dept. of Archaeology. Occasional Paper No. 6 (1981). Forthcoming in the new edition of the *Cambridge Ancient History*.

D. Ridgway and F.R.S. Ridgway, eds., *Italy Before the Romans* (London, New York, San Francisco 1979).

F. Roncalli, "*Carbasinis uoluminibus implicati libri*. Osservazioni sul *liber linteus* di Zagabria," *JdI* 95 (1980) 227–64.

————, *Le lastre dipinte di Cerveteri* (Florence 1965).

J. Rykwert, *The Idea of a Town: The Anthropology of Urban Form in Rome, Italy, and the Ancient World* (Princeton 1976).

H.H. Scullard, *The Etruscan Cities and Rome* (Ithaca, New York and London 1967).

C. de Simone, *Die griechischen Entlehnungen im Etruskischen*, I-II (Wiesbaden 1968–70).

M. Sprenger, G. Bartoloni, and M. Hirmer, *The Etruscans:*

Their History, Art and Architecture (New York 1983). Translation of *Die Etrusker* (Munich 1977).

S. Steingräber, *Etrurien. Städte. Heiligtümer, Nekropole* (Munich 1981).

D.E. Strong, *The Early Etruscans* (London 1968).

Thesaurus Linguae Etruscae. I. Indice lessicale. Ed. by M. Pallottino, with M. Pandolfini Angeletti, C. de Simone, M. Cristofani and A. Morandi (Rome 1978).

M. Torelli, *Elogia Tarquiniensia* (Florence 1975).

————, *Storia degli Etruschi* (Rome and Bari 1981).

————, *Etruria.* Guida Archeologia Laterza (Rome 1980).

————, *Lavinio e Roma* (Rome 1984).

————, "Il santuario greco di Gravisca," *ParPass* 32 (1977) 398–458.

————, "Scavi di Gravisca," *ParPass* 26 (1971) 55ff.

J.M. Turfa, "Evidence for Etruscan-Punic Relations," *AJA* 81 (1977) 368–74.

O.-W. von Vacano, *The Etruscans in the Ancient World* (Bloomington, Indiana 1960).

K.W. Weeber, *Geschichte der Etrusker* (Stuttgart 1979).

Index

Larissa Bonfante is professor of classics at New York University. The author of numerous articles and reviews on Etruscan and early Roman studies, she is a member of the Istituto di Studi Etruschi e Italici, the Associazione Internazionale di Archeologia Classica, the international committee for *CSE,* and the governing board of the Archaeological Institute of America.

The manuscript was prepared for publication by Yvonne Cheryl Reineke, Jean Owen and the Press editorial staff. The book was designed by David Ford. The typeface for the text and the display is Galliard, based on a design by Matthew Carter. The text is printed on 70-lb. Sterling Litho Matte and is bound in Riegel's 10 pt. Carolina C1S.

Manufactured in the United States of America.